THE
BREVIARY EXPLAINED

By

Pius Parsch

Translated by

William Nayden, C.Ss.R.

and

Carl Hoegerl, C.Ss.R.

B. HERDER BOOK CO.

15 & 17 SOUTH BROADWAY, ST. LOUIS 2, MO.

AND

33 QUEEN SQUARE, LONDON, W. C.

1952

IMPRIMI POTEST

John M. Frawley, C.SS.R.

Provincial Superior of
the Baltimore Province

NIHIL OBSTAT

Frederic C. Eckhoff

Censor Librorum

IMPRIMATUR

✠ Joseph E. Ritter

Archiepiscopus

St. Ludovici, die 14a mensis, Januarii, 1952

Vail-Ballou Press, Inc., Binghamton and New York

Translator's Foreword

Pius Parsch needs no introduction to the American public. Several articles of his were translated for *Orate Fratres* during the war years. His *Messerklärung* appeared in English under the title, *The Liturgy of the Mass.*

This latest work of the zealous Augustinian from Klosterneuberg, *Breviererklärung*, is meant to be a companion to the *Messerklärung*. In the translation, the English Version of the New Psalter, prepared by members of the Catholic Biblical Association, has been used in excerpts from the psalms. A brief section treating of the difficulties of the Latin Vulgate has been omitted.

A glance at the table of contents will disclose the division of the book. The first part may be called theoretical, a study of the individual parts of the Breviary and of their special functions in the Office. The second part may be considered the practical application of the first part to the various seasons of the liturgical year. Since the author often refers to a passage of the Breviary without citing it, the reader will do well to have his Breviary handy while studying the explanation of the different Offices.

Whenever the New Testament is cited with chapter and verse numbers, the version used is that of Monsignor Knox, for which permission was granted by A. P. Watt & Son of

London. Due thanks must also be expressed to His Excellency, Most Reverend Edwin V. O'Hara, Chairman of the Episcopal Committee of the Confraternity of Christian Doctrine, for permission to use the English translation of the New Version of the Psalter.

Finally, I wish to thank all who helped to prepare this translation, especially my brother, Frater John Nayden, C.Ss.R., who collaborated extensively when Father Hoegerl was unable to continue the work; Father James Galvin, C.Ss.R., who offered valuable suggestions; and my sister, Margaret M. Nayden, who prepared the manuscript for the publisher.

W. A. N.

Author's Foreword

WHEN I was a seminarian, more than thirty-five years ago, I used to wonder that in the vast field of German publications, no commentary on the Breviary had ever been written. Each branch of theology was abundantly treated, but only a few feeble attempts were made to explain the Breviary. Then and there I resolved, in my youthful zeal, to write an exhaustive commentary on the Breviary. But, once ordained, I was occupied with ministerial and other labors. Then came the World War in which I served as chaplain. But as the war in the Carpathian Mountains amounted to little more than maintaining the lines, I found time for spiritual labor too. It was here that I hit upon the two ideas that were to dominate my later years: the Bible and the liturgy. I realized that we must bring our people to the very fountainhead of God's word. My flair for the Breviary had returned. I wrote an explanation of the psalms as they occur in the Breviary, though the manuscript was later lost. At the end of the war I was entrusted with the training of novices. Once again my old love for the Breviary came to the fore.

Out of all these hours of training and instruction, my first work was born, an explanation of the weekly Psalter, a work that never saw print. Pustet had actually accepted it; but with the post-war inflation its publication was indefinitely postponed. Meanwhile I began popularizing the liturgy, and all work on the Breviary took second place. This spadework in the Breviary, however, proved useful to me in work on my other books: *Jahr Des Heiles* (a commentary on the Church's liturgy throughout the year), *Wochenpsalter* (an explanation and commentary on the weekly arrangement of the psalms); but I did not return to any explicit work on the Breviary.

Even the present work is not a comprehensive commentary on the Breviary. However, for priests and interested laymen it will serve as an introduction to the daily prayer of the Church, which has regard not so much for what is external and material, but for the internal and spiritual. I have omitted entirely from this treatise rubrics and rules for recitation of the Breviary, e.g., the concurrence of feasts, commemorations, octaves, ranks of various Offices. My sole purpose is to help those who pray the Breviary to understand the Church's prayer, and to say this prayer "in spirit and in truth." This book, then, an Explanation of the Breviary in the spirit of the liturgical revival, is a counterpart to my *Messerklärung* (*The Liturgy of the Mass*).

PIUS PARSCH

Contents

CONTENTS

PART I

FUNDAMENTAL NOTIONS

CHAPTER I

Why Pray the Breviary?

I CANNOT remember whether anyone ever told us young seminarians why we should pray the Breviary. We have had to wait for the liturgical revival to enlighten us and to reveal the true grandeur of this prayer. Let us put it frankly: the Breviary is a clerical Cinderella. Most priests, without understanding it properly, say the Office merely to fulfill their obligation. When they really wish to pray, they say their Rosary or some other prayer. What is even more unfortunate, they do not realize why they are praying the Breviary. They have scant notion of the nature of the Church's prayer. In my own opinion, the very name, Breviary, is largely to blame for this misfortune. It is a misnomer. For there is really nothing brief about a daily prayer that takes up an hour or more. The name is misleading. "Breviary" indeed! The word almost prompts one to sarcasm.

Why do we pray the Breviary? It is the prayer of the Church. The word "Church" now takes on a new meaning. "Church" here is not the legislator formulating the rubrics of the Breviary or the moral theologian making each canonical hour of grave obligation; nor is it the temporal element of the Church permitting certain errors and defects to slip into the Breviary. The Church, as we consider it here, is the mystical body of Christ, the sacred spouse of the God-man, the vine whose root is Christ. When I speak of the prayer of the Church,

3

I have in mind the "Church" in this exalted sense. This mystical body has various functions, but four in particular: to offer sacrifice, to suffer, to pray, and to preach. As Christ, during His earthly life, performed these four duties especially, so the Church through her members continues them, and "supplies what is yet lacking to the body of Christ." This prayer, then, is one of the primary manifestations of the Church's life, which can never be suppressed or extinguished.

I am deeply moved each time I read in the Gospels that Jesus prayed. The accounts of the Evangelists bear out the fact that Christ held prayer in high esteem. For Him it was not an occupation of secondary importance as it is for some of us priests, who use the Breviary to fill in leisure moments. For Christ, prayer was something of essential import, that went hand in hand with His teaching; it was intimately bound up with the lofty mission of mankind's redemption. Christ began the work of redemption with earnest prayer, on the occasion of His forty days' fast. In prayer at the Jordan He heard the Father declare His Messiahship. ("When He prayed, the heavens opened and the Holy Spirit, in the form of a dove, descended upon Him.") Busy as He was with His work for souls, He withdrew from the circle of His apostles and spent the night in prayer. Till late in the evening He cured the sick at Capharnaum: "Then, at very early dawn, He left them, and went away to a lonely place, and began praying there." [1] Especially before important occasions, such as the choosing of His apostles, the promise of the Eucharist, and His passion, He passed whole nights in prayer: "It was at this time that He went out onto the mountain side, and passed the whole night offering prayer to God." [2] His prayer

[1] Mark 1:35.
[2] Luke 6:12.

must have been profound, even ecstatic, so that at His baptism it was accompanied by a manifestation of the Holy Trinity, and at another time by a transfiguration of His countenance: "and even as He prayed the fashion of His face was altered and His garments became white and dazzling." [3] Just before His passion Christ gave us a glimpse of the intentions for which He prayed. His was a high-priestly prayer that in its petitions embraced the Church of all centuries with its head and members. With His soul groaning in prayer, Christ entered upon His passion on the Mount of Olives; in prayer He died on the cross. Indeed, Christ prayed long and fervently; it was an important part of His life here on earth.

This duty of prayer must be continued by His mystical body, the Church. Thus the infant Church awaited in prayer its birth on the first Pentecost: "all these, with one mind, gave themselves up to prayer." [4] The early Church at Jerusalem retained the usual daily visit to the Temple, the daily "breaking of bread," and the daily song of praise to God. Wherever a Christian community was established, prayer, and in fact common prayer, became one of its chief activities.

Perhaps we can express the idea by saying that prayer is the breathing of the mystical body. Breath is an unmistakable sign of life. Consequently, where there is prayer, there the life of the Church is manifest, whether it is the prayer of the parish, the family, or individual souls, all of which are cells of the one Church. Here we may insert a practical, pastoral idea that for many is surprisingly new: every community realizing that it is a part of the Church has the task and duty of praying and, moreover, of praying in common. The cloistered religious communities fulfill this duty. But I ask, how do par-

[3] Luke 9:29.
[4] Acts 1:14.

ishes and the majority of families accomplish it? Even in the parish and the family the Church's prayer must play its part. What spiritual powerhouses parish and family would become if the pastor, with the devout members of his flock, held community prayer, if father, mother, and children morning and evening joined in the Church's prayer! How few pastors and parents are aware of this duty!

Why, then, pray the Breviary? This question is somewhat easier to answer now. This duty of common prayer, which belongs to the whole Church with its members, has actually fallen on priests and religious, for whom it is of serious obligation. Through them the mystical body breathes and thereby lives. It is they who continue Christ's prayer in the Church. This ought to be for us priests and religious, not a heavy yoke or a distasteful duty, but a sublime task, to which we should prefer to devote our best efforts, heart, will, and mind, and the best time of our day and life.

I would not, however, wish this situation, in which only priests and religious take upon themselves the obligation of community prayer, to be construed as something ironbound and unchangeable. It should be but a stepping stone: all Christians have the duty, or rather the right, to pray together, as a community. In this matter the priest has not the slightest advantage over the layman.[5] Our confident expectation is that the time will soon come when not a few Christians, entire families and parishes, will join in and maintain the Church's prayer.

We can now view the Breviary with a new attitude. Besides the Missal, the hallowed book of the Sacrifice of the Mass, the

[5] Here Parsch is speaking of that radical right to community prayer, inherent in all Christians, prescinding from the special right priests obtain by virtue of the sacrament of orders, or religious by their profession. Cf. *Mediator Dei* (America Press ed., pp. 61 ff.). Tr.

Church treasures another precious book, her prayer book. The Breviary is the Church's official prayer book at which the Holy Spirit and the Church herself have been engaged for more than nineteen hundred years. It is a priceless anthology containing the prayers, thoughts, and aspirations of the greatest saints of all time. This prayer book has two important functions: it is the official common prayer of the Church, and it is a norm and guide for private prayer.

1. The Church, from day to day and from hour to hour, prays to God the Father through her divine Bridegroom, with the tongues of her priests and religious, and, we trust, soon of her lay children. Those who join in this prayer join not as mere individuals, distinct persons, but as members of Christ's mystical body. The Breviary, therefore, is first of all not a private prayer. Consequently the marked difference between private and liturgical prayer should be clear. In private prayer I pray mainly for myself and things that concern me. Here the prayer is focused on me, it is a more or less egocentric prayer. In liturgical prayer, and consequently in the Breviary, it is not so much "I" who pray, but the Church, the bride of Christ, who prays for the vast needs of the kingdom of God on earth. In praying the Breviary I am a member of a great community, a leaf on the tree that is Christ's Church, in whose life and growth I have a definite part. Thus he who prays with the Church rises above his own petty self, lending the Church his tongue to pay God a tribute of praise and thanks, and to pray for the graces and needs of the Church.

In the Breviary prayers, we weep, or rather the Church, through our tears, weeps with those who are sad, and through our joy she rejoices with the joyous and repents with the penitent. Every feeling of our Mother the Church finds its echo in our own expanded hearts. Our prayer takes on a richer meaning. We make our own the interests of the Church, even Christ's interests in man's redemption. It is a sublimely liturgical prayer that fashions us into true shepherds of souls, a work in which the laity also ought to have its share.

The Breviary is the Church's prayer. This fundamental thought should animate our hearts whenever we take up the Breviary. The Church is praying with these our lips.

2. The Breviary has another function. Individual souls are not overlooked in this world-wide prayer. The one who prays should himself grow spiritually along with his prayer. The Breviary should be the ladder on which the soul mounts to heaven. As the seasons of the year have their effect on nature, giving the trees growth and blossom and fruit, so too the Church year with its course of feasts and seasons should affect the soul. Through contact and "exposure" to the Church year, our soul matures for heaven; no book offers more contact with the life of the Church's liturgical year than does the Breviary. With this prayer book, moreover, the Church accompanies us through the day, and for each hour of the day she gives us a sword and a shield to spread and defend the kingdom of God in our soul: all this accomplished by the marvelous arrangement of the hourly prayer.

The Breviary is prayer on the hour. As the prayer that paces the Church year, it is in a sublime sense our guardian angel, our guide through life. We surely ought to make our guide's acquaintance and allow him to show us the way.

Here the universal, objective, pastoral prayer is wedded with personal prayer, the individual growing up into Christ. The one widens the vistas of the soul, breaking through the narrow walls that coop us up. The other leads us up into the secret citadel of our own spirit. You can hear in the Breviary two distinct voices praying in unison: the Church and your own soul, now one, now the other, usually both together, for they are as like one another as mother and daughter. For as man carries within himself a tiny world of his own which resembles the mighty universe, so every child of God bears within his soul a kingdom of God that closely resembles God's kingdom on earth, His Church.

Another striking thought that may help to a better understanding of the Breviary: the Breviary and the Mass form a unit: the spiritual, liturgical day. The Mass may be compared to the sun in the Christian day, a sun around which the hours of the Church's common prayer rotate like seven planets. The "hour-prayers" are a preparation for Mass, they hark back to it, they seek to garner its fruit and graces through the day. Or let us put it this way: Mass does not begin with the *Introibo ad altare Dei,* nor does it conclude with the *Ite missa est.* Rather it begins with the First Vespers of the day before, advances through Matins, Lauds, Prime, and Terce. These hours are a remote preparatory part of the Mass. In Sext and None and Second Vespers we hear the echo and hark back to the morning's Mass. Thus the Breviary serves the very heart and core of our worship, the Holy Eucharist, the Holy Sacrifice of the Mass.

CHAPTER II

Some Historical Notes on the Breviary

IN offering the reader a brief history of the Breviary, I intend to mention merely the more notable phases of its development from the beginning to its present form. My aim is simply to impart a deeper understanding of the prayer we have today, and at the same time to evoke respect and reverence for the age-old arrangement. I shall set my sights for these three marks: 1. the Church's prayer as an hourly tribute to God; 2. the Church's prayer as a public, social act of worship; 3. the development of this prayer into its present form.

The history of the Breviary can be divided into three periods which correspond fairly well with the divisions of profane history: the early ages, until Gregory I (*c.* 600); the Middle Ages (to 1520); modern times, from Pius V to Pius X. By the end of the first period, the form and arrangement of the Breviary were so completely established that there have been no substantial changes since. The second period sought to improve and enhance the heritage of the early ages, not always in accordance with the idea and nature of the Breviary, inasmuch as many errors slipped in. The third period is marked by the reform or revision of the Breviary; this reform is not yet completed. The three pontiffs I have mentioned exercised a profound influence on the development of the Breviary.

First period: the time from the apostles to Gregory I (*c.* 600). Since the Christians of apostolic times (until about the year 65) held their prayer services in common with the Jews both in the Temple and in the synagogues, it is evident that Jewish practice had a definite influence on the formation of our Christian prayer service. We must, therefore, first acquaint ourselves with the synagogue service.

At the Temple in Jerusalem the day was sanctified by three fixed hours of prayer and sacrifice. These three sacred hours, with their prayers and blessings, were carried over into the synagogue service but without the sacrifice, and even the private prayer of pious Jews was recited at these customary prayer hours: the third, sixth, and ninth hour of the day (Terce, Sext, and None). We might therefore say that the Jews had an official "hour prayer," which was held partly in private and partly in common, and which included three prayer periods.

Let us examine these three prayer hours more closely. The first was the hallowed time of the morning sacrifice (the continual sacrifice) that took place between sunrise and the third hour, about 9 o'clock. At the end of this sacrifice, psalms were sung, and festive prayers were recited. The act of worship closed with the priest's blessing. The essential part of the prayer service was a sort of Creed (*Shma:* Attend, O Israel) to which were added other prayers (called *Shemone Esre*). Among the psalms used, we are familiar with several: Sunday psalm 23, Monday 47, Tuesday 81, Wednesday 93, Thursday 80, Friday 92, Saturday 91.[1] In addition there was the daily morning prayer, consisting of psalms 5, 21, and 62, later psalms 148–150. Of these, psalms 62 and 148–50 have found their

---

[1] Even today this psalm is retained in the Roman Breviary in Lauds for Saturday.

way into the permanent contents of Lauds of the Roman Breviary. It was, then, similar to our Terce.

The second sacred hour was that of the daily peace offering (*Minchah*) shortly after midday. The rite for this prayer service was simpler and less rigidly defined. Frequently this noon prayer was combined with the evening prayer.

The third sacred hour was that of the evening sacrifice, which began at the ninth hour and lasted with various prayers till sunset. Our knowledge of the contents of this evening prayer is not precise. It seems, however, that the Hallel psalms (112–117) as well as psalms 120–136 were sung at this time. If such is actually the case, then we have in the Roman Breviary a continuation of this custom, since psalms 109–144 are divided among Vespers for the week. Such, then, were the prayer hours of the Jews.

The Christians of apostolic times participated in this prayer service at the Temple as well as in the synagogue and even in their private prayer. The Acts of the Apostles relates something of the worship of the early Christians. For prayer service they gathered together every day in the Temple; to celebrate the breaking of bread, they met in private homes. These meetings took place at a time coinciding with the daily morning and evening sacrifice in the Temple. These three prayer hours are even mentioned expressly in the Acts of the Apostles: "the third hour," [2] in which the Holy Spirit descended on the infant Church,[3] "the sixth hour," at which "Peter went up on the roof to pray," [4] the "ninth hour," at the hour of prayer when Peter and John went up into the Temple.[5]

---

[2] This third hour is not mentioned in the New Testament specifically as a prayer hour. Tr.

[3] Acts 2:15.

[4] Acts 10:9.

[5] Acts 3:1.

When the Christians began to withdraw from participation in the synagogue worship, they retained this division of prayer hours, at least in private prayer, with developments of their own.

We find the first evidence of an ordinance concerning prayer in St. Paul's first letter to Timothy [6]: "This first of all, I ask: that petition, prayer, entreaty, and thanksgiving should be offered for all mankind especially for kings and others in high station, so that we can live a calm and tranquil life. . . . It is my wish that . . . men everywhere lift up in prayer hands that are sanctified, free from all anger and dispute."

We cannot, it is true, determine from this passage whether or not the Apostle is speaking of a definite hour prayer. Nevertheless it is the earliest mention of a common-prayer service, which finds its continuation in the solemn orations on Good Friday.

The *Apostolic Teaching* (*Didache*) of the first century also bears witness to the three Christian prayer hours. It prescribes that three times a day all the faithful should recite the Our Father. There we clearly see a substitute for the Jewish hour prayers, which the Christians had now rearranged. Of course in this passage there is still question merely of private prayer.

Further, by the beginning of the third century, the number of prayer hours of the Christian day had mounted to six: the night prayer, morning prayer, Terce, Sext, None, and evening prayer. Still for the most part there is question only of private prayer. The *Apostolic Tradition* (*c.* 218) of St. Hippolytus offers significant testimony about these prayer hours of the early Christians. In chapter 32 we read:

All the faithful, men as well as women, on waking in the morning and before beginning their work, should wash, and raise their

[6] I Tim. 2:1 ff.

hearts to God in prayer, and only then betake themselves to work.
If, however, there is to be an instruction given about God's Word,
then everyone should rather go to the place of instruction. With
all his heart he ought to believe that he is listening to God Himself
speaking through the preacher. Then, after prayer in the Church,
he will be able to overcome the day's worries and difficulties. The
truly pious Christian, especially one who can read, will consider
it a great loss if he fails to attend an instruction in the Faith. So
whenever a teacher visits you, do not fail to go to the place where
he is to speak about the Faith, for this instructor may well preach
something profitable for each of you. You will hear something you
will not expect to hear, and you will derive fruit from what the
Holy Spirit offers through the mouth of your teacher. Thus your
faith will grow strong through what you hear. Furthermore, at
these instructions you will learn how you are to act at home. For
this reason, let each one try to go to the place where the Holy Spirit
is speaking.

If some day there is no instruction, then take up the Holy Scriptures and read for a while a goodly portion whatever seems profitable to you. If you are at home at the third hour, then say a prayer
of praise to God. If you are elsewhere at this hour, pray secretly in
your heart. For at this hour, we know Christ was nailed to the
cross. For this reason the law of the Old Testament prescribed
that a special loaf of bread (the loaves of show-bread or of
"proposition") should be presented each hour as a foretype of
the Body and Blood of Christ, and as a figure of the slaughtering
of an innocent lamb which in turn was a type of the perfect Lamb,
Christ. Christ is a shepherd too; again, He is the bread that came
down from Heaven. In the same way, you should pray again at
the sixth hour. When indeed, Christ was nailed to the cross, the
sun disappeared, and darkness shrouded the earth. Thus at this
sixth hour, we should offer an ardent prayer, in an effort to imitate
Him who prayed at that hour when the faithlessness of the Jews
cast its shadow on all creation. Then too, we should bring the
ninth hour to a close with a majestic prayer and song of praise,
that all may see how the soul of the just man praises the Lord our
God who remembered His chosen people and sent them His Son

to enlighten them. For at this hour Christ's side was pierced with a lance and blood and water issued forth, and thereupon it was light for the rest of the day till nightfall.

Thus you too, when you sleep, should begin a new day which should be for you a figure of the Resurrection. Before you go to bed, you ought to pray once more. Then, around midnight, arise, wash and pray; wash with clean fresh water. If you have a wife, pray alternately with her. If she is not yet a Christian, withdraw, and pray by yourself, and then return. However, even when you are obliged to your marital duties, do not omit your prayers, because you are not thereby defiled. For those who have washed once need not wash again, since they are fresh and clean. Breathe upon your hand and make the Sign of the Cross thereon with the spittle from your mouth, and you will be clean from head to foot. For this is a gift of the Holy Spirit, and a few drops of water form a cleansing that flows from a fountain that is the heart of the faithful, to cleanse those who believe in it. It is necessary for us to pray at this hour too, for the priests have passed on this practice to us, and taught us to wash also at this time. For at this hour slumbering creation pays its tribute of praise to God. The stars, the trees and the rivers seem to stand still; the vast host of Angels worship together with all the souls of the just. At this hour they sing their praises to God. Thus spoke the Lord when He declared "At midnight the cry arose: Behold the bridegroom cometh, go forth to meet Him." Then He added a word saying: "Watch therefore, for ye know neither the day nor the hour when the Son of man shall come." In the same way, arise at cockcrow, to pray. For at this hour the sons of Israel disowned Christ, whom we, the faithful, have acknowledged by our faith. Full of hope, we await the day of eternal light, that, through the resurrection of the dead, will give us light for all eternity.

Thus the instructions of St. Hippolytus regarding the hours of prayer. There was a practice, therefore, even at this time, of six prayer hours, though, in fact, it was still mostly private prayer. We should note, however, the remarkable depth of thought in this night prayer. Nowhere in ancient literature can one find so simple and yet forceful an appreciation of nature.

If you were to ask the origin of these six prayer hours, I might answer the following: Jewish as well as ancient Roman custom contributed to the development of Terce, Sext, and None, the three little hours; even in civilian Roman life these three hours were the principal divisions of the day. The other prayer hours are specifically Christian, and their origin I shall soon explain.

Besides the hours used for private prayer by the Christians, there began a public prayer of the Church, which was, however, quite independent of the public prayer in the Temple and the synagogue. It was of this prayer that Paul spoke in the passage cited above. Clement of Rome, one of the disciples of the apostles, mentions in a letter written about the year 96, that the apostles, at the behest of Christ, made certain prescriptions concerning the time and procedure of the celebration of the Christian worship. Since Clement distinguishes the sacrifice from the other acts of Christian worship, there must have existed a public prayer service. The pagan Pliny, too, mentions in his famous Report to Trajan that the Christians had the practice "*stato die ante lucem convenire carmenque Christo quasi Deo canere.*" Here for the first time we find mention of an official night prayer, the vigil. It became a common practice among the Christians to meet for public night prayer and vigil before Easter and the other Sundays of the year. Before Easter, the vigil lasted the whole night, at other times, only part of the night, because it was considered sufficient to spend the beginning of the night watch, and the end of the same from cockcrow on, in prayer. In this way Vespers and Lauds took their origin from the vigils. In the beginning the official prayer of the Church consisted of these three hours: the vigils, Vespers, and Lauds. The ecclesiastical writers of the second and third centuries testify to this nocturnal prayer service of the early Christians.

Tertullian (*c.* 200) writing to a Christian girl whom he would dissuade from marriage with a pagan, says: "What [pagan] husband will view with pleasure the fact that his wife leaves him when it is time for the evening assembly in the Church? Or what [pagan] husband would willingly allow her to spend the whole night of the vigil at Eastertime away from him?" [7] If the question should be raised how the public night prayer of the Christians came about, I would first of all insist that such a thing was quite unknown to the Jews, but was an innovation of the infant Church in the days of the martyrs. Surely the persecution of the Christians was a main factor in establishing the practice of public prayer worship at night, since the Christians could no longer assemble in daylight. So they combined the rite of prayer and sacrifice, both to be held at night. Perhaps too, the widespread belief that Christ's second coming (His Parousia) would occur around midnight occasioned the introduction of this custom of observing the vigils. St. Jerome approves this opinion, when he writes in his commentary on St. Matthew: "There is a tradition among the Jews that the Messiah will appear around midnight, as He did once in Egypt in time past, when the Passover was being celebrated, and the avenging angel stalked the land. Thus I believe that it was considered a custom handed down from the apostles, that it was wrong to dismiss the faithful before midnight on the vigil of Easter, inasmuch as they were awaiting Christ's second coming." [8] Since they considered each Sunday another Easter, it was natural to celebrate it in

[7] *Ad uxor.,* II, 5.
[8] Matt. 4:5.

somewhat the same fashion. But as a vigil that lasted the whole night would place too heavy a demand on the faithful, the observance of the vigil was usually limited to the beginning (Vespers) and the end of the night (Lauds).

That was the state of the prayer life of the Church until the beginning of the fourth century. Night prayer was public, divided into Vespers, Vigil, and Lauds; the three other "hours" were privately observed. But when the Church emerged from the catacombs under Constantine the Great in the year 313, her worship also began to enjoy the light and the freedom of the grand basilicas and thus experienced further development and elaboration. Vespers and Lauds now belonged to the daily community prayer of the Church, and even the little hours were at times held in public. At this point the spread of monasticism had a definite effect on the contents and make-up of these prayer hours.

Monasticism, which spread rapidly over the whole Church at the beginning of the fourth century, enthusiastically embraced this new practice of community hour prayer. What the layfolk performed of their own free will, the monks considered a sacred obligation and their main occupation in life. Consequently we find now that in the cloisters, the hour prayers with which the monks were familiar, were recited with some solemnity in common. Even the laity recited the hours with the clerics in the Church, usually only the more solemn and festive hours, as Matins on Sundays, and Vespers and Lauds during the week.

St. Hilary mentions that, around the year 365, Lauds and Vespers were recited daily in the whole Latin Church. We have many accounts of the observance of vigils before feasts and Sundays by both priests and laymen. There is the classic description of the divine worship as held in Jerusalem (which was famous as a place of pilgrimage), found in the memoirs of the French nun Aetheria (*c.* 385), according to which both the clergy and the laity celebrated all the hours.

St. Basil, the founder of monastic life in the East, describes in detail the Office of his day. It consisted of six hours: night prayer, morning prayer, Terce, Sext, and None, and lastly, evening prayer.

The first clear ordinances concerning prayer are found in the *Apostolic Constitutions* of the fourth century. There we can see the beginning of the development of the Office in both the East and the West. Morning and evening they prescribe a daily visit to the church. At the morning service psalm 62 was to be recited, and at Vespers psalm 140. Both of these psalms have retained their respective places in our Roman Office. Psalm 140 occurs in Friday Vespers and also in the ancient Vespers for Maundy Thursday and Good Friday; parts of it are used elsewhere in the Breviary as versicles, and so on (e.g., *Dirigatur oratio mea . . .*). By this time even the longer *preces*, or prayers at Vespers, had made their appearance. Certain prayers were prescribed for the third, sixth, and ninth hours because at these hours our Savior was condemned, was crucified, and died (VIII, 35). To answer the question regarding the make-up and contents of the hours at this time, we can say that they consisted for the most part of readings from Sacred Scripture, followed by the singing of psalms and hymns and concluded with certain prayers. Even today we have remnants of these ancient prayer hours. For example, the twelve prophecies we read on Holy Saturday formed a part of an ancient Christian vigil.

Now a few words about the ancient Vespers. It was an evening prayer which began when darkness set in and the evening star appeared. It was also called *Lucernarium,* that is, the hour at which the lamps were lit. Those prayers which were recited by the Christian assembly when the lamps were lit in the evening also bore the name *Lucernarium*. *Lucernarium* and Vespers were originally not one and the same hour; but because the one followed so closely on the other, the distinction gradually disappeared. Most probably the *Lumen Christi Deo Gratias*, and the blessing of the paschal candle are remnants of the ancient *Lucernarium*. It was only at the time of St. Benedict that Vespers became a daytime prayer hour.

About this time Prime and Compline were introduced into the cloister. John Cassian in his *Collationes*, written about 417, recounts how Prime was introduced at a monastery of Bethlehem. Among the monks the custom arose of returning to their cells after the night Office (Matins) and Lauds to rest, or to pray in private. The tepid, however, used to go to bed and sleep even to Terce. The more fervent confreres complained about this to the superiors, who, after long consultation, decreed that the monks should rest until sunrise. Then, however, all were to leave their beds and recite a morning prayer consisting of three psalms and certain prayers to begin the day's work. This practice gradually spread over the whole Church. Thus Prime originated some time between 390 and 400.

Compline is mentioned for the first time by name in the Rule of St. Benedict. Though already in St. Basil's time there were traces of an evening prayer distinct from Vespers, with psalms 4 and 90, yet we must acknowledge St. Benedict as the one who made Compline a separate prayer hour.

It is worthy of note that the first complete, detailed description of the Office of the Western Church is found in the Rule of St. Benedict. Benedict did indeed make his own independent arrangement of the Psalter; but the text he borrowed from the Roman Church. On the other hand the Church owes to St. Benedict much of her arrangement of the psalms and the make-up of the hours.

The Rule of St. Benedict lays down five principles or norms for the arrangement of the hours which in a general way were employed also in the Roman Office. 1. The entire Psalter was to be recited in the course of the week, and the whole of Scripture was to be read each year. 2. The mystic number of twelve psalms should be retained for the night Office (this norm prevailed in the Roman Office until the time of Pius X). 3. During the summer and in the day hours, the Office was to be shorter; on Sundays, and in the night hours, longer. 4. Since prudence is the mother of all virtues, consideration for human weakness should prevail and keep the Office from being too prolonged. For this reason Benedict made Vespers a part of the day Office, and introduced the hour of Compline. 5. Each hour was to be a well-defined unit which through a balanced arrangement of psalms, hymns, and other prayers was to form a harmonious composition.

Before introducing the most important figure in this first period we wish to mention two other men who had considerable influence upon the arrangement and formation of the Roman Breviary: St. Ambrose and Pope St. Damasus. In his spiritual dealings with St. Basil, Ambrose brought from the East to the West the practice of singing the psalms in alternate choirs, and also introduced the hymns, thereby contributing much to the enrichment and dramatization of the Office. The role of Pope Damasus with regard to the Breviary is not entirely clear. Nevertheless he did have an active part in the arrangement of the Office (whether he is responsible for the arrangement of the Psalter in the Roman Breviary is not definitely known). From what was at first but custom, for the

Roman clergy the obligation of reciting the hour prayer gradually developed. It became an *officium*. The East Roman emperor Justinian had this situation in mind when he decreed
in the year 528 that the clergy throughout the Empire in the
East and West should recite the night, morning, and evening
Office (Code I, 3).

This first period of Christian antiquity terminates with the
magnificent personage of Pope Gregory I. It was he who gave
the Roman liturgy the form that it possesses today. We may
also say that he brought the development of the Roman Breviary to a close, and thus established uniformity of the Breviary in the entire West. We cannot, it is true, discern precisely
what was already established in the Breviary with regard to
text and melody, from what Gregory himself contributed. In
any case the Antiphonary and the Responsale justly bear the
title "Gregorian."

The sons of St. Benedict were mainly responsible for the
spread of the Gregorian Office. They presided over the Office
in the basilicas and they were active also as missioners.

Second Period: the Middle Ages to the Council of Trent.
With regard to its text and formation, the Office was now complete. Throughout the Middle Ages no essential addition or
development occurred. At the most only accidental changes
and embellishments took place, but nothing along the classic lines of the Gregorian Office. Only a few notable additions
became a permanent part of the Breviary. Even the length-
ening of Compline through the addition of the *Nunc Dimittis*
can be traced back to Gregory I. Chrodegang von Metz (*d.*
766) added the second part of Prime, the Chapter Office
(*officium capituli*). The concluding antiphons to Our Lady
come into use after the thirteenth century. Thus the minor ele-

ments of the Breviary we have today were added one by one
in the course of the Middle Ages. In this period too, most of
the hymns were introduced, though at Rome itself hymns
were not to be found for yet some time. During this period
most of the festive Offices were composed; for example, the
Office at Tenebrae, the Advent Office, and the Office of the
Dead. The only festive Office whose author and date of composition we know is that of Corpus Christi, by St. Thomas
Aquinas in 1264.

It would be too tedious to enumerate all the details of the
development of the Breviary through the Middle Ages. Still
we should mention a fact which made the hour prayers the
Breviary which we use today. Up to this time, several books
were used for the community prayer: the Psalter for the
psalms, the Bible and homilies of the Fathers for the readings
(lessons), and the Antiphonary and Responsale for the choral
prayers. The length of the readings was left to the discretion
of the one who presided; it was anything but cut and dried.
Now, for the convenience of the officials of the Roman Curia,
who were often engaged in travel, a single book was compiled,
containing all the parts that were hitherto found in sundry
tomes. It was called *Breviarium secundum consuetudinem
Romanae Curiae (Breviary Used by the Roman Curia)*. There
was this difference however, that, in contrast with the ancient
Roman Office, the readings besides being shortened were
also well-defined. This book was the origin of our present Breviary. What actually guaranteed the successful spread of this
form of the Roman Office was the fact that the newly-founded
Order of Friars Minor began to use it. On their missionary
journeys, a small handy book that contained the whole Office
was quite welcome. We may note here that the Roman Office,
in comparison with that of the rest of the Church, had already

suffered many curtailments which were now absorbed into the Breviary. But we should note that the Breviary thus abridged and divided, often without regard for sense or continuity, considerably diminished the spiritual value of the ancient hour prayers. The broad, swift stream of community prayer now slackened, became an exactly defined obligation that the individual had to fulfill. Because of this book, what was once only a common and public prayer, was now recited privately by the individual priests bound to recite it.

Third period: This was the period of Breviary reform, undertaken by the two pontiffs, Pius V and Pius X.

In the course of the Middle Ages the Breviary suffered several abuses. For example, the great number of saints' feasts precluded the recitation of the whole Psalter during the week, as well as reading the whole of Scripture in the course of the year. In all three nocturns of a saint's feast, the readings were taken from the lives of the saints, and the psalms from the Common of the feast. Consequently the scheduled reading of Scripture often fell far behind, while the same few psalms were recited over and over, with the rest recited perhaps only once a month. These and other abuses clamored for reform toward the end of the fifteenth century.

The reformers comprised three groups: 1. The humanists, who were chiefly concerned with correcting the uncouth Latinity of the Breviary. For them the ideal would be a Breviary couched in Ciceronian Latin; one whose hymns would match as closely as possible the Horatian odes. At the behest of Leo X, one of this group, Zacharia Ferreri, made the first attempt at reform by composing a hymn book for the entire Church year. For these classicists considered the hymns the most insipid part of the Breviary. All the hymns are new in form; none of the old remain. Actually it was no improvement, but a pale and shoddy imitation of the splendid ancient chants of a grander and holier age.

The second group clung fast to the liturgical traditions and wished to relinquish nothing of the ancient text and form, though by no means did they close their eyes to the defects of the Breviary of their day. Their partiality for antiquity, however, was too great for them to attempt any radical change. At the Council of Trent these men began the reform which Pius V brought to a close. But before this happened, a third group had entered the field of reform. The latter in their tendencies stood somewhere between the other two groups: they might be characterized as the practical group. Even at this time they were influenced by the Reformation that threatened in Germany, and wished to comply with some of its just demands. One of this group, Cardinal de la S. Cruz Quignonez, a Spanish Franciscan, led the way by publishing at the Pope's request, in 1535, a new Breviary, called the *Breviarium Sanctae Crucis* ("The Breviary of the Holy Cross"). It was a radical departure from the ancient traditions. Though indeed it was the fruit of sincere religious zeal, and a great advance on the formalistic attempt of Ferreri, yet it was composed too much after the fashion of a private prayer. It did away completely with chapters, versicles, and responsories, and partly abolished the antiphons and hymns. Each hour had three psalms, which remained the same even on feast days. The Office remained uniform on Sundays, week days, and feast days. There was some leeway with regard to the readings from Scripture. Most of the Old and New Testament was read in the course of a year. In judging the merits of this Breviary, however, we should remember it was not intended for choral or community use; thus all the parts which the community usually recited (e.g., antiphons and responses) were omitted.

With the Pope's permission, the secular clergy was permitted to use this *Breviarium Sanctae Crucis* in private recitation. It is quite understandable, however, that such a radical change would provoke a storm of protest. Before long some renowned theologians viewed it askance, and in 1558 Paul IV, a champion of the second class of reformers, forbade its use.

If the *Breviarium Sanctae Crucis* had been of no other value, at least it served as a call for reform of the Breviary. The Council of Trent began this reform, which Pius V brought to a close with the publication of the revised Breviary (*Breviarium Pianum*) in 1568. The spade work for this revision was done, behind the scenes, by the cofounders of the Theatines, St. Cajetan and the future Paul IV. The new Breviary held fast to the ancient traditions, endeavoring only to cut away the weeds that had found their way into the Breviary. The number of feasts was reduced, the devotional Offices (Office of the Dead, the Little Office, and the gradual psalms), which were gradually becoming obligatory, were suppressed or abrogated. The yearly reading of the entire Scriptures and the weekly recitation of the Psalter were restored. The apocryphal lives of the saints were either expunged or amended, and finally a general list of rubrics was appended.

The new Breviary was well received, for it put an end to the variations and uncertainty that prevailed up to that time. That it was subject to criticism, of course, was to be expected. For example, the lessons of the second nocturn were not yet sufficiently reliable from a historical viewpoint. The new Breviary was introduced into most of the Churches of the Latin rite. Only those dioceses and orders which possessed their own Breviary for more than two hundred years, were exempted from the use of the new Breviary.

In the next few centuries, various improvements were made on the Breviary of Pius V but they were only of secondary importance. Clement VIII amended the lives of the saints, altered the rank of many feasts, and revised the Vulgate text of the Bible. Of great consequence, however, was the attempt of Urban VIII to revise the hymns. In an effort to lend a classic polish of meter and prosody to the hymns, he tried to improve the hymns of Prudentius, Fortunatus, and St. Ambrose. Altogether 952 "mistakes" were "corrected." For example, the hymn for the dedication of a church was completely recast. Unfortunately we have kept these "corrected" hymns in our Breviary even to this day, though they fairly shout for restoration to their original form.

Meanwhile, since the time of Pius V, nearly a hundred feasts had crept into the calendar, producing the usual situation of suppressed ferial offices and even Sunday offices, as before the reform of Pius V. For this reason the scholarly Pope Benedict XIV wished to inaugurate a new reform. He resolved to introduce no new festive Office during his pontificate, and he kept his resolve. However, he never succeeded in any further reform.

In France in the seventeenth and eighteenth centuries there arose a movement against the Roman Breviary, which effected the introduction of a special Breviary in several dioceses tainted with Jansenism. But this Gallican Breviary did not endure, and it was doubtlessly the greatest accomplishment of the Abbé Gueranger that the whole of France embraced the Roman Breviary again.

Only in recent times Pius X undertook a reform of the Breviary; by dividing the reform into two parts, he was able to bring it to temporary conclusion. Anything that required lengthy preparatory work (e.g., the historical lessons, the general rubrics) was postponed, and unfortunately even today remains "unfinished business." Yet Pius X did accomplish a thorough rearrangement and abridgment of the Psalter in the Breviary. We shall treat more precisely of some of the details of this revision.

We must admit that even today the Breviary is a sort of black sheep, a Cinderella of the clergy. It still cries for reform and revision. I hope this may soon come, but the Breviary will always be like the "father of the family" we read of in the Gospel, who brings forth from his treasures things ever new and old. I trust it may always remain true to the ancient traditions, whose heritage the Church guards so carefully, but may it always bear in mind the wants and needs of modern times. I hope especially that the number of saints' feasts may be reduced, so that the classic beauty of the liturgy with its Offices of the temporal cycle, and the Scripture readings may shine forth once again.

The Office, then, in its form and arrangement is most venerable, and certainly belongs to the most precious gems of our liturgy. Even these brief historical notes must have suggested this to the reader.

CHAPTER III

The Breviary as Hourly Prayer

T HE Church lives in and along with time, a fact we see plainly in the Church's liturgical year, and even more so in her Office. Through the latter we can sanctify and consecrate our entire day to God. Christ's words, "Pray always and faint not," become a reality in the Office. For each part of the day the Church has its special prayers to form an hour whose contents are suited to the needs of that hour of the day. The day is somewhat like a journey through the dry desert of life, where every three hours we come upon an oasis with the cool water of God's grace in the pleasant shade of His protection. This is what each hour of the Office is, an ardent turning to God in our passage through the day.

I recall here what I mentioned in the historical account of the origin of the different hours. After the period of the persecutions the main hours were the vigils, Lauds, and Vespers; Terce, Sext, and None were almost invariably private prayers, though frequently enough in monasteries even these were recited in common. Since the vigils were usually composed of three parts (i.e., the three nocturns), there was indeed a sort of balance in the arrangement of the hours: a morning and an evening prayer. The three divisions of daylight corresponded to the three "watches" (nocturns) of the night. Thus the whole day was sanctified in its principal divisions. The two most recent hours of Prime and Compline were born in the cloister, and were developed almost exclusively out of the life and circumstances of the monasteries. After the monks had chanted Matins during the night, and then Lauds, they went to rest; at sun-up they rose again, and, since they did not wish to begin the day's work without prayer, the hour of Prime was introduced as a sort of second morning prayer, and a consecration of the day's work to God. St. Benedict made Vespers a part of the daytime Office, to be held before the evening meal; then, before going to bed, several other religious exercises were to be held in the dormitory (spiritual reading, chapter of faults, etc.). This practice gradually evolved into the hour of Compline.

Thus the evolution of the hours was completed. Today we have three (in ferial offices, only one) night hours or nocturns, and three day-hours; two morning prayers and two evening prayers: in all, ten (or eight) hours, most of which serve to sanctify the three-hour period that follows them, and in the Roman Breviary they are divided into three parts in such a way that practically each hour of the day has its own special prayers. Only Vespers and Lauds are composed of five parts, and these hours, the morning and evening prayers, enclose the whole spiritual day, the one ushering it in, the other bringing it to a close.

For an understanding of the Office, two other ideas are important: the historical-redemptive background, and the special thought that belongs to each hour. The Church likes to recall on certain days and at certain hours the events in the history of our redemption that happened at the same time or hour. Thus, as we pray each hour of the Breviary, some such event is presented to us, to serve as a pictorial background for that particular hour; it can stimulate the imagination and thereby increase our devotion, somewhat like the mysteries of the Rosary. The special thought for each hour is that which arises from the very needs of the hour; it is the intention for which the Church prays at this hour, and is often closely related to the historical-redemptive background. Some thought and meditation on these two points make the best preparation for the devout recitation of an hour. Let us glance at the various hours, and examine these two ideas.

I. MATINS

It is night, and the noise and bustle of day are hushed: everything is still. The Church is at prayer, recalling the nocturnal vigils of Christ her bridegroom on the mountains of Galilee. She thinks of the prayer of the early Christians at night in the catacombs. Though times have changed, the Church insists that the night is not only for slumber, but is also the time for prayer. In ages past, the thought of the Parousia predominated in Matins, the longing for the return of the Lord, during the night until dawn broke: a thought that still finds its echo in the hymns for Matins.

Nowadays, Matins for Sunday reminds us that the three nocturns used to be prayed at the beginning, the middle, and the close of night. The first versicle runs: "In the evening I think of Thy name, O Lord." In the second nocturn: "I rise at midnight to praise Thee." In the third nocturn, "I looked for Thee even before the dawn." However, of all the hours, we have to admit that Matins has the fewest characteristics of an hour prayer and, since it is but loosely coupled with the hours of the night, it can just as readily be recited, without any great loss of devotion, on the day before or even on the morning of the day itself. Instead of a special hour thought, the thought of the feast prevails, finding its expression in the lessons and other variable parts of the Office. Feast-day Matins are a meditation, a sort of prayer drama for the feast; one must study Matins in order to find the true meaning of a feast. Many feast-day Matins are masterpieces of prayer composition (e.g., the Matins for the last three days in Holy Week, the Matins for the Office of the Dead, for the Dedication of a Church, for Corpus Christi). The psalms for Matins during the week are mostly a prayerful, prolonged meditation on God's kingdom, to prepare us for each new day of redemption. Only on the greater feasts (so-called doubles) and on Sundays are there three nocturns for Matins. Otherwise all nine psalms are combined to form one nocturn, concluding with the oration. Matins has a magnificent introduction, the Invitatory, and also a splendid conclusion, the *Te Deum* on Sundays with festive office, feast days, and during Paschaltide. The Invitatory song, with the venerable psalm 94, is a liturgical masterpiece. But to sense the full effect of this "Invitation," one must hear it chanted at night, with all the solemnity of the liturgy. Hear, for instance, the joyous tidings, *Christus natus est nobis,* "Christ is born to us" (Invitatory for Christmas): truly the "good news," ringing out like the merry cry of the herald in the stillness of the night, a splendid prelude to the day's feast. The *Te Deum* is a song of praise of the whole Church to the triune God, and especially to Jesus Christ, which closes with an earnest plea for protection. It is at the same time an excellent transition to Lauds.

II. Lauds

Lauds is a joyous hour, fresh as the morning dew, and perhaps the most beautiful of all the hours. We can afford to dwell awhile on its symbolism: It is still night, men and all nature are asleep. In the distant east the dawn is breaking, gray at first. Then a reddening colors the sky, the herald of day, and all nature begins to awake. This is but a comparison, an image of an event in the story of our redemption; it was just about this hour that our Savior burst the bonds of death. He is celebrating His resurrection once again, and that is the historical thought, the background of this hour. These two sublime ideas suggest a third: the spiritual awakening of mankind. There is, then, a threefold awakening: nature awakes, our Savior arises from the tomb, and man celebrates his own spiritual resurrection. With these three ideas in the back of our minds, we recite the hour of Lauds. It is evidently a song of praise, and praise is the theme of the hour. Anybody who turns these three ideas over in his mind, and immerses himself in this theme of resurrection, who rejoices and praises and prays along with nature, if possible even outdoors in the early morning, will certainly grasp the spirit and meaning of the hour. Indeed, Lauds is a clear example of what the spiritual background and the actual hour of the day can do to further our devotion in the recitation of the Breviary. For this very reason the psalms chosen for Lauds are songs of praise. We can readily discern in them the theme of nature. And the idea of resurrection appears mostly in the antiphons at Lauds, especially the frequent Alleluia. We can see this particularly on Sunday, which is in truth our weekly Easter. Here the day and the hour of the resurrection coincide.

The climax of Lauds is the Gospel canticle, the Benedictus. It is a song of praise and thanksgiving for the redemption, a greeting for the new day of redemption given us, to be a further step in the perfection of God's kingdom on earth. The Church is the one that prays now, taking the place of Zachary. Our Redeemer comes to us each day, and the Church salutes

Him as the "Orient on high," the divine "Sun." Thus Lauds is also a song of praise to the "Sun."

III. Prime

Prime is the Church's second morning prayer, but quite different from Lauds. The latter is actually the ideal morning prayer, the prayer of all creation on awakening. Prime is rather the morning prayer of poor sin-ridden man, more of a subjective prayer, if we can speak of subjective prayer in the liturgy. The idea behind Prime is the good intention, or a sort of girding for the day's battles and the day's work. This thought pervades the whole hour, and there is no definite historical-redemptive background. The idea of the good intention and preparation for the day's work and struggles commands all our attention, so that thoughts and ideas proper to feast days are somewhat suppressed in this hour. The hymn for Prime dedicates all our thoughts and deeds to God, our Creator, and forearms us against the day's perils, thus neatly crystallizing the prayer sentiments of Prime.

Prime also has a part that does not vary from day to day, and that makes of Prime a beautiful morning prayer. After the psalms, comes the usual conclusion for the little hours: chapter, responsory, versicle, and oration. The chapter *Regi saeculorum* ("To the eternal King"), a pledge of fealty to the King of heaven: "love, peace, and truth," a program for the day. The responsory is an earnest plea, with the realization of our own weakness. The blind man of Jericho sits by the roadside. Jesus passes by, and the man cries out: "Have mercy on us." Today in the Office, I am the blind beggar crying out to Christ as He passes. The beautiful oration never changes and contains all the elements of a good morning prayer: gratitude, petition, good intention, preparation for the day's work;

particularly the lovely petition "that I may commit no sin to-day." With the oration, the first part of the hour of Prime, called the choir office, comes to a close.

At this point the monks adjourned to the chapter hall for the daily chapter and chapter office. This consisted of four parts of their daily order which can still be traced in the following part of Prime: 1. The reading of the Martyrology, the Church's official register of her canonized children. From a psychological point of view, it is profitable to call to mind the day's heroes as our models, at the very time when the day's struggles are to commence. 2. Distribution of chores for the day, by the Father Abbot. The next prayers and verses refer to this and express in beautiful phrases the good intention and consecration of the day's work to God, all of them masterpieces of prayer. 3. The reading of a chapter from the Rule, or a passage of Sacred Scripture (even today, among the Benedictines, the rule is read at this point). 4. The Father Abbot gives his blessing. Like little children we receive God's paternal blessing before we go out for the day's work. This blessing occurs twice in the Office, in Prime at the beginning of the day, and at Compline at its close. Prime also serves as the hour prayer for the following three hours (i.e., from six to nine o'clock). Note also the beautiful blessing before the capitulum that sums up in terse and forceful language the theme of Prime, preparation for the day's work: "May almighty God direct our actions and our days in His peace."

IV. TERCE

Nine o'clock. The Church wishes us to turn our hearts to God for a brief while during the day's work. This is the meaning of the little hours. They are breathing spells for the soul, oases in the journey through life's desert. We should not recite all these hours at one sitting, but rather each at its appointed time, so as to consecrate that particular hour of the day. Since the day is meant for labor, the little hours are purposely short.

In Terce, the historical-redemptive background plays a part. It was about the third hour on Pentecost that the Holy Spirit descended on the infant Church (the hymn for Terce at Pentecost is the *Veni Creator*). The Church recalls that mystery at this hour. Thus Terce spiritually invigorates and fortifies us for the day's battles. The theme of the hour, then, is the invocation of the Holy Spirit. The themes of the little hours are aptly expressed in the hymns. Two particularly beautiful thoughts are to be noted in the hymn for Terce: 1. Our body is the dwelling, the temple of the Holy Spirit, a temple which we must adorn as best we can. Every power and every faculty of our body must tell of the beauty of this divine temple. 2. Love for God and for our neighbor is a gift of the Holy Spirit.

V. SEXT

Twelve o'clock. Theme: The day's struggle is at its height. The heat of our passions is at its strongest. Hell has its greatest power over men; man's fallen nature has the upper hand. Historical-redemptive background: Our Savior is hanging on the Cross (twelve to three o'clock). Hell unleashes all its might against Him. Good Friday forms the background for sext, while in the foreground we and the Church wage the battle against sin. "Lead us not into temptation" summarizes the meaning of this hour.

The hymn recalls the beautiful symbolism of noon. In the morning the dawning sun brings us light; at noon, with its fiery brilliance, it gives us warmth. This noonday heat is a symbol for two evil and two good elements in man's life. (a)

The heat of strife and quarrel—hatred; the fire of passion—concupiscence. (b) Health of body (heat and warmth are medicines for life and health); peace of heart (the stillness at midday in the Orient is a figure of this peace).

VI. NONE

Three to six o'clock. Another day given for our salvation is slowly drawing to its close; our thoughts are of the end of life. Man, looking into the future, asks himself: "Will I persevere?" The theme, then, is perseverance. There is no real historical redemptive background, at most the last things.

The hymn gives us a beautiful view of the symbolism of this hour: 1. Evening closing in (three to six o'clock) reminds us of the fickleness of life: the contrast between the immutable God and the ever-changing world, implicitly including fickle, inconstant man. This unexpressed thought paves the way for the second stanza.

2. Negative ideas. The close of evening is a figure of anxiety, of temptation and inconstancy. The soul hurries to the light, to Jesus Christ. If Christ gives us light in the evening of temptation and affliction, in the evening of our life, then the divine life of grace will never leave us. Positive ideas: Evening time is also a figure of the end of life and, in fact, of a holy and happy death. This we ask as a reward for a truly pious life.

VII. VESPERS

Vespers is the ancient evening prayer of the Church, the *Lucernarium* or candle-light worship, the evening tribute of praise to God that corresponds to Lauds, the morning hour of praise. There is a difference inasmuch as our praise is also a tribute of thanks as we glance back over the past day, given us to work out our salvation. Our Mother the Church reviews the favors and graces which her divine Spouse has lavished on her and her children through the Holy Spirit; she thanks God for them. Vespers is, then, a prayer of praise, and especially of thanks. The climax of this expression of gratitude we find in the Magnificat, the Church's glorious song of thanks. Here it is the Church and the soul, mother and daughter, that pray; they put their sentiments of gratitude on the lips of the greatest of creatures, God's own Mother. The theme is simple: thanks for the past day's blessings. In Vespers, too, there is a historical redemptive background: the Last Supper. It was about the time when one prays Vespers, that Christ sat at the Last Supper with His apostles; thus we can relate Vespers also with the Holy Eucharist; in fact, a great many of the Vesper psalms are Eucharistic songs, or can readily be applied to the Eucharist; especially the so-called Hallel psalms (112–17) which were sung at the Last Supper, and the gradual psalms (119–33), which were sung by the pilgrims on their way to the Temple. This Supper is itself a figure of the heavenly banquet. Nevertheless Vespers suffers by comparison with Lauds, for, whereas the psalms for Lauds are specially selected, those for Vespers merely follow the order of the Psalter. For this reason we do not find exclusively psalms of thanksgiving as we might expect.

VIII. Compline

Compline is the Church's second night prayer. It differs from Vespers by being rather the personal prayer of the sinful soul seeking to return to rest and peace with God. Mark well again the difference between these two night prayers: Vespers is an objective song of praise and prayer of thanksgiving for another day given for our salvation. Compline, on the contrary, is a subjective prayer of repentance and plea for a restful night. Vespers glances back over the past day in a spirit of gratitude; Compline reviews the day only briefly, in a spirit of contrition, then prayerfully looks to the coming night, asking God's protection.

Compline is a masterpiece of composition, the work of St. Benedict himself, and can be called the ideal night prayer. Its symbolism is beautiful. The hour begins straightway, without any introductory prayer, pauses awhile for an examination of conscience and an act of contrition. Both in Holy Scripture and in the liturgy, the sun and light are favorite comparisons and figures for the Godhead, for Christ, and the divine life. Christ is the divine Sun, the Christian is a child of this Sun. Such thoughts as these recur frequently in this hour. The opposite of light, night with its darkness, is also a favorite image in the liturgy and the Bible for the sinister powers of hell. This thought of night and of darkness predominates in Compline. The darkness we recognize as the devil's trademark. Night is the mantle of the Prince of this world. The Christian, being a child of light, is afraid of this darkness, and like a little chick it scurries beneath the wings of the hen to escape Satan, the wheeling hawk. I would stress the point once again, that in liturgical prayer we think not only of ourselves, but also of our fellow men for whom "night" is falling, whether the night of trial, of sin, or of death. And is it not true that the enemy lays his snares under cover of darkness? It is as though when night falls, hell disgorged all its inmates upon the earth, to prey upon men. How many sins indeed night enfolds in its darkness! And for this very reason the Christian prays at night for protection against the powers of hell, for himself and all his fellow men.

Sleep too is a symbol, a figure of death. As man thinks of death almost spontaneously on going to sleep, Compline be-

comes also the night prayer of life, a prayer for a happy death.
It contains many striking thoughts on this point. The blessing
at the very beginning is a crisp but thoughtful summary of
these two ideas: "May Almighty God grant us a restful night
and a happy death." For a historical-redemptive background
for our prayer, we have the agony of Jesus at Gethsemane, and
consequently we can pray Compline for the Gethsemane in our
own life and in that of our fellow men. It is, then, prayer of petition. Contrition, plea for protection, and deep confidence are
the chief ideas involved. The section following the psalms
is unusually beautiful. After the hymn we have the lovely
capitulum, "Thou art in the midst of us." God and Jesus are in
our midst; we are gathered in their name. "Forsake us not" is
the main thought, the main petition, to which is added the
following versicle and response. Next are two images of death.
The first is found in the responsory: Jesus is hanging on the
cross, breathing out His last words: "Father, into Thy hands
I commend My spirit." And we, mindful of this scene, say the
very same words: "To you, my Redeemer, now in the night of
this day, and of my life, I commend my spirit." The versicle
that follows contains two favorite images of night: (a) Guard
me as the apple of your eye. I need your protection as much
as the eye does, and I wish to be as dear to you as your eye.
(b) Like chicks we fly to shelter under your wings. Now the
second figure of death: in the Gospel canticle, *Nunc dimittis*,
Simeon, the old man, is chanting his swan song. We are in a
similar situation, for we bear in our hearts and hands the
mystical Christ. We pray now for release from God's service
on earth. This is the "night off" after our day's work, and perhaps, even after our life's work. The antiphon for Simeon's
canticle is full of meaning, too. There is an alternation of sleep
and vigil for soul and body. In this prayer also we can see that

Compline is a prayer for a peaceful night as well as for a happy death. The Oration crystallizes in brief but thoughtful phrases the theme and leading ideas of Compline.

Now our night prayer gradually concludes with several versicles and the blessing of our heavenly Father. We bid our heavenly Mother Mary "good night" with the antiphon to Our Lady. Then all is quiet in the choir. We pray silently the Our Father and the Apostles' Creed, with which the Office for the day terminates, just as it began (with the Creed). For faith is truly the beginning and end of our whole life. We can arrange these leading thoughts on the hours in the following schema.

	Theme or Thought for the Hour	Historical - Redemptive Background
Matins	(Awaiting the Parousia)	Thoughts of the feast predominate
Lauds	Praise: spiritual resurrection	Christ's resurrection
Prime	Preparation for the day's struggles	
Terce	"Come Holy Spirit"	The descent of the Holy Spirit
Sext	Sin: "Lead us not into temptation"	Christ on the cross
None	Perseverance	The last things
Vespers	Thanksgiving: preparation for Holy Eucharist	Last Supper; heavenly wedding feast
Compline	Contrition: protection for the night	Christ in the Garden

The busy priest may shake his head on reading through the sketch just given above. It would indeed be an ideal schedule for the day's prayer. But who would have the time to adhere to such a distribution and arrangement of the hours? Of course, I admit that no one can adhere to such a schedule slavishly; still we should try to observe at least the principal divisions in the morning and evening office. Especially we ought to avoid treating the Breviary as something of secondary importance, as a sort of pastime for idle moments, with the idea that "now I have a few minutes free, I can breeze through a few hours." This prayer must have a central place in a priest's life, and precisely this attitude is of the greatest importance: I must take up my Breviary with a holy reverence, as one of the most important works of the day. It would surely be a mistake if I were to find my devotion in private prayers, and scurry through the recitation of the Breviary. No, the Breviary should be the golden paten on which I place the best fruits of the day's prayer.

Further, I should not recite the Breviary all at one sitting, as they say. The value of this prayer increases according as the hours are recited separately. The ideal must always be to pray each one separately at its special hour. The Breviary is intended to sanctify the whole day, to accompany us through the day, to give us for each period of the day just the proper medicine and strength. This aim can be achieved only if we recite each hour at its proper time.

My resolutions, then, are: 1. to say at least the liturgical morning and night prayers at their right time, even though the sequence of the hours is broken. This is quite permissible in private recitation.[1] Therefore I shall recite Lauds and Prime

---

[1] Therefore Matins may be anticipated, and Compline may be recited afterward, before going to bed.

early in the morning, with Vespers and Compline in the evening; better still, Vespers before supper, and Compline before going to bed. One needs no other morning or evening prayer; these are the best of all.[2] 2. I shall recite each of the three little hours separately: Terce after Mass, Sext at noon, None after siesta. 3. I can readily anticipate Matins, though not with Lauds following immediately.

[2] This should not be understood as discouraging private prayer, which ought to be the complement of public, liturgical prayer. Cf. *Mediator Dei* (America Press ed., p. 70). Tr.

PART II

THE CONSTITUENT PARTS

Introductory

Upon examination, we find that the hours are composed of various parts, some larger, some smaller, like a mosaic made up of many little pieces of stone. Each part has its own definite function and purpose with which we must become familiar if we would completely understand the make-up of the hour. When the hours are reduced to the most important elements, we find three salient parts: the psalms, the lessons, and the orations. The psalms, among which are also included other poems of Sacred Scripture, constitute man's upward turning to God; the lessons, taken, for the most part, from Sacred Scripture or commentaries on Sacred Scripture, are God's turning to man. The very essence, then, of the Breviary prayer is a dialogue between man and God, with man usually speaking first and God answering.[1] The orations crystallize our petitions for divine help and are usually at the conclusion of the hours, or at the conclusion of the subdivisions of the hours. The remaining minor parts of the Breviary (antiphons, responsories, hymns, verses and versicles, blessings, introductory and concluding verses) are bound up with and grouped around these three principal parts. Moreover, these minor parts can be rightly understood only in their relationship to the principal parts. In the following pages we shall treat first the principal parts; the minor parts will then follow naturally.

[1] We shall see that originally the very opposite was true.

47

CHAPTER IV

The Psalms

I F one should ask why a great portion of the clergy is more or less at odds with the Breviary, we must answer that the fault lies with the psalms. A whole series of complaints can be arrayed against them, complaints that state why the psalms are difficult or unsuitable for prayer. I shall present these difficulties in the psalms in all frankness, taking into account those positive aspects which reveal their worth, while at the same time candidly noting those negative aspects which give rise to the difficulties.

A. There are three main positive arguments for the value of the psalms.

1. At all times the psalms have been an essential and indispensable part of the Christian liturgy. Even in the synagogues, the psalms were the official prayer for centuries. From the very first days of its existence and down to the present time, the Church has always made use of the psalms as an essential element of her prayer life. There has never been a time when either theoretically or practically the psalms were excluded from her liturgical prayer, and there are no indications that matters will be otherwise in the future.

Christ Himself prayed the psalms and stressed the fact that they speak of Him: "All that was written of Me in the law of Moses, in the prophets, and in the psalms, must be fulfilled" (Luke 24:44). We have reason to believe that in all the critical incidents of His life and even while hanging on the cross, Christ prayed the psalms or portions of them. The apostles, the Blessed Virgin, the early Church prayed the psalms. In the Church of the Cenacle, in the Church of the catacombs, psalms were sung, and psalms accompanied the martyrs to the place of execution. As the Church was waging its fierce wars against the heretics, lowly hermits prayed the psalms. And in the basilicas of ancient Rome the chant of psalms rose up before the dazzle of golden mosaics. In thousands and thousands of monasteries night and day, there was a continual chant of psalms. All his life the lonely village pastor prayed the psalms in the name of the Church, and wove all his sorrows, his struggles, and his privations around them. And so it shall remain, for the Church will ever consider the psalms her best and dearest prayers. The psalms, thus considered, have indeed very great value.

2. Esthetically and theologically the psalms are invaluable. For among them are poems which hold a high place in world literature. That this was frequently overlooked is due, no doubt, to the imperfections of the Latin Vulgate translation, where the poetry, the arresting phrases, the glowing imagery, the delicate balance of strophe against strophe—the whole artistic pattern—can no longer be savored. Thus it happens that members of the laity who use a good translation marvel at the brevity of the psalms, while priests who use the Vulgate rarely do. I will later on note some examples of the poetry found in the psalms.

Moreover, the theology contained in the psalms is remarkable. Note, for example, how strikingly the eternity of God is contrasted with the mortality of man in psalm 89. Psalm 138 admirably extols the omniscience and omnipresence of God, and many psalms voice firm, unswerving trust in God. Psalm

102 describes the fatherly kindness of God in such a way that one would almost think it a prayer written after the coming of Christ. And again, what a deeply religious feeling for nature we find in the psalms! The Messianic psalms picture Christ in all His greatness both as man and as God. More than one author has attempted to compose a theology of the Psalter. Inasmuch as the psalms are also prophetical poems, they truly speak of things that belong specifically to the Church; e.g., the Eucharist, the external society. We can rightly conclude that the psalms are prayers and hymns of truly high value. They are worthy to be the prayer formulas of all times.

I note the opinion of but one from among many renowned scholars. Friedrich Delitzsch, a noted Oriental scholar, who in his studies of the Old Testament was somewhat of a liberalist and often denied its divine inspiration, wrote a long essay on the psalms, in his collected works, *Deutsche Reden in schwerer Zeit*. It was entitled "The Psalms and Modern Times" and had exalted words of praise for the psalms. The following is an excerpt from his essay:

> "I lift up my eyes toward the mountains;
>   whence shall help come to me?
> My help is from the Lord,
>   who made heaven and earth" [2]

When, as fifth form students at the University, we were reading this 121st psalm during our Hebrew course, our professor, who had quite a reputation as an authority in Latin and Greek literature, told us that he knew of no poem in classic literature to match this psalm. This made a deep impression upon our youthful susceptibilities and aroused in us a desire for deeper research into the Old Testament. Later, when my various studies led me first to the banks of the Ganges to the sacred literature of

[2] Ps. 120:1 f.

the Brahmans and Hindus, and then to Babylon, along the Euphrates, I could not fail to remark, and this I have maintained many times, that several ideas of the sages of Babylon, about the creation of the world, the origin of sin, have had a deep influence upon the authors of the Old Testament. But I have never failed to maintain that neither Babylonian nor Indian nor Semitic literature has a collection of poems that can bear the faintest comparison with the Psalter of the Old Testament. This is true because of the poetic beauty of many individual poems, but in particular because of the sincere preoccupation with the riddle of human life, and the stirring recurrence of unalloyed religious sentiment, forming a veritable paean of trust in God ranging from a silent *piano* to a thundering *fortissimo*. Indeed this book is unique in world literature. The short, truly remarkable words with which human life is not only described, but also plumbed to its depths, have in their poignant simplicity and truth, resounded through the world.

But much more telling is the testimony of men of prayer, because the Psalter is primarily, even exclusively, a book of prayer. We can indeed say that saints of all times have vied with one another in praising the psalms. How deeply St. Augustine was affected by psalm 4, shortly after his conversion! He describes this for us in his *Confessions* [3] and at the same time gives us an example of how the psalms should be prayed. We can go so far as to say that during the first centuries of Christianity the prayer life of the faithful found its sole expression in the psalms. It sounds strange for us today to hear that in the time of St. Jerome farmers hummed psalms while plowing, as did the workman at his trade. The psalms, it seems, did not belong to the priest only, but were vital in the lives of the laity as well. And the homilies and explanations of the psalms, written by Origen, Eusebius, Gregory of Nyssa, Chrysostom, Ambrose, and Augustine show us that in those days people did not pray the psalms mechanically, but found

[3] *Conf.*, IX, 4.

in them fruit for their everyday lives. St. Augustine's *Enarrationes super Psalmos* ranks among the profoundest works of that prolific writer.

3. There is yet another cogent argument. The psalms are inspired works. Since they are included in Sacred Scripture we believe that they were composed under the inspiration and guidance of the Holy Spirit, and therefore they are not merely free from error, but proclaim the very truths of God. We must believe that the psalms are prayers which God Himself has given us. God, then, in hearing the psalms, hears His own words. As St. Augustine says, "God praised Himself that men might fittingly and worthily praise Him." This fact compels us to have a deep reverence for the psalms. They are prayers that incomparably excel all other merely human prayers. For this reason the Church clings tenaciously to the psalms in her liturgy and prefers them to all other prayers.

Only in recent times have we Catholics once again begun to recognize the importance of the Scriptures as the Word of God, as God's revelation. We have even begun to see the sacramental character of the Bible. The same is true of the Psalter. Where the psalms are sung or prayed, there God is present, there grace abounds, there the power of hell is banished. We ought to approach the psalms with deep reverence, for through them the Holy Ghost speaks to us "in unspeakable groanings."

B. Still we must be honest enough to see and admit the difficulties and shortcomings of the psalms. Practically speaking, these are more noticeable than the positive considerations, and they can be such as to embitter one's love and esteem for the psalms. Therefore I will by no means ridicule or conceal these difficulties with small talk. And yet we will have to admit that the positive arguments far outweigh the negative ones. I shall mention several such negative objections.

The first objection is weighty. How can I use the psalms as prayers since they belong to a time long past, and to a foreign country; since they come from a people whose mentality and mode of life are so different from our own? From the fact that they are inspired poems, and therefore sacred prayers, does it follow that I can use them to give expression to my own prayer life? I cannot make my own all the prayers of the saints. Food which I cannot digest and assimilate will give me no nourishment. Can I then digest the psalms to nourish my life of prayer? We must admit that these reflections present real difficulties which we by no means intend to minimize. As a matter of fact, we know from experience that many who have prayed the Breviary have ruined their spiritual stomach (we mean no disrespect) through the undigested diet of psalms; that is, through the unintelligent praying of the psalms, they have put their life of prayer in serious jeopardy.

These are real difficulties; even the language of the psalms is unfamiliar to us. In the first place, the Jews think differently, and express themselves differently from us. We must become acquainted with Hebrew idiom. To a large extent the pictures and images are strange to us, because they take for granted the Orient with its deserts, its sea, and scarcity of water, with different social, civil, and national institutions. Without doubt, prayers that stem from our modern and Christian mentality would impress us more deeply. But then the Gospels and the other books of Scripture, in their imagery and terms of expression, present the same difficulties. God has so ordained things once and for all, and we must accommodate ourselves to them. Perhaps we moderns, with our greater nationalistic spirit, feel these difficulties more keenly than did our fore-fathers.

For many of those who pray the Breviary, those specific things of the Old Testament which have been abrogated by Christianity, cause more trouble. I have in mind, for example, these fundamental ideas: the virtuous man will be blessed with worldly goods, and the evil man will be punished with misfortune; or still more to the point, love your friend, hate your enemy.

And then there are the cursing passages, even entire cursing psalms (e.g., 108). These bring the Psalter into disrepute. These, together with the complaining, the grieving, the perse-cution psalms are all so foreign to our way of looking at things.

Nor shall I try to argue away this further difficulty, because it is only with reluctance that any of us pray such psalms, un-less, of course, we have the proper outlook. These psalms do not talk about personal enemies, but about the tremendous spiritual battle between heaven and hell. This battle rages through the course of time, and it is vividly present to the Church in her prayer. We can hate the devil and can desire his destruction and defeat.

The following reflection can be of great help in the recita-tion of the cursing psalms. The complaint and petitions of these psalms are worded in the natural, primitive form of the curse. The natural man always expresses his revolt against evil in just this way. It is understandable that we as Christians cannot wish evil upon a sinner who is still capable of doing good. The psalms actually have nothing to do with personal enemies. The theme of all our prayers is the kingdom of God and sin; in the psalms, the curse is only the primitive expres-sion of our absolute protest against sin and hell. As Christians we can tolerate no sentiments of revenge in our hearts; we hope and pray that all those who are capable of improvement do abandon their sin and turn to God. If we change the wish into something that is actually taking place, then the curse is an expression of God's justice and it does not come from us, but from the mouth of Christ or His Church. The psalm is then something similar to Christ's "woe" to the Pharisees and the city of Jerusalem. It is precisely in the cursing passages that I see something extremely moving and grand. The just God and Judge comes before the one who is praying. The mouth of hell gives us warning of its abysmal depths. If the Church reminds us of eternal damnation just before the Consecration, "*Hanc igitur,*" etc., then it seems to be in order that here and there the prayer of the Church warn us against a just God who punishes sin. The Church is truly a pleading mother who is always praying for us, but also a stern father who threatens punishment and hell.

If while praying the psalms we are thoroughly convinced that they are concerned not with petty, earthly, selfish motives, but with the great battle between heaven and hell, we shall soon find ourselves warmly attracted to them. Both the Church and the soul have a part and interest in this prayer; the Church in whose heart are gathered together all the needs of the soul, and the soul which is lifted up above itself from the mere human to the divine, which is Christ. I repeat that this objection presents a real difficulty which we cannot easily overcome. On the other hand we must not exaggerate it. The Old Testament is not so separated from the New as many often suggest. To be sure, in the field of morals, the Old Testament is imperfect alongside the New, as we see in the doctrine of love of one's neighbor. But otherwise, with regard to their doctrines of belief and their relationships with God, we can go a long way with the Old Testament. For us the Old Testament is not a book of secondary importance, but is as precious as the New Testament, if only we know how to appreciate the contents of both.

Anyone who has become familiar with the psalms finds in them a faith, a charity and, in general, a spirituality which is entirely in harmony with Christian sentiment. Indeed there are psalms which are entirely Christian. Whoever takes the trouble to separate the difficult psalms or passages from the others will find that the difficult ones are a notable minority.

Another objection is often raised. Many passages, which presuppose conditions prevalent during the time of the Old Testament, are a source of annoyance. Jerusalem, the Temple, the Law, Israel, are often spoken of, not to mention those psalms in which incidents and especially the aberrations of the Jews are drawn out to some length (e.g., psalms 67, 77, 104, 105).

Here too, we must admit that there are difficulties for the modern user of the Breviary; we do not pray these psalms with much relish, especially when there is mention of incidents entirely strange to us, as in psalm 107:

"Mine is Galaad, and mine Manasse,
Ephraim is the helmet for my head; Juda, my scepter;
Moab shall serve as my washbowl."

Some things can be said to defend and to remove these difficulties. Once and for all, the history of the Old Testament has been given new life through revelation; God has so ordained it. Moreover, many of the incidents and topics of the Old Testament are a type of the New Testament. God permitted many things to happen in the Old Testament that were symbols of Christ and His Church. For this reason Holy

Scripture is interpreted in two senses: the literal sense, and the spiritual or symbolic sense. The literal sense is that thought expressed by the words in their ordinary meaning. The spiritual sense sees the deeper image contained in the incident or topic treated. When we pray the psalms we must keep in mind this spiritual sense. Therefore Christ is for us the King mentioned in the psalms; under His eternal rule, His sufferings and work of redemption are described. The city of Jerusalem (Sion) is for us the Church of Christ, both in our pilgrimage here on earth and glorified in heaven. The Temple is the house of God filled with the riches of the Messiah. Israel, Jacob, God's people, signify the people of God of the New Testament. The sacrifice, the holocaust, the bloody sacrifice, represent the sacrifice of Christ in the Eucharist, and the Law is the Gospel of Christ.

Only the Christian is able to discern in the psalms the complete meaning of the Redemption. This, however, is not something arbitrary; but, owing to divine inspiration, exists in the psalms from the beginning; still, those who used them in the Old Testament could only guess at this meaning.

"Because of this spiritual sense, the psalms, besides their general prayer content, express Christ's entire work of Redemption. Nothing constrains us to revert to the imperfect state of affairs of the Old Testament or to remain with purely theoretic, sterile, and historical considerations. We can give value to the whole thought world of the Old Testament, give it new meaning, complete it, and give it its true prayer content. Experience will soon teach us how easily this revaluating, this completion, so far as it is really necessary, can be effected." [4]

[4] Miller, *Die Psalmen*, pp. 11 ff.

These reflections will lighten many of the difficulties we may encounter in praying the psalms. Still, they are real difficulties, and all of us must cope with them.

C. The problem regarding the psalms is reduced to two important points: understanding the psalms and learning to pray them. In the following pages I purpose to give some hints on the solution of these problems, relying on the experience of thirty years.

I. UNDERSTANDING THE PSALMS

It may interest the reader to hear how I came to understand the psalms myself. I devised a system of cards, with one card for each psalm. On this card I noted, the title of the psalm, the nature of the psalm, whether it was one of praise or complaint, and the historical circumstances if any, then the author of the psalm. Thirdly I noted what is most important for an understanding of the psalm, the division or sequence of thought. Often this corresponds to the arrangement of the strophes.[5] For this reason I adhered strictly to the strophic divisions and those poetic forms closely related to it (refrains, similar initial verses), and the exchange of dialogue. I did not do this to become involved in minutiae, but solely in order to understand the psalms better. For it can be seen that the strophes correspond with the thought sequence. The study of the strophes was what brought me to the heart of the psalms. I adverted to this fact in an essay of Cardinal Faulhaber. Later on I shall give some examples of the strophic structure of the psalms.

To continue, then, I wrote this strophic arrangement of the

---

[5] In several of the Breviaries containing the new version of the Psalter, the strophic division is indicated by a dash at the end of the verse that concludes the strophe. Tr.

psalms minutely upon the card. Besides, I also noted certain words and topics that needed explanation, historical facts and translations of difficult passages, Hebraisms, and so on. The other side of the card was devoted to the liturgical use of the psalm. It is most important that we know why this particular psalm is used on this feast or in this Office. Later we shall note that the best key to the liturgical use of a psalm is the antiphon. Here an understanding of the psalm has already become a prayer.

My first work was to acquire a proper understanding of the psalm. The particular advantage of these short notes was that by quickly rereading them I could recall the whole psalm in a very short time, and that with this meager foundation I had something upon which to build. For I must here remark that treating the psalms only once in this manner was not enough; I worked over them often again, and indeed had to do so. Every priest must do this work at some time, otherwise the psalms will always remain for him a book sealed with seven seals. For this reason even the young seminarian ought to be obliged to perform this task. In olden days no one was ordained a priest unless he knew the Psalter by heart. Today no one ought to be ordained who has not studied the Psalter at least once.

However, let no one think that merely a study of the psalms will obviate all difficulties. There will remain some psalms which, despite study, will still be difficult to pray.

I have one more suggestion to make for a better understanding of the psalms: annotating your Breviary. There is a great difference between desk and kneeling-bench. Who has not experienced how during study the psalms seem so full of life, but at prayer all that vanishes? At prayer the psalms go along so quickly that we cannot grasp the thought sequence or the unity of the psalm. Therefore this second bit of advice: annotate your Breviary. With a pencil, put markings in it. You will hardly believe how far a few lines can go toward a better understanding of the psalms. At the beginning of the psalms it is well to note the title and a brief summary of the contents, or even the circumstances in which the psalm was written (e.g., evening song, psalm in exile). The divisions of the psalm are also important; these ought to be numbered and noted with terse catch phrases.

Another suggestion: some of the verses in the Vulgate, even with the best of intention, do not make sense; or if they do, it is extremely far-fetched. We are discouraged with such verses because they take all the satisfaction out of praying the psalm. I put brackets around such verses, and thus know beforehand that I do not have to bother with the meaning. The remaining verses still make sufficient sense. For example, psalm 115 is a beautiful prayer of thanksgiving which we often use as a prayer after Holy Communion; add to this its beautiful strophic structure. Still the first two verses do not fit too well with the meaning of the whole psalm: "I believed, even when I said. . . ." But why take time to discover the meaning? Let us put brackets around these two verses. Begin to look for the meaning with: "How shall I make a return to the Lord . . . ?"

On the other hand, taken as a whole, the unity and thought sequence of some psalms is difficult to grasp; yet, these psalms have some striking verse or verses. I put a check in the margin next to these verses so that I will take note of them. These verses are the "jumping off" points for my devotion. I have in mind, for example, the lengthy, somewhat monotonous, 118th psalm. It contains many beautiful verses on which we can fasten our devotion. Often it is one of these verses that affords us great spiritual joy. Here are some examples. In psalm 41: "As the hind longs for the running waters, so my soul longs for You, O God. Athirst is my soul for God, the living God." In psalm 35: "The children of men take refuge in the shadow of Your wings. They have their fill of the prime gifts of Your house; from Your delightful stream You give them to drink. For with You is the fountain of life, and in Your light we see light." In psalm 72: "Yet with You I shall always be; You have hold of my right hand; with Your counsel You guide me, and in the end You will receive me in glory. Whom else have I in heaven? And when I am with You, the earth delights me not. Though my flesh and my heart waste away, God is the rock of my heart and my portion forever." This is one of the loveliest passages in the Psalter. In psalm 22: "Even though I walk in the dark valley I fear no evil; for You are are at my side." I could adduce a whole array of such striking verses. Our praying of the psalms would greatly improve even if we fixed our attention only on the beautiful passages.

One last hint. Write the liturgical usage, or the principal ideas of a psalm, in brief catch words at the beginning, so that a glance is sufficient to give the idea of an hour or a psalm. I call this word the key. A longer explanation or application would be hard to keep in mind, but a catch word or a short sentence brings to mind all I have studied and worked out. I am also accustomed to give a key for an entire hour. Thus the hour is characterized by one principal thought which I can easily keep in mind. This is something that is actually a part of praying the psalms. My book, *The Weekly Psalter*, is built upon these ideas. This book embodies all the principles and suggestions I have noted above. It is an attempt to facilitate an understanding of the psalms for those who pray them. Hundreds of priests have told me that reading this book has considerably improved their recitation of the psalms.

II. Praying the Psalms

Once we understand the psalms, we have made a great advance; but our problem is not yet completely solved. We must learn to pray the psalms. We must, so to speak, make the content of the psalm the form into which we pour our personal prayer; we must learn to place the incense of our prayers in the censer of the psalms. This is quite possible, and not too difficult.

We can see this fact from the consideration that God has given us the psalms to pray; we see it from the liturgical use of the psalms for two thousand years, and we see it from the experience of thousands of those who have played the harp strings of the Psalter with a master's touch. We know, too, from the complaints and objections raised against the psalms that there are also difficulties against learning to pray the psalms.

No instrument plays of itself. The Psalter is like a harp that one must learn to play. Virtuosos are not born. Lovingly and reverently we must penetrate into the secret chamber of the psalms, we must especially ponder and meditate on them, we must carry them over into our lives. We well know that the psalms strike all the chords of our soul, from the darkest sadness, fear, and despair to the brightest joy. With the psalms we are led from hate to the most fervent love. Our soul, so to speak, must be the sounding board where all these tones can find an echo. The psalms contain two great themes: God and man. Since these two themes are the focal points of all our prayers and meditation, we can easily learn to pray the psalms.

But we must not race through them, as we often do in fact: mouthing mere words with no idea of their meaning and no feeling at all. To pray is indeed a great art, and nothing is more harmful to it than hustle and haste—distraction and meager attention.

We can easily turn many of the psalms into prayers of our own, without too much preparatory study. I have in mind the psalms of praise, the psalms of nature, the psalms of penitence and confession. To be sure, we must become proficient in extracting the prayer content from the psalm form. I would advise the following preparation. After I have worked over a psalm and understand it, then I run through it in my mind. I meditate upon it and try to make it practical for my life and for my soul. In a word, the psalms must find an echo in my own soul. Then I pray it once or twice a day, go with it to church and to the open fields. Soon it becomes as dear and as intimate as a childhood lullaby. Sweetness fills my soul upon merely beginning it or praying one or the other verse. A definite experience accompanies the words: I have absorbed it; it has become a part of my treasury of prayers.

I admit we cannot do this with all the psalms. We shall be able to pray some psalms only with our minds and wills. Some will find no echo in our souls. At such times we must let the Church pray in us. If we have a kindly apostolic heart, then we shall be able to pray well even those psalms which do not correspond entirely with the sentiments of our own soul. Then we shall pray the psalms of suffering and of persecution, as coming from the heart of the Church for those who are suffering, for those who are in sin, for those who are persecuted.

One more thought: as a rule the sentiments of the psalms are forceful; so much so that a Christian ensconced in a peaceful existence can hardly put himself in tune with them at all.

For this reason the psalms often leave us cold. They strike no kindred chord in our own souls. But once a man meets the same situation as the psalm presumes, then the psalm takes on new meaning for him. Those who were in the late wars or in prison camps, or who have suffered greatly, will bear me out on this. As a rule the psalms presume men in dire straits.

Whenever we meet psalms that we cannot absorb point blank into our prayer life, we must do two things. (1) We must lift them out of the historical situation in which they were composed (e.g., a war, a persecution, the exile) and give them a new meaning vital to ourselves. We should make them suit a present-day situation in the Church or in our own souls. (2) We must Christianize the ideas, translate them into Christian terminology. This is possible since the Old Testament is not inseparably divorced from the New Testament, for it is the same Holy Spirit who speaks in the psalms and who prays in our hearts.

Without a sense of the mystical we shall never be able to grasp either the psalms or the Breviary. Anyone who approaches the psalms in a critical or rationalist frame of mind, will derive little benefit from them. He will rather be repelled by many items. There are so many fine and delicate relations and references that only a friend of the liturgy can perceive them. It is like a fine web which may not be touched with awkward hands.

A word about translating the psalms into prayer. The whole prayer content of many of the psalms consists in a poetical comparison. We find the key to a comparison in the point which both members of the comparison have in common. This focal point is what we have to search for. And once it is found, we can see at a glance what is to be translated into our prayer and what is to be passed over as merely the embellishment of the image. As every detail of an image need not have an application in a comparison, so in the psalms not every verse or thought need be translated into our own prayer. If we fail to see this fact, then those far-fetched explanations crop up, against which any thinking man revolts. A glance at the point of comparison will save us from such aberrations. This method has the advantage of resting solidly on the literal sense; for only a comprehensive grasp of the original image will enable us to see the object of comparison. We first look for this common feature of the Psalmist's comparison in our own souls or in the Church. Sometimes it is a strong sentiment that the psalm is to arouse in us, for example, psalm 136, an elaborate elegy written during the exile. Here the common point of comparison is a deep and loyal love for Jerusalem. We can refer this to the Church, to the Eucharist, or to Christ. When this has been done, the curse in the last two verses no longer jars. It is merely the embellishment of the image intended to evoke this sentiment in us.

Let us not be insincere when we pray the psalms. When we pray, we must have something to pray for. It is insincere to pray for refuge in persecution when actually we are secure from danger. When we pray a psalm it must express a true need, either in the soul or in the Church, otherwise the psalm is for us "sounding brass and tinkling cymbal." We are always in need of something, if not for our own souls, then surely for the Church. We have only to recall what that needed something is.

If you wish to pray the psalms well, you must meditate upon them lovingly. Only hard work reveals their beauty and adaptability for prayer. But is not that the case in every field of endeavor? You will not become enthusiastic over the classics unless you eagerly delve into them. A symphony will not yield its secret if you do not penetrate it yourself by listening to it frequently. How much more is this true of the profound words of Sacred Scripture and consequently of the Psalter? The Fathers of the Church and the saints tell us of the gold that can be mined from the psalms. Here is an example from the *Confessions* of St. Augustine. He shows how after his conversion he experienced and prayed psalm 4.[6]

When I read the Psalms of David, songs of faithfulness and devotion in which the spirit of pride has no entry, what cries did I utter to You, O my God, I but a novice in Your true love, a catechumen keeping holiday in a country house with that other catechumen, Alypius: though my mother also was with us, a woman in sex, with the faith of a man, with the serenity of great age, the love of a mother, the piety of a Christian. What cries did I utter to You in those Psalms and how was I inflamed towards You by them, and on fire to set them sounding through all the world, if I could, against the pride of man! But in truth they are already sung throughout the world and *there is none who can hide himself from Thy heat.* I thought of the Manichees with indignation and a burning anguish of sorrow. I pitied them because they did not know our sacraments and our healing, but were insanely set against the medicine that would have cured their insanity. I wished that they might be somewhere close at hand— without my knowing that they were there—and could see my face and hear my words, when in that time of leisure I read the Fourth Psalm; and that they could see what that Psalm did in me: *When I called upon Thee, Thou, God of my justice, didst hear me; when I was in distress, Thou hast enlarged me: have mercy on me, O Lord, and hear my prayer.* Would that they could have heard me —without my knowing that they heard me, lest they might think it was on their account I was speaking as I spoke when I recited these words: and indeed I would not have said those things or said them in the same way, if I had realized that I was being heard and seen by them: nor, if I *had* said them, would they have under-

[6] *Conf.*, translated by F. J. Sheed (Sheed and Ward, New York, 1943), IX, 4.

stood how I was speaking with myself and to myself in Your presence from the natural movement of my spirit.

I was in fear and horror, and again I was on fire with hope and exultation in Your mercy, O Father. And all these emotions found expression in my eyes and in my voice when Your Holy Spirit turned to us and said: *O ye sons of men, how long will you be dull of heart? Why do you love vanity so much and seek after lying?* For I myself had loved vanity and sought after lying. *And Thou, Lord,* hadst already *made Thy holy one wonderful,* raising Him from the dead and setting Him at Thy right hand, whence He should send from on high His promise, the Paraclete, the Spirit of Truth. And He had already sent Him, though I knew it not. He had sent Him because already He was magnified and risen from the dead and ascended into heaven. For till then the Spirit was not yet given, because Jesus was not yet glorified. And the prophet cried aloud: *How long will you be dull of heart? Why do you love vanity and seek after lying? Know ye also that the Lord hath made His holy one wonderful?* He cries out "How long," he cries out "Know ye." And I so long was ignorant and loved vanity and sought after lying.

I heard these things and trembled to hear them, for they were spoken to such as I remembered myself to have been. For in those phantasms which I had taken for truth were vanity and lying. And I cried out many things strongly and earnestly in the grief I felt at which I remembered. If only those could have heard me who still loved vanity and sought after lying. Perchance they would have been troubled, and have vomited up their error: and You would have heard them when they cried to You: for He who intercedes with You for us died for us with a true death of the body.

I read, *Be angry and sin not.* And by this I was much moved, O my God, for I had by then learned to be angry with myself for the past, that I might not sin in what remained of life: and to be angry with good reason, because it was not some other nature of the race of darkness that had sinned in me, as the Manichees say: and they are not angry at themselves, but treasure up to themselves wrath against the day of wrath and of the revelation of the just judgement of God.

The good I now sought was not in things outside me, to be seen by the eye of flesh under the sun. For those that find their joy outside them easily fall into emptiness and are spilled out upon the things that are seen and the things of time, and in their starved minds lick shadows. If only they could grow weary of their own hunger and say: *Who shall show us good things?* And we should say and they should hear: *The light of Thy countenance is sealed upon us,* O Lord. For we are not *the Light that enlightens every man* but we are enlightened by Thee that *as we were heretofore darkness we are now light in Thee.* If they could but see the Light interior and eternal: for now that I had known it, I was frantic that I could not make them see it even were they to ask: *Who shall show us good things?* For the heart they would bring me would be in their eyes, eyes that looked everywhere but at You. But there, where I had been angry with myself, in my own room where I had been pierced, where I had offered my sacrifice, slaying the self that I had been, and, in the newly-taken purpose of newness of life, hoping in You—there You began to make me feel Your love and to give *gladness in my heart.* I cried out as I read this aloud and realized it within: and I no longer wished any increase of earthly goods, in which a man wastes time and is wasted by time, since in the simplicity of the Eternal I had other corn and wine and oil.

It was with a deep cry of my heart that I uttered the next verse: *O in peace! O in the selfsame!* O how he has said: *I will sleep and I will rest.* For who shall stand against us *when the saying that is written will come to pass: Death is swallowed up in victory?* You supremely are that selfsame, for You are not changed and in You is that rest in which all cares are forgotten, since there is no other besides You, and we have not to seek other things which are not what You are: but You, Lord, alone have *made me dwell in hope.* All these things I read and was on fire; nor could I find what could be done with those deaf dead, of whom indeed I had myself been one for I had been a scourge, a blind, raging snarler against the Scriptures, which are all honeyed with the honey of heaven and all luminous with Your light: and now I was fretting my heart out over the enemies of these same Scriptures.

To be sure, we shall not be able to scale these lofty heights of prayer, but God will give us the gift of prayer also if we seek it with a good will.

A beautiful soul of simple life who had prayed the psalms for years and acquired a great love for them wrote:

The simplicity and candor with which the psalms speak to the soul have made them dear and even indispensable to me. They awake in the soul acts of faith and trust in God, as well as acts of love and thanksgiving. I could never do without them; in joy and sorrow they have carried me through the years. The psalms always strike the right note in the human heart whether it cries in deep anguish or sings with great joy. The psalms prepare the soul for reverent prayer, which brings peace to the afflicted, conversion to the penitent, consolation for the sorrowful, and happiness for those who love God. Precisely those passages that express a deep communion with nature, make for peace and banish all anxiety in prayer. The psalms are teachers as well as guideposts; and can have a great influence upon our lives. Thus psalm 31 has evoked a complete change in my life—turning away from sin and temporal things, turning to God and eternal things. The motto of my life is "Opera mea regi"[7] taken from psalm 44, and above all, verse 11, which gave me a great deal to think about. Through the psalms, each day has its own special blessing. Upon awakening I pray psalm 24:1–3; and as a morning prayer, psalm 62. I use psalm verses to accompany me to Mass and Holy Communion and, according to the dispositions of my soul, they give me guiding thoughts for the whole day. During my work or after some annoying incident, verses from the psalms restore my peace and composure of mind again. When I have some sacrifice to make: "Behold I come" (Ps. 39:8). My night prayers consist of psalms 90, 114, 129. At night a psalm of praise is very uplifting. Psalm 56 works wonder when I cannot sleep or when I am frightened at night. As a preparation for confession I use psalms 6 and 42, and as a thanksgiving afterward psalm 102. It is good to stamp on one's mind those verses which impress one the most. It is not necessary

[7] Old Version.

to constrain oneself to an entire psalm, for at times one verse means more to me than the whole psalm together. Generally I try to steer clear of the cursing psalms. At most when I do use them, I direct them against the devil and his cohorts. To sum up, I thank God for the day He let the psalms fall into my hands.[8]

III. Examples

In the following pages, I will give several examples of how we may acquire an understanding of the psalms and then how we can make them a part of our prayer life. First of all I will show this with a very simple psalm, psalm 1. A mere knowledge of the thought sequence carries with it an understanding and appreciation of the psalm itself.

The Title Page of the Psalter

The first psalm is the preface to the Psalter. St. Jerome calls it the *Praefatio Spiritus Sancti* (the Preface of the Holy Spirit). As a matter of fact, this psalm gives the principal theme that runs through most of the psalms: Blessed are those who fear God; woe to the godless. It also expresses a thought that was especially dear to the early Church: the two ways: the way of life and the way of death. This psalm is easy to grasp, expressive, and uplifting.

Psalm 1

I

1 Happy the man who follows not
      the counsel of the wicked,
    Nor walks in the way of sinners,
      nor sits in the company of the insolent,
2 But delights in the law of the Lord
      and meditates on his law day and night.

[8] Miller, *op. cit.*, pp. 16 ff.

3　He is like a tree
　　planted near running water,
　That yields its fruit in due season,
　　and whose leaves never fade.
　　[Whatever he does, prospers.]

II

4　Not so the wicked, not so;
　　They are like the chaff which the wind drives away.
5　Therefore in judgment the wicked shall not stand,
　　nor shall sinners, in the assembly of the just.
6　For the Lord watches over the way of the just,
　　but the way of the wicked vanishes.

Thought sequence of the psalm:

    I. The man of God (vv. 1–3)
        1) Negative: three degrees of sin (v. 1)
           walking (sin)
           standing (habit)
           sitting (depravity)
        2) Positive: faithfulness to the law (v. 2)
        3) Comparison: the fruitful tree (v. 3)
   II. The man of sin (vv. 4–6)
        1) Comparison: straw upon the threshing floor or
           the withered tree (v. 4)
        2) Judgment (v. 5)
        3) Conclusion (v. 6)

This division of the psalm makes it clear. We have before our eyes a just man who is first of all described negatively. Let us consider the threefold gradation: walking, standing, sitting. Living according to the counsels of the godless is a picture of sinning. But it is a sign of hardheartedness to stand still on the path; and to sit upon the seat of vice, is to be fettered with sin. This, however, is not the case with the just man; on the contrary, the law upon which he meditates night and day is the joy of his heart. It is therefore the same as with sin: not merely an isolated compliance with the law, but it is virtue, faithfulness, complete conformity to the will of God. But the Psalmist, wishing to give us a picture, does so with the appealing figure of the fruitful tree. A similar passage is found in Jeremias 17:7: "Blessed is the man that trusteth in the Lord, and the Lord shall be his confidence. And he shall be as a tree that is planted by the waters, that spreadeth out its roots toward moisture: and it shall not fear when the heat cometh. And the leaf thereof shall be green, and in the time of drought it shall not be solicitous: neither shall it cease at any time to bring forth fruit." The similarity of these two passages is so great that we can see a dependence of one upon the other. Notice especially the impression that would necessarily be made by this picture in a region as arid and treeless as Palestine: the verdant tree by the banks of the stream. How rare is such a tree and how delightfully it lifts its head above the other withered and scrawny trees.

The just man, therefore, is like a tree which

  a) is planted beside a stream,
  b) is always clothed with fresh green foliage,
  c) and bears fruit in due season.

The Psalmist immediately explains the image by saying: "Whatever he does, prospers."

In the second part we see the opposite: the godless, to whom the Psalmist does not give as much attention as to the just man. The Psalmist immediately seizes upon the image of the tree and says: The godless have an entirely different lot; they are not like the green tree, but rather like straw which is whirled about by the wind. We should have expected a different picture, that of the withered foliage. According to the original text, the image of withered foliage is also a possibility. Then the Psalmist thinks of the last judgment: sinners will have no recourse at the time of judgment. The thought is repeated in order to emphasize it (this is called parallelism of members). At the conclusion we hear sentence passed: "For the Lord watches over the way of the just, but the way of the wicked vanishes."

Liturgical usage. This didactic poem is used in the liturgy frequently, and its application is not difficult to perceive. In general we can find two such applications. Among the just are comprised the saints, martyrs, and confessors; for this reason this psalm is found on their feasts. The feast of one martyr has the antiphon: "Day and night, his delight was in the law of the Lord." Still more beautiful is the antiphon for the feast of several martyrs: "Alongside the running water, he planted the vineyard of the just, and their delight was in the law of the Lord." [9]

It is the same on the feast of confessors. In the early Christian mosaics there is usually a palm tree next to the saint. The image of a tree is beautifully applied to the saints. Planted beside the stream of grace, whose source is the hill of Calvary, the Christian always flourishes and is not subject to any diminutions of grace. He produces fruit in due season; not all the time, for a tree also has its rest period, in which it bears no fruit.

Actually, in the realm of grace there is no such thing as failure: before God an external failure is often more meritorious and full of grace than success.

[9] Both passages are adapted from the old version of the psalm. Tr.

The liturgy applies this poem to another "Just man," to Jesus Christ Himself. We cite two examples to show this: at Matins for Easter we sing this psalm to honor the risen Christ. Far removed from sin, He is the mighty conqueror of sin and the devil. The basic motto of His life, His food, was to do the will of Him who sent Him (John 4:34). Christ has become the tree of life, from which we pluck the fruit of our eternal life. "Planted near running water," that is, the grace laden stream of His blood. Before His death the source of this stream was dried up; through His death and resurrection it has become our salvation.

We also sing this psalm at Matins of Corpus Christi; in the antiphon St. Thomas Aquinas gives a commentary on its usage. Our Lord, at the time of His death, gave us life, giving fruit to taste. Here again the image of the tree is especially significant. Before us stands again the tree of life in the kingdom of God; it is planted beside the stream of Christ's blood; it spreads out its branches far and wide. As children of God we are permitted to break the health-bringing fruit of the Holy Eucharist. The fruit matured at the death of Christ.

Meditate upon this simple poem; it is not lyrical, but flows along quietly like a brook, and yet it will lead you along the way of life and keep you from the way of death. Consider yourself a tree in God's garden, planted close to the waters of salvation; take care always to be like the verdant tree, and bring forth sweet fruit. You will soon be drawn to this psalm and you will pray it eagerly.

Psalm 136, a Song of Longing

A student of German philology once told me that he was making a collection of the most beautiful poems and songs of various literatures. I asked him if he had read through the

Psalter, as there were literary pearls among the psalms. He went to work. I drew his attention to a number of psalms, but he dismissed them all except psalm 136, which he added to his collection. From this I concluded that, though there are better poems among the psalms, this makes the deepest impression upon people who had not penetrated deeper into the spirit of the Psalter. This psalm is easy to understand, and is deeply moving. It is a stirring elegy.

Psalm 136

I

Grief in Babylon

1 By the streams of Babylon we sat and wept when we remembered Sion.

2 On the aspens of that land we hung up our harps,

3 Though there our captors asked of us
Songs of Sion   the lyrics of our songs,
And our despoilers urged us to be joyous: "Sing for us the songs of Sion!"

II

4 How could we sing a song of the Lord in a foreign land?

Love for   5 If I forget you, Jerusalem, may my
Jerusalem   right hand be forgotten!

6 May my tongue cleave to my palate if I remember you not,
If I place not Jerusalem ahead of my joy.

III

Curse on Edom   7 Remember, O Lord, against the chil-

dren of Edom, the day of Jerusalem,
When they said, "Raze it, raze it down
to its foundations!"

Curse on Babylon 8 O daughter of Babylon, you destroyer,
happy the man who shall repay you
the evil you have done us.

9 Happy the man who shall seize and
smash your little ones against the
rock!

Division. The poem is strophically symmetrical, having three strophes, each of which is again divided into two distichs. Each strophe gives a complete thought which is taken up by both distichs. The strophe structure corresponds nicely with the thought structure. First strophe, a description of the grief in Babylon; second strophe, longing for and devotion to Jerusalem; third strophe, a curse upon the enemy.

Literal meaning. The poem takes us back to the miserable days of the Babylonian capitivity (the author in a mood of melancholy reminiscence, sings this psalm after his return home). Far from Jerusalem, from the Temple, the source of all blessings and joys, the chosen people sit disconsolately under the aspens by the great river of Babylon. There is no singing, no playing of harps; only nostalgic tears of longing and sorrow (1a). The scene soon becomes more intense. Either out of malice or out of good fellowship, the Babylonians ask the Jews to sing some of their native songs, songs that are known the world over (1b). But they refuse such a request: "How could we sing a song of the Lord in a foreign land?" That would be to desecrate them, that would be to forget Jerusalem, that would be ingratitude toward our beloved Sion.

Then the Psalmist lifts his right hand in oath, and vows solemnly that he will never use his hands or his tongue again for such songs. He calls down punishment upon himself if he should be unfaithful to his vow; may his right hand be forgotten, and his tongue cleave to his palate (2). In the natural, unredeemed man, burning love is always united to a deep hatred of whatever disturbs that love. And thus the same love which has evoked this oath of fidelity from his lips also evokes the fiercest curses against the authors and perpetrators of his misfortune. During the destruction of the city, nothing had enraged the people so much as the malicious conduct of their ancient enemies, the Edomites, whose sadistic shouts of encouragement to the conquerors still ring in their ears: "Raze it, raze it down to its foundations" (v. 7). The Psalmist hurls a final curse at the merciless Babylonians who have brought such unutterable misery upon the people. The curse sends shivers up and down our spine: "Happy the man who shall seize and smash your little ones against the rock" (v. 9). Indeed such words can come only from one who does not have the "Law of Christ." This short but psychologically masterful psalm actually comes to a close with this frightful curse.

Evaluation. Perhaps some one will say: The poem is beautiful when I consider it from an esthetic standpoint, but how can I make it a part of my prayer life? What can I do with the curses?

I repeat what I have said about the psalms of imprecation. Complaints and petitions in the psalms are often cloaked in the natural, primitive form of the curse. That is how the natural man expresses his opposition to evil. We do not need to mention that we Christians cannot wish evil upon anyone. But the psalms are not concerned with personal enemies. The theme of all our prayer is the kingdom of God and sin; and the curse in the psalms is the natural expression of our absolute protest against sin and hell.

I call your attention, further, to what I have said about comparisons drawn from the psalms. Here the comparison is twofold: negative, the feeling of banishment and exile; positive, the deep love and longing for Jerusalem. We can easily apply the first of these to the exile of this earthly life. We are strangers and pilgrims here on earth, we have here "no lasting abode." Love of Jerusalem is longing and love for the heavenly Sion. When we take this into consideration, the curses in the last two verses will not disturb us at all, because we know that they belong merely to the embellishment of the picture intended to arouse this strong outburst of feeling.

There are two periods in the Church year when we should be especially mindful of the exile and strangeness of this earthly life: during the preparation for Easter, i.e., Septuagesima and Lent, and during the autumn of the Church year, the preparation for the coming of the Messiah. In the Middle Ages the seventy days before Easter (Septuagesima) were frequently compared to the seventy years of the Babylonian captivity. In the Middle Ages there was also a ceremony on the Saturday before Septuagesima celebrating the departure of the Alleluja, and in this ceremony psalm 136 was often used in hymns as a picture of the approaching season. Durandus, a liturgist of the Middle Ages, says: "We omit the Alleluja of the angels because through the sin of Adam we are excluded from their company; and we are sitting in the Babylon of this earthly exile and are moved to tears at the thought of Sion; and as the children of Israel in a strange land hung their harps upon the aspen trees, so we at a time of sorrow must put aside the joyous Alleluja in a spirit of penance and sadness." The psalm fits just as well for the autumn of the Church's year, when we are to prepare a throne for the returning Lord. This preparation has a positive and a negative side; on the one hand, a longing to be dissolved and to be with Christ, a homesickness for heaven; on the other hand, a sense of exile on this earth. Thus we can well see how splendidly this psalm expresses the spirit of the season. Hence it is also used, even though only once, but then very effectively, on the Twentieth Sunday after Pentecost as the Offertory antiphon. Formerly, when the Offertory chant was prolonged, nearly the whole psalm was sung.

In the Roman weekly Psalter this psalm is sung at Vespers on Thursday. The antiphon for this psalm indicates that the liturgy wishes to impress upon us a love for the Church and the heavenly Jerusalem.

Psalm 129

Psalm 129 is one of the few psalms that have become ingrained in the religious consciousness of the ordinary people; we hear it at every funeral. From early childhood we associate the thought of a prayer for the dead with these familiar but unintelligible words and, as a matter of fact, it is actually the Church's exclusive prayer for the dead. We shall see what a deeply impressive and highly poetical prayer it is. This psalm is the classic model of a poem artistically constructed and delicately perceptive from a psychological viewpoint.

Psalm 129

I. Prayer

1 (A song of ascents)
  Out of the depths I cry to you, O Lord;
    Lord, hear my voice!

2   Let your ears be attentive
      to my voice in supplication.

II

3   If you, O Lord, mark iniquities,
      Lord, who can stand?
4   But with you is forgiveness,
      that you may be revered.

III. Meditation

5   I trust in the Lord;
      my soul trusts in his word.
6   My soul waits for the Lord
      more than sentinels wait for the dawn.

IV

    More than sentinels wait for the dawn,
7   let Israel wait for the Lord,
    For with the Lord is kindness
      and with him is plentous redemption;
8   And he will redeem Israel
      from all their iniquities.

Structure. Let us consider, first of all, the structure of the poem. The psalm can be divided into two parts each of which has two strophes. The infallible external sign of the division is the transposition of the persons. The first part is a prayer addressed directly to God, using "you" and "your" five times: "Out of the depths I cry to you, O Lord." The second part is a meditation or reflection on the merciful heart of God, in the third person: "My soul trusts in his word."

Each part is again subdivided into two equal strophes, the second of which gives the basis for the first. The first part

describes the striving for confidence, the second the consoli-
dating of the confidence already acquired. The psalm has
therefore the following evident divisions.

Part I: the budding forth of confidence.
1. From the depths of my misery I cry to Thee, O Lord
   (vv. 1–2).
2. Basis:
   a) It is true I am a miserable sinner, but are sins an
      obstacle?
   b) Because of your mercy I hope for help (vv. 3–4).

Part II: consolidation of the confidence.
1. Consoled and full of longing, I trust in His word (vv.
   5–6).
2. Basis:
   a) Because the Lord is kind and merciful and will
      bring salvation from sin (vv. 7–8).

The psalm begins with urgent petitions and ends with confidence, even with certainty of salvation. Every true prayer
contains just such a development: forgive me, help me; I trust.

Literal meaning. We shall find the application easier for us
if we try to grasp the poem in its original circumstances. The
poem originated in the Babylonian exile. The nation lies in
abysmal disgrace, the Temple and the city have been de-
stroyed, the kingdom has been devastated, the people have
been delivered over to the contempt and caprice of the heathens. It is evident that this great misery is punishment for
sin. From the abyss of its misfortune the nation cries loudly
to the Lord, fully conscious of its unworthiness. (If we could
only feel what a strong outburst of emotion is contained in the
first verse.) Still the nation has full knowledge of the God

who is bound to them by convenant, and who has forgiven them many times. It knows that all men are sinners and that sin is no obstacle. Consequently it places all its hope in the mercy of God, on His promise that He has given often. Thus the prayer attains the first stage: we are trustful, and He will help. From this stage we rise up to passionate longing. Observe what forceful sentiments are expressed in the picture of this "night watchman." In the midst of the night of misfortune, of exile, the nation looks longingly toward the first faint gleams of sunrise that will announce the dawn of salvation. Again the Psalmist reviews all the reasons for his confidence, but he is more sure of them and more consciously joyful over them. God is full of mercy and plentiful in His redemption. It closes with an utterance of joyful certitude; the Lord will free us from all sins (and thus from the consequences of sin). From passionate cries of desolate fear the psalm rises to sweet expectation of divine mercy, to earnest patience, and closes with complete confidence of salvation.

Evaluation. In the liturgy this psalm has various applications. In the first place, as already mentioned, it is the Church's psalm of the dead; secondly, it is one of the seven penitential psalms; in the last Sundays after Pentecost it is sung as several of the proper parts of the Mass, it is to be found in the Second Vespers of Christmas; in the Psalter for the week it is used in the Vespers of Wednesday. We can take the psalm into our prayer life just as it is, using it either as a penitential psalm, or praying it in the name of the poor souls. For the idea of exile is one frequently used by the Church as an image and symbol of this earthly life and of purgatory. In both, it is sin which has caused the exile and forestalled a return home. And in both the great motive is the mercy of God. Thus it is any easy matter to pray this psalm. If we use it as a psalm for the dead, then we say it in the name of the poor souls. How strikingly do the pictures of abyss and night watchman fit here! Thus we may picture purgatory to ourselves: the poor souls are still in utter darkness, far from the light of God. With what longing they keep watch toward the East to perceive the first faint dawnings of release! How great is their consciousness of sin, their confidence, their longing, their certainty of salvation! This psalm is also the sixth of the seven penitential psalms. We use it with a deep sorrow for sin and confidence in salvation. At first it might seem strange to see this psalm used in the Vespers of Christmas, but the antiphon throws light upon it; the psalm should joyously bring to our attention the superabounding salvation of the new-born Savior.

Psalm 99

This psalm is one of joyous praise, an invitation to go to church. We can also regard it as a dialogue between the priests and the people. In fact, we will get much more out of it if we divide it according to such a thought pattern. The first part (vv. 1–3) comes from the people. The first two verses are in praise of God and command the service of God; the third verse gives a threefold reason for this. The second part (vv. 4–5) comes from the priests. Verse 4 declares their invitation to the people to come to church to praise God; verse 5 again gives a threefold reason why they should do so. I shall present the psalm according to this division and note the thought sequence alongside it.

Part I (The people)

1 A psalm of thanksgiving.

Praise God.　　　　Sing joyfully to the Lord, all you

	2	lands; serve the Lord with gladness; come before him with a joyful song.
Reason: God, Creator, Shepherd.	3	Know that the Lord is God; he made us, his we are; his people, the flock he tends.

Part II (The priests)

Praise God.	4	Enter his gates with thanksgiving, his courts with praise;
Reason: He is good, kind, and faithful.	5	Give thanks to him; bless his name | for he is good; the Lord, whose kindness endures forever, and his faithfulness, to all generations.

That is how the psalm looks in skeleton form. In the first verse of each part there is an invitation to worship God, given in three short phrases. In the second verse of each part, we find a threefold reason: the Lord is God, Creator, and Shepherd. In the second part, the reason is more fervent, more emotional still: God is good, merciful, and faithful. Knowing this division, you will understand the psalm more completely. Since the arrangement of the verses in the Breviary does not of itself indicate the division of thought, you can note the proper arrangement and division with lines or little marks.

CHAPTER V

The Lessons

WHEREAS the psalms convey to God our spiritual needs, the lessons bring God's answer back to us. We talk with God in the psalms; in the lessons, God talks with us. Our prayer worship, then, is really a two-way conversation: we plead and promise through the psalms; God replies through the lessons. Thus our recital of the Breviary is a sort of a dialogue between God and mankind.

We have already met with the same form of dialogue worship in the Mass of the Catechumens. This, as you well know, has two parts. Man speaks to God in the first; in the second, God speaks to man. You might call it a meeting halfway. Man makes, as it were, four steps toward God: 1. an act of contrition (the prayers at the foot of the altar); 2. an act of desire (the Kyrie Eleison); 3. an act of praise (the Gloria); and finally, 4. an act of petition (the oration). God in His turn then comes down to man, speaking in the Epistle, the Gospel, and the sermon. The Creed then comes like an echo to God's threefold message. Something quite similar to this we find in Matins, where each Nocturn is constructed in a similar fashion. First there is our talk to God in a trio of psalms; then God's reply in a trio of lessons.

We must not overlook the fact that in past ages quite a different emphasis was laid on this twofold relation than obtains today. God's message was more dominant according as the

Christian viewpoint was more objective and theocentric. As this viewpoint grew subjective and anthropocentric, man's talk with God came more and more to the fore. It can be observed in the vigil service, as well as in the Mass of the Catechumens, since both have the same origin. The vigils were, in the main, a reading service in which prayer served only as a response to what was read. This fact can be seen from what is perhaps the one relic we have of such a vigil service: the twelve prophecies for the liturgy of Holy Saturday.

In the Middle Ages, as the Christian mentality grew more subjective, the lessons were gradually shortened, their place in our worship losing much of its former prominence. The psalms took precedence, with God's word following in the lessons as an answer. The Mass of the Catechumens followed a similar development. Opening straightway with a lesson, the ancient Foremass then passed on to prayer. A lingering trace of this can still be found in the opening lesson of Good Friday's Mass of the Presanctified.

Prayers were later prefixed to the lessons, and from this a prayer service gradually developed. The lessons, then, reduced in number from three to two, were made to follow the prayers, and the *orationes solemnes* which formerly followed the lessons, after a while disappeared. The time may come when we shall revert to the more objective mentality of the early Church, and once again give the lessons more prominence in our worship.[1]

Here too is a place for reform and revision in the Breviary; the lessons are far from perfect. In the early Church, until the

[1] Such an objective mentality or "piety," as it is called in *Mediator Dei* (no. 28), is not meant to exclude or derogate from the so-called subjective or personal piety. Tr.

Middle Ages, in the course of each year, not only the whole of Scripture was read at Matins, but commentaries on it as well. How these readings should be apportioned and how long they should last was left to the decision of the one presiding. But when the *Breviary for the Roman Curia* was drawn up in the Middle Ages, though the Scripture pericopes for the Missal were chosen with remarkable care, the lessons for the Breviary seem to have been chopped out in a mechanical and almost careless fashion. The explanations of the Scriptures, too (the homilies and sermons), and the lives of the saints even more so, leave much to be desired. We hold our Breviary too dear to allow anything mediocre, historically inaccurate, apocryphal or haphazard, in its pages. In view of the wealth of early Christian literature, the lessons could well present only the choicest passages of Sacred Scripture, the best writings of the Fathers, plus lives of the saints which are not only devotional, but which are concise and historically reliable as well. In our personal opinion, the lessons of the most recent offices have by no means measured up to this ideal. (For example, the feast of the Immaculate Conception, the Holy Family, Christ the King, and the Sacred Heart of Jesus.) They neither stir our devotion nor do they add any enjoyment to our recitation of the Breviary.

We can conclude, then, that the lessons, and especially the Scripture lessons, formed an original and, we may say, even an essential part of the Office. This was particularly true of the night office.

In the Office at present there are two kinds of lessons: at Matins the longer lesson called *lectio* or "reading," and in the other hours, the shorter lesson, which is styled the *capitulum* or *lectio brevis* ("short lesson").

I. The Lessons, or Readings, at Matins

These can be subdivided into three groups: Scripture readings, readings from the Fathers, and readings from the lives of the saints.

a) The Scripture Readings

In the synagogue we find a venerable custom of reading regularly prescribed portions of the Scriptures. The frequent presence and participation of our Savior sanctified this synagogue worship. St. Luke records one of these hallowed scenes for us: "Then He came to Nazareth where He had been brought up; and He went into the synagogue there, as His custom was, on the Sabbath day, and stood up to read. The book given to Him was the book of the prophet Isaias; so He opened it, and found the place where the words ran: The Spirit of the Lord is upon me; . . . Then He shut the book, and gave it back to the attendant, and sat down. All those who were in the synagogue fixed their eyes on Him, and thus He began speaking to them, This Scripture which I have read in your hearing is today fulfilled." [2]

The Christians of the ancient Church used to take part in this synagogue service. When Paul established Christian communities there, this was the case in the lands outside of Palestine too, as well as in Jerusalem. The Acts of the Apostles offers a striking example of this at Antioch in Pisidia: ". . . where they went and took their seats in the synagogue on the Sabbath day. When the reading from the law and the prophets was finished, the rulers of the synagogue sent a message to them to say, Brethren, if you have in your hearts any word of

[2] Luke 4:16–21.

encouragement for the people, let us hear it." [3] However,
when they separated from the Jews, the Christians carried this
heritage of the synagogue over into their own worship, at the
same time giving it a Christian character. These readings find
a continuation in the ancient vigils; and from the time of the
persecutions they were held at night. Later still, the readings
became a part of Matins. Hence we can say that the Scripture
lessons of Matins belong to the oldest elements of our liturgy.

Just as the synagogue had its prescribed order of lessons, so
too the early Church soon developed a fixed arrangement. But
before the time of Gregory I (*c.* 600) we have no satisfactory
account of the prescribed order of lessons in the Roman
Church. All we know is that both Old and New Testaments
were read, as well as the works of the Fathers and the Acts
of the martyrs. The Rule of St. Benedict (d. 543) provides the
first detailed description of the lessons for the different hours,
principally for Matins. There were three different readings
from the Scriptures: 1. Parts of the Old Testament were
selected for the first nocturn. 2. Passages from the New Testament, other than the Gospels, were read in the third nocturn
. . . because 3. the Gospel pericope for the day's Mass was
read at the end of Matins. Pope Gregory I, a Benedictine himself, adopted this arrangement of lessons for the Roman
Church, and it continued thus until the ninth century.

To read the whole of Scripture in the course of the year,
together with the commentaries of the Fathers, was the
principal norm for the lessons, just as the whole Psalter was
to be recited in the course of the week. Since individual readings often lasted so long that in one Matins, especially in the
winter nights, fifteen or twenty chapters were read, this goal

[3] Acts 13:14–16.

was not too difficult to attain. Not infrequently, whole books
were read at one reading; for example, the book of Ruth,
Baruch, the Minor Prophets, or the Catholic Epistles. It is said
that Abbot John of Gorze (d. 962) once permitted the whole
book of Daniel to be read in the three lessons.

Until the ninth century the third nocturn was reserved for
the reading of the New Testament. It has, since that time, been
relegated to the first nocturn of the post-Christmas season,
. . . an arrangement which has remained unaltered to the
present day. The only notable change occurred in the Middle
Ages, after the composition of the *Breviary for the Roman
Curia*. The latter provoked the subsequent division and
abridgment of the lessons. Where previously the entire Bible
was read in portions marked only by the nod of the one presiding, now the unfortunate and artless hacking of the lessons
considerably reduced the amount of Scripture read in the
course of the year. . . . Hence the name "Breviarium." It was
certainly a shortening of the Office.

The following is the present order of Scripture lessons. Advent, from the first Sunday on: Isaias. Christmastide to Septuagesima: St. Paul's Epistles. The Sunday after Christmas
until the twenty-ninth of December: the Epistle to the
Romans. The first Sunday after Epiphany: the First Epistle to
the Corinthians. The second Sunday: the Second Epistle to
the Corinthians. The other epistles of St. Paul then follow. The
sixth Sunday after Epiphany concludes with the Epistle to
the Hebrews.

Pre-Lenten time and Lent: the five books of Moses. On
Septuagesima: the first book, Genesis. On the four Sundays of
Lent: the second book, Exodus. Oddly enough, the rest of the
Pentateuch is not officially read at Matins during the Church
year. At Passiontide, beginning on Passion Sunday: Jeremias.

Then on the last three days of Holy Week: the Lamentations of Jeremias.

Eastertime: only the New Testament. On the Monday after Whitsunday: the Acts of the Apostles. On the third Sunday after Easter: the Apocalypse (an ancient Easter-book). The Catholic Epistles then follow; indeed on the fourth Sunday after Easter: the Epistle of St. James. From the first Sunday after the Ascension on: the first, second, and third Epistles of St. John. On Saturday: the Epistle of St. Jude.

From the Octave of Pentecost until Advent: only from the Old Testament; first the historical and didactic books, then the prophets. On the Monday after Trinity Sunday: the First Book of Kings. On the fifth Sunday after Pentecost: the Second Book of Kings. On the seventh Sunday: the Third Book of Kings. On the ninth Sunday: the Fourth Book of Kings. The order thereafter follows according to the months of the year.

In August. On the first Sunday, the Book of Proverbs; on the second Sunday, Ecclesiasticus; on the third Sunday, the Book of Wisdom; on the fourth Sunday, Ecclesiastes.

In September. On the first Sunday, the Book of Job; on the third Sunday, the Book of Tobias; on the fourth Sunday, the Book of Judith; on the fifth Sunday, the Book of Esther.

In October. On the first Sunday, First Machabees; on the third Sunday, Second Machabees.

In November: first, two of the major Prophets; then the twelve minor Prophets. On the first Sunday, Ezechiel; on the third Sunday, Daniel.

From all this we can readily perceive that this order of the lessons is not haphazard. On the contrary, it is well adapted to the course of the Church year. Let us take notice especially that the reading of the first book of the Bible, Genesis, begins not with Advent, but with Septuagesima Sunday. It is thus that the liturgy points out how the Church year begins, not with Advent, but with the pre-Lenten period. How well though, the Book of Genesis fits this season, we can see from the line of patriarchs that the liturgy presents for these Sundays: Adam, Noe, Abraham, and so forth. There is excellent reason, too, for the portions of the New Testament chosen for Eastertime: the Acts of the Apostles, the Apocalypse, and the Catholic Epistles. The same holds for the sapiential books in mid-summer; the prophetical books in November; the didactic books in autumn; Isaias in Advent; Jeremias in Passiontide. It is not too difficult to harmonize these books with the various thoughts and ideas in the liturgical year.

The following consideration will perhaps afford a better understanding of the symbolism of the Scripture lessons:

The spirit of the liturgy in the Church year until Pentecost, is correlated with the story of Christ's life, and thereby those special graces are renewed through the commemoration of the historical events in our Savior's life. On the other hand, in the time after Pentecost, in presenting the kingdom of Christ, the liturgy employs a prototype, taken from the annals of the Old Testament theocracy. As unfolded in the liturgy, the historical account of the *civitas Dei* is accordingly a prophetical vision, fulfilled in the course of the ages by the Church of Christ. We can distinguish three great periods in the history of this mystical fulfillment. The founding and the spread of Christ's kingdom is the first period. Samuel prepared the way for the kingdom by uniting the people. (First to the Third Sunday after Pentecost.) The two promoters of this gradual fulfillment, David (Fourth to the Seventh Sunday after Pentecost) and Solomon (the Eighth Sunday after Pentecost) at the same time were prototypes of our Lord. Yet, even at the time of the downfall of the theocracy, the mighty arm of God held sway over king and people alike through His emissaries, Elias (Eighth to the Tenth Sunday after Pentecost) and Isaias (Eleventh Sunday after Pentecost).

The second epoch in the history of Christ's kingdom begins with the first Sunday of August. After the external history has been recounted, we turn our attention now to our own interior formation by the reading of the sapiential books: the Proverbs of Solomon (first Sunday), Ecclesiastes (second Sunday), the Book of Wisdom (third Sunday), and Ecclesiasticus (fourth to the fifth Sunday). These deepen our knowledge of God and at the same time strengthen the principles of our moral life. In the garb of historical narratives, the two Books, Job (September: first and second Sunday) and Tobias (third Sunday) offer practical moral lessons. These books afford a transition from the speculative considerations of the sapiential books to the concrete realization of their ideals, as manifested in the lives of Judith (fourth Sunday) and Esther (fifth Sunday). Their heroic love for the true God and for their people, because it is a woman's love, is all the more impressive. In October we read the two Books of the Machabees. These describe the strenuous battle devoted to the protection of the theocracy and to the defense of its spiritual goods.

The prophet Ezechiel introduces the third period: the perfection of Christ's kingdom, to which it lends an eschatological character. His visions, and the promises of the other prophets down to Malachy, who ends the line of prophets, treat of the last things, of the passage from the *civitas Dei* on earth to that in heaven, and of the eternal dominion of God.[4]

I wish that all who pray the Breviary might rightly appreciate the value of the Scripture lessons, and open the ears of their heart to these lessons. Here indeed is the opportunity to read each year and spiritually to digest the very kernel and essence of Holy Writ.

b) The Lessons from the Works of the Fathers

Not only ought we read, or rather listen, to the words of Holy Scripture, but we ought also learn to understand their meaning. That is why it was a practice from the early ages to

4 Herwegen, *Alter Quellen neuer Kraft*, pp. 109 ff.

read, besides the Holy Scriptures, an explanation of them. In the synagogue service an oral exposition was given after the reading from Scripture. Christ, and St. Paul too, took advantage of this practice to speak of the kingdom of God. The passage cited above, from Luke 4:16 ff., shows that Christ actually explained the lesson read from the Scriptures. So it was, then, that quite early in the ancient Church the custom was established of explaining the Scripture lessons at the vigils, by reading excerpts from the works of the Fathers. Even for the later Matins, this remained the case. It is true that formerly the readings were not specified, and the matter was left to the one presiding. There were individual collections of homilies by the Fathers, and explanations were read from these. Even to this day we have some of these collections from the seventh and eighth centuries. With the introduction of the *Breviary for the Roman Curia,* however, even these lessons from the writings of the Fathers were abridged and strictly defined. Since that time the homilies in our Breviary have been definitely prescribed.

The Breviary lessons from the Fathers have yet another characteristic: the writings of the Fathers of the Church are a great Christian heirloom. They hold for us the heritage of the Church's traditional teachings. They give us an over-all picture of our faith. This is why the ancient councils based their doctrinal decrees on patristic testimony. The unanimous agreement of the Fathers in doctrines of faith or morals is a sure and infallible guide for our faith. The same holds true for the Fathers' interpretation of Holy Scripture. We can well say that the Fathers are past masters at understanding and interpreting the Scriptures. In scientific exegesis of the Bible, we have indeed made greater advances than the Fathers. However, they have plumbed far deeper the spirit and meaning of

the Scriptures. The understanding of God's word requires
more than mere science or knowledge. There is also a question
of grace and sanctity, of love and faith; the Fathers possessed
all these to a far greater degree than we do. I can aptly quote
here the words of St. Paul: "Knowledge puffs up; charity, on
the other hand, edifies." For a proper understanding of the
Scriptures, then, the study of the Fathers is invaluable.

We must admit that not all the lessons from the Fathers
which we now have in our Breviary are of equal merit. Besides much gold, we find also much gravel in with the gold.
Hence the mere fact that a phrase is from a lesson of the
Fathers does not imply that it is flawless or infallible. Not by
any means. But we can deem ourselves fortunate indeed to
have in the Breviary many lessons from the Fathers brimful
of beauty, genuine masterpieces. And yet we dare express the
hope that when the Breviary is revised, at some future date,
more of these passages of genuine excellence will be culled
from the pages of the Fathers of the Church. As a matter of
fact much of the blame for the ill-chosen lessons in the
Breviary devolves not only on the *Breviary for the Roman
Curia,* but also on those who shared in later revisions. For
many such lessons, better and richer passages could readily
be substituted. Here again, I maintain, we possess such a rich
treasure of early Christian literature that we have a right to
expect to find the best of it in our Breviary. Any revision
should, first of all, remove those apocryphal lessons falsely
ascribed to certain authors, or at least see that they are
ascribed to their correct authors.[5] Frequently we can blame
the strictly mechanical division of the lessons taken from the
Fathers for the fact that their beauty is not properly appre-

[5] P. G. Morin, O.S.B., has shown that no fewer than fifty sermons and
homilies in the Breviary are attributed to the wrong authors.

ciated. I have in mind a book, *Vaterlesungen*,[6] by Wintersig (a German work from the collection "Ecclesia Orans," Herder and Co. Germany), which continues and completes the excerpts we have in the Breviary lessons, and thereby reveals their beauty and richness. I could observe this in my own case: only after I had carefully translated it and pondered over the translation did a lesson really impress me.

Now I wish to give a general survey of the lessons of the Fathers. Our Roman Breviary contains more than five hundred sermons and homilies of the Fathers, including even those of the later doctors of the Church: St. Bernard, St. Peter Canisius, and St. Francis de Sales. There is a total of nearly forty Fathers whose words occur in the Breviary. The earliest are Irenaeus (died *c*. 203) and Cyprian (d. 258), from whose pen we have six beautiful lessons. The Fathers of the classical period come next: Athanasius, Cyril of Jerusalem, Hilary, Basil, John Chrysostom (who has given us no fewer than forty-six lessons), Ambrose with seventy-two lessons, and Jerome with thirty-nine. St. Augustine leads with one hundred and forty lessons. Those of Pope Leo the Great, totalling thirty-two, are particularly beautiful. Gregory the Great addresses us in sixty-six lessons. To enumerate all the other Fathers and to discuss their works would be too much of a digression. This one thing is positive: we have collected for us in the Breviary a precious treasure of spiritual thought that pleads for our full attention and appreciation.

c) The Lives of the Saints

It was a custom, even in Christian antiquity, to have the Acts of the martyrs and accounts of the lives of the saints read aloud at the vigils. The lessons of the second nocturn were

---

[6] "Lessons from the Fathers." Tr.

added to Matins expressly to continue this custom. Toward
the end of the Middle Ages the lives of the saints had attained
such a preponderance in the lessons that they were read
throughout the three nocturns. Even the Scripture lessons
were eliminated. What is more, these accounts of the saints'
lives were often historically unreliable, interspersed with a
certain amount of legend, plus dubious reports of miracles,
and so forth. It was precisely these lessons that cried persist-
ently for revision. Much still remains to be corrected, though
the Breviary of Pius V did improve many things. The reform
of Pius X included in its program also the revision of these
lessons taken from the lives of the saints. However, because of
the long research involved, this particular correction was
postponed. The matter, unfortunately, still hangs in abeyance.

Admittedly, this problem of the lives of the saints is a difficult one. The lives should be historically reliable, devotional,
and concise. Many of our present lessons fail to meet the re-
quirement of historical reliability, which actually was one of
the important points in all past Breviary reforms, including
the latest reform of Pius X. Our modern age especially demands historical accuracy. However, these lives of the saints
should not sound like biographies from the encyclopedia; they
were meant to be devotional and edifying accounts. I readily
admit that it is difficult to harmonize this latter quality with
historical accuracy. In our Breviary there are few of this kind:
perhaps the classic lives of St. Scholastica or St. Hermenegild,
both from the pen of St. Gregory the Great. Several of the
sermons read in the second nocturn on certain saints' feasts
are also of devotional and classic character; for example, the
sermon of Bishop Fulgentius on the feast of St. Stephen, on
the feast of St. Agnes, St. Lawrence, and certain others. To
let the saint himself, whose feast is being celebrated, speak

either in the homily or the lessons of the third nocturn, is also a favorite practice of the liturgy. Thus, on the feasts of the doctors of the Church, Hilary, Gregory I, Isidore, Leo I, Athanasius, Venerable Bede, Basil the Great, Paulinus, Irenaeus, Augustine, Jerome, Peter Canisius, Alphonsus Liguori, and Robert Bellarmine, we find homilies from their own pens. The same could be done for other saints, as for example, Ignatius of Antioch, Peter Chrysologus, Cyril of Alexandria, Cyril of Jerusalem, Justin, and Gregory Nazianzen. On the feasts of St. Ignatius, St. Perpetua and St. Felicitas, their accounts from the Acts of the martyrs could fittingly be read. These are all goals for a future Breviary reform.

d) Introduction and Conclusion of the Lessons

The lessons at Matins are surrounded with their own special prayers and ceremonies which are not sufficiently appreciated. The lector introduces the recitation of a lesson by requesting a blessing of the one presiding at choir. The lector says: "*domne*," which means "Sir" (as distinguished from "*Domine*," which means "Lord," that is, Jesus or God), "please (give me) your blessing." The one presiding then replies with a blessing in words that vary for each of the nine lessons. For the reader the prayer expressed by the blessing asks help that he may read the lesson well; for those present it asks grace that they may hear and accept with profit what is read. The choir approves the prayer by its answer: "Amen."

This custom of asking a blessing before the lessons existed even in the fourth century. In a similar way St. Benedict prescribed in his Rule that the abbot give his blessing before the lessons. The wording of these blessings was variable. Individual feasts, like Christmas and Easter, had their own proper blessings, allied to the mystery and meaning of the particular feast. The present blessings in our Breviary first appeared in the twelfth century.

We ought not skip over these blessings simply because they are so short, for often a profound thought is hidden in a few simple words. In the first nocturn the blessings refer to the Trinity, suggested, perhaps, by the fact that there are three lessons. 1. "May the eternal Father grant us a perpetual blessing." 2. "May the only-begotten Son of God deign to bless and help us." 3. "May the grace of the Holy Spirit enlighten our minds and hearts." Similarly in the second nocturn: 1. "May God, our all-powerful Father, be kind and merciful to us." 2. "May Christ grant us the joys of eternal life." 3. "May God enkindle in our hearts the fire of His love." In the third nocturn, the blessings refer to the Gospel: 1. "May the reading of the Gospel afford us protection and salvation." 2. "Through the words of the Gospel may our sins be forgiven." 3. "May Christ, the Son of God, teach us the words of the Gospel." Notice that the first two of these blessings express the sacramental character of the Gospel. The alternate blessings for the third nocturn refer to the saints: "May he, whose feast we celebrate, intercede for us with God." "May the King of angels lead us to the society of the citizens of heaven."

In ancient times there were various conclusions for the lessons at Matins. Of these the only remaining example is found in the lessons at Tenebrae: "Jerusalem, Jerusalem, return to the Lord, your God." Now the customary ending is: *Tu autem, Domine, miserere nobis* ("You then, O Lord, have mercy on us!"). We should regard this as a plea for gracious forgiveness of all the faults made through inattention in reading the lesson. This conclusion has a history of its own. In former times the length of the lesson was determined only by the wish of the one presiding; by a knock he would signal the reader to stop, saying: *Tu, autem,* "*You there (stop).*" The reader then would bow and reply: *Domine, miserere nobis* ("*Lord, have mercy on us*"). Later on, when the length of each lesson was determined, the lector said, as we say now: *Tu autem* . . . ; and the choir answered: *Deo gratias,* to thank God for what was read in the lesson.

II. The lectio brevis ("short lesson") or the capitulum ("little chapter")

At present long lessons occur only at Matins. Only short Scripture lessons are found in the other hours. In two cases, at Prime and at Compline, this lesson is called the *lectio brevis.* It is a remnant of a longer lesson. Even today, among the Benedictines, a passage from the Rule is read at Prime. At Compline a lesson was read from Scripture in the dormitory before going to bed. Today this lesson is invariable and harmonizes beautifully with the thoughts and ideas of a night prayer. At night the evil one prowls around the castle of our soul like a lion, roaring to strike terror into our hearts. We must stand courageously. We must calmly keep alert.

At Prime nowadays the lesson either corresponds to the season of the Church year, or, on feasts, is the same as the capitulum read at None. The reason for this, I do not know. The lessons at Prime, as a rule, propose some dominant idea of the current liturgical season. Get them by heart and repeat them over and over through the day; they are short, meaty excerpts from Scripture. Here are some examples: "May the Lord direct our souls and bodies in the love of God and in the patience of Christ." In Advent: "Lord, have mercy on us; we have awaited Thee; be our defense in the morning, our salvation in the time of affliction." In Lent: "Seek the Lord while He can yet be found; call on Him while He is near at hand." In Passiontide:

"I did not hide my face from those who rebuked me and spat upon me; Lord God, Thou art my helper, wherefore I am not ashamed." At Easter: "If you have risen with Christ, seek the things that are above, where Christ sitteth at the right hand of the Father; think of what is in heaven, not of what is on earth."

Nor may we overlook the two blessings that introduce these lessons. They express the thought and meaning of each hour in one brief sentence. At Prime: "May God almighty guide our days and deeds in His peace." (Prime is a preparation for and a consecration of the day and its work.) At Compline: "May almighty God grant us a peaceful night and a happy death." (Compline is not only a night prayer, but also a prayer for a holy death.) Besides the two short lessons in Prime and Compline, there is the so-called capitulum in each of the little hours. This is a short lesson too, but it has a meaning different from that of the ordinary lesson. The fact that it is commonly read by the one presiding, or by a subdeacon at Solemn Vespers, while the choir stands, makes this quite evident. The capitulum always follows on the psalms, to express in terse, scriptural phrases one of the main thoughts for the day. Thus the capitulum, which is always the same for Lauds, Vespers, and Terse, succinctly expresses the thought for the feast or the day. You might say that the capitulum leads up to the high point of the hour. At Lauds and Vespers the hymn follows like an echo to the capitulum; then comes the Gospel canticle with its antiphon, the dramatic climax of the hours. In the little hours (Prime to None) an entire responsory follows the capitulum; after a versicle the Oration for the day follows. While in most of the hours the capitulum varies from day to day, in Prime and Compline it remains unchanged. These latter are of course the least variable of all the hours. Genuine morning and night prayers as they are, the thought proper to the hour so predominates as nearly to suppress all reference to the feast. It would be well to study the thought behind the capitulum for each of these hours. Prime is a girding for the day's struggle. Its capitulum is like a pledge of fealty to our heavenly King (*Regi saeculorum*): "May honor and glory be given to the King of ages, immortal and invisible, the only God, for all eternity." On ferial days the capitulum is worded thus: "The almighty Lord saith 'Love peace and truth.'" Peace and truth are the sum total of the fruits of the Redemption, . . . a brief but weighty truth God provides us with for the coming day. At Compline the capitulum is especially impressive. We have eluded the snares and allurements of the world and of sin; we scurry to shelter beneath God's wings, like little chicks. Hidden safely now, we have but one plea to make: "Desert us not." The capitulum reads thus: "Thou, O Lord, art in the midst of us; . . . O Lord, God, desert us not." The beautiful responsory follows: "O Lord, into Thy hands I commend my spirit. . . ." This one example will show how dramatic and artistic an element the capitulum is in the structure of the Office.

On many Sundays the core and essence of the Epistle is selected for the capitulum. Thus the Office for the day is coupled and correlated with the Holy Sacrifice, the focal point of our Christian worship. We usually find as capitula in festive Offices, three appropriate Scripture texts which throw light on the feast. In the common of saints the capitula generally present a group of the saints for our imitation.

On Sundays and ferial days during the year, and in the various liturgical seasons, as Lent, Advent, and Easter, the capitula are especially rich and expressive. There we find genuine pearls of Scripture. For example: [7] "God is love, and who abides in love, abides in God, and God in him" (Sunday at Terce). "Carry one another's burdens, and thus fulfill Christ's command" (Sunday at Sext). "A great price was paid to ransom you; glorify God by making your body the shrine of His presence" (Sunday at None). "Do not let anyone have a claim upon you, except the claim that binds us to love one another. The man who loves his neighbor has done all that the Law demands" (Sext during the week). "Look anxiously then to the ordering of your lives, while you stay on earth. What was the ransom that freed you from the vain observances of ancestral tradition? You know well enough that it was not paid in earthly currency, silver or gold; it was paid in the precious blood of Christ; no lamb was ever so pure, so spotless a victim" (None on weekdays). There is no doubt but that such passages are truly magnificent.

Summarizing, we may say that even these little lessons, especially the capitulum, have a part to play in the make-up of the Office. They provide us with brief excerpts of God's word to accompany us through the day. In the rich, pregnant language of the Bible, they express the idea of a feast or season. They constitute the dramatic as well as the artistic element in the structure of the Office. What is more, for the man of prayer these words will resound like chimes through the whole day.

[7] The examples are quoted according to Msgr. Knox' version of the New Testament. Tr.

CHAPTER VI

The Orations

THE third element of the Office is the oration, or prayer in the strict sense. It has a definite importance in the make-up of the Office, though in comparison with the psalms and lessons it occupies the smallest space. But for the most part these orations are not taken from the Scriptures, but are rather the Church's own free compositions, they form the climax and conclusion of the hours. Serving to introduce an hour, the psalms are found at the beginning of it. The lessons follow in the middle of the hour. The orations, however, are usually last, something like a quiet pool into which psalms and lessons spill like lively brooks. The whole choir is to recite the psalms, whereas the lector, commissioned by a blessing for the task, is to read the lessons. Only the one who presides, however, is to read the orations.

It is true that these statements hold in full only for the liturgical oration which the hebdomadary recites at the end of an hour. Other orations that do not enjoy this important position are set within the structure of the Office. I shall mention something about the various kinds of orations.

1. The oration. That the Office should conclude with a prayer by the one presiding over the choir is an ancient custom, and even a law, of liturgical prayer compositions. As we noticed above, it is as though all the petitions, aspirations, and desires were fused into one brief prayer and presented to God

by the priest as mediator. We can establish two ancient customs in regard to this practice. Older indeed, and by far the more beautiful, is the one of concluding the hours with the Lord's Prayer. The Our Father is the epitome of all prayers, even of the whole Gospel ("A breviary or compendium of the whole Gospel." Tertullian). All our prayers and reading should culminate in this prayer. So it was that St. Benedict, following the practice of the Lateran Church at Rome, concluded the hours with the Lord's Prayer. Other churches, especially St. Peter's in Rome, either added to, or substituted for the Our Father, a special oration that corresponded to the oration or collect of the day's Mass. This custom spread gradually and eventually came into the *Breviary for the Roman Curia.* It suppressed the other, far more beautiful practice. Since that time most of the hours close with the oration for the day, which is also the principal oration of the Mass. Still, there can be no doubt that the ancient use of the Our Father gives this oration its special value and esteem.

We still have a few instances of the Our Father concluding the Office in our present Breviary. At Matins, the Our Father is the conclusion for each trio of psalms. Then follows the concluding prayer (called *absolutio;* here the word means "conclusion," not "forgiveness"). This is the last trace of an ancient practice that, perhaps, began in Gaul. The so-called *preces* found at the end of many hours, as, for example, Prime in the chapter Office, contain the Our Father too. This usage takes its origin from the concluding prayer or *absolutio.* The ancient *Teaching of the Apostles* (the *Didache,* from the first century) prescribed the saying of the Our Father three times a day by Christians. This was a part, in any case, or perhaps the conclusion, of the early Christian hour-prayers. The latter certainly finds its continuation in the custom I mentioned above.

Even our Breviary still has some faint traces of this; for example, the Pater Noster and Creed at the beginning of Matins and Prime, and at the end of Compline.[1]

The oration for the day stands, at present, at the end of the hours. It is the priest's prayer, "directed to God in the name of the community (by the priest), somewhat like one who heads a deputation and makes his appeal" (Jungmann) Like the celebrant in a procession, it always comes at the end. This oration is principally a *collecta*, a summary of a great complexus of prayers. A summary is to embody the basic thoughts in a logical manner. It contains, as a rule, what is applicable to all. In this way a chairman at the end of a meeting, in his summary of what was proposed in the discussion from a more or less subjective viewpoint, casts aside anything incidental or merely personal and individual. He confines himself rather to the essentials, and expresses them as briefly as possible. This is the task of the priest in the oration.[2]

Since I considered it at length in my book, *The Liturgy of the Mass,* I shall not treat of the structure and form of the oration here. We know that the orations are exquisitely constructed prayers, that their crisp terseness recalls the lapidary style of the old Romans. Feast-day orations express the leading ideas of the feast in a very brief prayer formula. Sunday orations contain a terse yet often profound expression of some idea that corresponds to the current liturgical season. Again we note that by means of the oration the Office is correlated with the Mass. Like planets around the sun, the hours rotate around the Mass. Eventually crystallized in the oration are the thoughts and petitions of the Office; and the orations of

---

[1] Jungmann, S.J., *Die liturgische Feier,* pp. 91 ff.
[2] Taken, for the most part, from Jungmann.

the Office are all fused into the collect of the Mass, to be borne aloft to the heavenly altar by God's angel.

In Prime and Compline, two of the hours which are somewhat personal morning prayers and night prayers, the oration does not vary from day to day. The oration, as a result, is not the collect of the day. Genuine morning prayers and night prayers, and of exquisite classical caliber, are the orations at Prime and Compline. At Prime the oration is worded: "O Lord, God almighty, who hast brought us to the beginning of this day, save us today by Thy power, that we may not fall into sin this day, but that all our thoughts, words, and works may be directed to the fulfillment of Thy will." With its address, its motive, and its petition, this prayer is in its entirety constructed like a collect. The motive contains our implicit gratitude: God has kept our lives safe until today. The petition is suited to the idea of Prime as a girding and preparation for the coming day. May the assistance of God's grace make us able to accomplish two things; first, negatively: may we today keep far from all sin; and second, positively: today may we fulfill God's will in thought, in word, and in deed. Notice that, strictly speaking, Prime ends with this prayer. What follows is the rite of the chapter assembly in the cloister. This section's structure is quite independent of the structure of the hours themselves. Here we find a splendid oration. Because of its French origin, it differs from the Roman collects somewhat in its form. In content, it resembles the oration given above, but its expression is richer and more positive: "O Lord God, King of heaven and of earth, deign this day to direct and sanctify, to rule and govern our hearts and bodies, our thoughts, words, and deeds, in Thy law and in the fulfillment of Thy commandments, that now and always, with Thy help,

we may attain salvation and freedom, O Savior of the world;
Thou who livest . . ."

The oration for Compline is just what it should be, a summary of the whole hour: "Visit this house, O Lord, we beseech
Thee, and drive all the snares of the enemy far from it; let Thy
holy angels dwell therein to watch over us in peace, and may
Thy blessing be upon us always." This prayer is an echo of
some of the verses of the psalms. Psalm 90 has a vivid description of the devil's snares, and it speaks also of the angels who
guard us in all our ways. Psalm 4 sings of rest and peace, and
psalm 133 refers to God's blessings. Thus the oration actually
is a collect, a summary of the hour.

To the class of invariable orations belong also the "absolu-
tions" which, after the Pater Noster, conclude the prayer part
of Matins. They are not, of course, as richly expressive as the
orations just mentioned. This would hardly be possible, because the psalms change from day to day. Somewhat like the
Libera nos quaesumus after the Pater Noster in the Mass, they
are intended to amplify and conclude the Our Father. And
what is more, they make special references to Jesus Christ,
whereas the Pater Noster addresses God the Father. They are
rather meager in content: "Graciously hear, O Lord Jesus
Christ, the prayers of Thy servants, and have mercy on us."
"May His loving kindness and mercy help us, who liveth, etc."
"May the almighty and merciful God release us from the bonds
of our sins." This last prayer is really an absolution in a double
sense: actual absolution from sin, and also a "conclusion." In
fact, the idea of its being a "concluding prayer" seems almost
to have been lost.

2. *The preces* (prayers). Besides the summary prayers,
there is a second group of prayers in the liturgy, which we can
include under the term "common prayer." This prayer also

stands at the end of the hour, but it precedes the oration. When liturgical prayer followed the ancient laws on the matter, it conformed to the following pattern: first, a reading from Scripture; then the responsory, the prayers recited by the people; and finally the oration, the prayer of the priest.[3] Even in the early Middle Ages, we must admit, these norms and laws were laid aside to make room for other laws. Still, there are some traces of these laws in the Breviary, and as a result some remnants of the people's prayer. To this, the so-called *preces* at the end of the hour, just before the oration, mainly belong. The common prayer in the early ages consisted chiefly of invocations in the form of litanies; the Kyrie Eleison is the most frequent of these. The Greek *Ektenie* (litany) is an example of such a form of prayer. In the present *preces* we find a further development in the addition of a series of psalm verses and prayers of contrition, like the Confiteor. These *preces,* for the most part, were recited kneeling, and this practice has an excellent foundation. The people should pray and make their petitions on their knees; to the priest reciting the oration, belongs the position of mediator—that of standing. In the *Oremus, Flectamus genua, Levate* the liturgy preserves this double norm for us.

As the people's prayers, the *preces* are prescribed in the Breviary for all the hours on days of penance (Lent, Embertide, Advent, and vigils), and for Prime and Compline, the two subjective hours, on ferial days and lesser feasts.

The *preces* for Lauds and Vespers are sacred for yet another reason; they are the last vestige of an ancient community prayer that we can trace to apostolic times, the prayers for all the various stations in life. Paul was referring to this prayer when he requested (I Tim. 2: 1–7): "This, first of all, I ask;

[3] Jungmann, *Liturgical Worship.*

that petition, prayer, and entreaty be offered for all mankind, especially for kings and others in high station, so that we can live a calm and tranquil life." Even as early as the year 95, in his letter to the Corinthians (chaps. 59–61), St. Clement of Rome gives the text of such a community prayer. We can find this prayer in the ancient liturgies too; for example, in the *Apostolic Constitutions* of the third and fourth centuries. The *Oratio fidelium* is found after the lessons, in the early Roman liturgy. Good Friday's liturgy keeps this venerable relic for us. In ancient times, every Foremass (Mass of the Catechumens) contained this prayer. Even before the time of Gregory the Great, it had, unfortunately, dropped out of the Mass more and more frequently; eventually it disappeared altogether. Yet, contrary to what you would expect, it keeps its original form fairly well in the *preces* at Lauds and Vespers. Whenever we recite these *preces,* we ought to realize that we are following the most ancient traditions.

If you study our present *preces,* you see that the second part keeps the original form, but the first has been somewhat simplified. The petition for forgiveness and the Our Father (prayed aloud here) used to come at the end, but now you find them at the beginning of the *preces.* Several of these versicles hearken back to very ancient times, for example, *Pro afflictis et captivis;* this recalls the days of the martyrs. Prayers for the pope, bishop, civil authorities, for the people, and for peace, made up the chief part of the ancient community prayer. We find these petitions too in the solemn orations for Good Friday.

The so-called *suffragia,* where we pray for the intercession of the saints, are more or less like these *preces* in character.

3. *Pauses for prayer.* In conclusion, let me call attention to the silent, wordless prayer, found in certain places in the

liturgy of the early Church. At the summons of the celebrant's *Oremus*, the faithful knelt and prayed awhile in silence. This is why the deacon called out: *Flectamus genua* ("Let us kneel down"). A pause followed here, then the call *Levate* ("Rise"), whereupon the people stood up to listen to the celebrant's prayer. There were similar pauses in the course of the Mass. Thus, when after the *Dominus vobiscum* the priest called out *Oremus*, he waited until the oblation was completed before he recited the Secret prayers. There were, and are, such prayer pauses in the Office too. At the start of every hour there is a brief pause so we may recollect ourselves, and another is found just before the Confiteor in Compline so we can examine our consciences. The pause was to last the length of a Pater Noster.[4] Later, however, the Pater Noster itself took the place of the pause for silent prayer. Then, at the beginning of Matins and Prime, and at the end of Compline, the Apostles' Creed was added to the Our Father. Still, even now, as a matter of principle, we should remember that they are pauses for silent prayer. The Our Father is far too sacred to serve merely as a preparation and means of recollection for our prayer. What is more, wherever possible, it stands in the liturgy at the end of an hour, as we have mentioned, as a summary of all our petitions and desires.

This chapter shows us particularly that the liturgy is like the loving father in the Gospel, who is perpetually bringing out things new and old from his treasure. The Breviary, at the same time, has remnants of the most ancient prayer services, and some things too of modern composition.

---

[4] I recall that housewives sometimes use the Our Father to measure the time for boiling eggs.

CHAPTER VII

The Verses and Versicles

T HE psalms, lessons, and orations are the framework of the Office. Smaller parts are added to surround and embellish them. These minor elements can be divided into four groups: the verses, the antiphons, the responsories, and the hymns. We shall treat these in the pages that follow.

The short verses are the smallest parts of the Breviary. They are called versicles (the diminutive of "verse"). A verse whose first half is said by an individual and whose other half is answered by the choir, is a versicle. What is its purpose? We must first see if the versicle occurs at the beginning, in the middle, or at the end of the Office. At the beginning, it is like a springboard from which we can take off into the prayers that follow. For example, the introductory verse, *Domine, labia mea aperies* ("Lord, open my lips"). The ancients called this the *versus aperitionis* ("the opening-verse"). So it is that the first verses are meant to open the heart and lips for prayer. The versicles at the end of the Office are the farewells the soul calls back to God, as though it did not wish to part from Him so quickly. From an esthetical viewpoint, such versicles are actually required at the beginning and the end of the hours. It would not seem right to us if a jubilant chorus of bells broke off ringing abruptly. If their ringing diminishes gradually, it suits us better, with the bells one by one growing fainter and fainter. This would make an apt transition from the jubilant

112

pealing of the chimes to complete silence. On the last three days of Holy Week we can see what an effect such an abrupt and imperfect ending has. Here the sudden conclusion of the Office takes us by surprise. Something is missing. This, of course, is the proper way to express our grief for the departed Bridegroom. But what evokes fitting sentiments for Good Friday would on other days be cold and inartistic. How differently a festive Office sounds, especially at Matins! It is like an exultant pealing of bells. First a tiny bell, then a second, a third, and finally all the bells, small and large, blend in full harmony. The pealing ends in reverse fashion. It dwindles gradually, starting with the big bells, down to the smallest ones, little by little, until all are silent again.

The Office begins with silent prayer: the Pater Noster and the Creed. We know already, from the previous chapter, that the Pater Noster is merely a pause given for us to recollect ourselves. Actually the rubrics should say: "Let each one recollect himself for the space of an Our Father." This Our Father then, like the smallest bell, is but a preparation. The opening verse comes next, the second bell. Then a hymn, the third bell. Finally come the psalms, the full chorus of bells.

The versicle in the middle of the Office has a different meaning. There it has the following purposes. 1. It serves as a transition from one to the other among the major parts of the Office. 2. It summarizes the principal idea of the hour. Like a second Invitatory, it is a summons to prayer, a sort of spiritual cockcrow to rouse the sluggish from their lethargy (*gallus somnolentos increpat*). 3. Above all, notice that the versicle always refers to what follows, and not to what has gone before. It stands before the oration, the Pater Noster, and especially before those passages which deserve our particular attention and devotion. At Lauds and Vespers the versicle looks to the climax of the hour that follows immediately, namely, the Magnificat and the Benedictus. In ancient times there were but four versicles in an ordinary Office, and each of these occured at a fixed place in the Office.

Let us consider this now as it actually exists. We have two types of versicles that stand at the beginning of an hour. With the exception of Matins, every hour begins with the versicle, *Deus in adjutorium* ("O God, look to my aid! Lord, hasten to help me!"). "Glory be to the Father and to the Son and to the Holy Ghost; as it was in the beginning, now and ever shall be, world without end. Amen. Alleluja." (In Lent, and the pre-Lenten season, instead of "Alleluja," we have: "Praise be to Thee, O Lord, King of eternal glory.") The first verse (*Deus in adjutorium, etc.*) comes from psalm 69:2. Even by the early ascetics, it was used as an effective prayer against temptation, especially against distraction in praying.[1] St. Benedict too [2] prescribed its use at the beginning of an hour, as a prayer or petition for grace. So it is that this piercing cry is meant to be our plea for the grace to pray properly. Yet St. Paul says: "When we do not know what prayer to offer, the Spirit Himself intercedes for us with groans beyond all utterance" (Rom. 8:26).

The "Glory be to the Father" is added to this verse so we can express the intention of our prayer immediately: to honor God. The Breviary is essentially a prayer of praise, not of petition. It is an effort to duplicate the eternal praise of God that is sung in heaven. That is why the Office is perpetually returning to this theme. Though the soul may rejoice to the heavens, or be afflicted even to death, at the end of each psalm with the

[1] Cassian, *Coll.*, X, 10.
[2] *Rule*, chap. 9.

Gloria Patri, we invariably revert to the intention we made at the beginning of the hour.

The Alleluja is the third call to prayer. We are familiar with this favorite chant of the liturgy. Translated literally, it means: "Praise the Lord." But long ago it lost this literal sense. Now it is rather an exclamation of joy. It is the Church's "resurrection song," and the theme song of the saints in heaven. There we hear the Kyrie no longer; only a perpetual Alleluja. We declare the joyous character of the Office by this Alleluja at its very beginning, and we blend our voices with the heavenly choirs. Only from Septuagesima Sunday to Good Friday do we discontinue the "Song of the Lord," as it was formerly called. We hang our Alleluja harps on the aspens in our longing for the Sion of heaven. In place of the Alleluja we sing and pray: *Laus Tibi, Domine, Rex aeternae gloriae* ("Praise be to Thee, O Lord, King of eternal glory"); a song of praise to Christ, our divine King.

These three versicles, then, the first little flutterings of our prayer, give us not only an expression of the nature and character of the Office, but also a theology of Christian prayer.

With the exception of Compline, which prefaces a lesson and the "chapter of faults," and Matins, which inserts the prayer, *Domine, labia mea aperies; et os meum annuntiabit laudem tuam,* before these three versicles, all the hours begin with them. The insertion at Matins takes its origin from the rules prevailing in the cloisters. The great silence began for the monks with Compline, and lasted until Prime of the next day. Matins were sung during the night. The monks, accordingly, asked permission to open their mouths that they might chant God's praises. So much for the opening verse.

At the end of the hours too, there is a series of versicles and verses that are intended, perhaps, to bring the hour to a gradual close. The ending that occurs most frequently is made up of the following prayers: *Amen. Dominus vobiscum. Et cum spiritu tuo* ("So be it. The Lord be with you. And with thy spirit"). *Benedicamus Domino. Deo gratias* ("Let us praise the Lord. Thanks be to God"). *Fidelium animae per misericordiam Dei requiescant in pace. Amen* ("May the souls of the faithful departed through the mercy of God, rest in peace. Amen"). The "Amen" is the customary ending for prayers in the liturgy. (It is a Hebrew word that means, "So be it.") As a result, it is the people's approval of the priest's prayer. The *Dominus vobiscum* is the liturgical greeting used by the priest. Here it is used also as a liturgical farewell. Notice that the laity, and those not yet ordained deacons, may not use this greeting. They cannot be answered with "and with thy spirit," because "spirit" here signifies the power of orders received from the Holy Ghost. In its place then, they must use *Domine, exaudi orationem meam. Et clamor meus ad Te veniat* ("O Lord, hear my prayer. And let my cry come unto Thee"). Like the *Ite, Missa est* in the Mass, the *Benedicamus Domino* is the dismissal signal in the Office. The hour opened with a prayer of praise to God. The end of each psalm returned to this theme. Now, with a last tribute of praise to God, it draws solemnly to a close. We recall the poor souls at the ending of an hour. This is a lovely feature of loyalty and fellowship that our liturgy shows. There is not a single hour (with the lone exception of Compline) in which the Church does not recall her poor, afflicted members, the Church suffering. In her official table prayers even, she does not forget the poor souls.

Two of the hours, Prime and Compline, have an ending that differs from the one just mentioned. Both of these conclude with a petition for a blessing. Their cloister origin explains this, too. The last part of Prime (called the *Officium capituli* or "chapter office") is the liturgy's good-intention for the day's work. Right here the abbot gave the monks the day's chores and then dismissed them with a paternal blessing. For us now, this is the fatherly blessing God gives us, His children, before we go out into the world, as into a foreign land. There was something like this in the night prayer the monks recited in the dormitory. At the end of this they got the abbot's blessing for a restful night. We, however, seek this blessing from the Father Abbot in heaven.

Now I wish to mention several ideas about the versicles that are found within the hours. First of all, they form a transition between the major parts of the hour. For an example, take the end of the prayer service (i.e., the psalms) at Matins. Here the versicle is also a summary of what the preceding psalm expressed. As a rule, the versicle is an apt verse from one of the psalms, which sheds some light on the feast. For instance, on the feast of the Epiphany: "The kings of Tharsis and the isles shall offer gifts"; or on Holy Saturday: "As soon as I lie down I fall peacefully asleep."

Another type of versicle shows up just before the climax of the various hours: before the Magnificat at Vespers, the Benedictus at Lauds, and before the oration in the other hours. Here the versicle is planned as a preparation for the climax that follows. I like to compare it to the run you take before you jump.

At this point it may be well for us to recall the versicles proper to the various liturgical seasons. Advent has two: *Vox clamantis in deserto* ("The voice of one crying in the desert, prepare ye the way of the Lord"), and *Rorate coeli, etc.* ("Drop down dew, ye heavens, and let the clouds rain forth the Just One. Let the earth open up and sprout forth the

Savior"). Thus, throughout Advent, morning and evening we
have before us the two famous Advent preachers, John the
Baptist and Isaias. All during Lent we pray a verse from psalm
90: *Angelis suis mandavit* . . . ("For to His angels He has
given command about you, that they guard you in all your
ways"). It is as though all during Lent the Church would
make good the words Satan used with evil intent when he
tempted our Lord. The words of the disciples going to Emmaus are appropriate, as used at Vespers during Eastertide:
Mane nobiscum ("Lord, stay with us, Alleluja; for evening is
falling, Alleluja"). We could pick out other characteristic
verses like these for the whole church year. Once again, how
very evident it is to us what a wealth of artistry is ours in the
liturgy!

   In conclusion, I would point out that it is precisely these
versicles which lend a stirring vitality and a touch of drama
to the Breviary. We should remember that the Office, as well
as the Mass, is a prayer drama, and not merely a meditation
or a form of mental prayer. Nor is it meant to be a private
prayer. It is rather the prayer of the community, paying its
tribute of praise to God in active participation. The versicles
are, then, continual and regular summonses to community
prayer.

CHAPTER VIII

The Antiphons

W<small>HAT</small> the setting is for a gem, the antiphon is for the psalm. What is the antiphon? It is a verse or sentence recited before and after a psalm. It indicates the psalm tone, and suggests a particular thought for the psalm or psalms that follow it. Thus, the antiphon has a musical as well as a spiritual or intellectual purpose. If we wish to understand its meaning, we must inquire into its history.

a) History. Only in the light of the various methods used to recite the psalms, can the origin of the antiphon be understood. The faithful of ancient times were familiarized with the psalms in the following manner. First a soloist, called the precentor (one who sings first), sang a verse of a psalm. The faithful repeated this verse. The precentor sang another verse, and the people sang the first verse again, and so on. The faithful always sang the same verse, one that was particularly impressive. The precentor proceeded with the remaining verses of the psalm. This is the so-called responsory method. Typical examples of this manner of recitation are the litanies. One person leads; the others show their approval and agreement by responding with the same verse each time. It is easy to understand that this method was an ideal way to sing the psalms for the simple folk who had no books or who perhaps could not even read. Yet it was somewhat rudimentary and tedious. I might mention that this could well be the way for

119

our Catholic people, unfamiliar with the psalms, to gradually regain a knowledge of some of the psalms at least. But we know that the responsory method would not satisfy the liturgy for long. It soon changed over to the chant method of the Greeks; that is, alternate choirs, with antiphonary chant. In the responsory method, only one person proceeded with the singing of the verses; the rest merely expressed their agreement. In the antiphonary chant, two equal choirs sang the verses by turns, although in a different pitch. One choir was made up of men and the other of women, so that there was a difference of nearly an octave in the pitch. This chanting "in turns" was called "antiphon"; that is, alternate voice or chant. This manner of singing the psalms flourished especially at Antioch where, according to an ancient tradition, St. Ignatius (d. 107) had introduced it after, in a vision, he had heard just such an alternate chant by the cherubim and seraphim before the throne of God. The monks of the East used this method in the fourth century, whence it spread over the whole Christian world. Pope Celestine I (d. 432) accepted it in Rome; and somewhat earlier St. Ambrose had introduced it at Milan, at the very time St. Augustine was sojourning there. St. Augustine describes the profound impression this manner of chanting the psalms made on himself, his mother, and the other faithful.[1]

I wept at the beauty of Your hymns and canticles, and was powerfully moved at the sweet sound of Your Church's singing. Those sounds flowed into my ears, and the truth streamed into my heart: so that my feeling of devotion overflowed, and the tears ran from my eyes, and I was happy in them.

It was only a little while before that the church of Milan had begun to practice this kind of consolation and exultation, to the great joy of the brethren singing together with heart and voice. For it was only about a year, or not much more, since Justina, the mother

[1] *Conf.*, IX, 6 f.

of the boy-emperor Valentinian, was persecuting Your servant
Ambrose in the interests of her own heresy: for she had been se-
duced by the Arians. The devoted people had stayed day and night
in the church, ready to die with their bishop, Your servant. And my
mother, Your handmaid, bearing a great part of the trouble and
vigil, had lived in prayer. I also, though still not warmed by the
fire of Your Spirit, was stirred to excitement by the disturbed and
wrought-up state of the city. It was at this time that the practice
was insituted of singing hymns and psalms after the manner of the
Eastern Churches, to keep the people from being altogether worn
out with anxiety and want of sleep. The custom has been retained
from that day to this, and has been imitated by many, indeed in almost all congregations throughout the world.[2]

Thus writes St. Augustine in his *Confessions*. This method
of singing the psalms may be pictured in the following way.
The clergy, divided into two choirs, assumed the chanting
of the psalms. A certain verse that deserved the special attention of the people was chosen from the psalm to give the
faithful, too, a share in these prayers. This verse was called
the antiphon. It was repeated by the faithful after each verse
sung by the choir. So there began a double choir. The priests
chanted the psalm; the faithful wove the antiphon in after
each verse, a golden thread in the fabric of the liturgy. Each
time this emphasized the thought that was to kindle the devotion of both choirs. From history comes a remarkable example of this custom. Julian the Apostate, who desired to
restore the pagan worship, was in power in the year 362 when
the Christians carried the relics of the martyr Babylas to Antioch. The priests chanted psalm 96 as the procession made
its way. After each of the priests' verses, the people repeated
verse seven: "All who worship graven things are put to shame,
who glory in things of naught." A better antiphon could not

[2] *Confessions of St. Augustine*, translated by F. J. Sheed (Sheed and Ward,
New York, 1943).

have been chosen, and it had a profound effect on the people. Soon afterward a young Christian was thrown into prison. All through his torments he sang this antiphon. Because of his courage under the greatest torture, though he did not deny his faith, he was set free.[3]

To make it easier for the faithful to sing the antiphon, the chanter, called the precentor, sang the antiphon first, before the psalm. After a while, however, the repetition of the antiphon after each verse of the psalm became too tedious. Perhaps after but two or three verses of the psalm, it was sung less and less frequently. In the end, what once was an alternate chant became a "frame-verse" to encase the psalm at beginning and end. This is the development to the present day.

But even our present-day liturgy bears some trace of the antiphonal chanting of the psalms. At the blessing of candles on February 2, *Lumen ad revelationem gentium* ("a light of revelation for the Gentiles") is sung after each verse of the Canticle of Simeon. The consecration of a church or altar calls for several chants to be sung in this fashion. For instance, the Benedictus with the antiphon *Quam terribilis est locus iste* ("How full of awe this place is!"). The Breviary shows us the transition stage of the use of the antiphon too. In the third Nocturn of the Epiphany we find psalm 94 with the antiphon repeated after every two verses. Until recently, several dioceses and orders (Cologne, Munster; the Premonstratensians) were repeating the antiphon on the most solemn feasts, before the psalm, and before and after the Gloria Patri.

Today the antiphon is sung in the Roman rite only twice, before and after the psalm. It is merely intoned before the psalm if the feast is less than a double. The whole antiphon is not heard until the end of the psalm.

[3] Sozomen, V, 13.

b) Significance. From the historical development of the antiphon something of its nature and purpose is apparent. Viewed esthetically, it should be seen as lending beauty, variety, and completeness to the psalms. You do not hang a picture on the wall without a frame to enhance its value and beauty. Just so, the antiphon is the frame for the psalm. It would be hard to measure how much it improves and enhances the recitation and, even more, the singing of the psalms. Incidental stress might be laid also on the antiphon's technical importance from a musical viewpoint. The choir knows immediately in what tone it is to sing the psalm from the antiphon intoned by the chanters.

The liturgical meaning of the antiphon in the Office is even more important. Though the psalm offers several thoughts and dispositions, the antiphon is intended to stress a particular thought and arouse a single disposition in the one who prays. Often it is the key to the psalm. It links the psalm with the theme of the feast or, on ferial days, with the burden of the oration. You might say that the antiphon is supposed to tell us why we pray this psalm at this place in the Office, and how we are to apply it to the feast. It is a sort of commentary for the psalm. This is, of course, what the antiphon should do ideally. It is not always realized. One other type of antiphon has little, if any, intrinsic relation to the psalm. It serves only as a frame, and is not unlike the border of a picture. Then too, the antiphon may be intended to focus our attention on the leading thought of the feast. Antiphons from the life of a saint belong to this class, the rather common ones used for Vespers and Lauds too.

Our Office has both the antiphons that give us the key to the psalm, and the ones that have no intrinsic relation to it, but merely serve to frame it. But between these two types is a whole range of variations, the one or the other predominating.

Some examples will illustrate this point. An antiphon that is true to its purpose is taken from the psalm itself and suggests the proper disposition for praying it. The same psalm, related to two different antiphons of this caliber, can arouse entirely different dispositions. It is like looking at a landscape through glasses of different colors. As an example, psalm 129, the *De profundis,* is the Church's favorite for the dead. The laity, too, know it well. It is used not only in the Office of the Dead, but as a penitential psalm as well. Who would ever dream then, of finding this same psalm in the Second Vespers of Christmas? Only an antiphon could make this possible: "With the Lord there is mercy, and with him plentiful redemption" (old version).

Christmas is really the feast of our Redemption. In praying the *De profundis* we pass lightly over any sadness in the verses, but we stress God's mercy and His desire to redeem us, manifested so touchingly in Christ's birth. Here is proof, then, how masterly the antiphon can show us the way to pray the psalms.

If you would study how the antiphon can serve as a key to interpret the psalms, consider the Office for Corpus Christi. At the same time, you cannot fail to notice the genius of St. Thomas, its composer. Psalm 1 at Matins treats of the just man and the sinner. It compares the former to a tree that bears its fruit in due season. St. Thomas sees Christ in this upright man: Christ, the ideal for all the just. We think also of the tree of the cross. For us now it is the tree of life and bears the saving fruit of the Holy Eucharist. The antiphon reads: "At the time of His death, the Lord gave wholesome fruit to be eaten."

On Sundays and ferial days, the antiphon usually expresses a general idea or picks out a special verse from the psalm. This bears some resemblance to the original antiphonal chant of the faithful. Sometimes the entire content of the psalm is to be emphasized. In this case the first verse of the psalm serves as the antiphon. It is not repeated, but the recitation of the rest of the psalm moves right along. It is when a single antiphon must serve to frame several psalms or parts of psalms (as in the little hours) that the antiphon has the special duty of pointing our attention to the theme of the hour or feast. In this the liturgy is unrestricted. To study the antiphons of the daily Psalter from this viewpoint would be worth our while.

Very often, though, the antiphon serves merely to enclose the psalm. Lauds at Christmas and Easter exemplify this method. The antiphons at Christmas spotlight the events of the night and morning. They tell that the shepherds heard the message of the angels and went to see the divine Child. Easter's antiphons describe the moment of our Lord's resurrection: the appearance of the angels, the earthquake that set the guards to flight, and the approach of the holy women. These antiphons have no connection of ideas with the concurring psalms. They do no more than frame them. Better still, they set the scene of action, and the psalms present a meditation on it. The psalms of Lauds, for the most part, are morning prayers or songs of praise. These fit in with the theme of the hour. Almost invariably they stress the morning prayer's relation to the feast also. There is nothing to prevent each one from making this connection in his own mind and weaving his own thoughts into the psalms. With the help of the antiphons, for instance, it would be easy enough to pray the psalms at Easter Lauds from Mary's heart, or from the hearts of the holy women. It also often happens that historical antiphons

are closely related to their psalms. The feasts of the protomartyr, St. Stephen, and of St. Lawrence point this out. The
lips of the martyrs themselves speak the third psalm at Lauds
(*Deus, Deus meus, ad te de luce vigilo*) for us: "My soul
cleaves to Thee, since my body has been stoned for Thee, my
God." A slight change is made for St. Lawrence: "because
my body has been given to the flames."

Some liturgists of renown have decried the so-called in-
complete antiphons (*antiphona imperfecta*). They are rela-
tively unimportant for the thought expressed since they are
merely intoned before the psalm. But from a musical standpoint, they are valuable inasmuch as they indicate the chant
tone for the psalm by giving a hint of the melody of the full
antiphon.

The antiphons for the *Benedictus* and the *Magnificat* have
a special purpose. They stress the leading thought of the feast
or the feria. In style and music, they are carefully fashioned
works of art and often form the climax of the day's liturgy.
Gracing, as they do, the key points of the day, sunrise and
sunset, they are like the focal points of an ellipse. Linked
with the Gospel canticles, these antiphons propose some particular motive for praise and thanksgiving. Drawn usually
from the Gospel on Sundays, they show us how we can play
our part in the Gospel drama. Much more could be said about
the antiphons, but perhaps these few suggestions will gain
for the antiphons the attention their importance deserves.

I will say in conclusion that the antiphon definitely enjoyed
a greater importance originally as the alternating verse. Now,
however, serving merely as a frame for the psalm, it has not
entirely lost its significance. Just as a river's banks determine
its course, so the antiphons channel our praying of the psalms.

CHAPTER IX

The Responsory

E<small>VEN</small> more important in the Office than the antiphons, are the responsories. These are chants that follow a lesson and give a reflection on it. It is an arrangement in which the faithful use certain phrases to reply to the main sentence, recited by one or more precentors. Essentially, then, the responsory is the task of a soloist; short verses let others join in at intervals. Because it is to voice the choir's reflection on the lesson, it should apply what was read to the individual soul. This use of responsories was the oldest and most popular method of chanting. The litany is a familiar example of this form of prayer. The precentor recites the invocations, and by a brief reply to each, the community expresses its participation. As a prayer of quiet reflection, the responsory chant is appropriately placed after the lesson as a brief meditation. And still, these antiphonary chants serve well to rouse us and stir us to action. (As processional chants, the Introit, Offertory, and Communion of the Mass are ranked as antiphons.)

I. Types of Responsories

Our Breviary has two kinds of responsories, the long and the short responsory. How these differ can best be seen by an example.

The Long Responsory (Matins on the Saturday before Low Sunday)

R. Isti sunt agni novelli qui annuntiaverunt, alleluja, modo venerunt ad fontes,

Chanter: These are the youngling lambs, who have proclaimed alleluja, they have come just now to the fountains.

* Repleti sunt claritate, alleluja, alleluja.

All: They are filled with light, alleluja, alleluja.

V. In conspectu agni amicti sunt stolis albis et palmae in manibus eorum.

Chanter: Before the lamb they stand clad in white garments, with palms in their hands.

* Repleti sunt claritate, alleluja, alleluja.

All: They are filled with light, alleluja, alleluja.

The Short Responsory (Terce at Easter)

R. Surrexit Dominus de sepulchro, alleluja, alleluja.

Chanter: The Lord has risen from the tomb, alleluja, alleluja.

Surrexit Dominus de sepulchro, alleluja, alleluja.

All: The Lord has risen from the tomb, alleluja, alleluja.

V. Qui pro nobis pependit in ligno; alleluja, alleluja.

Chanter: He who hung for us on the cross;
All: Alleluja, alleluja.

Gloria Patri et Filio et Spiritui Sancto.

Chanter: Glory be to the Father and to the Son and to the Holy Ghost.

R. Surrexit Dominus de se-   All: The Lord has risen from
   pulchro, alleluja, alleluja.   the tomb, alleluja, alleluja.

Let us study the structure of each of these more closely. The
first part of the long responsory is the main sentence, marked
with the sign R (responsory in the stricter sense). A little star
or asterisk marks the second part. This is called the *repetenda*
and is sung by all. Another verse comes next, marked with
the sign V. The *repetenda* is sung after this too. The last responsory of every Nocturn adds the *Gloria Patri* and concludes
with the *repetenda*. This long responsory is found only in
Matins; the short responsory occurs in the little hours (Prime
to None, and Compline). The latter differs from the long responsory in its structure. Everybody repeats the first verse.
When the second verse has been said, the second half of the
first verse follows it up. At the end after the *Gloria Patri*, the
entire main sentence is repeated.

The English translation of the examples given above indicates who is to recite the various parts. The chanter or precentor leads the chant. He goes on alone through the prayer,
and the people have their say at intervals. It is easy to see how
this resembles the structure of a litany.

II. Contents of the Responsories

The liturgy has always used a chant to echo what was read
in a lesson. It borrowed the practice from the synagogue where
a psalm was usually sung after a lesson. The tracts in our
Mass point to the fact that the early Church had not yet divided the responsory into parts. Good Friday's ceremonies
and the prophecies on Holy Saturday show this ancient form
very clearly. It could very well be that the choir of ancient
Greek and Roman drama influenced the masterly division and

arrangement of the responsory. In those classic tragedies, it was the choir's function to reflect and voice the sentiments of the audience about the action of the drama. As a matter of fact, the choral passages take their place among the most beautiful parts of the ancient dramas. Though the choir was to a considerable extent an intrinsic part of the play, it always kept far from any show of excessive emotion or passion. It would rejoice with the joyful, mourn with the sorrowful. But the dignity and tact of its manner kept the hearts of the audience in that tranquillity without which there is no enjoying a masterpiece.

The responsory has functions of a similar nature. It too narrates, admonishes, instructs, prays, rejoices, bemoans, and laments, all according to the tone of the lesson. From an artistic standpoint, some of our responsories are good matches for the Greek choral passages. As examples, consider those in Holy Week, in Advent, and in the Office of the Dead.

Primarily then, the responsory is an echo to, or a reflection on the lesson. The listener should let the lesson work on him; he should work on the lesson, and ponder over it in his heart. A responsory first of all, then, must correspond to the contents, or at least the general ideas, of its lesson. Ideally, lesson and responsory would be linked by a perfect unity of matter. This, however, does not always happen; each lesson otherwise would require its own responsory. Yet, leaf through the Breviary and, especially at Matins on feast days, you will find a fair number of these ideal responsories. But if the responsory merely suggests and touches upon the theme of the feast— and this is more often the case—we are satisfied. When this happens, certain characteristic verses are repeated again and again, on purpose. Short responsories do this especially.

As far as the esthetic aspect of the responsories is concerned, no one need hesitate to rank them among the most beautiful and poetic parts of the Breviary. In this ultra-dramatic part of our liturgy every phase of poetic art is represented. Sometimes lyric, the responsories are epic and didactic too.

It would be impossible to demonstrate the diversity of the responsories in detail. At one time they proceed objectively with the account given in the lesson. Again, they provide instruction and admonitions, or voice the petition of the one who prays. Listen to the various voices that speak: now the voice of God, now an individual's . . . the patriarchs, kings, and prophets, from God's servant Abraham to the Apostle of the Gentiles, St. Paul, the spouse in the Canticle, the Mother of God: all speak to us in the responsories. In the Tenebrae Matins for Holy Thursday and Good Friday there is a regular alternation of Christ's voice with the people's. Sometimes we find a dramatic dialogue in one and the same responsory.

It is to be expected that not all of the nearly 850 responsories in the Roman liturgy are of classic beauty. Different periods of history have influenced their composition. Nevertheless we can say that many are of outstanding beauty and are rightly classed with the pearls of religious poetry. Let me call your attention to the responsories for the principal feasts of the Church, for instance, Christmas, the Epiphany, and Easter. See the almost extravagant richness of the responsories in Advent, especially the famous first responsory of the First Sunday. And the so-called historical responsories, how they have enhanced the Office as they echo scenes and words from the life of the day's saint! For example, study the responsories for the feast of St. Martin (November 11), St. Cecilia (November 22), St. Andrew (November 30), and especially St. Agnes (January 21). The third, sixth, and seventh responsories, which are used also in the profession ceremony of nuns, are worded (feast of St. Agnes):

It is Christ I love, in whose chamber I shall enter, whose Mother is a virgin, whose Father knows no woman; and the sound of His music falls rhythmically on my ear.

After I have loved Him, I am chaste; after I have touched Him, I am pure; after I have received Him, I am a virgin.

His flesh is already united with mine, and His blood has reddened my cheeks.

He it is, born of a Virgin-Mother, He it is whose Father knoweth no woman.

I am wedded to Him whom the angles serve, at whose beauty the sun and moon do marvel.

To Him alone do I keep my troth, to Him do I give myself with all devotion (seventh responsory).

The Tenebrae responsories are quite moving also. They sustain the tenebrae drama. It would be well worth the reader's time to study the responsories in Holy Week, keeping in mind the ideas we have indicated.

The responsories that follow the Scripture lessons of the temporal cycle deserve some attention too. They give us the essence of the lesson and reaffirm its main thoughts and incidents. The lessons' account of these matters is objective and factual, but that of the responsories is poetic and full of feeling. The Church's heartfelt pondering on the lessons finds warm expression in the responsories. These indeed furnish devout meditations on the Scripture lessons and the Church's festive seasons. Very often, too, at Matins the main figure of the Scripture lesson is the theme of nearly all the responsories. On Quinquagesima Sunday, for instance, it is the patriarch Abraham. During Lent, even though there is no reading from the Old Testament, the Sunday responsories continue

all through the week at Matins. The liturgy uses the responsories, then, to teach us to let the Scripture lesson echo not
merely through one day, but through the whole week. The
lesson is God's word conveyed objectively. The responsories
rephrase that same word subjectively, as it re-echoes in our
own souls.

Thus they teach us to meditate on Sacred Scripture. As a
matter of fact, be it noted that, though we listen to the objective presentation in the lesson, we sing the responsory ourselves; and what we sing becomes the concern of our own
heart. The responsories that treat of Sacred Scripture are
with us from Septuagesima Sunday to Passiontide, and then
from the First Sunday after Pentecost to the last Sunday.
New responsories appear and accompany us through the
whole week whenever a new section of a book is read (Adam,
Noe, Abraham, Jacob, Joseph, and Moses), or a new book begins (Books of Kings, Sapiential Books, Job, Tobias, Judith,
etc.). The responsories that occur in the lengthy period for
reading the Books of Kings throw much light on the passages
read. At the very beginning the main characters and salient
events are presented. For example, we are just considering the
birth of Samuel and already the responsories sing of Saul, of
David, and of Elias. It is as if the spirit of these men pervaded
the Books of Kings from the very beginning.

III. Form

On the whole, in the responsories classical form and exquisite melody match the choice thoughts. Let us note some
of the structural niceties of the responsories. That type and
antitype may be juxtaposed, some have their main sentence
from the Old Testament, and the verse from the New Testament. The majestic feast of Corpus Christi has seven of its

eight responsories fashioned in this way. Here is an example.

R. Immolabit haedum multi-
tudo filiorum Israel ad ves-
peram Paschae.

Chanter: The multitude of
the sons of Israel shall sacrifice a kid on the eve of the
Pasch.

* Et edent carnes et azymos
panes.

All: And they are to eat the
flesh and the unleavened
bread.

V. Pascha nostrum immola-
tus est Christus: itaque
epulemur in azymis sin-
ceritatis et veritatis.

Chanter: Christ, our paschal
Lamb, has been sacrificed:
therefore let us dine on the
unleavened bread of sincer-
ity and truth.

* Et edent carnes et azymos
panes.

All: And they are to eat the
flesh and unleavened
bread.

Antiquity had yet another requisite for a well-constructed
responsory. The verse chosen should be so phrased as to flow
naturally and logically into the opening of the *repetenda*, the
phrase that is repeated. This actually happens in a great number of responsories. Yet in many others such a logical connection is lacking. This, however, should not make them any
the less esteemed. The ninth responsory for the Third Sunday
of Lent shows how this requisite can be fulfilled.

R. Jacob wept bitterly over his two sons: Woe is me,—my
heart is sad for Joseph whom I have lost, and I grieve
deeply over Benjamin too, who has been taken away to obtain sustenance for us.
* I pray the King of Heaven in my grief ardently, that He
let me see them both.

V. Jacob, for grief, threw himself weeping on the ground, and
praying earnestly, he cried out:
I pray the King of Heaven in my grief ardently, that He
let me see them both.

(See how the *repetenda,* marked by the asterisk, affords in
both instances a natural continuation to what precedes.)

Some responsories have two *repetenda,* and such invariably
stand at the end of a Nocturn. This type has the *Gloria Patri*
as a kind of second verse. The first *repetenda* is heard after the
verse; the second, after the *Gloria Patri.* The ancient responsories had even more *repetenda,* and some are still to be found
today, such as the first responsory for the First Sunday of
Advent, and for Matins at Christmas, and the famed *Libera*
from the Matins of the Office for the Dead.

If we look at their musical status we find that the responsories rank among the most beautiful even though most difficult passages of the chant. This difficulty comes from their
being specifically solo chants. Because we have not yet an
official edition of the *Horae matutinae* (Book of Matins) these
chants are seldom used.

CHAPTER X

The Hymns

C LOSELY related to the responsory is the hymn. It lends the lyrical and emotional touch to the make-up of the Office. By a hymn, as found in the Office, we understand a definite piece of prayer chant, a self-contained song with text and melody united through meter and rhythm, and sometimes even rhyme. The hymn is not merely a poem; it is rather a song. The Church uses it as a prayer to stoke our devotion. This prayer resembles a poem in form and content. But better still, it is a prayer song that voices the thoughts of the whole community, as does everything in the liturgy. Once again let us go to history, and learn what it can teach us about the hymns.

I. HISTORY

In the broad sense of songs of praise to God, hymns are as old as the Church. St. Paul mentioned the Christians' hymns in his epistles. "Now there will be psalms, hymns, and spiritual music, as you sing with gratitude in your hearts to God." [1] Paul has, in fact, left us even some fragments of these early hymns. For example, in Ephesians 5:14:

> Awake thou that sleepest,
> And arise from the dead,
> And Christ shall give thee light!

[1] Col. 3:16.

136

Or in his First Epistle to Timothy (3:16), when he speaks of the mystery of godliness:

> Revelation made in human nature,
> Justification won in the realm of the Spirit,
> A vision seen by angels,
> A mystery preached to the Gentiles,
> Christ in this world, accepted by faith,
> Christ on high, taken up into glory.

The Apocalypse contains several prayers fashioned like this. Finally, there are the three hymns or chants from the Gospel, the Benedictus, the Magnificat, and the Nunc dimittis. These found their way into the liturgy at an early date. It is in this sense, too, that the Te Deum and the Gloria in excelsis are hymns of the early Church. It is true that the ancient Church knew nothing about hymns in the stricter sense of metrical chants. The Oriental Church did use hymns in its Office much earlier, but these were not metrical. In fact the Orient introduced metrical hymns long after the West had done so. Very early in the history of the Church, besides the Gloria in excelsis, we find the lovely evening chant *Lumen hilare.* This belongs to the ancient Greek hymns.

By the third century the Greek Churches had fully adopted the custom of singing hymns. St. Hilary of Poitiers (d. 369), doctor of the Church, learned some hymns in the East and introduced them to the West. He did not, however, leave the Church any from his own pen. St. Ambrose is the father of the hymns in the Latin liturgy. He also originated the meter for the hymns. It may well be said that St. Ambrose set the standard for all future composition of hymns. Even to this day several of his hymns are considered among the gems of the Breviary. The Roman Church had kept aloof from hymns until well into the Middle Ages. After St. Benedict broke away from this tradition in his Rule, prescribing a hymn for every hour, his monks spread the use of hymns over the whole West. Hymns were not used in the Office of the Roman basilicas until the latter half of the twelfth century. Even today you can find traces of this attitude of reserve toward the hymns. Look, for instance, at the Office for the Dead, for the last three days in Holy Week, and surprisingly enough, in the Easter Octave, where we find no hymns at all. Of the ancient Breviary hymns those sung each day of the week at Matins, Lauds, and Vespers (ferial hymns) have come down to us unchanged from the ninth century. These weekday hymns sing of the six days' work of creation. Eighty of the 180 hymns in our Breviary were written at an early period or in the Middle Ages. They found their way into the Office for the first time when the *Breviary for the Roman Curia* was composed. Before that they had been gathered in individual hymnals. At the beginning of the modern era, the hymns posed a stumbling-block for the humanists, whose classical standards made them look askance at the lines and form of the Breviary hymns. Hence Ferrari (1525), a humanist, undertook to compose new hymns that would follow the classical rules—an attempt doomed to failure from the start. The old hymns were retained. But under Urban VIII the attempt at reform was more disastrous. At his command, four Jesuits were to correct the hymns according to the rules of ancient prosody and classic Latinity (1629). We know today that this "correction" was nothing more than gross barbarism. What the humanists pedantically labelled "mistakes," were, in fact, quite idiomatic peculiarities of popular, late-Latin poetry. We have every good reason to hope that some day we shall see these hymns restored to our Breviary as they were before their mutilation.

Here I shall list some of the outstanding poets whose hymns

we find in the Breviary. But first, let us admit that it is impossible to ascertain the authors of many of the hymns, especially those of the ferial Office. In the liturgy, the practice of putting the name of the author of the words or melody at the end of a hymn, is not followed. Yet it is possible to determine many of the authors with a reasonable degree of certitude. Eight to fourteen of the classic hymns of St. Ambrose are known today; of these, four or five are in our present Breviary. Among them are the famous *Aeterne rerum Conditor* of Sunday's Lauds, and *Splendor paternae gloriae* of Monday's Lauds. Besides these, probably the hymns for the three little hours (Terce, Sext, and None) are from his pen. We find, too, several fragments of the longer works of Aurelius Prudentius (d. *c.* 405). Caelius Sedulius (*c.* 430) wrote the hymn for Christmas, *A solis ortus cardine.* The initial letters of its stanzas follow the sequence of the alphabet. Venantius Fortunatus (*c.* 600) has left a lasting monument to his genius in his hymns about the Cross: *Pange lingua gloriosi praelium* and *Vexilla regis prodeunt.* (Fortunatus also wrote the Easter processional chant, *Salva festa dies.*) The four poets just mentioned belong to the first period of Christian antiquity. Precisely what part Gregory the Great had with regard to the hymns is not clear. The second period embraces the early Middle Ages. Here belongs Paul the Deacon, who composed the hymn for St. John the Baptist: *Ut queant laxis.* (This hymn has a place in the history of music. Guido d'Arezzo borrowed the initial syllables of its first three verses and used them to designate the six tones of the diatonic scale: "ut-re-mi-fa-so-la." The first strophe of this hymn could well be used as a "tuning-fork.") Also of this period is Hrabanus Maurus. He composed the hymn for St. Michael, and the hymn for the martyrs: *Sanctorum meritis,* and, most important of all, the celebrated

Pentecost hymn: *Veni Creator Spiritus*. A greater élan characterized the third period, which included the late Middle Ages and modern times. Here rhyme came to the fore. St. Thomas Aquinas ranks first with his hymns for the feast of Corpus Christi. These impress us all the more since we find them as an integral part of the entire Office of the feast which seems to have come forth in one outpouring from his pen. The composers of many of the hymns of this period, however, are unknown. Of the more recent composers, we know St. Robert Bellarmine, the author of the hymns for the feast of the Guardian Angels and of St. Mary Magdalen. We know, too, that Urban VIII (d. 1644) composed the hymns for the following saints: Martina, Hermenegild, Venantius, Elizabeth, and Theresa; that Clement IX was the author of the hymns for the feast of St. Joseph; and finally, that Leo XIII gave our Breviary the hymns for the feast of the Holy Family.

II. PURPOSE AND APPRECIATION

If you are to understand the real value of a hymn, you must consider it as a song. And psychologically, what potentialities lie hidden in song! Of its nature, thought looks to words for external embodiment, though they may be ever so calm and softly spoken. Yet, of itself, thought is not obliged to have song. With feeling and sentiment, however, it is quite otherwise. These find their natural expression in song. It is the heart, the feelings, then, that are the source of song. *Cantare amantis est* ("He who loves, sings"), says Augustine. On the other hand, feelings and sentiments cannot last without thought. Thought must lead and govern them. Actually then, heart and mind are a twin source for song. We can apply all this to the hymns. In the Office, the hymn fills the affective, emotional role. It is either the feast or the hour that arouses the soul and stirs the heart. The hymn, then, draws its ideas from these two sources. As a result the hymns sing either of the feast or of the hour in which they occur.

We find hymns in three different places in the Office: after the psalms and capitulum at both Lauds and Vespers, after the psalms but before the capitulum at Compline. (In both these cases it serves as responsory and echo to the psalms and lessons.) The hymn at Matins stands at the beginning of the hour, so too with the little hours, Prime to None. Here it is meant to enliven heart and mind to pray. You can really say that the hymn so placed rouses us. Matins is a part of the night Office. Here, then, hymn and Invitatory are to wake our minds to full attention. The start of an hour must not lull us to sleep. At the little hours, the hymn calls us from the occupations of our daily life to think of spiritual things. The two functions of hymns in the Office are clear, then. At the beginning of an hour, the hymn is to rouse our fervor and fasten attention. But if our fervor is already at its peak and the heart is full, then the hymn lets us speak our hearts.

There is no need to be ashamed of the hymns from an esthetic point of view. Of course we must use the proper norm to measure their value. They are not the compositions of one group of poets. They are, rather, an anthology of songs in whose composition the whole Church has had a part. "Popes and kings, cardinals and bishops, brilliant luminaries of science and learning, ordinary teachers, influential politicians and simple monks,—usually not even bothering to leave their names to posterity—all these wrote the hymns. No more eloquent testimony could be given to their magnificent spirit of love and devotion, of joy and poetry." [2] In a certain sense, I like to compare the hymns to folk-songs. Though these, too,

_____
[2] Baumgartner, *Geschichte der Weltliteratur.*

are nameless and clothed in plain language, still they portray
the soul of the people better than would any classic composition. As a result the hymns of the Office do not bear comparison with profane, or even spiritual, poetry composed in the
modern era. The Church's heritage of song has its own special
value. Even at that, there are some less worthy ones among
our hymns, particularly those of more recent composition. The
vast majority of those that antiquity gave us, however, are of
outstanding magnificence and beauty. A future revision of the
Breviary that gives us these hymns in their original form
would certainly be well received.

Even with things as they are, two factors prevent us from
fully perceiving the beauty of the hymns. First, the laity who
do not understand Latin, find a translation a poor substitute.
Everyone knows that a poem loses its effect in any but its
original language. What is more, we have no classic translations. Besides, the unique character of the hymns is quite alien
to modern poetry. The poetry we know, stresses rhyme,
whereas meter is secondary. In Latin poetry, as found in the
hymns, meter is all-important. Rhyme appeared only in com-
paratively recent times. Consequently, the more closely translations try to adhere to the Latin meter, the more inexactly
they express the ideas. That is the first factor that puts the
hymns out of our reach. On the other hand, if we pray the
hymns in Latin, a new problem arises. We have to work over
them if we are to plumb their spiritual content. A poem, even
in English, will not fully reveal its beauty and depth of thought
at the first, cursory reading. We have to meditate and study
it. This holds, all the more so, for foreign, and especially
ancient, poetry, as are the Breviary hymns. Unfortunately,
few of us have ever studied and translated the hymns leisurely,
in an effort to understand them. Finally, the Latin of the

hymns is somewhat strange. It can lead to difficulties comparable to those encountered in translating the odes of Horace. On the other hand, once we give the hymns serious study, they become an enduring part of our spiritual treasures. Hence a word to all who pray the Breviary: Study the hymns. We should here recommend *The Hymns and Canticles of the Roman Breviary* by Father Britt (Benziger Bros., New York), an excellent work on the hymns.

III. EXAMPLES

1. The Cockcrow Hymn

To give the reader an idea of their beauty, we shall now translate and briefly explain several hymns. First, one of the most beautiful hymns in the Breviary, the work of St. Ambrose, the father of church hymns. As we mentioned already, St. Ambrose was the first to bring hymns into the Western Church. He deserves all the more credit when we recall that the Greek Church did not use meter, so that he had no model to follow. Through his own compositions, then, Ambrose set his imprint on those that followed, since the majority adhered to the meter he had chosen for his own. The "Cockcrow Hymn" is without doubt one of his best. For the most part it is a splendid description of nature. Here we give the original text and the English translation of W. J. Copeland, as found in Britt's *Hymns of the Breviary and Missal*.

AETERNE RERUM CONDITOR

(Sunday at Lauds)

Aeterne rerum Conditor	Maker of all, eternal king,
Noctem diemque qui regis,	Who day and night about dost bring,
Et temporum das tempora	Who weary mortals to relieve,
Ut alleves fastidium.	Dost in their times the seasons give.

Nocturna lux viantibus	Now the shrill cock proclaims the day
A nocte noctem segregans,	And calls the sun's awakening ray
Praeco diei jam sonat,	The wand'ring pilgrim's guiding light
Jubarque solis evocat.	That marks the watches night by night.
Hoc excitatus lucifer	Roused at the note, the morning star
Solvit polum caligine:	Heaven's dusky veil uplifts afar;
Hoc omnis erronum cohors	Night's vagrant bands no longer roam
Viam nocendi deserit.	But from the dark ways hie them home.
Hoc nauta vires colligit,	The encouraged sailor's fears are oe'r
Pontique mitescunt freta:	The foaming billows rage no more
Hoc, ipsa petra Ecclesiae,	Lo! e'en the very Church's Rock
Canente, culpam diluit.	Melts at the crowing of the cock.
Surgamus ergo strenue:	O let us then like men arise,
Gallus jacentes excitat,	The cock rebukes our slumbering eyes
Et somnolentos increpat	Bestirs who still in sleep would lie
Gallus negantes arguit.	And shames who would their Lord deny.
Gallo canente spes redit,	New hope his clarion-note awakes
Aegris salus refunditur,	Sickness the feeble frame forsakes
Mucro latronis conditur	The robber sheathes his lawless sword
Lapsis fides revertitur.	Faith to the fallen is restored.
Jesu labantes respice,	Look on us, Jesu, when we fall,
Et nos videndo corrige:	And with Thy look our souls recall
Si respicis, labes cadunt	If Thou but look, our sins are gone
Fletuque culpa solvitur.	And with due tears our pardon won.

Tu lux refulge sensibus,	Shed thru our hearts Thy piercing ray
Mentisque somnum discute:	Our soul's dull slumber drive away
Te nostra vox primum sonet	Thy Name be first on every tongue,
Et vota solvamus tibi.	To thee our earliest praises sung.

The hymn describes nature and closes with a petition. It reveals the spiritual symbolism of night's transition to early morning. Its matchless phrases depict the breaking of dawn, heralded by the shrill crow of the cock. The first strophe addresses our Creator. To His kindness we owe the practical alternation of day and night. Then the cock, the herald of day, lifts up his voice (2). Nearly all the rest of the hymn is taken up with recounting the effects of the cockcrow. It gives us the cock in his three related roles. First he is the light that guides late and lonely wayfarers. Though moon and stars are shrouded in darkness, his cry assures them that near-by are men's homes. Then, his cry marks off the three night watches and finally announces the dawn of a new day. The verses that follow go more into detail about the effects of this cockcrow. It rouses the morning star from its slumber, and its appearance in the sky drives off darkness. With no mantle of darkness to hide him, the criminal flees the shadowy paths of crime he had walked during the night. The crow of the cock stirs new hope in the breast of the sailor while in a small boat he battles wind and waves beneath a starless sky. The heaving seas remind the poet of the Church, the Rock that towers above the storm of time in impregnable security. Then he remembers Peter, the fisher of men; the cockcrow recalls Peter's denial, the Lord's glance of pity, and Peter's tears of remorse.

Here in this strophe the poet makes a lyric transition from the general to the particular, from a fisherman to Peter. Almost before we know it he has conjured up these scenes before our souls. He cannot let the thought of Peter's tears go now. Throughout the rest of the hymn he weaves it in and around the main thread of thought. In the fifth strophe he describes the effect of the cockcrow on us. The cock wakes us up too; let us rise quickly. If you do not get up, his crow reproaches, even rebukes you. Notice the gradation in this strophe. The cock awakens the slumbering (*excitat*). It chides anyone who does not heed it (*increpat*). If he persists in disregarding the call, and falls into temptation, the cock rebukes him (*arguit*). Still more striking events are recounted in the sixth strophe. Hope returns to the heart. After a sleepless night the bed-ridden welcome the dawn and take new hope. But the wicked hide from the approaching daylight, a realistic picture of the murderer concealing his poniard. The sinner takes new courage now, somewhat as did the cowardly Peter. The last two strophes rise to an ardent prayer. This unfolds the spiritual symbolism of morning. First, negatively, it reminds us of our Lord's gracious glance at the sinful Apostle and of the wonderful effect this glance had. Then, positively, it extolls Christ as the true light of the world, the "Orient on High," who drives spiritual sleep from our hearts, and lets us offer God the first fruits of the day. It is on a chord of praise that this immortal hymn concludes. By this composition Ambrose proves himself a master of vivid, forceful language that can voice the depth of his thought and his appreciation of nature. Above all, it shows he was fully possessed of the dignified reserve in thought and language that characterizes the ancient Roman culture.

2. *Ave Maris Stella*

Our second example of a classic hymn is the lovely song to Our Lady: *Hail Star of the Sea.* No one knows who wrote this pearl of medieval poetry. An indication of the Church's high esteem for this hymn is the rubric that the entire assembly kneel during the recitation of its first verse. Very few hymns share such a distinction. Profound thought, masterly division and arrangement, shine forth from its simple, unpretentious phrases. In the following we give the English translation of Rev. G. R. Woodward (Britt, *op. cit.*).

AVE MARIS STELLA

Ave maris stella,
Dei Mater alma
Atque semper Virgo,
Felix coeli porta.

Ave, Star of Ocean
Child Divine who barest,
Mother, ever-virgin
Heaven's portal fairest.

Sumens illud Ave
Gabrielis ore,
Funda nos in pace,
Mutans Hevae nomen.

Taking that sweet Ave
First by Gabriel spoken
Eva's name reversing,
Be of peace the token.

Solve vincla reis,
Profer lumen caecis,
Mala nostra pelle,
Bona cuncta posce.

Break the sinner's fetters,
Light to blind restoring,
All our ills dispelling,
Every boon imploring.

Monstra to esse matrem
Sumat per te preces,
Qui pro nobis natus,
Tulit esse tuus.

Show thyself a Mother
In thy supplication;
He will hear who chose thee
At His Incarnation.

Virgo singularis,
Inter omnes mitis,
Nos culpis solutos
Mites fac et castos.

Maid, all maids excelling,
Passing meek and lowly,
Win for sinners pardon,
Make us chaste and holy.

Vitam praesta puram,
Iter para tutum,
Ut videntes Jesum,
Semper collaetemur.

As we onward journey
Aid our weak endeavor,
Till we gaze on Jesus
And rejoice forever.

Now a brief explanation. The first strophe gives us in four lines the basic concepts of the Church's entire doctrine of Mariology. The first line is a greeting and an address. The other lines in turn mention Mary's three principal prerogatives: her divine maternity, her virginity, and her power of mediation. These five thoughts expressed in the first stanza are the themes of the next five stanzas: strophe two, *Ave* (Hail!); strophe three, *Maria* (Star of the Sea); strophe four, Mother; strophe five, Virgin; strophe six, Gate of heaven (Mediatrix).

Strophe one. Mary is addressed as "Star of the Sea," because in the Middle Ages people thought this was the translation of the name "Maria." The first verse, then, paraphrases the greeting "Ave Maria."

Strophe two. This treats of the "Ave." O Mary, you reversed Eve's name (*Eva*) when you heard the greeting "Ave" for the first time from the lips of Gabriel, Eva to Ave. You transformed Eve's curse into a blessing. In the next sentence, however, not to the past, but to the present the poet alludes as he prays: So may you now bring us peace! Establish us in peace, and in us too change Eva to Ave, change us from the "old" to the "new man."

Strophe three. This varies the name "Star of the Sea." What the star at night is to the sailor at sea, Mary should be to us in the night of life. We have a twofold darkness to battle against: the darkness of sin,—for we are prisoners of the devil —so we pray: "break the bonds of sin"; the other is the darkening of the intellect, our heritage from original sin. The second petition, then, is: "Give light to the blind." A third petition follows: "Ward off the robbers that make the sea of life so dangerous, Satan, concupiscence, and sin." The fourth petition is worded: "May the star of the sea shed its light so our voyage through life may be peaceful, pleasant, and successful." What a beautiful reflection on Mary, Star of the Sea!

Strophe four. Show that you are Jesus' Mother; that you have influence with your Son, Mary the all-powerful advocate.

Strophe five. Mary, purest of virgins, we ask you to obtain for us purity and meekness, the two virtues that characterize virginity.

Strophe six. Mary, gate of heaven. She is the great Mediatrix, the refuge of sinners, the way and the guide to Jesus. Through Mary to Jesus.

"Where can we find another hymn that within the space of six short stanzas combines such depth of thought and balance and symmetry of structure with such simplicity and candor of expression, as does this unpretentious but fragrant flower of Latin hymnody?" (G. M. Dreves)

To round off this section I offer now a brief explanation of the hymns for the little hours. The special purpose of these hymns is to point out the leading thought of the hour, and to express vividly the spiritual significance both of the position of the sun and of the hour of the day. T. Michaels, O.S.B.[3] (I, 115) shows how the idea of the sun in these hymns came to serve as a pole star for the various hours. At Lauds, in the light of dawn, the Church rises to meet Christ, the spiritual sun. At Prime, the first hour, she places the day's work and deeds beneath the light of Eternal Light. At Terce, the third hour, the sun fills the soul with increasing warmth, and with the Holy Spirit too. At noon (Sext) the Christian is exhausted by the heat and oppressed by his passions; so he flies to the protection of the all-powerful Ruler of the universe, because at this time, according to ancient tradition, the evil spirits prowl over the world. At the ninth hour (None) we turn our eyes

[3] *Jahrbuch für L.W.*

away from the setting sun to view the lasting brightness of eternity's evening, which holds out to us eternal glory as the reward of a holy death. This longing for eternal light is voiced again at Vespers in a simple but majestic petition to the Holy Trinity: though the light of the sun should fail, let Thy light always shine in us. With one last plea for God's omnipotent protection, the Church brings the sanctification of the daily life of her members to a close. In the pages that follow I shall give a translation and brief explanation of these five hymns.[4]

3. The Hymn for Prime: *Jam lucis orto sidere*

Strophe one. "The star of light being now risen, let us humbly beseech God that He may keep us from all harm in our daily actions." The hymn opens with the symbolism of light. The sun, that star which provides all our light, is just now risen. We rise from sleep. Prime is a girding for the day's battles. This explains our first request: that God may keep us from all harm.

Strophe two. "Bridling, may He restrain the tongue, lest the jarring discord of strife resound. May He lovingly veil our eyes lest they drink in vanities." Two of our senses are especially exposed to temptation: speech and sight. The Church always desires peace. That no quarrel may arise, we ask God to bridle our tongue, as we would an unruly horse. As for our eyes, we ask God to veil and protect them so that, in the words of the Psalmist, "they may see nothing vain and useless" (Ps. 118).

Strophe three. "May the inmost recesses of the heart be pure and may folly cease. May the sparing use of food and drink wear down the pride of the flesh." We have interior senses too, and these are much more dangerous. This is

---

[4] The prose versions of the hymns for the little hours are from Britt, *op. cit.*

particularly true of concupiscence. Only strict self-dicipline and moderation in food and drink can check it.

Strophe four. "That when the day has departed and Providence has brought back the night, still pure by virtue of abstinence, we may sing His glory." This strophe is looking already to the end of the day. The prerequisite for paying God a worthy tribute of praise is a day well spent, without any stain of sin. Still we think not merely of the present day and night, but of life, and of eternity too, the "night of life." This hymn harmonizes perfectly with the theme of Prime, the morning prayer of sinful man. At Lauds we were intent only on praising God. But at Prime our first petition is: "May we commit no sin!" Danger threatens on every side. Our tongue can run wild like an unbridled horse. Our eyes can drink up vanity. Our heart leans to levity, *cor ad vecordiam*. (The English cannot convey the play on words.) We might even say: "The heart plays foolish tricks on us." The flesh burns with concupiscence. Only a rigid self-control tempered by moderation in food and drink can quench this fire. Still we shall be able to glorify God with truly chaste souls only if we practice this restraint on all our senses.

4. The Hymn for Terce: *Nunc Sancte nobis Spiritus*

Strophe one. "Deign now, O Holy Spirit, who art one with the Father and the Son, to come to us without delay, and be diffused in our hearts." Terce is the Holy Ghost's hour. It was about nine o'clock that He descended upon the members of the infant Church on the first Pentecost. This explains why we do not address the Holy Spirit here with the customary *Veni*, but with an earnest plea that He take up His dwelling in our souls. Two words, perhaps, do not ring familiar to us: *ingeri* means "to be brought into us," and *refusus* means "poured out" (in our hearts). Then comes the prayer: May the Holy Ghost come and fill our hearts as on Pentecost.

Strophe two. "May mouth, tongue, mind, sense, and strength proclaim Thy praise; may our charity in its fervor glow brightly, and may its flame enkindle the hearts of our neighbors." This second strophe describes the effect and influence of the Holy Ghost's coming into our hearts. It is a threefold effect. All the faculties of body and soul praise God, because when they are filled with the Holy Ghost they serve God in word and in deed. Then too, the Holy Spirit especially enkindles our love for God ("enkindle the fire of Thy love"). This love of God urges us to love of our neighbor. Notice that this hymn apparently disregards the spiritual symbolism of the light, but only apparently. The second strophe gives it picturesque expression when it describes the effect of the coming of the Holy Spirit. Though their wording is extremely concise, on the whole you will discover that these hymns are rich and profound in thought content.

5. The Hymn for Sext: *Rector potens, verax Deus*

Strophe one. "O mighty Ruler, truthful God, who dost regulate the change of things, with splendor Thou dost light up the morning, and with burning heat, the noonday." It is noon. The sun burns down upon us. This strophe speaks of God, the Ruler of the world, who watches over the marvelous change of seasons in the year, of day and night, and of light and heat. At dawn He gives us the light to illumine the earth. At noon He gives us the sun's fiery heat. These lines form the background for the next strophe.

Strophe two. "Extinguish Thou the flames of strife, remove harmful heat, grant health of body and true peace of heart." The noonday heat can symbolize two bad and two good elements in man's life. First it suggests quarrelling and strife, then sensual passion. Both can make the blood boil in our veins. And as a matter of fact, in the noonday heat our lower nature is at its strongest. Yet on the other hand, warmth can be used as an excellent curative. Many ailments heal after its application. Finally, the tranquillity of the noon hour (especially in the Orient) suggests that genuine peace of heart which is the greatest gift Christianity offers.

6. The Hymn for None: *Rerum Deus tenax vigor*

Strophe one. "O God, the sustaining power of created things, who in Thyself dost remain unmoved, and dost determine our times by successive changes of the light of day": As in the preceding hymn, the first strophe forms the setting for the second one. God, the immutable Being, provides the alternation of night and day. Ponder individual words in these lines and see the profundity of thought they present. For instance: the sublime phrase *tenax vigor,* the basic power or force that sustains all things, the only source of all life and motion. But it is the second strophe, once more, that gives the application.

Strophe two. "Bestow Thou Thy light upon us in the evening (of life), that life may never fail us, but that eternal glory may await us as the reward of a holy death." This hour (None) consecrates the day's last quarter, from three to six o'clock. Our thoughts dwell on evening, on the twilight hours of the soul, and, in the end, of life itself. The hymn asks for light at evening-time, for Christ. Remember the words of the disciples at Emmaus: "Lord, stay with us for evening is falling." That the divine life may not leave our souls, we wish Christ to stay with us by His grace in the evening of temptation. With the night of death illumined with eternal light, then life's evening will be truly happy. This strophe reveals unusual wealth and depth of thought. Many authorities attribute these four hymns to St. Ambrose.

7. Compline hymn. *Te lucis ante terminum*

Strophe one. "Before the end of daylight, O Creator of the world, we beseech Thee, that in accordance with Thy mercy, Thou wouldst be our protector and our guard." As we would expect, a night prayer considers the approaching night; and night is a symbol of hell. Light is God's mantle. We beg Him for two things before the last trace of daylight disappears: that He be both master and guardian for us. In the language of the cloister, this would be: superior or abbot (*praesul*) and porter or gatekeeper (*custodia*). God should be King in the interior of our hearts. He should be our protector against the wicked enemy from without.

Strophe two. "Far off let dreams and phantoms of the night depart; restrain Thou our adversary lest our bodies become defiled." Night is hell's domain. Phantasies that entice the senses and stir the passions usually invade the soul at night. We pray God to drive these away. In fact, it is now that the devil himself prowls about the earth like a roaring lion. The hymn alludes to nocturnal pollution. Though it is no sin in itself, it can be an occasion of sin.

CHAPTER XI

The Ordinary of the Breviary

THE first part of the Breviary is the Ordinary. It contains parts that occur every day, or at least regularly during the different liturgical seasons. We will now explain the more important of these prayers. Their frequent recurrence merits them a more thorough treatment; otherwise the adage might hold good: Familiarity breeds contempt. We shall treat: 1. the Invitatory psalm, 2. the Te Deum, 3. the Benedictus, 4. the Magnificat, 5. the Canticle of Simeon, 6. the concluding antiphons to Our Lady.

I. THE INVITATORY PSALM (94)

We already know what the Invitatory is expected to do. Matins is said at night, and the Invitatory is a cry to wake up. It is the herald announcing tersely what the feast is about. It is for Matins what the Introit is for the Mass, a festive, highly dramatic introduction. In modern language we would call it the overture to the drama of Matins. Envision Matins celebrated in a grand abbey with full choir and perfection of rubrics. Then you can see the Invitatory as it should be, a masterpiece of prayer composition. To St. Benedict, most probably, goes the credit for fashioning this introduction out of psalm 94.

No matter how feast or season may vary, the liturgical reveille stays the same throughout the year. There must be something about its contents to enable it to act the important role of introduction to Matins. The psalm reads:

I

1 Come, let us sing joyfully to the Lord;
   let us acclaim the Rock of our salvation.
2 Let us greet him with thanksgiving;
   let us joyfully sing psalms to him.
3 For the Lord is a great God,
   and a great king above all gods;
4 In his hands are the depths of the earth,
   and the tops of the mountains are his.
5 His is the sea, for he has made it,
   and the dry land which his hands have formed.

II

6 Come, let us bow down in worship;
   let us kneel before the Lord who made us.
7 For he is our God,
   and we are the people he shepherds, the flock he guides.

III

   Oh, that today you would hear his voice:
8   "Harden not your hearts as at Meriba,
   as in the day of Massa in the desert,
9 Where your fathers tempted me;
   they tested me though they had seen my works.
10 Forty years I loathed that generation,
   and I said: They are a people of erring heart,
   and they know not my ways.
11 Therefore I swore in my anger:
   They shall not enter into my rest."

The psalm has two parts, sharply distinct. Its sequence of ideas is not hard to follow. The first part (strophes I and II) invites us to praise God. We have two good reasons for doing this: God is our Creator and, what is more, our Shepherd who has made a covenant with us.

The second part (strophe III) begins with a thought entirely new, but consequent upon the first. Action follows thought, the law follows faith. We should listen to God's voice today and obey Him. Yet we should not follow the example of our forefathers in the desert. They disregarded God's commandments and paid dearly for it. Now God Himself speaks. He tells how the fathers in the desert tried His patience, how, despite His miracles, they murmured against Him and left Him, despite the manna, the water from the rock, the rain of quail. This is why the whole generation died in the desert without even seeing the Promised Land.

This psalm is impressive, poetic, and dramatic. Even in the Old Testament it was very likely an antiphonal chant.

It is not hard to see how it applies liturgically. The main reason this psalm plays its role at the beginning of Matins is the opening verse: "Come, let us sing joyfully to the Lord," a natural invitation to take up the Office. But the rest of the psalm, too, fits in at the beginning of Matins. We cannot help but notice that the liturgy speaks more of Christ than of God, Christ the King of apostles, of martyrs, and of confessors. The psalm too, then, refers to Christ. The first part invites us to greet Him and praise Him. We are invited to adore Him as our Creator and Savior. The Church lifts a warning finger in the second part: "Today. . . ." Today is upon us, a momentous "today." Let us not ignore His voice today. Certain feasts give these thoughts an even greater significance.

The Invitatory, of course, heightens the effect of this psalm. Let us weave it in, then, with Easter's Invitatory as our example: "The Lord is truly risen, Alleluja!" Picture the scene

to yourself: Matins is being sung, at night of course, and the
church glows with light. All of a sudden, Mother Church announces to her children: "The Lord is risen." Do not be incred-
ulous as the disciples were; the Lord has truly risen. What is
more, your own resurrection will be just as real.

Psalm 94 sounds, like a fanfare, an alternating echo to the
Church's joyous cry. 1. Let your hearts rejoice. Joy, jubilant
joy is in order. It is Easter; the Church has no more joyful feast.
"Let us greet Him with thanksgiving." In the fullest sense, our
Lord is death's conqueror. 2. He is the same God that fashioned the world, that carries this globe in His hand. He is the
God who molded the mountain peaks and set limits for the
seas. Nature rejoices at the Resurrection, and wishes to rise
also. Lauds daily commemorates the Resurrection; it is made
up chiefly of poems of nature. 3. But man has more reason to
pay homage to the risen Christ, and especially today: "Come,
let us bow down in worship; let us kneel before the Lord," the
victor over death and sin. And why? More than King and
Master, He is our Good Shepherd who has given His life for
the "flock He guides," who is faithfully leading us now. Bowed
with grief on Good Friday, the Church sang: "Our shepherd
has departed, the fountain of living water" (fourth antiphonal
chant). But now, full of joy she sings: The Good Shepherd
has arisen, who delivered His life for His sheep. 4. Then the
Church utters a maternal wish and hope: "Oh, that today you
would hear His voice." Once again that momentous "today."
And why should not this present day preach us a stirring
sermon? Today you may hear again the Master's gentle voice
and loving words. You may hear Him speak such words to
Magdalen, to Peter, to the disciples on the road to Emmaus,
to the apostles, to all of us. "Peace be to you." Today God
speaks eloquently to your heart; do not let it be hardened. Do

not be stony ground; be rich and fruitful soil. 5. Toward the close of the psalm the Church warns us against indifference and lack of confidence in God. She sets the example of the Jews before us; they died in the desert after their first Pasch, without ever seeing the Promised Land. This is almost too stern a conclusion for a day of such great joy. Again and again we hear: "The Lord has truly risen, Alleluja!"

As a concluding thought, we may think of psalm 94 standing like a Roman arch, faced with a series of tableaux: the Good Shepherd, the Jews in the desert. We pass beneath this arch every day to pay our homage to Christ. Let us recall the principal ideas: 1. praise to Christ, the Creator and Redeemer; 2. the all-important "today."

II. The Te Deum

The Te Deum, the so-called Ambrosian hymn of praise, takes the place of a responsory to conclude festive Matins. It supplies the transition needed to enter into the spirit proper to Lauds, that joyous morning prayer of praise.

The Te Deum, which dates back to the first Christian centuries, was not composed by any one author in particular. Like its twin sister, the Gloria in excelsis, it took shape gradually. The story that St. Ambrose and St. Augustine sang it at the latter's baptism is without foundation.

The hymn divides easily into three sections. As a matter of fact, it was not until a later date that the three were combined. A well-founded tradition names Bishop Nicetus of Remesiana (c. 350–400) as the one who compiled, arranged, and completed this hymn. The first part (vv. 1–10) sounds the praises of God the Father, concluding with a doxology. In this part customs are referred to that date from very early times. For example: the classification of saints into apostles, prophets, and martyrs. At that time "confessor" was not used in the sense now accepted; thus the threefold classification embraced the entire common of saints. *Martyrum candidatus exercitus* is a phrase that deserves special attention. *Candidatus* means "clad in white." The martyr's color in those days was white, not our present red. Aside from the doxology, this first part has all the earmarks of a second-century Greek hymn, translated into Latin at some early date. Even as early as the third century St. Cyprian knew of it.

The second part (vv. 14–21), of a later date, was originally a Latin hymn in honor of Christ. Its pithy expressions borrow heavily from phrases of the different Creeds. A comparison of the two parts is highly revealing. Again and again in the first part *Te* and *Tibi* recur; in the second, it is *Tu*. The first part praises God the eternal Father. It does not linger long over His person but goes on to unfold His kingdom to us, the angels and the Church. The three divine persons are mentioned only at the conclusion. The second part addresses Christ and recounts all His offices and dignities. Here we are given the glorious portrait that the ancient Church had of Christ. First we see the King of glory; only afterwards, the eternal Son of God. Christmas and Easter are the only incidents of His life that are presented. His birth is an act of humility: "He did not shrink from entering the Virgin's womb." To redeem mankind He assumed human nature. (That is characteristic Latin brevity.) The hymn barely touches Christ's sufferings and death. It lingers rather over His resurrection and depicts His victory over hell and death: "You have conquered the sting of death and opened the kingdom of heaven to the faithful." We are reminded of Easter's oration: "You have conquered death and unlocked the gates of eternity." Instead of stressing our Lord's ascension, the hymn rather reveals the manner of

Christ's presence in heaven: "You sit at the right hand of God, in the glory of the Father." This, then, is the picture that the ancient Church has of Christ. Birth and Resurrection belong to the past; but the King, the Son of God, His place at the right hand of God, these are of the present. This verse focuses our thoughts on the future: "Our faith professes that You will come as Judge." The Te Deum floods our minds with the light of profound and beautiful thought.

The third part (vv. 22–29) is comprised of several verses from various psalms.[1] This at any rate is of later compilation. The emphasis shifts now from praise to petition, petition to Christ. The Church reminds us that: "He had redeemed us with His precious blood." The petitions are varied. First, general pleas for help are heard, then comes a specific petition for eternal happiness: "Let us be numbered among the multitude of Thy saints in the kingdom of eternal glory." A petition for the protection of Christendom follows this. "Bring salvation to Thy people, O Lord, and bless Thy portion, and guide and bring it to eternity." See the image of the Good Shepherd filling out the background. Next are two verses of praise that the Good Shepherd's loving care evokes. More petitions follow, that resemble the concluding phrases of the Our Father, liberation from sin: "Deign, O Lord, to preserve us this day without sin." At its close come general but urgent pleas for mercy. Like its twin, the Gloria in excelsis, the Te Deum has its Kyrie too: "Be merciful to us, O Lord, be merciful to us." "Let your mercy come upon us, Lord, as we have expected it of Thee." The finale resounds, a cry of unwavering confidence in God and Christ: "In Thee, O Lord, I have hoped; I shall not be confounded forever."

Judged by any standard, this hymn is one of the Church's

---

[1] Ps. 27:9; 144:2; 122:3; 32:22; 30:2.

grandest treasures. Its antiquity and prayerfulness made it doubly precious. And I might add, it is an exclusively Christian and Catholic prayer. The laity has to a great extent adopted the Te Deum as its own. The Holy God, We Praise Thy Name, our standard hymn of thanksgiving nowadays, shows this admirably.

III. The Benedictus

St. Luke [2] records this song of praise uttered by the priest Zachary after the birth of his son, John the Baptist. For a fuller understanding of his prayer, let us look at the events that evoked it. While Zachary was offering incense in the Temple, an angel told him that his wife, despite her old age, would conceive a son. As he doubted that this would happen, he was deprived of speech until the promise should be fulfilled. This affliction served both as a punishment for his incredulity and as a pledge of the fulfillment of the promise. It was after the child's birth, during his circumcision, that the bonds of Zachary's tongue were loosed and he could speak again. His first words were this hymn which he sang during the rite of circumcision. Since relatives always attended this festive rite, Mary was also present. The customary rite of circumcision is the basis for this hymn. First the father gave the child his blessing and wished him the best of good fortune. After that the father gave the child its name. The blessing reads: "Blessed art Thou, O Lord, King of the world, who hast sanctified us through Thy commandments, and hast ordered us to enter into the covenant of our father, Abraham." The halves of this blessing form the heart of the hymn. The Benedictus is a Messianic hymn. Most important for us, it is a greeting that we address to our Savior. The hymn can be divided according to

[2] Luke 1:68–79.

its literal meaning into two parallel parts. Each division describes the fact, the motive, and its effect.

Part I, in praise of salvation (Luke 1:68–75)

1. Fact: God has brought salvation.

   a. He has sent us grace (68–70).
   b. He has brought us deliverance and help against our enemies.

2. Motive: God has done this

   a. because of His mercy (72a);
   b. because of His fidelity to His promises (72b, 73).

3. Effects of salvation:

   a. peace from our enemies (negative) (74);
   b. grace (positive) (75).

Part II, vocation of the child (76–79)

1. Fact: John will be a prophet

   a. to herald the Savior (76);
   b. to proclaim the forgiveness of sin (77).

2. Motive: the mercy of God (78a)

3. Effects: The Orient from on high has visited us (78b).

   a. liberation from darkness (negative) (79a);
   b. peace (positive) (79b).

The length of its sentences and its theological terminology make this hymn somewhat difficult to understand. (The whole hymn consists of but two long sentences.) Let us compare it with the Magnificat as regards terminology. Simple in its language and sentence structure, the Magnificat fits the character of the humble handmaid perfectly. The Benedictus, however, is the work of a theologian. This makes it clear that the two canticles in question are the products of Mary and Zachary, and by no means from the pen of St. Luke himself.

The Benedictus gives us the same portrait of the Redeemer as the Old Testament does. Salvation is cast in more somber language and becomes a ransom from the enemy, liberation from the clutches of the heathen. The religious aspect of the Messiahship is emphasized also. Salvation is the fulfillment of the promise made to their father Abraham. In true, biblical style, Christ is described as the sun. "The Orient from on high," He rises on mankind to drive away error and darkness and to bring peace. Christ called Himself the "Light of the world." This hymn is a good example of that device of Hebrew poetry found so often in Scripture, "parallelism of members."

How can we employ the Benedictus as a personal prayer? It is usually found as a sort of sunrise song at Lauds, the Church's solemn morning prayer. Through His great mercy the Orient from on high has visited us; this divine Sun gives light to all of us who sit in darkness and in the shadow of death, that we may walk in the path of peace. Because it voices the fact of this blessing so convincingly and, at the same time, can be used as an earnest petition, it is not hard to see the reason for its selection as a part of Lauds. Our own personal application begins here. The theme is the Redemption. In the eyes of the Church every day is a day of redemption. Each morning she experiences the same emotions as Zachary did when he held the child John in his arms and saw in him a pledge of future salvation. Zachary, in spirit, beholds the rising Sun, Jesus Christ, the Light of the world. In the reddening of the east, in the rising sun, the Church sees the Savior rising from the dead. At dawn the priest, or the Church, lifts up in her hands the mystical Savior, the graces men need for the new day. The Benedictus is like the good intention, a petition: "May men use this day of Redemption profitably."

Part I. Praised be our God, our Savior, for today He visits us and brings us the grace of salvation. 1. In the text let us underline *visitavit* (He has visited). Under the guise of sorrow, inspiration, temptation, or in the person of our neighbor, how often He will knock today at the doors of our hearts! Let us sound the depths of this thought: God visits us today. To overshadow even this generosity, He gives us a mighty Savior, as He promised He would. He helps us conquer our fiercest enemy, the devil.

2. The motives remain the same too, even today, mercy and fidelity. If we carry out our obligations, He will be faithful to us. If we have failed in anything, He will be merciful. Again and again these two motives recur in the psalms (e.g., Ps. 88).

3. The effect. Cleansed from sin, we can serve Him in holiness and justice all the days of our life. A beautiful program for the day: to be free from sin and able to look up to our Father as His child, full of confidence; to love and obey God; to be considerate of all men. Grant us this grace, O God.

Part II. "And you, O child." (Here we must change the original meaning of the text radically.) You are this child. It is you, O child of God, that the Church addresses. You are the prophet of the Most High. What a glorious thought: to put yourself in the place of John the Baptist! At the very start of the day you have a model to light your path: "The lamp lit to show you the way" (John 5:35). Bring to mind his love for Jesus, his zeal, his humility, the greatness of his character. You are prophet too, in a further sense. Your duty it is to announce, to explain, to expound the word of God. What a beautiful phrase: "to go before the Lord"! You go before the Lord to prepare His ways. By word and deed the child of God, the true precursor, who prepares the way, who precedes. Christ follows with His grace. God awaits your cooperation today because you are an instrument of salvation. It is a pity if you kindle God's wrath instead of preparing men's hearts. "Because of the compassionate kindness of our God," superabundant mercy is to be found everywhere. It appears in the very fact that you are a Christian, that Christ has redeemed you. His mercy is more than sufficient to give you another day of salvation, to let you see salvation's rising Sun, Jesus Christ, the Savior. Christ in the Eucharist is the spiritual Sun of my day and every Christian's day. All light, all warmth, all life, all joy must emanate from Him. He ought to be the main concern of the day, of life itself. "He has visited you," especially today in Holy Communion. Why has He come? 1. To enlighten our darkness; 2. to give us peace. A sad picture of poor human nature follows: "in darkness and in the shadow of death." Estranged from God and without grace, many men are living corpses. "Into the way of peace." Peace is the essence of the gift of salvation because salvation brings sanctifying grace, which is peace with God. It brings fraternal charity, which is peace with men. It brings peace of soul and a harmony to all man's faculties.

Today Christ, our spiritual Sun, brings us His light and peace of soul. The Benedictus unfolds the whole program of the Christian life. This life has the following two important obligations. First, a Christian must save his own soul, he must live each day "in holiness and justice." Secondly, he must help others save their souls, especially by the good example of his life. "You are the salt of the earth, the light of the world, the city built on a hilltop, the light upon the candlestick" (Matt.

5). He must drive darkness away and bring men peace of heart.

IV. THE MAGNIFICAT

This is Mary's prayer. In it she praises God and thanks Him for the dignity of being chosen as His Mother, and for the salvation of mankind. Our understanding of this hymn will deepen if we transport ourselves to that stupendous moment when it was first spoken. From an angel Mary hears the good news that she is to be the mother of the Savior. The meaning of this tremendous grace is beyond her grasp. Yet no one is near to whom she can open her heart. She sets out for Judea's hills to visit Elizabeth, her cousin, whom God had favored with a great grace too. It was God who inspired Elizabeth to greet Mary as the mother of her Lord. "She [Elizabeth] cried out with a loud voice, Blessed art thou among women, and blessed is the fruit of thy womb. How have I deserved to be thus visited by the mother of my Lord? . . . Blessed art thou for thy believing; the message that was brought to thee from the Lord shall have fulfillment." [3] Mary can contain the sentiments of her soul no longer. Her grateful heart sings this hymn of praise, the Magnificat. Let us consider first its literal sense; it is composed of three strophes.

The Magnificat

Luke 1:46–55

I

46 My soul magnifies the Lord,
47   and my spirit rejoices in God my savior,
48 Because he has regarded the lowliness of his handmaid,
    for behold, henceforth all generations shall call me blessed,

[3] Luke 1:42–45.

49 Because he who is mighty has done great things for me,
  and holy is his name;
50 And his mercy is from generation to generation
  toward those who fear him.

II

51 He has shown might with his arm;
  he has scattered the proud in the conceit of their heart.
52 He has put down the mighty from their thrones
  and has exalted the lowly.
53 The hungry he has filled with good things
  and the rich he has sent empty away.

III

54 He has given help to Israel his servant,
  mindful of his mercy,
55 As he promised our fathers,
  toward Abraham and his descendants forever.

The divisions of the hymn are simple and easy to grasp. The first strophe praises God, (a) for the grace and the dignity of the divine motherhood; (b) a motherhood given because of God's omnipotence, holiness, and mercy. Strophe two tells how God despises the proud and exalts the humble. Strophe three is a thankful picture of the Savior's coming in fulfillment of God's promise.

To get a clearer view of the contents, let us paraphrase the hymn.

1. I give thanks to the Lord with joyful heart. Why? Because poor, worthless slave that I am, in me He has accomplished a great work of mercy (the divine maternity). I will be venerated by all mankind because of this grace. God the Almighty, the Holy One, the Merciful, has exalted me. God's omnipotence has no greater manifestations than the Incarnation and the Redemption. Both of these began with my exalta-

tion. Through them God reveals His holiness and His loathing for sin. Through them He proves His boundless mercy toward men.

2. By praising God's attributes, Mary shifts the prayer from her own person to the divine plan of salvation. In the second strophe she outlines the reasons for this plan and for her own election as Mother of God. God reveals His might by reducing the pride of the powerful to nothing, and by favoring the weak and lowly with blessings before the whole world.

3. Mary joyfully announces, after this reflection, that God in His mercy and faithfulness intends to redeem Israel. His mercy is the motive because Israel is too weak to help itself. God's fidelity shares this role of motive because He had promised salvation to the ancients. This hymn displays the utmost simplicity, like the poetry of the Old Testament and the early Christian centuries. The rhythmic recurrence of the thought is obvious, the well-known parallelism of members. Perhaps it was during Mary's three-month stay at Zachary's house that this outburst of her heart received its ultimate poetic form. Perhaps it is Zachary himself, who certainly knew how to write, whom we are to thank for preserving the hymn for us. It found its way into the liturgy at an early date. As early as the fourth century it was a part of the Office, and according to tradition it was first used for Vespers by St. Benedict.

It is important for us to assimilate this hymn into our spiritual life. In the liturgy, indeed, it is no longer Mary who utters the Magnificat, but rather the Church and our own souls.

The Magnificat is the climax of Vespers. Upon hearing the hour chanted, you realize this easily enough. During the incensing of the altar this hymn is sung, more solemnly than the psalms. It is a hymn of thanksgiving; indeed the most sublime

outburst of joyful gratitude. But who is giving thanks? The Church and the soul. And to give thanks fittingly they borrow the words and sentiments of the noblest creature in heaven or on earth. You might say that Mary is the interpreter of our thanksgiving. For what things are the Church and the soul giving thanks? First of all, for the graces of salvation granted during the day, in particular for the feast's grace, because God grants special graces for each feast of the Church year. The soul adds its thanks for personal favors received. In short, Church and the soul join their voices in this magnificent hymn to thank God for all His graces and benefits. The Church's reasons for being grateful are much like Mary's. She bore the Savior beneath her heart; the Church bears the mystical Savior with all the graces of salvation within her bosom; the soul bears the Savior through grace and Holy Communion. Gathering together all the graces of salvation, Church and soul jubilantly thank God for them. Every one of Mary's thoughts and sentiments in this hymn apply easily to the Church and individual souls. "My soul magnifies the Lord, and my spirit rejoices in God my Savior" (Jesus). The reason for this is that He has deigned to look upon His poor handmaid. Reduced to beggarhood by original sin, our miserable soul recalls its sinfulness, its weakness, its attraction to evil. Its new dignity is in every respect a gift of God since the soul could never dream of the right to such an honor. Is not the Church a poor outcast too? Yet God has so exalted her that all nations shall praise her. She has become the mother of nations. The miserable soul has become God's child and His temple. What exalted dignity, what unexcelled blessings accompany sanctifying grace! "Because He who is mighty has done great things for me" (the holy one, the merciful). How many souls has God converted through the Church? How many of His children have again returned to Him? How many graces and blessings have we received, the graces of today's feast especially? Is there any way this Mover of hearts has not shown His power and holiness, by His victory over sin, by His mercy in forgiving our sins?

The second part of the prayer teaches and consoles us. The burden of the teaching is that we should remain a little child, be a stranger on this earth, stay humble. Let us keep in mind Mary, our great model. God has exalted the lowly handmaid, He has fed the hungry with good things. A short sermon, but its few pointed sentences proclaim the fundamental law of God's kingdom: humility. Now the Church offers us a sweet consolation. In truth, the scene is compelling. The enemies of the Church rage around her. They drag her down into the mire and rob her. The rich and proud view her in disdain. But each day within the walls of God's house, the afflicted Church's Magnificat ascends to heaven on clouds of fragrant incense. These words stand out: "He has scattered the proud . . . put down the mighty from their thrones . . . sent the rich empty away." As a matter of fact, the Church has always carried her point. She well knows after two thousand years of experience that all the proud topple from their thrones. What consolation in the thought! Here, too, are verified the words: "Heaven and earth shall pass away, but My word shall not pass away."

Thirdly, we give thanks for our salvation. The words "Israel, His servant" refer to us. In gratitude we recall God's faithfulness and mercy. Though we became His debtors by sin, He still kept His promise. We voice our heartfelt thanks because again today He has fulfilled that promise.

V. The Nunc Dimittis

A third Gospel hymn, recorded by St. Luke also, found its way into the Breviary. It is the hymn of Simeon, and it occurs at Compline. Though otherwise identical with that of the Roman Breviary, the Benedictine Compline does not have this hymn. Common opinion would have it that Pope Gregory the Great (c. 600) added the Nunc dimittis to the Office of Compline. There is little doubt but that it was a thing well added. The situation that gave it birth can readily teach us its literal sense. Simeon, though far advanced in years, had received a promise from God that he would not die until he had seen the Redeemer. It was Simeon who accosted the holy family when Mary brought the Child to the Temple in fulfillment of the law. In this poor Child he sees the Redeemer of the world. His joy is full; once again his heart is young. Would Mary, please, show Him the Child? At her offer he takes the Child into his arms with trembling hands and lovingly presses Him to his heart. He asks nothing more from life. What more can it offer him? He sings his swansong. His lips pronounce the night prayer of his life:

Canticle of Simeon

Luke 2:29–31

29 Now you dismiss your servant, O Lord,
     according to your word, in peace,
30 Because my eyes have seen your salvation
     which you have provided in the sight of all the peoples:
31 A light of revelation for the Gentiles,
     and the glory of your people Israel.

Simeon considers himself a servant of the divine Master. Now he will be released from that service as the Holy Ghost promised, because he has seen the Savior with his own eyes.

He is not sad. Death, for him, peacefully removes life's heavy burdens from his tired shoulders. Enlightened by God, he beholds the Savior in all His grandeur as the "Salvation from God" which He had prepared before the eyes of all the peoples of the world. He calls the Savior "the Light of the world," remaining impersonal and using an image that the Bible is fond of and Christ Himself often used. Because He is the world's Light, He is its Sun. He is to the supernatural world what the sun is to the natural world. Light has two purposes: it drives away darkness; and secondly, it gives growth and beauty to nature and joy to the hearts of men. This is why Simeon exclaims: "A light of revelation for the Gentiles." It puts us in mind of the night of unbelief, of vice and blindness. This light is "for the glory of God's people, Israel." Although the Jews already enjoyed the light of faith, truth, justice, and morality, that light had not yet reached its full brilliance. Complete and perfect enlightenment comes with Christ and Christ's grace. We can see how Simeon's picture of the Savior is better than Zachary's. Zachary is still the representative of Jewish thought. Simeon sees the "Catholic" Church embracing Jew and Gentile. Filled with the spirit of the Messiah's kingdom, his interest is not enemies to be conquered, but salvation, enlightenment, and eternal glory. As nightingales are said to sing themselves to death, so Simeon in an excess of joy at seeing his longing fulfilled, died with this song on his lips.

How can we fit this hymn into our prayer life? At night we find ourselves in a situation like Simeon's. We, too, are in God's service. Life for us is like a term of military service, and at the day's close we look forward to our release from it. Thoughts like these develop the proper attitude for a true Christian. Detached from all earthly affections, day after day he is prepared for death. There is another point of similarity.

Like Simeon, we also carry Christ. Through faith, through grace, and by Holy Communion, the Christian bears Christ within him. In Lauds the Orient from on high floods our soul's eyes with divine light of salvation. To drive away darkness Holy Communion has brought us light and glory. But we must not forget the Church and the rest of men, for a light has been enkindled in the world too. Each day brings all of us a step nearer that everlasting glory which will drive darkness away forever. As Simeon closed his life, we ought to close each day with a prayer of gratitude that our longing has been fulfilled. And how well we may use this song as a night prayer for this life, since, as we know, Compline is also a prayer for a good death!

VI. The Concluding Antiphons of Our Lady

In the monasteries of the Middle Ages more prayers were said than simply the Divine Office. For example, the monks said the Office of the Dead and the Little Office of the Blessed Virgin. In time this custom became universal. As a result, the opening of the modern era found this aggravated obligation of common prayer clamoring for reform. In the sixteenth century, as a conclusion for each hour, the antiphons to Mary were substituted for the Little Office of the Blessed Virgin. In the Middle Ages, not to mention any earlier period, there were no such antiphons in the Office. In Rome at Eastertime, however, the Regina Coeli was sung, not at the end of an hour, but as the Vesper antiphon *de sancta Maria*. Our present usage seems to date from the thirteenth century. In the chapel of St. Louis IX it was the almost invariable custom to sing the antiphon Salve Regina at the end of Compline. In 1239 Gregory IX decreed that the Salve Regina be sung after Compline on Fridays.

Today four different antiphons to Our Lady are used to conclude the hours during the various seasons of the Church year.

1. *Alma Redemptoris Mater,* from the beginning of Advent to Candlemas Day.
2. *Ave Regina Coelorum,* from February 2 to Easter.
3. *Regina Coeli Laetare,* from Easter to the close of the octave of Pentecost.
4. *Salve Regina,* from Trinity Sunday to the beginning of Advent.

It is improper to call these hymns antiphons, if by "antiphon" we mean a chant which stands before and after a psalm. Originally, as a matter of fact, several of these at least were antiphons in the strict sense, inasmuch as they accompanied a psalm or a canticle. We have already mentioned the fact that hymns without psalms are of a fairly recent date in the liturgy.

Even today these antiphons are not in harmony with the classic lines of the liturgy. They form a subjective epilogue to an objective prayer. This would explain why we recite them kneeling.

1. *Alma Redemptoris Mater*

Alma Redemptoris Mater, quae pervia coeli
Porta manes, et stella maris, succurre cadenti,
Surgere qui curat, populo: tu quae genuisti,
Natura mirante, tuum sanctum Genitorem,
Virgo prius ac posterius, Gabrielis ab ore
Sumens illud Ave, peccatorum miserere.

(The following is an English prose translation)

O loving Mother of the Redeemer, who dost remain the ever accessible portal of heaven, and the star of the sea, aid thy fallen people who strive to rise: thou, who, a Virgin both before and after receiving that Ave from the mouth of Gabriel, didst, while nature wondered, give birth to thy holy Creator; have pity on us sinners.

As far as we can ascertain, this hymn is the work of a Benedictine of Reichenau, Hermanus Contractus, "the Cripple" (d. 1054). He borrowed heavily from the older hymn *Ave Maris Stella*, in composing it.

Alma Redemptoris Mater . . .	Dei Mater alma
Pervia caeli porta	Felix caeli porta
Et stella maris	Ave maris stella
Gabrielis ab ore	Sumens illud Ave
Sumens illud Ave	Gabrielis ore

Exceptionally rich in ideas, this hymn is a guide to the proper spirit for Advent and Christmas. It uses two favorite images to describe Mary: the gate of heaven, and the star of the sea. This "star" gives the poet the lead to trace mankind's need of a Savior. Beautifully he cries: "Help those falling and seeking for someone to lift them up." He amplifies the image of the sea. With their ship about to sink, the passengers scan the horizon for rescuers. The second part of the hymn considers Mary's divine maternity. All nature is astonished at her. Full of faith and humility, she receives the angel's greeting. She gives birth to her own Creator. Yet before and after Christ's birth she remains a virgin.

The oration following the antiphon varies for Advent and Christmastide.

The antiphon's melody tells us clearly the date of its composition. It is a joyful melody that surges upward, traversing a whole octave on the first syllable of the word *Alma*. *Genuisti* and *Virgo*, words that express the marvel of the Incarnation, are especially emphasized by the music. This hymn's masterful form and ornateness show clearly it is not from any of the older collections of Gregorian melodies but is a composition of the later Middle Ages. Its tonality also suggests this. The Gregorian fifth mode, the Lydian scale, with *ti* flattened throughout, definitely has the tonality of the modern major scale. We can practically say, then, that the medieval composer's sensibilities here were already distinctly modern.

Let us end our remarks about this hymn with the reflection that both the melody and the text of the *Alma Redemptoris Mater* strike a sympathetic chord in our hearts, and definitely influence our spirit and dispositions for Advent.

2. *Ave Regina Coelorum.* From the feast of the Purification on February 2 to Wednesday of Holy Week, the Church concludes the hours with the antiphon *Ave Regina Coelorum.*

> Ave Regina coelorum,
> Ave Domina Angelorum,
> Salve radix, salve porta,
> Ex qua mundo lux est orta:
> Gaude Virgo gloriosa,
>
> Super omnes speciosa,
> Vale, o valde decora,
> Et pro nobis Christum exora.
>
> (A free English translation)
>
> Hail, O Queen of Heaven,
> Hail, O Mistress of the Angels,
> Hail Thou Root (of Jesse), Thou Gate (of heaven)
> Whence rose true light into the world;
>
> Rejoice O glorious Virgin,
> More beautiful than all others,
> Farewell, O Thou exceeding fair!
> And plead with Christ for us.

Neither the author of the text nor the composer of the melody of this antiphon is known. All that can be said is that evidently the same person should receive credit for both. The date of its composition can be established only approximately. It appears for the first time in a Parisian manuscript that dates from the twelfth century.[4] Its composition, however, certainly does not antedate the tenth century. The liturgist is especially interested in this period (tenth to twelfth century) because of the sequences, tropes, and the rhyming offices being composed everywhere at the time. Rhyming offices were those whose antiphons (texts) boasted rhyme and meter. At first, only one or the other of a feast's antiphons was thus ornamented. Later, however, all the antiphons of a feast shared this distinction. Undoubtedly these sequences and tropes which the faithful of the time were so fond of, were in great measure responsible for the introduction of numerous metrical compositions among the antiphons of the Office. In view of its evident rhyme and meter, and the fact that it was formerly used as an antiphon at None on the feast of the Assumption, it seems likely that at one time the *Ave Regina Coelorum* was a part of a rhyming office. It must have occurred to those who have sung or recited this hymn, that its words have little reference to the time of Septuagesima or Lent, even though the *Alma Redemptoris Mater* and the *Regina Coeli* clearly express the main ideas of their respective seasons. As in the other texts of the present-day office of the Assumption, in the *Ave Regina Coelorum* Mary is praised as the Queen of heaven and Mistress of the angels. You would expect that in the antiphon for Lent, Mary would appear as the intercessor for sinners, or at least, as the Mother of sorrows.

Both the thought and the expression of this hymn are exquisite. The Latin *Vale* can mean either "farewell," or "good

[4] Cf. P. Wagner, *Ursprung und Entwicklung der liturgischen Gesangsformen,* p. 157.

health to you." Here is a possible interpretation. The feast of the Assumption is our celebration of Mary's departure from this earth. High above the choirs of angels she will reign in the glory of heaven as Queen. We rejoice at the great honor shown our Mother. Yet our souls are filled with sorrow at her going, and we wish her a heartfelt "Farewell." "Farewell, thou elect of God; and when thou art with thy Son, intercede for us."

The definite festive character of this antiphon's music is impressive. It is written in the sixth mode. Our joy is kept somewhat subdued in the opening *Ave,* but it moves on to jubilant expression in the *Salve* and *Gaude.* Line two repeats the melody of the first line. *Salve* introduces a new musical thought which already possesses the genuine hymnodic élan. But the very next phrase rises merely to the fourth. Only at the *Gaude* are we permitted to hear the clear triad resound, which then finds not only a repetition, but a strengthening and a broadening of its resolution. This melody is a blend of melismatic and syllabic chant, with the melismatic predominating. Thus the metrical verse form of the text is hardly noticeable, lost as it is in the background.

As usual, the antiphon is capped by a versicle and oration. It is worth noticing that only the oration makes any mention of the penitential season and the feast of Easter.[5]

3. *Regina Coeli.* Just before the Introit of the Mass for Easter Sunday, in accord with an ancient Roman custom, we find the note: "Station Church at St. Mary Major." This indicates that on Easter the pope celebrated his Mass in that Church. An old tradition links this church with the composition of the *Regina Coeli.* A legend of even older times re-

[5] I have taken the explanation of these antiphons in part from the articles by D. A. Weissenbaeck in *Bibel und Liturgie,* 1927–28.

counts that angels sang this hymn while the church was being blessed. Actually, however, according to the research of Peter Wagner, the *Regina Coeli* is the most recent of the antiphons.[6] The first traces of it date from about the year 1200, when it was used as an antiphon for the octave of Easter in the Antiphonal of St. Peter's at Rome, published by Tommasi. Here is another instance of a former psalm-antiphon graduating to the dignity of a concluding antiphon to Our Lady.

> Regina coeli laetare, alleluja.
> Quia quem meruisti portare, alleluja,
> Resurrexit sicut dixit alleluja,
> Ora pro nobis Deum, alleluja.

> (A free English translation)

> Rejoice O Queen of Heaven, alleluja,
> For He whom you merited to bear, alleluja
> Has risen as he said, alleluja,
> Pray to God for us, alleluja.

The Gospels tell us nothing of any meeting of Mary with her gloriously risen Son. Could anyone have experienced greater joy at His resurrection than His mother, who witnessed His suffering and death on Calvary? Her joy is ours too. While we rejoice to see her unbounded happiness, the accomplishment of our Redemption fills us with gladness, too. It was this Redemption that required His shameful death as man, and His glorious resurrection in victory over death and hell. The Alleluja, expressing the deepest faith and joy, closes each verse. The liturgy uses this cry of jubilation to characterize the whole Easter season.

The *Regina Coeli* is the shortest of all the antiphons of Our Lady. Pregnant brevity is an especial feature of the Office

---

[6] Wagner, *op. cit.*, p. 158.

during Eastertide. The period of the rhyming Offices may well have been the time of the composition of the text.

The choral tone of the *Regina Coeli* differs strikingly from that of the three other antiphons. The others for the most part resemble the ordinary office antiphons, though they consist to some extent of melismatic chant. Nowhere in the older antiphons, and only rarely in the later ones, are found compositions built up as the *Regina Coeli* is of melismatic chant. It is also evident that in the *Regina Coeli*, as in choral music in general, there is question not so much of the composer echoing the thoughts by the music, but of his adhering in the main to a definite law of musical composition. The first two lines express the thematic upward surge of the melody; the third line is like a secondary theme; the fourth is a melismatic conclusion that embodies great richness. The use of the most explicit melismatic chant in the first two lines emphasizes the riming words *laetare* and *portare*. Indeed the word *portare* receives an even stronger musical expression than *laetare*, and this is done by the use of a repetition of neums within the melisma itself. Yet the text seems to demand that *laetare* be stressed rather than *portare*. We are surprised, too, that the music accompanying *Regina Coeli*, is of lesser musical intensity than that of the *quia quem*. A melody on a higher plane stresses *resurrexit*, so very important in the text. But even at that, it is treated rather briefly, as is true also of the *alleluja* right after it. Joy and exultation get free rein only in the last line; however, even here, only in the *alleluja*. On the whole, this kind of tonal treatment of the text is but another proof of the rather thorough musical formalism of the composer's notions of composition.

4. *Salve Regina.* The fourth and last antiphon to Our Lady

is the *Salve Regina*. It occurs in the liturgy from the First Vespers of Trinity Sunday until the Saturday before the First Sunday of Advent. This means it is employed for a full half-year, longer than the periods of the other three antiphons together.

There are different opinions as to the author of this antiphon. Most frequently mentioned are Hermanus Contractus (*c.* 1050) and Bernard of Clairvaux (1091–1153). P. Wagner, on the contrary, holds that these two had nothing to do with its composition, but that it may probably be attributed to Bishop Ademar of Puy (d. 1098). At any rate, it was most likely composed in the eleventh century.

A Cistercian antiphonal of the thirteenth century gives the *Salve Regina* as the Magnificat antiphon at First Vespers for the feast of Mary's Nativity. We have already called attention to the fact that all the antiphons to Our Lady formerly had a place in the Office. We also know that Pope Gregory IX gave the *Salve Regina* its official status in the Office in 1239.

Of these four antiphons this is the most profound in its ideas. Full of feeling, it is a perfect example of devotion to Mary during the Middle Ages. It also brings out Mary's central position in the work of salvation as the mediatrix of all graces. Man's life upon this earth is sketched as an exile in a valley of tears. Man himself is the banished child of Eve. But Mary is the kindly mediatrix who will lead us to her Son, Jesus, when this life is over. She is the mediatrix of grace and we call her "our life, our sweetness, and our hope." It is not difficult to understand why this prayer found its way into people's hearts and readily became one of their favorite private prayers. It is the happy fusion of a hymn and a prayer of petition.

Regarding the musical settings of the *Salve Regina,* the

following is to be noted. In the Gregorian repertoire there are two tonal vestures for this antiphon. The one found in the official antiphonal is undoubtedly the older. It is written in the first mode, called the Doric. At the time when this melody came into being, musicians were no longer holding fast to the medieval rules of musical theory because, according to these rules, melodies in the first mode were never to descend more than a whole tone below the final. However, we find only one such departure from the rule in the *Salve Regina*, where the melody on the word *Jesum* descends to the fourth below the final. For the composition of this melody it clearly enters here the compass of its parallel plagal mode, the second or Hyperdoric mode. We can easily see that the composer here wished to emphasize the word *Jesum* in a special and prominent way. That is why he exceeded the bounds of the first mode and entered the second; or, as we would say today, he modulated into another key to highlight *Jesum*. Since the chant of this era does not yet make use of the devices of harmonic modulation, the desired effect could be attained only by a melodic means, which today we would call linear or "horizontal" writing. According to our modern musical sensibilities, the word to the emphasized would require at least this: if not a special group of neums so striking that it would stand in marked contrast to all the others, then at least that the word be placed at the very top of the modal range, or even go above it.

The old theory of chant placed compositions like the *Salve Regina* in the "mixed tone" category, because it employed the tone range of both the authentic mode and its corresponding plagal mode.

The text of the *Salve Regina* is the longest of the four Mar-

ian antiphons. As a musical composition, according to Peter
Wagner,[7] it has held an undisputed place of honor for nine
hundred years as an impressive masterpiece among the chant
melodies of the Middle Ages. In general its melodic pattern
is built up quite freely. Only at the beginning do we find a
more or less identical repetition of a closed-off musical period.
Wherever in the text we find a phrase completed, the music,
in exact cognizance of this, makes the melody achieve a ca-
dence that will conclude it on the final of the mode.

[7] *Gregorianische Formenlehre.*

PART III

THE SPIRIT OF THE BREVIARY

CHAPTER XII

Structure and Spirit of the Hours

W HAT have we accomplished so far in our study of the Breviary? We first considered preliminary questions about the meaning, history, and thought of the hours. Then we stopped to gather the stones and mortar that we need to build the Breviary's spiritual edifice: psalms, lessons, orations, and the minor parts. But the real test of the architect's skill is to take those materials and produce a house that is both habitable and pleasing to the eye. Our task now is to build from the parts of the Breviary we have explained the spiritual edifice of the hours and of the entire Office.

I. LAW OF DEVELOPMENT

When an architect sits down to draw plans for a building, he does not proceed haphazardly, merely as his fancy dictates. The materials at hand, the purpose of the building and its architectural style, determine hard and fast laws of construction that he must follow. The Church's hour prayer is also a building, spiritual indeed, but none the less subject to definite laws. Private prayer and popular devotion may choose their own way. In this they are like bubbling springs or forest brooks that spill over the ground wherever they have a will to. But norms and laws govern the construction and maintenance of communal prayer. Two thousand years of experience have given the Church a thorough mastery of the art of community prayer. An accomplished architect has fashioned the Breviary for us.

Perhaps we have not given this point sufficient thought, and hardly advert to how nicely the individual prayers coalesce. Just such a lack of thought is often responsible for so-called modern liturgical devotions. Some persons are foolhardy enough to think that they have composed a liturgical devotion by a haphazard lining up of liturgical texts. By no means. The liturgy must be studied. We must familiarize ourselves with those definite laws according to which each hour is fashioned.

Every prayer is a conversation between God and man. God speaks, and man speaks. Right here arises a fundamental problem. Who speaks first, God or man? Prayer is the manifestation of a religious disposition of mind, of spirituality if you will. Two types of religious attitudes have arisen in the course of the Church's life, the objective and the subjective attitude. Both are good; both have flowered into sanctity. The objective attitude begins with God. It obtains its inspiration from grace and from the sacraments, the objective sources of holiness. But the subjective attitude begins with man, and strives to rise up to God. A joyous consciousness of salvation immerses the one, a contrite consciousness of sin the other. One lets God speak; it listens and answers. "Speak, Lord, for Thy servant heareth." The other speaks first to God, and prepares itself to hear God's voice. With childlike simplicity the objective attitude goes directly to God. It does not bother to knock, but asks God to teach it Himself. Not so the subjective attitude. Before it even knocks, it brushes the dust from its feet. In acts of preparation and introduction it speaks to

God first. Only then is there a care for the sound of His voice. One favors God's words; the other, man's words. But each, in its own way, carries on a conversation with God. Objective spirituality lets God take the lead; it answers in prayer. Subjective spirituality leaves the initiative to man, striving to make himself receptive of God's word. Even from such a short analysis we can deduce two principles that are basic to the structure of liturgical prayer. First, however, let us see what history has to say about this matter.

It was the objective attitude that received the stress during the first centuries of the Church. But the Middle Ages, and the Modern Era even more so, gave the subjective attitude the preference. The prayer life of the various periods shows this clearly. A glance at the early Christian Foremass, which was a prayer service, and the earlier forms of the vigils (Matins) confirm this opinion. Good Friday's liturgy gives us an example of the Foremass; Holy Saturday's twelve prophecies exemplify the vigil. In both of these it is the objective attitude that predominates. The Foremass starts in with the word of God by the reading of a lesson. Almost as an echo, a psalm (tract) is sung after this. The *orationes sollemnes* then bring common prayer on the scene. These orations always conclude with the prayer of the celebrant. Notice how the program of this service is built up: lesson, responsory, and only then prayer. It is a perfect example of the objective attitude in action. The vigils show the same thing. Long readings from Scripture come first and predominate. These were followed by meditative chants (tracts). At the end, after a pause for private prayer by the whole community ("Let us kneel down: Arise") came the prayer of the celebrant. Predominance of position, and length too, fell to the readings from Scripture in these ancient vigils.

It was the beginning of the Middle Ages, and even earlier, that saw the subjective element coming more and more to the fore. Both the Foremass and the hour prayer witness this. Various prayers were placed before the reading from Scripture. A trend is noticeable toward making some sort of preparation and saying introductory prayers before the reading. There develops what you might call a ladder of human prayers that are to lift men up to God: sorrow (prayers at the foot of the altar); desire (Kyrie), praise (Gloria), petition (oration). Besides this there was the festive overture of the Introit. And it is only after all these prayers that God speaks.

In the meantime, the prayers customary after the reading fell out of use. By the time of Gregory I (c. 600) these solemn orations had already become a rarity. Nothing shows the transition from objective to subjective prayer more clearly than the Foremass. In times past the word of God took the initiative; prayer was but a response to it. Now man's word takes the lead, and the role of answering falls to the word of God.

At this time too, the hours of the Office underwent a considerable transformation. This change was due especially to the influence of the contemplative monks. At first the prayers received equal emphasis with the readings. Later they got an even greater emphasis. More and more the praying of psalms was introduced into the Office, a definitely subjective element. Here the psalm no longer serves as echo or responsory. Now it takes precedence over the readings, as these grow shorter and shorter. The psalms are prolonged conversations with God. They bring Him the feelings and sentiments, all the needs and troubles, the joy and sorrow of the soul. Man takes the spotlight in the psalms. But not until the reading from Scripture does God answer. We need only to

compare our Matins with the ancient vigils to notice the tremendous change.

From what has been said we can deduce two distinct laws
of formation that hold throughout our Office. These spring
from the two distinct attitudes of soul. Actually, however,
each hour reveals the influence of both attitudes.

a) The Law of Objective Prayer

J. A. Jungmann, S.J., the well-known liturgist, in his book,
Liturgical Worship, has taken the very usage of the liturgy
to demonstrate this law of objective prayer. He says (pp.
55 ff.):

The fundamental plan that plainly dominates liturgical practice
from the third and fourth century is (to have) first a reading, then
a chant, and finally a prayer. This prayer is twofold, first on the
part of the community and then of the priest. In ancient times
every devotion, every service, even the Vigils followed this plan.
In fact this plan even repeated itself several times in the course of a
complete Vigil, that is, one that lasted the whole night or the greater
part of it (at Easter and the Sundays of Embertide). According
to the arrangement of the early Middle Ages there were twelve
Lessons, chants and Orations.

Jungmann points out examples of this plan in the Foremass
and in the hour prayers. But he shows that this plan is basic
to all the hours of the present Breviary too.

Except for Lauds and Vespers which are older and which the
people attended in the churches, the Hours as we now have them
were developed since the fourth century by the monks. The objective plan is discernible in all the Hours, especially in the second
half after the Psalms. In the Little Hours it is clearest. First a short
Lesson which today we call the "Chapter"; then a short chant, the
little Responsory; then the prayer, which often is twofold,—first
petitions for various needs, followed by the Oration strictly so-

called. The second half of Lauds and Vespers shows this plan also. First the Chapter, then a chant, a Hymn and a Canticle (Benedictus or Magnificat), finally the prayer portion, the Oration with or without the petitions. There is a slight difference in the individual Nocturns of Matins. But here too the plan holds true for the second half of the Nocturn, from the reading on. Each of the three Lessons that make up a Nocturn is followed by a chant, but there is no Oration. In a nine Lesson Office the chants are Responsories; but the ninth time the chant is something more festive,—the *Te Deum!* Only if the recitation of the Office is to conclude with Matins is the Oration added after the *Te Deum.* Otherwise, the Oration is found after the entire unit of Matins and Lauds,—more precisely, after the Responsory of Lauds. . . . To sum up, then, we find this ancient plan in the second half of all the Hours (p. 60).

Jungmann's exposition is adequate proof of the presence of the objective form of prayer in our Breviary. But a question likely to be raised is: What about the first half of the hours? After all, since the psalms take up the greater portion of the hour, the first half ought to be more important. Jungmann answers that the first half is the more recent portion, a later addition to the original plan. According to my terminology, the first half exemplifies the subjective attitude of prayer found in the liturgy.

b) The Law of Subjective Prayer

What has been said about objective prayer should make this section easier to grasp. We saw that objective prayer begins with God. It opens with the reading of His word, continues with a meditation on it, and closes with a prayer. Subjective prayer takes the opposite direction. It starts with man. That is why it needs an introduction, the Introit or Invitatory, a hymn, at least an introductory verse. Then come the psalms, the meditative element. But the psalms also need something to introduce them, the antiphons. Only when these two elements have been presented does the subjective plan consider the soul ready to hear the word of God. In the objective plan the reading was more important than the chant or oration. In this subjective plan, the psalms are more important.

Since the fourth century, together with the growth of monasticism, and indeed through the growth of monasticism, there arose a movement which emphasized the antiphonal psalmody as the most important element of the Office. Thus it came about that every Hour was prefaced with a number of Psalms. It is more or less similar to a custom that prevails among certain peoples. When an evening devotion is to be held, a large number of people assemble beforehand to recite the Rosary. Here the laity is gathered together and recites Psalms.[1]

At a later date the psalms were prefaced with an apt introduction and fitted in more organically with the other portions. The psalms and the second or more ancient part of the hours join directly with no transition of any sort to connect them. Only at Matins do the psalms conclude with an oration. Here the Pater Noster fills the role, exemplifying the custom we have already mentioned of using it to conclude an hour just like an oration.

The distortion and curtailment of the older objective element, especially of the readings, went hand in hand with the growth of the subjective element which the recitation of psalms pointedly attested. Lengthy readings were retained only at Matins. And since the time of the *Breviary of the Curia,* even these were restricted. (We saw this already in the historical section.) Though they kept their dignity as the word of God, the readings in the other hours were reduced to the chapter. With the place of meditative prayer before the read-

[1] Jungmann, *op. cit.,* p. 62.

ing thus enlarged, we can understand why both the chant (responsory) and the prayers, especially the community's petitions, were much abbreviated, and even entirely removed. Here, then, we have the plan for subjective prayer: introduction, antiphonal psalmody, abbreviated reading with a short responsory and an oration.

c) Transition

In very old churches we often find an architecture that is really the blending of two styles, usually of the Romanesque and the Gothic. There may be a Romanesque façade and Romanesque windows. But the same church will have Gothic arches and vaults, and a Gothic tower. The styles blend well and the result is pleasing. Portions of some buildings are constructed in this so-called transition style. This latter provides an excellent image of the blending of the two attitudes of prayer in our Breviary. Each hour is built up of objective and subjective prayer. The two styles are so woven together into a harmonious unity that we can well speak of this as a transition. Fundamentally it is the subjective style, or Gothic style if you will, that prevails. Every hour has psalms at the beginning. Still we find the old objective, or Romanesque, style in the second half of every hour. In my opinion, an understanding of what is said above will add much to a deeper appreciation of the prayer of the Breviary.

II. Structure of the Hours

Classified according to structure, the hours fall into three types: a) Matins; b) Lauds and Vespers; c) the remaining little hours.

a) Matins

Matins has not only the longest but also the most beautiful structure of all the hours. None of the others is so dramatic; none has such clear structural lines. Despite the fact that very often First Vespers introduces the feast, the long pause for recollection at the beginning of Matins (*Pater, Ave,* and *Credo*) indicates that this hour begins the Office. Of all the hours, Matins has the longest and most ornate introduction. Many things about this hour appear clearer when we keep in mind that it is a night office intended to be sung in choir.

"O Lord, open my lips." Strict silence is observed in a monastery after Compline. This silence lasts the whole night and can be broken only for prayer. Only God can, as it were, give permission to speak. ". . . so that my mouth may utter Your praise." Praise of God is the essence of prayer in the hours. Each hour is introduced by the verse: "O God, come to my help." A cry of urgency even, is added: "Lord, hasten to my assistance." We may remark that such a verse was a bit too strong for the classic age of the liturgy, which placed praise of God before all else. "Glory be to the Father. . . ." Praise of the Trinity is the whole purpose and contents of the hours. Though its prayer may be urgent or peaceful, though the psalms run the gamut of spiritual emotion from contrition and despondency to boundless joy, the Office always returns to the praise of the Blessed Trinity. That praise is the deep-toned tolling that is sounding throughout the Office. That is the purpose of the "Glory be to the Father" after each psalm. The "Alleluja" is the bursting forth of Easter joy, a song to evoke pictures of our heavenly home, to put into words our jubilation that all things are new in Christ. At the opening of each hour stand three phrases: "O God," "Glory be to the Father," and "Alleluja." On each hour they set the seal of these three sentiments: petition, praise, and Easter joy.

Two heralds step to the middle of the choir and proclaim the liturgical character of the feast. They recite the Invitatory, the hymn of invitation. We might also call it reveille. This type of hymn goes back undoubtedly to the old assemblies where custom had a herald announce the day's procedure. When the Invitatory is heard sung at night by a full choir, its beauty excites far greater appreciation. In such a setting, the cry, "Christ is born to us, come let us adore Him," strikes the ear like the shouting of trumpets. Actually the Invitatory is an act of homage to Christ the King. But at the same time it announces the theme of the feast. The verses of psalm 94 lace the parts of the Invitatory together. The Invitatory taken as a whole, let me repeat, is a masterpiece of liturgical prayer.

The Invitatory has aroused us and warmed our hearts. Now we need something to release the stress of emotion. A hymn is just the thing. This explains why Matins really has three introductions: the first verse, the Invitatory, and now the hymn. Before they begin the restful psalms and lessons, the monks, who have just risen from sleep, must be thoroughly awakened by all the means hymns and singing can bring to bear.

The nocturns, three uniformly constructed units, confront us after this majestic introduction. They are actually three self-sufficient hours, which used to be said at the beginning, middle, and end of the night. (The three versicles of Sunday Matins bring this out beautifully.) Though completely alike in form, in content these three nocturns show a gradation. The Old Testament dominates the first nocturn. We know that at the first night watch in ancient times there was never any reading from the New Testament. That was reserved for the third night watch. One of the Church's fundamental principles shows up here: to begin the readings with selections from the Old Testament since it foreshadows the New. The second night watch touches on the subject of the day's feast. Its lessons give either the saint's life or an exposition of the mystery of the feast. The third watch has the highest rank because it is concerned with the New Testament. In ancient times it was more beautiful than now. Then the lessons were entirely from the New Testament, and at the end the Gospel of the day was read.

The number three dominates Matins: three nocturns, three psalms, three lessons, three responsories. It is not hard to think then of the Blessed Trinity. If we look closely, the liturgy helps us in this by the blessings so called, before the lessons (first and second nocturns). In early times the number twelve predominated. The primitive vigils had twelve lessons. (The number twelve is traditionally expressive of completeness and perfection.)

If we examine each watch, we notice that they are true to the subjective attitude of prayer. Each begins with the psalms; only afterward come the lessons. As a rule the psalms follow one another in numerical order. (This is an ancient principle of the liturgy. Recent usage, however, has departed from it more and more.) Each psalm is bracketed with an antiphon, which is usually taken from the psalm and can thus often supply a clue to its meaning. The prayer portion of the watch ends with the Our Father, which takes the place of an oration here, and with the absolution. The reading portion of the watch begins with the reader's request for a blessing. The lesson begins after the blessing, and closes with the lesson's usual ending. The responsory follows. The degree to which its contents re-echo or restate the thoughts of the lesson determines its greater or lesser effect as a response. Both lessons and responsory have their origin in the objective attitude of prayer. In all, the responsory is a highly dramatic element of the Office. The majestic Te Deum closes Matins, a fitting conclusion for this prayer drama.

We would not be far amiss in saying that Matins is a masterpiece of prayer. It is beautiful in its construction, it has a fine sense of the dramatic. It begins joyfully in the Invitatory, mingles prayers with readings, lets the responsories re-echo the thought of the readings, and ends, as joyfully as it began, with the Te Deum.

b) Lauds and Vespers

If judged by form, these two hours belong to the second type. Both have exactly the same structure and, since both are hours of praise, the same purpose. Originally they were the morning and night prayers of the Church.

The number of psalms is the first thing that strikes us in these hours. All the others have only three psalms; these two have five each. Why they should have five I do not know. (The Benedictines have only four psalms in their Vespers.) The absence of any special introduction, apart from the usual initial verses, is another peculiarity of these two hours. Matins has an elaborate introduction, and all the little hours begin with hymns. Lauds differs slightly from Vespers inasmuch as a canticle takes the place of the fourth psalm. I can find no reason for this either. The most notable characteristics, however, are the canticles taken from the Gospels. They constitute the climaxes of these two hours.

A consideration of their parts shows that these hours are built of three ascending steps. The peaceful, meditative recitation of the psalms is the first step. Here, as in Matins, each psalm is framed by an antiphon. On greater feasts, as a rule, Vespers and Lauds have the same antiphons. This fact indicates somewhat more clearly their ornamental duty rather than any close connection with the psalms they frame. The psalms for Lauds have been more carefully selected than those for Vespers. At Lauds they are almost exclusively psalms of praise or actual morning prayers. Those for Vespers usually follow the numerical order of the Psalter. Later we shall see also that the psalms for Lauds build up to a climax. The Vesper psalms do not.

The chapter and the hymn form the second step. We saw already that these two parts stem from the ancient objective attitude of prayer. Besides, this second step is more festive. If possible, we must always keep before our eyes festive Vespers as sung in some monastery. The entire community sings the psalms, but the chapter is sung by the subdeacon alone, from the Epistle side of the altar. Our attitude of prayer grows more fervent. Even the context of these two parts shows this. Although it is true that the antiphons draw our attention to the feast, often the psalms stir up only ordinary thoughts and sentiments. The chapter, however, is a selection neatly chosen from Scripture to place even stronger emphasis on the predominant thought of the feast. This thought is emotionally re-echoed in the hymn that follows immediately upon the chapter. I always imagine that an angel has come down from heaven and read a selection from Scripture to impress the day's feast on my mind.

The hymn here echoes the word of God. It has a different significance from the hymns found at the beginning of the hours. At the beginning, it is intended to stir up devotion. Here devotion is already roused, and the hymn is meant to give it free rein. The versicle that follows is a pause, and a spring-board to the Gospel canticle, the climax of the hour.

At the hour's climax, the third step, we are faced with prayers that, besides being the special characteristics of these hours, are among the most beautiful in the liturgy. In fact, they are the towering climaxes of the entire Office. They may be compared to the focal points of an ellipse. At festive Vespers the celebrant goes to the altar and fills the thurible with incense. During the chanting of the Magnificat or Benedictus (on a tone more solemn than that of the psalms), he incenses the altar and any reliquaries, then the clergy and the laity too. Praise of God floats up on clouds of incense. (Thus the customary verse: "May my prayer, O Lord, be lifted up in Thy sight as incense.") We note also the meaning of these canticles. They are hymns to the sun, perfectly suited to the hours; at sunrise (*the Orient from on high*) and at sunset. The sun symbolizes Christ. Sunrise and sunset are the day's important moments. The antiphons that bracket these two canticles are of special interest. For the most part they emphasize the feast. For example: the "O" antiphons, or the "Hodie" antiphons. At these two hours of the day the Church seems to collect its dearest and most beautiful thoughts.

Both hours close with an oration. Sometimes both the people's petitions and the priest's oration are found. We have already considered how sacred and ancient a tradition, harking back to St. Paul, underlies the petitions of the people. The thought that every time we pray them the centuries pray along with us ought to fill us with awe. Finally, Lauds and Vespers have a festive farewell in the *Benedicamus Domino* ("Let us bless the Lord"). This is analogous to the *Ite Missa est* ("Go, the Mass is finished") of the Mass. (At Easter and on the Saturday before Septuagesima, a double Alleluja is added.)

c) The Little Hours

The little hours constitute a third type of hour in the Office. They bear some resemblance to Lauds and Vespers. Because they have always had a subordinate place in the liturgy, they do not share the elaborate form that graces Lauds and Vespers. Lauds and Vespers were festive public prayers to which the laity was also invited. The little hours, however, often were private prayers. Only in the monasteries were they ever said publicly. They have two parts. With the exception of Compline, all of them begin with a hymn, which has the same purpose here as at Matins. It is to turn our mind from preoccupation with worldly affairs to spiritual things. For this very reason the hymn contains the key idea of each hour. All have three psalms, one for each hour that will pass before the recitation of the next part of the Office. (Prime, 6–9 o'clock; Terse, 9–12 o'clock; Sext, 12–3 o'clock; None, 3–6 o'clock.) These hours differ from Lauds and Vespers in having one antiphon to bracket all three psalms. Even at that, before the psalms, only the first word or two are intoned. The significance of the antiphon is to a great extent lost because of this. Its purpose is to direct our praying of the psalms and, like the banks of a river, to channel the stream of prayer for the whole hour.

The objective form of prayer supplies the pattern for the second part of these hours: lesson, chant, community prayer, and the oration. It is to be noted that this second part expresses the thought of the feast or the hour much more than the psalms do.

In the first part usually the antiphon brings the particular

idea of the hour to mind. But in the second part all the compo-
nents share this task. As in Lauds and Vespers, the chapter is
a Scripture passage that gives the character of the feast. (On
Sundays they are usually striking passages from the Epistles.)
The short responsory follows the chapter. (It is called "short"
to distinguish it from the longer responsories at Matins.) At
Lauds and Vespers, the hymn followed the capitulum. The
responsory, which is rather a Roman custom, is an echo to the
lesson, and like the responsories at Matins it lends a dramatic
touch to the Office. It is intended to be a choral or sung prayer.
The versicle is a remnant of the community prayers or *preces*.
The latter are rarely said and, except at Prime, they are rather
short. The hour closes with the oration of the day.

Two of the hours deviate somewhat from this third type,
and even have some new additions. They are Prime and
Compline, the two most recent of the hours. We saw already
that Prime is divided into the office that takes place in the
choir and that which takes place in the chapter-room. The
first is exactly the same as the other little hours: hymn, psalms,
chapter, responsory, versicle, and oration. But the second, the
part after the chapter, is unique. It is always the same and has
no reference to the feast of the day as the other little hours
do. Prime, as a result, more than the others, emphasizes the
thought of the hour. The chapter office is a custom that
originated in the monasteries of Gaul. It does not fit into any
of the forms we have mentioned, but has a structure all its
own. Noteworthy is the fact that this second part also contains
a reading now much abbreviated, and that here the first Our
Father of the day is said. (That is, if we do not count the Our
Fathers prescribed as pauses for reflection.)

Compline too, especially in its first part, deviates from the
third type. Consisting of a reading and a chapter of faults,

this also stems from monastic customs. The three psalms follow, just as in the little hours. But they are not preceded by a hymn, which would be pointless here. Compline needs no song at its beginning to give the theme of the hour. It has a reading and a public confession to do that. The second part of the hour resembles Lauds and Vespers somewhat, because of the hymn which follows the psalms, and more especially because of the Canticle of Simeon. As we have already seen, even more so than Prime, Compline disregards the feast of the day, and always stays the same. The thought of the hour permeates it through and through. That is why many can use it for a night prayer though they may know nothing of liturgical practices and customs.

Looking over the three types of hours, we conclude that they are genuine, well-formed prayers, replete with drama, vitality, and variety. We have every reason to believe that in the field of prayer the Breviary is a classic without equal.

CHAPTER XIII

Structure of the Psalter for the Week

FROM the earliest times of the Church a custom prevailed that the entire Psalter of 150 psalms be said each week. Though it is not entirely certain, tradition mentions Pope Damasus (d. 384) as the originator of the "Psalter for the Week" that was commonly used in the Roman liturgy until 1911.

Pius X began a thoroughgoing reform of the Breviary, but was able to bring it to only partial completion. The part achieved concerned itself especially with a new distribution of the psalms for the week. With the publication of the bull *Divino afflatu* on November 1, 1911, the new arrangement became obligatory.

Two reasons prompted this radical change. In the first place, the old axiom, "The entire Psalter every week," was no longer verified in the Breviary. Because the old Psalter for the week was so long, various festive and even votive offices had been introduced. In practice, then, the ferial office was rarely said. In the course of an entire year only 30 of the 150 psalms were being said regularly. The rest were recited, perhaps, once or twice a year. A great achievement of Pius X was his restoring the ancient practice of saying the 150 psalms each week, and his giving the temporal cycle in general the preference it deserves over the festive offices. The first principle of his reform was: "Back to the entire Psalter."

Secondly, since the old weekly Psalter was very long, the Pope had to undertake a completely new distribution of psalms. He definitely wished to shorten the Office. When we consider the Church's conservative attitude in these matters, we must marvel that the Pope could decide upon a change that ran counter to a tradition of fifteen centuries. This change had as its purpose the shortening of the Breviary.

Just what did this change entail? In the old weekly Psalter certain psalms were said every day. For example: four were repeated daily at Lauds; at the little hours, the long 118th psalm; at Compline the same psalms recurred each day. The rest of the psalms had to be squeezed into Vespers and Matins with the result that Matins was exceptionally long. Pius X so arranged the new Psalter that no psalm occurred twice during the same week, except the Invitatory psalm 94. Arranged thus, the ferial offices were no lengthier than the festive ones.

Let us take a look at the present-day weekly Psalter. Since we recite it week after week, we ought to examine it more closely to see why certain psalms are placed where they are. This study will be not merely of scientific interest but also of profit for a deeper knowledge of the psalms.

Three fundamental principles were followed in carrying out the new arrangement: 1. Where possible, the old arrangement should be kept. 2. The thought of each hour should be emphasized. 3. The remaining psalms are to follow in order throughout the week.

Let us give a fuller explanation of these three principles.

1. Where possible, the old arrangement should be kept. If there was a special reason for using a certain psalm in the old Psalter, then where possible that psalm should keep that place.

a) Except for Matins, Sunday's office was not to be touched, because the psalms for its hours had been carefully selected.

b) The second schema of psalms for Lauds in the old ferial office remained.

c) The first psalms of Prime were also retained: psalms 23, 24, 25, 22, 21.[1]

d) Finally, Vespers begins, now as then, with psalm 109. Matins and the little hours of the week employ psalms 1 to 108, Vespers 109 to 146. Several psalms for Lauds are an exception to this rule. Thus all psalms chosen for a particular historical or liturgical reason were kept in their original order.

2. The thought of each hour should be emphasized. But only in Lauds and Compline is this the case. The psalms for these two hours are specially selected. In the other hours no selection was made with a view to conforming the psalms to the thought of the hour.

3. The remaining psalms are to follow in order. There are slight deviations from this norm for either technical or poetic reasons. In general, however, the psalms follow along in order.

Let us take a closer look at the psalms for Compline and Lauds.

a) Compline. Psalms that are evidently night prayers or that have a penitential character follow in numerical order from Monday to Saturday: Monday, 6 and 7; Tuesday, 11, 12, and 15; Wednesday, 33, 60; Thursday, 69 and 70; Friday, 76 and 85; Saturday, 87 and 102. We can notice how in places the psalms follow the Psalter's numerical order. In the Breviary

[1] The following is the history of these psalms for Prime. Psalms 21–25 originally belonged to Sunday Prime. When Pius V (d. 1572) shortened Prime, he divided these psalms among the days of the week in such a way that psalm 23 would be said on Thursday as a Eucharistic hymn, and psalm 21 on Friday; the others on Monday, Tuesday, and Wednesday.

(at Matins) and in part in the Missal, the liturgy has followed the principle of saying the psalms as they occur. In modern times we have departed from this idea. We stress the fact that appropriate night prayers were chosen for the psalms of Compline. This fact is important for an objective understanding of the psalms, for it makes a world of difference whether I apply my own ideas and thoughts, however so beautiful or apropos they are, or whether it is the Church's liturgy itself which suggests the application.

b) Lauds. The selection of psalms for Lauds is much more complicated. A different plan was used from the one for Compline. Lauds for Sunday was the model. Both form and content for the ferial Lauds were copied from Sunday Lauds. First of all, Sunday Lauds was shortened. Formerly psalm 62 was added to psalm 66, and psalms 148 to 150 were said in place of the omitted one. There remained, then, in Sunday Lauds, in the new arrangement of the Psalter for 1914, the Canticle of the Three Youths, and psalm 148. Psalms of similar contents replaced these five psalms in the Lauds for weekdays.

Sunday	92	99	62	Canticle	148
Monday	46	5	28	"	116
Tuesday	95	42	66	"	134
Wednesday	96	64	100	"	145
Thursday	97	89	35	"	146
Friday	98	142	84	"	147
Saturday	149	91	63	"	150

Psalm 92 is the first psalm for Sunday Lauds. It is a so-called royal psalm: *Dominus regnat*. God is King of the world, the heathens, the godless powers. For weekdays too the first psalm of Lauds is likewise a "royal" psalm. The arrangement of these royal psalms follows an ascending numerical order:

Psalm 46: Rex magnus super omnem terram.

Rex omnis terrae est Deus.

Deus regnat super nationes.

Psalm 95: Dicite inter gentes: Dominus regnat! (God, King of the world, of the Gentiles and of the Jews.)

Psalm 97: Exultate in conspectu regis Domini.

Psalm 98: Dominus regnat. (Psalms 95–99 are the "royal" psalms.)

Psalm 149: Filii Sion exultent de rege suo.

Thus the purpose is clear, namely, that the first psalm of the ferial Lauds should, after the manner of Sunday Lauds, sing of the kingship of Christ on earth.

The second psalm for ferial Lauds is the same as it was in the Breviary of Pius V. This is a selection of ancient origin. True to the first principle of the reform, all these psalms were taken over into the revised Lauds: psalm 99 (Sunday)—5, 42, 64, 89, 142, and 91,—again arranged in an ascending numerical order through the week with the exception of psalm 142 on Friday. In regard to the latter, we conclude that there is some special reason for departing from the usual pattern: that reason is the passion theme. Since psalm 142 is a "passion psalm," it is thus appropriate for Friday, the day dedicated to the memory of Christ's passion.

Later on we shall consider the third psalm of the ferial Lauds.

The fourth psalm has always been a canticle. Several additional canticles were chosen for the new Psalter.[2] I do not know why a canticle has found its way into Lauds.

The fifth psalm is one of praise, beginning usually with the word *Lauda* or *Laudate*. The name "Lauds" is taken from this

---

[2] That is, the revised Psalter (1918). Tr.

fifth psalm. Here too the psalms follow according to their numerical sequence:

Psalm 116: Laudate Dominum.
Psalm 134: Laudate nomen Domini.
Psalm 145: Lauda anima mea.
Psalm 146: Laudate Dominum.
Psalm 147: Lauda, Jerusalem.
Psalm 150: Laudate Dominum.

Now to consider the third psalm for Sunday Lauds. It is a beautiful prayer of longing, psalm 62 (*Deus, Deus meus es*). During the week the psalms are: 28, 66, 100, 35, 84, 63. I must admit I do not know any reason for this selection or order of psalms. There is neither numerical sequence here, nor does the thought have any relation to psalm 62 of Sunday Lauds. Let us try to explain it.

Psalm 28: A beautiful song of nature. The group of psalms 13 to 32 is said on Mondays, and our psalm is in that group. However, that is no reason for placing this psalm in Lauds. (The psalms for Lauds and Compline are of special selection. They do not follow along in order as they occur in the Psalter.)

Psalm 66: It was this psalm, together with psalm 62, that formerly made up the third psalm of Lauds.

Psalm 100: This is a girding for the day. But that is no special reason why it should be found in Lauds.

Psalm 35: A Eucharistic hymn: *Satiantur pinguedine domus tuae*. A fine psalm for Thursday.

Psalm 84: A psalm of Redemption for Friday.

Psalm 63: A psalm of the Passion.

It would help a great deal had the one responsible for the arrangement of the Psalter in our Breviary given us a commentary on his work. Then we could know why each psalm was chosen. This would hold for psalms, canticles, and anti-phons as well. As it is, we do not know even the author of the older offices and Masses, let alone his intentions. Had we some commentary we could know his mind. So much, then, for the structure of Compline and Lauds.

The psalms of the other hours were not of any special selection but follow along in numerical order, in such a way that Vespers employs the last third of the Psalter.

Several rearrangements show that the thought of each hour has been kept in mind.

On Monday, psalm 18 has been taken out of order and used for Prime. While it makes an appropriate morning prayer, it would be a poor evening prayer. On Friday, psalm 72 is used for Terce, probably because it fits better as a prayer to the Holy Ghost than as a night prayer. Psalms 101 and 103 on Saturday are similar cases, the latter being most suitable for Saturday Sext, since it sings of creation.

I would advise everyone who prays the Breviary to leaf through the entire weekly Psalter and ask himself at each psalm: Why is this psalm recited in this particular place?

A general answer would be that some psalms have been especially chosen for their positions, whereas others have not. This fact alone will give a clearer understanding of the psalms used in the various hours.

I mention here my book, *Wochenpsalter des römischen Breviers* ("The Weekly Psalter of the Roman Breviary"), in which I explain each hour according to its thought and the contents of the psalms. In this way the book furnishes a unified thought for each hour. I have tried to give both a subjective and an objective explanation.

In conclusion I would say that the present arrangement of psalms has attained the proper mean between a too artificial and a merely numerical sequence. It is not characteristic of the liturgy to hem in the free course of the psalmody. Her intention in each hour is first of all to praise God. She shies away from too much human prudence in her prayer life, and lets the Holy Ghost inspire the faithful with fitting thoughts and sentiments. I consider the arrangement of the new Psalter (1914) altogether fortunate; at least, I have not found any part entirely out of harmony with the rest. Many hours are beautifully arranged. I need no more than to mention Prime for Monday and Thursday, and Matins and Compline for Saturday.[3]

[3] For the history and structure of the new Psalter, consult *In Constitutionem "Divino Afflatu" Commentarium* by Dr. Peter Piacenza (Rome, Desclee, 1912). Unfortunately this book considers only the rubrics. Still, on page 29, Pascal Brugnani, O.M., one of the authors, promises us a work that will treat the reasons for the arrangement of the new Psalter. (Though the author refers here to the Psalter of 1914, the order of the psalms remains the same in the new version of 1945. Tr.)

CHAPTER XIV

Sunday Lauds and Compline

SINCE these two hours occur so often and since they have such a distinctive character, I shall explain them in their entirety.

Let me recall what was said above. The Church has two morning prayers, Lauds and Prime; and two night prayers, Vespers and Compline. Lauds and Vespers are the ancient, original, and more solemn prayers; Prime and Compline are more recent, and simpler in tone. Lauds and Vespers are the objective prayers in which the individual soul recedes into the background; it is the Church that prays in them. Prime and Compline, on the other hand, are more personal hours. They belong to the individual and reflect to a much greater degree man's consciousness of sin. Prime is the girding for the day's battles and the consecration of the day's work to God. In Compline we shake the day's dust from our shoes. I like to compare Lauds and Vespers to the first three petitions of the Lord's Prayer. These look to the increase and expansion of God's kingdom. Prime and Compline, however, are more like the last three petitions, since they are concerned with deliverance from sin.

I am even tempted to say that Adam could well have prayed Lauds and Vespers in the Garden of Paradise; but only after his fall, in exile on this earth, could he pray Prime and Compline.

I. Sunday Lauds

We are already acquainted with the symbolism of Lauds. It is the Church's early morning prayer, creation's song of praise to God, a "resurrection prayer." A thoroughly joyous hour, it joins Christ's resurrection and nature's awakening with mankind's spiritual resurrection. Its psalms are specially selected chants of praise and morning prayer. They contain many references to nature besides. The resurrection theme pervades the entire hour, particularly on Sunday, which is, in fact, "resurrection day." On it, the day and the hour of the resurrection coincide.

We know already that Lauds rises to the heights of its tribute of praise in three steps. The psalmody is the first step. The second is the capitulum as the authoritative word of God, with the hymn following as its echo. The third step, the climax, is the Benedictus. It has an antiphon that characterizes the day in a special way. The day's oration forms the conclusion.

One other point calls for mention. Lauds lays strong emphasis on the thought of the hour (praise and resurrection) as well as on the particular theme of the feast. In this, too, Lauds bears a resemblance to Vespers, but not to Prime and Compline. Both these latter hours almost completely ignore the theme of the feast. In Lauds, the theme for the feast and the theme of the hour are intrinsically related. The antiphons of the psalms, the capitulum, hymn, antiphon of the Benedictus, and the oration give expression to the theme of the feast. It is not difficult to link this theme with that of the hour. It is the mystical body, the Church, that celebrates the resurrection of its Head and members. We take up the mystery proper to the feast in the light of this truth, and praise and thank God for the day at hand.

The themes of the feast and the hour coincide on Sunday. As a result, only the antiphon for the Benedictus and the oration vary.

In the following pages I shall first explain the psalms in their literal sense, and then in their liturgical application as they are embodied in the prayer structure of Lauds.

Literal Explanation of the Psalms

Psalm 92. This song of nature is full of sublime poetry. Each verse of its three strophes contains three members. The following is the English translation of *Dominus regnat, majestatem indutus est,* arranged according to its strophic divisions.

Psalm 92

The Glory of the Lord's Kingdom

I

God, King;   1 The Lord is king, in splendor robed;
His raiment,   robed is the Lord and girt about with strength;
His sword,   And he has made the world firm,
         not to be moved.
His throne: 2 Your throne stands firm from of old;
the earth.   from everlasting you are, O Lord.

II

The raging   3 The floods lift up, O Lord,
flood.   the floods lift up their voice;
         the floods lift up their tumult.
God rules   4 More powerful than the roar of many waters,
  the flood.   more powerful than the breakers of the sea—
         powerful on high is the Lord.

III

Moral: 5 Your decrees are worthy of trust indeed;
  reverence,   holiness befits your house,
  trust.   O Lord, for length of days.

Even the first reading reveals the balanced structure and lofty poetry of this psalm. We behold a vision. In the first verse we see a king; nature is His ornament and garb; the powers of nature are His sword. The King has fashioned himself an eternal and unshakable throne, which is the earth. This is the second verse, and together with the first verse it forms the first strophe, which is the vision of the King of the universe.

The second strophe describes a vision of a conqueror. We behold the great flood that had covered the earth and been checked, and then had mounted toward this throne again (first verse). But God is victorious over the raging waters (second verse). As high as the tops of the mountains tower the waves, the waters rage, the flood roars. But louder than the roaring of the flood and higher than the surging of the seas, reigns God, marvelously enthroned on high. The third strophe offers us a conclusion. In humble adoration we witness this spectacle and pay homage to our victorious God in the temple.

Psalm 99 we have already spoken of in this book.

Psalm 62 is a song of ardent love and longing for God. Easy to understand and easy to pray, it ranks among our most beautiful psalms.

Division of strophes according to their thought:

The soul thirsting for God (2 to 4);

The soul united with God (5 to 9);

Verse 9 climaxes the song; the lovers embrace.

The enemies and the friends (10 to 12).

The Canticle of the Three Youths (Dan. 3:75–90). The three youths, Ananias, Azarias, and Misael, refused to worship the statue of King Nabuchadonosor. Though cast into the fiery furnace, by God's help they remained unharmed. It was here they sang this song. It was incorporated into the liturgy at a very early date.

The canticle invites all creatures to praise God. Specifically:

1. The heavenly creatures, those that dwell in the sky. Notice the observance of the order of descent from heaven to earth.
2. The earthly creatures, beginning with the inanimate, then the animals in their ascending order.
3. Men, in their ascending order; that is, from mankind to the individual.

The second last verse is a tribute of praise to the Most Holy Trinity. It was added by the Church and is not a part of the inspired text.

If we are to understand the first part of the canticle, we first must grasp the poetic image that the Bible offers. The sky is pictured as a vast and mighty dome, and above it the waters are gathered in gigantic sluices.

Out of a pagan world that is sunk in the worship of nature, a song of praise like this must sound all the more magnificent in the ears of the Creator.

Psalm 148. Heaven and earth chant their praise to God. The psalm embraces two strophes, each with a response from the choir.

1. Praise God all ye in heaven (1–4).

Choir: Let them praise their Creator (5, 6).

2. Praise God on earth (7–12).

Choir: Let them praise the God of the Covenant (13, 14).

Note the change of person. The strophes are in the second person, the choir's response is in the third. This psalm is much like the preceding one.

We are now about to pray Lauds. First we recall this hour's historical redemptive background. The Lord is risen from the dead. All nature is awakening from slumber, and man is undergoing a spiritual resurrection. Such is Lauds, a joyous song of praise, the morning prayer of all creation.

Dawn is breaking. After a hard battle, day has finally vanquished the night. Now nature celebrates its resurrection.

"Alleluja," the first antiphon begins; and thus every antiphon ends. In fact, the first and last antiphons have three "Allelujas," one at the beginning and two at the end. Thus "Alleluja" is the first and last word of the psalms, and the Church makes a resurrection song of Lauds from beginning to end.

Psalm 92. In the first place, this is a meditation on nature and the universe, to form an introduction to the hour. (a) The divine King, His robe the marvels of creation, the powers of nature His sword, and the earth His throne. (b) Symbolic of hell, the raging waters of the flood surge against the throne. Another picture then: night grapples with the new day and is forced to retreat. This is but an image of another battle and of another victory, that of spiritual light over the darkness of hell. Once again the risen Savior stands before us, the banner of victory in His hand. He has vanquished Satan. In His victory we see also the triumph of good in God's kingdom, in the Church and in the soul. Let the waters surge on high. Let them roar to the heavens. Let the powers of hell rage ever so fiercely. God is always the victor. This psalm crystallizes the history of the world. And how comforting are those two images: God the King, and God the Victor! God the King of creation; Christ, the Ruler of God's kingdom. "King" is the principal idea in Lauds. Again and again the natural and the supernatural are intermingling. Being a child of this victorious God, I too must trample the serpent underfoot.

We view awakening nature and the images she offers us in

a spirit of awe and adoration. God's witnesses they are indeed, images of the spiritual world. We cry out: O Lord, I believe the Savior is risen, and now man must rise, for the raging flood of hell must not be victorious.

The antiphon presents still another picture of the King of creation, but this time the "Alleluja" gives it a Messianic character. The risen Savior we see now transfigured as the King of the heavenly kingdom.

Psalm 99. In the midst of all this morning splendor, man now makes his appearance. (He kept in the background in the first psalm.) Joyfully we stand before our God, mindful of His and His Son's dominion over us. Nature can worship Him only as King and Lord, but we can do far more. Our God and Creator He is indeed, but He is also, and above all, our Good Shepherd. This naturally suggests the picture of the Good Shepherd that our Savior outlined, He who gives His life for us and who today leads us to pasture by Holy Communion. We linger for a time on this image in the second strophe. He is kind, He is merciful, and He is true to His word. These traits bear ready application to our Savior.

The antiphon: our hearts full of joy, we call on all the earth to join our song of praise. The first psalm described the break of day. The second spoke of man's awakening; he rises to make a pilgrimage to the temple. The third psalm is the high point of the psalmody, man's morning prayer.

Psalm 62. One of the most passionate of songs, the whole psalm is of ardent longing and love, a song of union with the Spouse, of the morning kiss and greeting of the bride. It presupposes the profound and mystical marriage of Christ and the soul. Lying like a drop of dew on the soul, our first thought on awakening is of what we love best. It is of Christ. "To you, my Jesus, I awake in the early morning. My heart, yes, my whole being thirsts for You as the desert sands thirst for rain. In this frame of mind I hasten to the sanctuary to adore and to offer the Holy Sacrifice. To be Your child, or even Your servant, to enjoy Your favor, is far better than a life of wealth and honor without You. That is why I shall be Your servant all my life; always I shall lift my hands and heart to You." The first part was the journey to the temple. Now I stand before my Spouse, and joy floods my heart. Earth cannot satisfy me; but, like a rich and bounteous banquet, Your love fulfills my every desire. On awakening, my very first thoughts belong to You. Now like a little chick, I am happy in the shelter of Your wings. The climax then, the embrace, the loving union of the spouses. "My soul clings fast to You; Your right hand upholds me." The last verse describes the soul's enemy who desires to curtail the happiness of its union with God. It flings the devil a warning challenge. The King Jesus Christ, however, rejoices over our spiritual resurrection. Only a saint can fully appreciate the stirring sentiments found in this psalm.

Antiphon. I will praise You not only this morning, but all my life long.

Lauds has passed from nature to man, for man, in fact, is creation's central figure. In psalm 62 we reached the climax of the psalmody. In long, deep draughts we "drank in" God. Now we take our place again among His creatures with Him in our hearts. But, as these hearts are too small, we summon all creation to praise our God. We blend our voices with the song of the whole universe in its morning prayer to God. Everything in this majestic world symphony takes on life and personification. All creation praises the risen Lord, for through His resurrection He brought complete redemption to nature too. Every creature, large and small, reflects God's perfections and tells me of God's love. At the same time, though irrational, these creatures preach a forceful sermon: We sing God's praise by the powers and laws He has established in us; through them we observe the Master's will in every detail. "He gave them a duty which shall not pass away" (psalm 148). So, you children of men, praise God also by fulfilling His will freely and consciously. This is our frame of mind as we begin the Canticle of the Three Youths, and psalm 148 also, which is closely related to this canticle. More sublime and stirring these canticles become if we pray them out of doors and early in the morning. Then it actually will be the morning prayer of all creation, of all the thousands of plants and animals, the forces of nature, the murmuring brook, the buzzing bees, the warbling birds, the rustling breeze, the mist-wreathed mountains. All things join in the prayer; I am but the leader.

Note too the fourth antiphon, for it reminds us of the canticle's history. The three brave youths have professed their faith so courageously; see that you do the same today. They sang God's praises in the midst of the flames; in the furnace of suffering and affliction, you do the same. Be steadfast and praise God.

The hour takes its name "Lauds" from *Laudate,* the opening word of psalm 148.

The antiphon affords a transition to the capitulum. "You spirits of heaven, praise God, for there the Alleluja is sung eternally." The capitulum is derived from the Apocalypse and is a part of the ancient liturgy. It is an echo of Lauds sung in heaven before the throne of the divine Lamb.

We are already acquainted with the cockcrow hymn. With its description of the transition from night to day, better than any other it fits in with the symbolism of Lauds. The versicle gives us once more the risen God and King. Again nature and grace are joined. We see the awakened creation as the garb of the victorious God. Now in the Benedictus, our prayer rises to its climax. The antiphon proposes a special motive for praising God. It is in this form (generally a Gospel portrait) that the *Oriens ex alto* ("the One who rises on high") appears to us today. This poetic hour concludes with the oration.

II. SUNDAY COMPLINE

Let us recall, first of all, Compline's role of a second and more subjective night prayer. It is the prayer of the individual soul conscious of sin, eager to cleanse itself of sin committed, and to protect itself from the sins that night threatens. Since Compline has no variable parts (formerly even its psalms were invariable), it is a perfect unit and can be explained as such.

It begins straightway, without any preparatory prayer. In itself this is a clue to the hour's earnestness. The blessing proclaims the purpose of Compline, terse and to the point: a restful night and a good death. A petition for protection in the spiritual night, to which is added a prayer for a happy death. The *lectio brevis* from St. Peter's First Epistle warns us that the situation is grave. We should be alert and watchful; that is, we should not be intoxicated by worldly pleasures nor, like the servant in the Gospel, slumber on while the Master knocks. Just now as night is falling, the devil prowls around the castle of our soul trying to find an entrance. A lively faith is our only defense. Such is the introduction. Now we begin to examine our consciences and to stir up sentiments of contrition. The Confiteor, which we know from the Mass, is the Church's concise and by no means sentimental act of contrition. It describes the judgment scene. In the presence of all the saints and of our fellow Christians, we stand before God's throne to be judged regarding our sins. The greatest of the saints are our accusers. The *mea culpa* is an outlet for the sorrow that floods the soul of the contrite sinner. But here he starts to take courage again. Those who were his accusers until now, turn to his defense and plead for him. The two petitions for forgiveness that follow are familiar to us from the Mass prayers at the foot of the altar. The next versicle, "Turn Thou to us once again," also bears a resemblance to the two verses at the end of the prayers said at the foot of the altar. It is the expression of our hope for the forgiveness of our sins. Only then, after the usual introductory verses, do we commence the psalms. At the beginning the antiphon is merely intoned; that is, merely the first word is said: *Miserere*.

Literal Meaning of the Psalms

Psalm 4. This is an evening song of consolation in affliction, composed by David in his flight from Absalom.

Division of the psalm:

Introduction: petition for help (v. 2).

1. Answer to the enemy (vv. 3–6).

2. Answer to his fainthearted friends (vv. 7–9).

This psalm guards a wealth of thought, but I warn you from experience that it needs frequent study before it is really made your own. It was a favorite prayer of St. Augustine, especially at the time of his conversion (*Confessions*, IX, 4). How much we could make this psalm our own if with Augustine we could pray it, "trembling with fear, yet radiant with hope and joy!"

Psalm 90. Blessed is the man who stands under God's protection. This song breathes the deepest trust in God.

Division (seven strophes):

1. Fortunate the man protected by God; he is safe from his enemy (vv. 1–3).

2.–5. A picturesque development of the same thought (vv. 4–10); description of the danger from the enemy, of the field of slaughter, of thousands falling, though not a single missile strikes the one whom God protects.

6. Guardian angels are appointed to protect him (vv. 11–13).

7. A direct address by God; the promise of a reward for placing his trust in God (vv. 14–16).

This psalm is most picturesque, the favorite psalm of St. Clement Mary Hofbauer.

Psalm 133. This is the greeting of the temple guards. It is a sort of liturgical greeting to the Levites about to commence their night watch in the temple.

1. The priest about to leave the temple; a call to the temple guards (vv. 1, 2).

2. The temple guards; a greeting to the priests in reply (v. 3).

Now we are ready to pray the three psalms.

Psalm 4. It is Sunday evening about nine o'clock. My window is open; from the street I hear the boisterous shouts of villagers and the frivolous titter of young girls, all returning home after a day of picnicking in the country.

I. Now I begin to pray. You children of men, why are you so preoccupied with mere trifles? Why do you hanker after vanities, why do you always seek deceit? And are not these vaporous, sensual joys of earth nothing but vanities and deceits? If you but knew. I realize the vanity of the world. But even at that, how often I too forget it! How often the world allures me too! How often I wade up to my neck in worldly things! I ought never forget that God has showered His saints, His consecrated, that is, every baptized person, with marvelous graces. Consider the graces of baptism and confirmation. Stand in awe of these gifts of God, and sin not. All this I say to myself. If you have sinned, if you have stained your soul today, if you have been wounded by vanity, the vanity and deceits of the world, then repent of your fault as you lie in bed. Make a sacrifice of appeasement by sincere contrition, and place your hope once more in God. Never give up your friendship with God even though things storm against you. Now is the time to return home to God.

II. Once more the "world" sneaks into the silent cloister. No rough obtrusiveness this time, however, since it intends merely to discourage us. "Why bother with all this asceticism, this renunciation of worldly pleasures? Why this mortification? You are not facing reality. Oh, if you but knew how pleasant things are outside." The psalm gives the reply of Holy Mother the Church. What advantage do I reap from my virtue? There are four important advantages: 1. As brilliant as the sun itself, God's favor shines down on me. I have the indescribably good fortune to be a child of light, of God; to be a knight of the divine King. 2. Joy, pure and full, floods my soul, a joy altogether different from that born of wine and cheap diversions whose end is nothing but intoxication and satiety. 3. Peace, that peace promised by the Messiah, dwells in my soul and enables me to enjoy tranquil sleep. 4. The hope of an everlasting home in the next life.

You cannot help but agree that this psalm is a magnificent night prayer. Every thought and word has a calming influence on the soul that has borne the assaults of the world's charms and allurements throughout the day. Now it has the "night off" from all such cares. All that is not God's we thrust from our hearts. With "our sights reset" on God and divine things, we return to peace and rest in Him. Thus it is that after the day's storms the psalm helps the soul to find peace. "As soon as I lie down, I fall peacefully asleep."

Psalm 90. Psalm 4 gave us a rather negative and defensive view. Psalm 90 now helps the soul regain its equilibrium; it is positive and active. Under God's wings the soul feels well sheltered. Yet this psalm sings too of conflicts and battlefields. The soul, however, is firmly grounded in its trust in God. Night throws its mantle over us; it is the devil's mantle at the same time. The physical and the spiritual night interplay. We can not help remembering our divine Protector:

> "You who dwell in the shelter of the Most High,
>   who abide in the shadow of the Almighty,
>   Say to the Lord, 'My refuge and my fortress,
>   my God in whom I trust.' "

The Satanic hunter will in vain lay traps for my soul. God will not let me fall into them. His trusty shield will guard me. Like a little chick, the soul scurries beneath God's wings as night falls. It is a dreadful picture the psalm offers now of life here on earth: a field of battle, arrows cut the air on every side, the terror of night, and pestilence stalking in its darkness, the devil's attacks during the heat of day. You ride over the battlefield: thousands falling on the left, tens of thousands on the right. On you stride, over vipers and asps. Poor fellow. I wonder if you will escape unscathed. But with a shout of joy and triumph you reply: "The Lord is my refuge and my stronghold; no evil shall befall me." Then another beautiful thought for the night: for the span of your earthly life God has given you a special spirit, a guardian angel who takes you by the hand lest you stumble and stub your foot on a rock. At the conclusion, from God's own lips we hear the comforting assurance: "Only trust in Me, and not a hair of your head shall be harmed. In affliction I shall always be near you." Then St.

Bernard's comforting words: "Lord, give me afflictions always, that You may always be with me." "From the battle of this life I will lead you to glorious victory."

This psalm likewise fits perfectly in Compline. It gives us the feeling that we are safely hidden in God's hand. It renews in us the happy conviction that we children of God will conquer all our enemies.

Theme: Safe in God's hands, Angel of God, my guardian.

Psalm 133 also affords some striking thoughts for the night. We children of God are indeed "temple guards," sent by Holy Mother Church to keep watch. You must not sleep now, but keep watch. The world needs the prayers you offer during the night that the enemy may not triumph. From the hand of the Church we receive the weapon we need, our Breviary, replete with so many appropriate night prayers.

Theme: Sleep not, you night watchmen of the temple.

Summary. 1. In retrospect: the vanity of the world, contrition, no faintheartedness, God's peace our greatest treasure. 2. Looking ahead: night the mantle of sin, shelter under God's protection, God's angels guarding us. 3. The Christian prays while during the night he keeps watch in the sanctuary. All three psalms are clearly night prayers.

The antiphon contains Compline's two leading thoughts: contrition ("Have mercy") and petition for protection ("Hear my prayer").

With the psalms finished and the soul hidden safely in God's protecting arms, there follows a part of truly remarkable force and vigor. The hymn pleads for protection during the night. God is our *praesul,* our abbot or superior, and also our *custos,* that is, our porter or gate-keeper. He is to be both King and Guardian of the house. The capitulum is especially stirring:

"Thou art in the midst of us." Jesus Christ is in our midst; we are gathered together in His name. "Do not desert us" is the main petition, linked with the responsory that follows.

Two images of death come next. The first is the antiphon in which Jesus, hanging on the cross, speaks His last words: "Father, into Thy hands I commend My spirit." And we repeat the very same words: "To You, O Savior, I commend my soul now, in the night of this day of my life and of my soul."

The versicle that follows contains two miniature figures. (a) Guard me as the apple of Your eye. I need as much protection as the eye does, and I ask that I may be equally precious and dear to You. (b) Like little chicks we scurry beneath Your sheltering wings.

The second image of death follows now in the Gospel canticle. Simeon, the old man, is singing his swan song. He holds the infant Jesus in his arms. Now his long yearning has been fulfilled. He has seen the Redeemer; now he asks for his release from God's service. We are in a similar situation. In our hands and hearts we bear the sacramental Savior, the graces given for the past day. Today our eyes too have seen again our "salvation." The divine Light has risen in us, and Christ is our glory. Now we ask for a respite from our service, a "night-off" after the day's work, possibly even after our life's work. For in very fact we are God's hired men, and each day we must be ready to be "dismissed."

These two images of death are truly sublime. And the antiphon for the Canticle of Simeon is no less expressive. There is an alternation of bodily and spiritual "watching" and "sleeping": "Protect us when we are awake (that is, in the daytime), watch over us when we sleep (at night), that we may keep watch with Christ (during life by means of His grace) and sleep in peace (in a happy death)." Here, too, we can readily see that Compline is both a night prayer and a prayer for a happy death.

A number of short verses are added to this antiphon on days of Lent, ferial days, and the lesser feasts. It is as though the soul could not break off her conversation with God. Having found Him again, she is searching for words worthy to praise Him. On the other hand, she is somewhat afraid of night, the night of sin. That is what makes her voice this petition: Deign to keep me this night from sin. Have mercy on me, have mercy.

The hour is drawing to a close. In the oration we find a concise summary of all the thoughts and ideas proper to Compline. 1. God's visit. He is invited to dwell with us by His grace and His protection. As in the Old Testament God dwelt among His people in the desert, so now may He visit and remain with us. 2. God also guards the castle of our soul; He refuses admittance to the enemy. 3. In fact, the angels too, our guardian angels, are to dwell in this house with us. We think without effort of the dream of the patriarch Jacob, where he saw the ladder reaching up to heaven. Up and down the angels go, carrying our prayers and good works to God and returning with His graces and favors for us. 4. May God's paternal blessing be upon us the whole night through.

Our night prayer draws gradually to a close: a couple of verses, the blessing of our heavenly Father, the Father of our house. Then we bid "good night" to our heavenly Mother in the antiphon to Our Lady. After this all is silent in the choir. We recite the Our Father and the Apostles' Creed to ourselves. And thus the whole day's Office ends as it began at Matins, with the Creed.

CHAPTER XV

The Advent Office

W E shall give some brief consideration to the Church year now, describing the peculiarities and characteristics of the Office in the various Church seasons and explaining the more important Offices one by one.[1] A detailed description of the latter will give us a much better understanding of the rest of the Breviary.

I assume now that the reader is familiar with the meaning and purpose of Advent. The name itself points to the contents of this season's Office: Advent, that is, "arrival." Christ is coming. Two distinct periods have influenced the formation of the Advent office. The older and more objective period sought to prepare for Christ's second coming, that is, the Parousia. Consequently it centered the Advent office on one of the favorite liturgical themes of the ancient Church. The more recent and more subjective period regards Advent as a preparation for Christmas. It makes the birth of Christ the focus of attention, and thereby is more intent on the first coming of Christ in the flesh. Since this first coming is now an historical event and can no longer be awaited and looked forward to, it is made an image or figure of the coming of grace into our souls. Thus these three "comings" alternate in the Advent office so that often it is difficult to determine which "coming" the liturgical

[1] I am following, for the most part, the plan indicated in *Bibel und Liturgie* by a confrere, Norbert Stenta, whom God called home at an early age.

text intends. But precisely this variation lends so much drama and poetry to the Advent office.

For a moment let us consider the four or five persons who enact the Advent drama: Christ, Mary, John the Baptist, and Isaias. Christ is both King and Bridegroom, Infant and Judge, man and God. The figure of the Mother of God is introduced tenderly (the Virgin who conceives, the Mother with her divine Child), so human, and yet so close to God. John is the man of penance, the one preparing the way. Isaias is the man of longing and expectation.

All these personages make a dramatic appearance, at one time speaking for themselves, at another portrayed for us by the Church herself. We do not hesitate to affirm that for poetry and drama, there is no part in the Breviary that can match the Advent office.

Two features of the Advent office contrast sharply with the liturgy of other seasons. Though Lent is the most important season of the Church year, it has but few exceptionally apt passages, whereas Advent teems with quotable texts. The second distinction of the Advent office is the matchless charm of its melodies, surpassed only by the Holy Week chants. Often the joyful expectation of each word and melody finds its expression in exalted, lyric strains. Speaking of these, I wish to point out that one can feel and experience the full mystic charm in the office of this richest of all the seasons only if one hears it chanted. Where the spoken word fails, and through inadequacy must fail, we enlist the aid of a melody. Among the excellences of the Advent office consequently, we find, first of all, antiphons and responsories that are obviously choral passages.

Now for a consideration of the individual hours. The new season opens with First Vespers on the Saturday before the

First Sunday of Advent. This hour is like an overture to Advent's first week. It suggests all the week's themes and leading ideas. To the antiphons falls the lot of showing us the proper picture for the entire season. We ought not overlook these antiphons, introductory chants that should re-echo in our ears all week. On this Sunday the same antiphons are sung four times, at both Vespers, at Lauds, and at the little hours. In addition, they occur in the little hours throughout the following week. We can find no better way, therefore, to grasp the spirit, the thought, and music of the Advent office, than frequently to repeat these antiphons.

1. In that day the mountains shall trickle with sweetness, and the hills will flow with milk and honey, alleluja.
2. Exult, O daughter of Sion, and rejoice exceedingly, O daughter of Jerusalem, alleluja.
3. Behold, the Lord shall come, and all His saints with Him, and a great light shall rise in that day, alleluja.
4. All you who thirst, come to the fountain: seek the Lord while He may be found, alleluja.
5. Behold, the great prophet cometh; He Himself will build a new Jerusalem, alleluja.

What joy and gladness in these verses! It is immediately clear to us that Advent is also a time of glad tidings. 1. "In that day," that is, the day of Redemption, which the liturgy sees in Christmas since Christ's birth was the beginning of our redemption. The Church sings it this way at Christmas: "Today, throughout the whole world, the skies drop down honey" (resp. lect. 2). The liturgy presents our redemption through this image of the fertility of the Promised Land. We Christians realize what these words mean. The kingdom of God in our souls and in the Church shall abound in treasures. Again we voice the fervent prayer: *Adveniat regnum tuum.*

Note also that each antiphon ends with an "alleluja." This is the Church's shout of joy. As a rule the liturgy closes each antiphon with an "alleluja" only in the joyous Easter season. Here in the Christmas liturgy it is, in truth, the celestial theme song resounding through the streets of the heavenly Jerusalem. Eschatological themes also appear from time to time in the Advent office; only in heaven will the kingdom of God be revealed in all its splendor. 2. Both Church and the individual soul are called on to rejoice. Does the kingdom of God actually afford us more joy and happiness than anything else? Do not material happiness and wealth make stronger claims on us? How can we long for the kingdom of God if we fail to esteem it higher than all else? 3. The third antiphon is thoroughly eschatological. The scene is the Last Day. The Lord is coming in great power and majesty; in His retinue are the saints of all ages. This is the Lord's last and most significant advent. The great light that rises now is the heavenly Jerusalem, eternal glory. That will be the Christmas par excellence. Our whole life is an Advent in preparation for it. 4. Here the liturgy strikes a new chord. It seems almost as if we were in the midst of Lent. Of course, Advent too is a time of self-examination and good resolutions. It is consequently of importance that we go to drink at the Savior's fountains. The Lord is nearer now than usual. It is a time of great grace, and we must seek the Lord. 5. Christ, the great Prophet, stands before the gate. He comes to renew the Jerusalem of the Church and the soul, that it may become the heavenly Jerusalem.

On the following three Sundays we sing antiphons similar to these. Profound sentiments and stirring appeals to the heart lie in each word and melody. There is a pleasant variation of poetic imagery and symbolism. Every antiphon, as a result, stirs the soul as a painting would. Psalms and antiphons have, at most, but a casual relation. Yet the antiphons do indicate the sentiments with which we should pray these psalms. The twenty Vesper antiphons for the four Sundays of Advent well deserve our deep meditation and our reflection.

In the capitulum we hear the most important passage of the Epistle read at the morning's Mass: "Brethren, you know that already it is high time for us to awake out of sleep." The great day of our redemption is dawning. The hymn, too, provides beautiful Advent thoughts. Its melody is fittingly styled Advent music. The versicle continues invariable through the season. At Lauds we hear John's voice preparing the way; at Vespers it is the longing cry of Isaias: "Drop down dew, ye heavens." These two versicles occur daily during Advent, and are the most typical of this season. An excellent choice was made for the Magnificat antiphon. We see the Lord coming afar off: "Behold, the name of the Lord cometh from afar, and His glory filleth the whole earth."

During the long nights of the Advent season (the longest of the whole year) the Church prays the true Advent prayer, Matins. To await the Lord was the idea behind the ancient vigils. Matins for the Sundays of Advent have their proper antiphons. As far as thought is concerned, these are closely related to the Vesper antiphons mentioned above. Full of joy and confident expectance, they invariably proclaim glad tidings. "Behold, I come quickly and bring My reward with Me, saith the Lord, to repay to each one according to his works." "Let the hearts of men be cleansed for the coming of the great King, that we may go to meet Him worthily; for behold He cometh, and doth not delay." We behold: God and man are going to meet each other. During the long Advent nights it is Isaias who speaks in the lessons. He is the Advent preacher and prophet for the whole four weeks. Prince among the prophets, he is the evangelist of the Old Testament. With strokes clearer than those of any other of the prophets, he outlines the picture of the Redeemer who comes. That is one reason why his book is read in Advent. The fact that his is the voice of mankind yearning for redemption, is another. With all this he preaches penance too, and would induce us to reform our lives. Such a voice should find its echo in our own souls. In the first lesson God sternly addresses His people. Though the prophet directed his words to the Jewish people, the Church has her own children in mind now. That God's love should go unheeded fills both heaven and earth with astonishment.

There is a definite break in the pattern of ideas of the four-week season of Advent. The first half is characterized by a longing for God's coming; the second half is marked rather by the joy of His actual coming. The difference of theme finds rich expression in the Invitatory, the overture to the prayer drama of Matins. "Come; let us adore the King who is to come." This is the antiphon for the first two Sundays. On Gaudete Sunday and on the last Sunday of Advent the Church sings with anticipated joy: "The Lord is now near at hand." In the Matins for the vigil of Christmas this joy is accentuated a third time: "Today you know the Lord shall come; and in the morning you shall see His glory." Even if Matins itself displayed no exquisite gems of prayer composition, we would still have to marvel at Holy Mother the Church for these three Invitatories. The hymn for Matins is the counterpart of that for Vespers. Its clear and deliberate phrases depict the Lord's triple advent. Strophe one describes the historical coming; strophe two, the coming of grace into our souls; strophes three and four, the parousia at the end of the

world. In outline within this hymn we find the essential ideas
and aims of all Advent prayer.

The responsories, breathing-spells in the prayer drama, are
of exceptional beauty. Indeed they are genuine pearls of liturgical prayer. The Advent responsories boast a richness
unexcelled by that of any other season. It is unfortunate that
I cannot treat these magnificent antiphonal chants in detail.
Through most of them run thoughts of the coming King.
Here too, it is Jerusalem the Holy City, that serves as the
foretype of the Church longing for its final redemption.
Thoughts of the parousia are flashes of joy to illumine this
night drama of the mystical Christ. On the first Sunday the
first two responsories at Matins form the climax of this yearning for the King who is to come. The first has remarkable dramatic and poetic force.

> From afar I look up;
> Behold, I see the power of God coming
> And a cloud covering the whole earth.
> Go out to meet Him, and say:
> Tell us if Thou art the One
> Who is to reign over the people of Israel?
> All ye inhabitants of the earth and sons of men,
> All together, rich and poor,—
> Go forth to meet Him, and say:
> Thou Who rulest Israel, listen;
> Thou Who leadest Joseph like a sheep,
> Tell us if Thou art the One?
> O ye princes, raise your gates,
> That the King of Glory may enter,
> To reign over the people of Israel.

Each year this passage stirs up a wholesome sentiment of
fear. Holy Mother Church penetrates deep into our hearts
with strong, impressive language. Only a soul thoroughly

hardened could resist its charm. Even though with its general theme of hope and longing Advent differs essentially from the somber penitence of Lent, it has this feature in common with it: the suppression of all elements that are specifically festive in character. The Te Deum, consequently, is omitted at the conclusion of Matins. Until the holy night itself the Church desires to maintain a certain reserve. Even on Gaudete Sunday, when for a day she lays aside the preparatory and penitential side of Advent, the liturgy holds to a gentle restraint.

The Sunday Lauds are quite joyous. That is why they are not from the second schema, that is, the Lauds for penitential days which we recite only during the week. In addition, the Church has composed special antiphons for the last days before Christmas. Lauds is in this way a genuine Advent hour. Light overcomes the darkness. This theme gathers eloquent expression to itself in the well-chosen capitulum: "The hour is now come, to arise from sleep." The hymn describes once more the threefold advent of the Lord. Its first strophe is particularly beautiful. In form and content it resembles the long responsory for Matins of the First Sunday in Advent. The antiphons for the Benedictus were carefully chosen too. They treat of the thought proper to the hour, that is, morning as symbolizing the dawn of our redemption.

There is always something uplifting about this morning hour of Lauds, chock-full of allusions as it is, to dawn and light. But its language is especially meaningful to the hearts of those who have been redeemed or who yearn for redemption. Christmas Eve finds this effect highly accentuated when, done with Matins and its ferial psalms, we turn to Lauds. Here each festive psalm has its own antiphon to trumpet forth the *"Hodie"* before the great morning (*crastina die*).

The little hours, Prime, Terce, Sext, and None, show the least characteristics of the season. They focus rather on the theme of the particular hour. Yet they have not altogether escaped the impress of the Advent season. Even Prime, though unaltered for the most part, suffers a slight change besides the special antiphons. The phrase, "Who art to come," in the responsory replaces the usual, "Who sittest at the right hand of the Father." The *lectio brevis* is special too. The other little hours borrow their variable parts from the proper parts of Vespers, Matins, and Lauds. Compline remains unaltered.

The antiphon to Our Lady, *Alma Redemptoris Mater,* is a true Advent prayer in content, style, and melody.

Another peculiar feature of the Advent office is that of having the so-called "O" antiphons sung as Magnificat antiphons at Vespers on the seven days before Christmas Eve. There is something extremely solemn and majestic about these antiphons which are sung in their entirety both before and after the Magnificat. Though they do not all have the same melody, in general structure and pattern of ideas they are the same. In fact, they have the structure of a collect of the Roman liturgy. 1. The address: The Lord who is about to come is addressed by some title, or through an image or figure. For example: O Wisdom, O Root of Jesse, O Orient. 2. A relative clause: here the image or figure is further explained and amplified. 3. The petition: introduced with the expectant "Come" (*Veni*). This is the emphatic point of the antiphon on which follows the petition for redemption.

These sublime chants likewise summarize all the prophecies about the coming Redeemer. Their melodies breathe a hopeful longing and astonishment. In them, too, we can glimpse the peoples of the Old Testament and of the pagan world yearning for a Redeemer. In truth, these antiphons are man-

kind's "Drop down dew, ye heavens." There is a definite progression of thought in the seven antiphons. In the first we
view the Son of God in His pre-temporal existence. He is
the uncreated Wisdom, who created the universe and "or-
daineth all things mightily and sweetly." This creation of the
universe prefigures the far loftier spiritual renovation effected
by the Redemption. We ask the Redeemer to accomplish this
renovation in us. In the next three antiphons, thanks to the Old
Testament, we see the Redeemer as the God of the covenant,
leading His people through the desert, as the Root of Jesse, the
Offspring of David, the victorious King, as the Key of David,
that is, as the fulfillment and realization of all the mysteries and
foretypes of the Old Testament. We pray that the Redeemer
may fulfill all these promises. In the fifth antiphon we enter the
realm of nature and see the sun as the symbol of the Redeemer,
a symbol that the Savior's own words have already made familiar to us. May He be for us, in truth, a spiritual sun. In
the sixth we see the heathen, arms outstretched, yearning
for the Redeemer who will make of all peoples the one people
of God. We call the Redeemer to a vast world of heathens
who yearn for him. The seventh antiphon is a summary of the
preceding six. It addresses the Savior by the name that the
prophet gave him: Emmanuel (God with us). In the monasteries these "O" antiphons are sung with great solemnity
and with special ceremonies. While the great tower bell peals,
the abbot himself, vested in pontifical robes, intones the first
antiphon from his throne. This bell continues ringing until the
end of the Magnificat, chanted on the solemn tone. On the
following days the one next in rank, vested in cope and standing before the lectern in the middle of the choir, intones the
antiphon.

CHAPTER XVI

The Office for Christmas and Epiphany

J OYFUL expectation and personal, spiritual preparation are, we have seen, the general theme of the Church's prayer texts for Advent. This season's last jewels are displayed on the Vigil of Christmas. To keep keyed at the highest pitch of expectation, the Church, it seems, wishes to flood this day with her thoughts and sentiments in their full force and beauty. Glowing throughout with the colors of joyous hope and expectation, the office for the Vigil of Christmas is a masterpiece of the art of prayer. This focal point in the liturgical year has as one of its unique features the gentle, almost imperceptible transition from Advent to the great feast of Christmas. In fact, with the Church's wish to the contrary so evident, I wonder that we make any interruption there at all. The liturgy makes the transition from the time of preparation to the feast itself very quietly. The season's texts and verses are moderate in the joy they express at the fulfillment of Advent's hope and expectations. And even in the Christmas liturgy we observe that gentle, poetic charm that characterized the Advent office. At any rate, the restrained joy of anticipation is now unleashed into the jubilant realization of our redemption. Our hymns before were full of hope and longing. Now we sing with these same hopes, certain and

fulfilled. Though the words and melodies are joyous and festive, they lack the vibrant vigor and emotion of those for
the Epiphany or for Easter. The intimate, personal, and cordial
tone that echoes from the Advent office makes the festive
Christmas cycle unique. This warm, personal element is so
reflected throughout the period that we might say it is the
characteristic feature of the Christmas office. Let us now
study the various days of Christmastide with their individual
hours.

The Vigil of Christmas

In Matins it is still Advent. We use the ferial psalms, and
the hymn is from the Advent office. Today is the last day
we sing it. But at the outset of the hour, we hear a joyous cry
of anticipation: "Today you shall know that the Lord is coming, and tomorrow you shall behold His glory." This theme
will ring out once again in the versicle at the end of the three
psalms. The joyous expectation of the Church is something
like the glee of little children peeking through the keyhole
on Christmas Eve, or spying pine needles on the floor and
guessing that the Christmas tree is already in the house. Some
such childlike attitude can fill us with the right sentiments
for praying this office. In the Gospel homily of St. Jerome
we relive the great dilemma that vexed St. Joseph's mind because of the conception of Mary, the miracle of which was
unknown to him. The great doctor's homily is indeed a canticle to St. Joseph. Poetic and emotional responsories relieve
its rather sober account. These repeat the word "tomorrow"
six times, and thus develop and amplify the Invitatory theme.
Since it is still Advent, there is no Te Deum at the end of
Matins. In Lauds, however, we glimpse the dawn of the festive cycle. Ferial psalms step back to make way for the festive

ones. Special antiphons further amplify the "tomorrow" we heard in Matins. In four of the antiphons it recurs with unmistakable emphasis, while "The Lord will come" is an able substitute in the one antiphon that lacks it. The capitulum is taken from the Epistle to the Romans and has as its subject our Lord's advent in the flesh. The hymn brings us back to Advent's sentiments and atmosphere, and the versicle stresses once again, "tomorrow." A classic Benedictus antiphon heralds the solemn morning hymn of our redemption. Its one brief sentence is a rare and beautiful blending of the theme of the hour, historical redemptive background, and the principal thought of the feast: "The Savior of the world will rise like the sun, and descend into the womb of the virgin as the showers fall on the fields, Alleluja." The oration is a rich combination of pleading for the special grace of the feast and petition for grace on the day of the parousia: still, then, an Advent prayer.

In the little hours we sing the festive psalms with the antiphons from Lauds. We find the "tomorrow" again in the responsories. Prime embodies a unique moment in the vigil's office, best appreciated, of course, only when the office is recited in choir. The lector opens the Martyrology and in unusually solemn style and with a gradual heightening of musical pitch, proclaims the birth of the Lord. The Nativity itself, however, is recounted in the rather pensive tone of the Passion; after all, the Savior's passion did actually begin in the manger at Bethlehem. Here we have the Easter liturgy at the extremity of its cycle throwing a shadow over the Christmas cycle. Christmas Eve arrives with the celebration of First Vespers. I can easily understand how diocesan priests and lay folk might envy the opportunity that religious have of assisting at solemn Vespers on Christmas Eve, clad in the festive robes of the liturgy with the chanting of Christmas melodies to help them celebrate the first moments of the feast. Believe me when I say I would not exchange my place at choir with anyone, or for anything.

Christmas Eve Vespers, like many other joys offered by the liturgy, is a part of the hundredfold received even on this earth by those who waive their claim to the world and its trifles. Vespers is the beginning of the great feast. Our Advent longing flows over now into fulfillment. Nevertheless many of the texts keep the Advent tone (especially the third, fourth, and fifth antiphons), and in the versicle we hear the "tomorrow" receive further repetition and stress. But the first two antiphons, and the capitulum and hymn in particular, are, definitely cast in the sentiments of Christmas. In fact, their texts anticipate the events of the feast. The splendid Magnificat antiphon is perfectly adapted to the theme of sunset. This picture of the setting sun naturally evokes pictures of its rising on the following day; all of this a figure of the great sun, Christ, emerging from the bridal chamber. The antiphon is taken in part from the "sun hymn" (psalm 18) which we shall meet again in Matins. The greeting to the Mother of God at the end of the hour, *Alma Redemptoris Mater,* is carried over into the Christmas season from Advent, but with a special versicle and oration now, from First Vespers of Christmas to the feast of Mary's Purification. Compline brings Christmas Eve to its close. Darkness moves in. At midnight the Church rises to sing the most beautiful office of the year. This is a true Christian vigil. About the very hour when the Lord was born, the Church re-enacts the great events of Bethlehem on the "swaddling clothes" of the altar. She prepares for the Mass a little earlier with the chants and lessons of the Matins drama. The night office, to which the

Church lends her whole heart and voice, is a vigil in both name and reality. Should you wish to hear the hymns and prayers of thanksgiving of the Church on this great feast, then assist at solemn Matins in some cathedral or abbey where the highest ideals of the liturgy are respected in the celebration of the office. Only then will you appreciate, to some extent at least, the wonderful treasures of the Church. Matins was the "Parousia prayer" of the early Church: out of the "night" of this life, a cry rising incessantly for the light of Redemption. It was the night *maranatha*. Christmas Matins is such an important hour that I shall afterward devote a special chapter to its detailed study.

Without chanting the concluding antiphon to Our Lady, the choir moves straightway from Matins to the celebration of the Mass for the great feast. It is midnight; the hour of Christ's birth has struck. This birth is re-enacted on swaddling clothes now too, symbolized by the altar linens. Matins was a powerful, thoughtful preparation for this great "Parousia" of grace. It was the last precious Advent hour before our coming to Bethlehem, "the house of bread," our own church. At dawn we witness the adoration of the shepherds in the grace drama. Holy Mother Church makes Lauds the introduction, and this hour is perfectly attuned to the simple, pastoral character of the occasion. I might say that Lauds is the Christmas hour par excellence. The friendly queries the shepherds whisper, the glorious hymns the angels sing, all find an everlasting echo in the warm tenderness of Christmas Lauds. The poetry of the shepherds and the theme of the hour (daybreak symbolizing the dawn of our Redemption) lend a special depth to the hour. The antiphons tell the story of the shepherd drama, and the psalms fill out the intermissions with their songs of morning praise. The hymn is full of the thoughts proper to the theme. The Benedictus, hymn of the dawn of our Redemption (*oriens ex alto*, "rising on high") has for its antiphon the jubilant song of the angels on the plains of Bethlehem: "Glory to God in the highest, and on earth, peace to men of good will." Terce, the third hour of the Office, introduces the feast's main act of worship, the Holy Sacrifice. The responsory at Terce reasserts the leading thought of the Gospel: "And the Word became flesh."

The Church brings the feast to a close with the Second Vespers. It has its own special psalms and texts (the antiphons are not the same as for First Vespers). Psalm 109 sings of Christ's eternal kingship; psalm 110, of God's fidelity as proved by the coming of the Redeemer; psalm 111 treats of the "light" that shines in the darkness for the just (those who are in need of redemption). The De Profundis takes on a special character and tone today. At this point the Church inserts her official "death psalm" as a sort of reminder that, while we rejoice and celebrate this anniversary of the Redemption, we should not forget the fact of the Redemption itself. She chose this somewhat somber Advent song because of the verse: "For with the Lord is kindness, and with him is plenteous redemption." Psalm 131 concludes the psalmody. Once more we are reminded of God's fidelity to the promise He made David that the Christ should come. In the Magnificat antiphon the Church seems to wish to stir up our memory of the theme of the three Christmas Masses. At Second Vespers with the commemoration of St. Stephen the Protomartyr, we start the celebration of the lesser feasts of the Christmas cycle. But as far as psalms and antiphons are concerned, the Christmas Vespers continues through the whole week. It seems that in the five psalms of Vespers the Church wishes to sing of her King; and of His "followers" only in the capitu-

lum and the other hours; then on the octave day (Circumcision) to give herself entirely once more to the celebration
of our Lord's birth.

THE LESSER FEASTS

Christ the King has come. He has descended to earth to
make men children of the King. Now around the King's crib
we find a carefully selected group of His children. First of
all there is Stephen, called "the crown." Naturally this Matins
does not rival Christmas' midnight office in splendor and ele-
gance. The Invitatory ties the mystery in very beautifully with
the theme of the feast: "Let us adore the new-born Christ
who today crowned blessed Stephen." The only texts proper
to the feast occur in the responsories. These are indeed vivid
and dramatic and give us a "close-up" of the death of the first
martyr. The lessons in the first nocturn recount the story from
the Acts of the Apostles, the why and how of Stephen's death.
In the second nocturn, St. Fulgentius the bishop makes clever
comparisons and contrasts between the feasts of Christmas
and of St. Stephen. Lauds gives more attention to the theme
and the mystery of the feast than does Matins. The antiphons
are small, scenic pictures that are fitted into the pattern of
morning praise. Appropriately psalm 62 (a canticle of a soul
that loves its God), with its antiphon aptly accentuated, pours
out from the soul of the protomartyr: "My soul cleaves to Thee,
for my body has been stoned for Thee, my God."

St. John, the beloved Apostle, follows as the King's next
"page." Although there is no exceptional wealth of proper
texts, a sort of sweet, pure fragrance, as of lilies, pervades the
whole office. The responsories especially give a tender, delicate picture of the chaste, virginal disciple "whom Jesus loved"
and who so well requited Christ's love. The lessons of the

first nocturn, as we might expect, are excerpts from the Epistle of a soul brimful of love (St. John's First Epistle). In the sixth lesson, St. Jerome speaks of the words long since proverbial: "Little children, love one another." On the Gospel, in the third nocturn, St. Augustine offers a rich meditation on the active Church, which he compares to St. Peter, and on the contemplative Church, personified by St. John.

Gathered about the crib of their King, we find the Holy Innocents too. As the violet vestments for the day scarcely harmonize with the festiveness of the octave, the more or less mournful tone of the office seems out of tune too. Thus the sorrowful strains that float up from the harp of the cross echo likewise around the crib, for in the poetry of the liturgy, this too becomes "the wood of suffering." Before the eyes of the Church praying her night office the infant martyrs pass in review, victims of a horrible crime. Two thoughts predominate: the martyrs' innocence, and the cry for vengeance. We find Parousia sentiments in some of the responsories. Matins has its psalms and antiphons from the Common of Martyrs. A special hymn gives vivid outline to Herod's motive for murdering the Innocents. The Book of Jeremias supplies the lessons for the first nocturn. In their literal sense, these passages are the laments of the Jewish mothers whose children have been carried off into exile. The Church has these laments sound from the mournful hearts of the mothers here in Bethlehem. In the third lesson there is a text that we refer to Mary: "A woman shall encompass a man." In the second nocturn St. Augustine preaches an eloquent sermon on the cruel, untimely death of the infants. The full significance of this act of God's providence he sets forth clearly. The violet vestments, the absence of the Gloria in the Mass and of the Te Deum at Matins has given rise to much thought as to why such a penitential character should predominate on this feast. I am of the opinion that sympathy with the grief-stricken mothers is not the reason. It seems, rather, that Herod's intention, his planning to kill Christ, foreshadows the somber events of Good Friday. The usually festive psalms of Sunday Lauds take on sober overtones from the tragic antiphons. A beautiful hymn traces an appropriate parallel between youth and the dawn of a new day (the theme for Lauds). We may also count in St. Thomas of Canterbury (December 29) and St. Sylvester (December 31) as part of the court gathered around the crib of the new-born King. In the offices of the two saints there are many references to the feast of the Nativity, though for the most part they seem far-fetched. The Church returns wholeheartedly to the Christmas theme on one occasion during the octave. This is on the Sunday within the octave; or if it is suppressed by the feast of one of the lesser saints, on the day this Sunday is resumed. With the exception only of the lessons, the whole Christmas office is repeated. Only at the Magnificat antiphon for First Vespers and the Benedictus antiphon at Lauds do we hear the magnificent text, the overture that rang out in the Introit of the Mass: "When everything was wrapped in silence and night had run half her course, Your almighty Word came down from heaven, O Lord, from His royal throne." The Church repeats this prayer three times in the Mass and offices to teach us that the fullest measure of this great mystery comes to us only in the silent depths of our soul and in the unobtrusive stillness of humility.

The Circumcision of Our Lord

Eight days after Christmas the Church once more prayerfully takes up the mystery of the holy night, and here brings it to a close. The office for this feast has a special character. For the most part, Vespers is a "Marian" hour. In fact, if the capitulum, hymn, versicle, and Magnificat antiphon did not show their Christmas character, the psalms (from the Common of feasts of Our Lady) and their antiphons would easily lead us to think the Church was celebrating a feast of Our Lady. Though unusually long, the antiphons are profound and rich in symbolic allusions and in the application of types from the Old Testament. It takes but a moment to see that these antiphons grew not in western, but in eastern soil.

Matins is a variation of the Christmas office, a meditation on the Invitatory of that great feast: "Christ is born to us." The psalms are short, some with antiphons taken from the psalms themselves, and others with special antiphons that bear but loose relation to the psalms. On the Sunday after Christmas the Epistle to the Romans makes its appearance in the office. Its fourth chapter treats of circumcision and is appropriately read on this feast. Here Paul means to show, as in the case of Abraham, that it is not circumcision (incorporation into the Jewish people) but faith that gives one a claim to redemption. We find another Christmas sermon from the pen of Pope Leo I in the first nocturn. This is a dogmatic discourse on Christ's two natures, the human and the divine. In the Gospel homily for the third nocturn, St. Ambrose discusses the reasons for our Lord's circumcision. The responsories are especially worth our attention. In the first nocturn they are like a solemn prelude to the Epiphany. John the Baptist speaks in the first responsory, "pointing out the Lamb of God"; in the second "the great light" appears; the third chants the praises of the new-born King. The responsories of the second and third nocturns paint a lovely picture of the Mother of God, accentuating her youth and virginity. There are no new prayer texts in Lauds. The antiphons for the psalms are the same as those for Vespers. However, we should take note of the special Benedictus antiphon, *Innovantur naturae*, which once more relates the theme to the feast at hand. All nature is transformed with the light of the rising sun; so too, the world takes on new life in Christ.

The Feast of the Holy Name of Jesus

This feast occurs on the Sunday after the Circumcision and is a parallel to it. The office is a meditation by the Church on the name of Jesus. All the psalms that mention the name of God sound forth now as hymns to the holy name of Jesus. The antiphons bring this out. The systematic arrangement of this feast is an evident departure from the pattern of the previous offices in the Christmas cycle. Especially manifest in the hymn, the type of devotion found here is definitely more in accord with the modern Christian mentality. Still it is this very contrast of old and new prayer texts that can teach us to appreciate the terse and austere style of the early Church. Even lessons and responsories are so exclusively concerned with the holy name of Jesus that they require no further commentary.

On the fifth of January the Church prepares for the second climax of the Christmas cycle, the Epiphany. The divine King, who at Bethlehem came into the world so unpretentiously and was recognized by so few men, reveals Himself now to the whole, wide world. Christmas, the intimate, almost personal feast, changes now to a universal, world feast, the great wedding feast of the King and His bride, the Church. It was this that the Advent preparation actually had in mind. The Church places us once more in the Christmas setting on the vigil, with the entire office of the Circumcision repeated. Only the

Magnificat antiphon for First Vespers, with its laconic account of Christ's youth, relates the day's office to the feast of the Epiphany, Christ's appearance in the world: "And the child Jesus grew in age and wisdom before God and man." The Gospel (Arise . . . and go into the land of Israel) indicates the chronological relation of Christmas to the Epiphany. It is at None on the vigil that we hear the last echoes of Christmas. The lovely Infant fades from the pages of the Breviary to make room for the triumphal epiphany of the *Majestas Domini*.

THE EPIPHANY OF OUR LORD

The Church combines three events of Christ's life into a liturgical unit to illustrate the feast of the Epiphany. She borrows the first incident from the Gospel record of His infancy, the story of the Magi. In the West, the feast of the Epiphany has actually become the feast of the three Magi. Christ's baptism in the Jordan is the second event, the "sanctification" of the Redeemer, to be placed just before His public ministry. Christ's first miracle at the wedding feast of Cana supplies the third mystery of the feast. Holy Mother Church threads these three incidents together to present His "theophany," His appearance, as the divine King of the world. Before us now we have the early Church's feast of "Christ the King." It found its origin in the East and breathes the spirit of early Christianity.

Only one schooled in the liturgy, who really lives the life of the Church, can thoroughly grasp the full significance of this feast and give it the place in his heart that is its due as the greatest feast in the Christmas cycle. There is an unusual depth of thought and a wealth of symbolic allusions in the artistic, liturgical unit that the Church fashioned of these three mysteries in our Savior's life. As we consider each part, I will point out the various features of this masterpiece of prayer drama.

Christ the King, now revealed to the world (the theophany at the baptism in the Jordan), celebrates His wedding (the marriage at Cana) with His bride, the Church; mankind hastens to give its wedding presents (the journey of the Magi). The Church's presentation of all this is far more vivid in the office of the feast than in its Mass. The Mass devotes itself almost exclusively to the idea of the Magi, whereas the office provides a thorough and dramatic treatment of all three themes.

This feast of the Epiphany should certainly convince us that, if the profound beauty of the great feast is not to be "wasted on the desert air," we must make ourselves more familiar with the Church's prayer. Compared to Christmas' tenderly pastoral office, this office is full of sublime, sacerdotal majesty. It is the universe bowing in solemn worship before its divine King. A feast of unique brilliance, it ranks among the gems of the Church's official prayer book. The feast begins, as usual, with First Vespers, pealing forth like great, resonant cathedral chimes. The Vesper psalms are the same as those of Christmas, but proper antiphons give them a special timbre. He who was born before the morning star (that is, from all eternity) makes His appearance in the world. Thus Vespers' first song, psalm 109, states the theme, like an overture for the whole office of the feast. The second antiphon tells of the illumination of the Holy City (the Church) in which a great light (Christ) has risen. The antiphon that mentions the gifts of the Magi frames psalm 111, the song of the just man. The roar of the sea and river waters (baptism theme) supplies the accompaniment for the fourth psalm

(psalm 112). The last, psalm 116, the hymn of the "Gentiles," is sung by the Magi, their noblest representatives. They were led by the star and were the first to recognize in Christ the divine King. The capitulum speaks once more of the illumination of the Holy City. The hymn has each of its stanzas treat a different mystery of the feast. Two stanzas give a vivid description of the Magi's meeting with Herod. Psalm 71, the psalm of the three Magi, lends the versicle that is a theme song re-echoing through the whole octave. In the Magnificat antiphon for First Vespers, special emphasis is laid on the Magi's visit to their divine King. Second Vespers is almost the same as First Vespers, except for its own proper antiphon whose few, masterly lines sum up the whole feast: "Three wonderful events enhance this sacred day we celebrate; today the star led the Magi to the manger, today at the wedding water was changed to wine, today in the Jordan Christ chose to be baptized by John that He might save us, Alleluia."

This summary of the leading ideas of the feast frames the Church's canticle of thanksgiving for Christ's "epiphany." This hymn wafts our evening sacrifice up as incense before God's throne, like the gifts of the Magi. Thus stands completed the re-enactment of the worship offered so long ago by these "first fruits" of the Gentile Church. The Church's Vesper prelude to the great feast concludes with the classic oration: may the star also lead us to the Epiphany (the Parousia).

Matins. By way of exception, Matins commences without Invitatory or hymn. Almost before we know it we are in the midst of the hour. The whole office is one grand symphony of prayer. All the psalms, and particularly the antiphons taken directly from them, stress the *adorare*. In this great canticle of adoration even psalm 94 relinquishes its place of honor. It mingles with the chorus of adoration that surges from the hearts of the wise men. However, as the Church dislikes too much repetition in her liturgy, psalm 94 falls out as the Invitatory as it introduces the trio of psalms for the third nocturn. All the psalms were selected with a view to the theme: adoration. Note especially psalm 46 which sings of the King of the world, psalm 65 which we may regard as the Gentiles' hymn of thanksgiving, psalm 71 which is the hymn of the three Magi, as we mentioned in connection with the versicle at Vespers, and which we may regard here as an Old Testament prophecy concerning the Magi, psalm 85 which we also put on the lips of the Gentiles, and finally the classic adoration psalm, psalm 94. With its distinctive antiphon, "Come let us adore, for He is the Lord, our God," this psalm is, by way of exception, sung antiphonally. In the fashion of the early Church the antiphon is repeated after every two verses. The psalmody concludes with the "royal" psalms 95 and 96. Nearly all the antiphons come directly from the psalms themselves and, either explicitly or with equivalent expressions, stress the theme: *adorare*. The Book of Isaias supplies the first nocturn lessons. Each is a separate passage and, viewed from a liturgical standpoint, each highlights one of the feast's three mysteries. The responsories that interrupt the lessons treat of the baptism of Jesus (quite apropos, after the first lesson) and the homage of the three Magi. Considering the prominence given to the baptism of our Lord, one would suspect that some Oriental influence was at work here. Pope St. Leo I, the famous Christmas preacher, gives us another discourse in the second nocturn. In the first lesson he explains the meaning of Christmas and the Epiphany; in the second he deals with Herod's terrible crime; in the third he shows the Magi as the beginnings of the Gentile Church. The responsories have us enter the recently illuminated city of Jerusalem to join with the Magi in making our offerings. The three responsories echo the thoughts and sentiments of the lessons. After the Gospel (at the appearance of the star) Pope St. Gregory offers a profound homily on the theme of the feast, telling us that for believers God gives prophecies, but for unbelievers, miracles. Both responsories of the third nocturn are appropriate meditations on the miraculous star. In the main we can say that scarcely any feast other than the Epiphany so well satisfies the theoretical requisites that the liturgy plots for the various parts. This holds true for its Mass as well as for its office.

For Lauds we use the festive psalms with antiphons borrowed from First Vespers. The hymn tells of the Magi following the light of the star; a fitting thought for the hour of Lauds since the morning star announces the dawn of the new day. The real diamond among the prayer texts of the feast is unquestionably the Benedictus antiphon. In a few, skillfully blended pictures it reveals the unity and beauty of the feast: "Today the Church was wedded with her heavenly Bridegroom, for Christ washed away her sins in the waters of the Jordan; the Magi hasten with gifts to the royal wedding, while the guests make merry with the water made wine, Alleluja." Holy Mother Church gives voice to her innermost thoughts with this classic antiphon to teach us the full significance of the feast of the Epiphany. She has not surpassed this masterpiece of prayer.

She develops the texts from Vespers, Matins, and Lauds in the little hours. The joyous "Alleluja" is added to the responsories. At Prime it is a phrase of the responsory that links the hour's theme to the feast: "Thou who hast appeared today," instead of the usual, "Thou who sittest at the right hand of the Father."

Conclusion. The office of the feast is repeated, with a few variations, all through the octave. At Matins we have the Invitatory: "Christ has appeared to us, come let us adore." Instead of psalm 94 in the third nocturn we find psalm 86. In addition to the special lessons for the octave, there are Magnificat and Benedictus antiphons proper to each day. These amplify the three mystery themes of the feast. The octave closes in the third nocturn for January thirteenth with the Gospel about Jesus' baptism in the Jordan. We should also mention the feast of the Holy Family, introduced in recent years, and celebrated on the Sunday within the octave of the Epiphany. Despite its appeal, this feast scarcely harmonizes with the thoughts and sentiments of the Epiphany. Once a person relives the Epiphany in its liturgy, he finds it hard any more to have a great taste for this feast. There are two worlds here. He can love but one of them.

CHAPTER XVII

Christmas Matins

IT is Christmas night, just about the hour Jesus was born. In the sacred silence of the darkness the Church is praying Matins, making her meditation on the great feast. *Christus natus est nobis* (*"Christ is born to us"*): the solemn Invitatory that opens the office as with a majestic chorus of chimes. These few words telegraph the theme, the leading thought for the feast. Note the "us." Christmas is a warm, almost personal feast for the vast family of Holy Mother Church. *Venite adoremus* (*"Come, let us adore"*); let us join the shepherds and kneel reverently in adoration before our infant God.

Psalm 94 offers an excellent background for the Invitatory. Whatever this psalm says of the God of the Covenant we refer to Christ. Come, let us rejoice. Filled with joy and gladness, we celebrate this feast in company with Jesus, our divine Savior and Redeemer, who is about to begin the work of our redemption. . . . Thus far the introduction. Now the first part of the psalm. This frail and shivering Infant is: (a) the great God and King of the universe, the almighty Creator of the lofty mountains and the vast seas; but (b) even more than that, He is our Savior and Redeemer, the Good Shepherd who pursued His sheep that strayed from heaven. If the first thought fills us with awe, this picture of the Good Shepherd melts our hearts. We fall on our knees before the Infant, for He is our God. In the second part we hear the teaching of

Holy Mother Church. Take these words to heart. "Today," indeed a momentous day that brought with it the dawn of our redemption. "Oh, that today you would hear His voice"; only a heart of flint could turn a deaf ear to the sermon of the Infant in the manger. And yet we Christians are much like our forefathers in the desert. They witnessed the many evidences of God's mercy, and for a time these made some impression on them. But soon their hearts turned to stone. In the desert God was in the midst of His chosen people for forty years. Still they neither knew His ways nor paid any attention to them. God, then, in His wrath swore they should not see the Promised Land. . . . And what about us? Today Jesus became the Emmanuel ("God with us"), not merely for forty years, but for all time, "until the consummation of the world" (Matt. 28:20). Nor do we know His ways any better than did our forefathers in the desert. This thought is a drop of gall to temper the wine of our Christmas joy. It will recur often. For example, in the prologue to his Gospel we hear St. John mention it: "He came to what was His own, and they who were His own gave Him no welcome." [1] "A light shines in darkness, a darkness which was not able to master it" (John 1:5). Such Good Friday thoughts are woven quietly and unobtrusively throughout the entire office of this feast. Was it in vain that Christ came on earth for you? And when He returns at some future date to His kingdom "in holy splendor," will you be numbered among those who knew Him not? Thus the psalm concludes on a serious, almost mournful note. It is as though the Church would tell us that the important thing in her great feasts is not that we should lose ourselves in sentiments of joy and exultation, but that we give true and sincere worship to almighty God, especially by fulfilling

[1] John 1:11.

His holy will. The psalm closes with the usual *Gloria Patri*. As often as we hear this little doxology in the Christmas office, we utter a heartfelt "thank You" to the Most Holy Trinity for the Incarnation. After all, this is a gift of the Holy Trinity: "God so loved the world, that He gave up His only begotten Son." [2]

The hymn, *Jesu Redemptor*, forms a transition from this solemn and rather serious introduction (the Invitatory) to the poetry and reflection of the psalmody. From the pen of St. Ambrose, this lovely hymn tells us the true meaning of Christmas. Beginning with the eternal generation of the Son by the Father (first stanza), it takes us straightway to the crib so that we may petition for favors (second stanza), since there can be no greater claim for favors than the Incarnation: Jesus has assumed our flesh and has consequently become one of us (third stanza). Today we celebrate the birthday of the Lord (fourth stanza), and all His creatures join in a song of praise (fifth stanza). But we, His ransomed children, have the most cause of all to sing His praises (sixth stanza).

Now we take up the psalms, first in a general view of the whole nocturn, then with a detailed study of each psalm, taking into account both the literal sense and its application to this particular feast.

FIRST NOCTURN

Here, in general, the psalms develop the Church's doctrine of the Second Person of the Trinity. Psalm 2 is first, and the eternal birth is its theme. Then in psalm 18 the temporal birth is described. Finally, psalm 44, the wedding hymn, describes the hypostatic union, the marriage in Christ of the two natures, human and divine. The Book of Isaias (Advent preacher

[2] John 3:16.

and evangelist of the Old Testament) furnishes the lessons. These are separated by picturesque and lyrical responsories. Now to study the individual parts.

Psalm 2. This poetic chant comes appropriately from the pen of David. Definitely and directly Messianic, it is a clear instance of the Holy Spirit's guiding the hand of the inspired author. St. Bernard refers to it as "the lion of Juda roaring at the enemy." It is divided into four equally balanced strophes, each with its own distinct thoughts. Note, too, how each strophe presents a different speaker or actor.

Strophe one (1–3): the revolt of God's enemies. (We are in the thick of the uproar.)

Strophe two (4–6): the King of heaven laughs in scorn. (Here the scene changes. God laughs at them from heaven, then the Messiah enters.)

Strophe three (7–9): the Messiah declares His commission. (The Father has made Him the ruler of the world.)

Strophe four (10–13): the Psalmist directs a word of instruction and warning to the kings of earth (and to us).

The scene that the Psalmist describes for us is indeed vivid, and timeless. Now we shall try to apply it to Christmas. The Messiah came into the world as foretold by the prophets. But His people Israel did not hail Him as a triumphant king. The world offered Him nothing, nor did He seek anything of the world. As a penniless babe He entered life, only to meet persecution a few days after His birth. The ancient serpent would wage ceaseless battle against the kingdom of God, especially against its King. The few expressive lines of the psalm's first strophe describe the battle. We cannot help but think of Herod, the first persecutor of Christians. The slaughter of the Holy Innocents is but a phase of the battle we keep before our eyes: hell versus Christ. Somber thoughts like these seem strange companions for the glad, joyous sentiments of Christmas. But they are not to be exaggerated. Today the emphasis is rather on the Redeemer's glorious appearance.

The second strophe contrasts the tumultuous revolt of the earthly kings with the scornful laughter of the King of heaven. That was the prophecy. Even more sublime is the fulfillment, the divine Son begging His Father: "Father, forgive them, for they know not what they do." Full of pity, the Father looks down on poor, blinded mankind: "For God so loved the world as to give it His own Son." No wrath or anger in His approach now, only kindness and love. And now, today, the Son of God enters the world. Poverty stricken ruler of the kingdom of God, already from the manger He proclaims the law of His kingdom. The following verse, however, is the main reason for this psalm's occurring on this feast. It is also the antiphon. "You are My son; this day I have begotten You." Try to read the Church's thoughts, and in this verse you can hear her saying: "This little Infant shivering in the crib is, in very fact, the true Son of God." If "today" He was born as man of the immaculate Virgin, we may truly say too that He was born also of God the Father from all eternity, the "today" which knows no yesterday and no tomorrow. This, then, is the theme of the psalm: a profession of our belief with regard to the Second Person of the Trinity.

Then we hear the Messiah declare His mission. The Father hands over to His Son all power and rule on earth. In vivid perspective we see the universal Church, and the Gentiles seeking admission into the kingdom of God. The sharp, stern strokes of the Old Testament are used to sketch the portrait of the Messiah in this psalm. That was prophecy. The fulfillment is far more excellent. Iron scepter softens into the shepherd's staff, on the cross of the Prince of Peace. Nor did He smash mankind like so much old pottery: "He will not snap the staff that is already crushed, or put out the wick that still smolders." [3] In the fourth strophe, from His pulpit in the crib, the divine Infant preaches a sermon to mankind: I have come to serve, not to rule. "Serve the Lord with fear, and rejoice before Him." Yield now, and listen to the Infant of Bethlehem. He comes this time as a little lamb, the "friend of sinners." At the end of the world, however, He will come as a roaring lion, to be our judge.

We have no difficulty in regarding this psalm as an appropriate meditation before the crib. The theme we saw outlined in the antiphon: Christ, born of the Father from all eternity; born in time, of the Virgin Mary.

Clouds of hatred of God and eternal judgment shroud psalm 2, but the next psalm is radiant with light. Psalm 18 is a "sun-hymn" in praise of the law of God; a parable on the sun. A view of the psalm, first in its literal sense, discloses two distinct parts. Commentators are not certain whether these parts were originally two separate hymns afterward combined for some reason, or whether they were intentionally united by the author, but only loosely related to each other. Actually the parts have entirely different ideas. The first is a lyrical nature song that reaches its climax in a vivid description of the sun. The second part is a hymn in praise of the Law. The psalm is practical for us, nevertheless, as we have it, so that we may well consider it a unit, a parable on the sun. The image is outlined in the first part. The second contrasts it with the Law, and applies the ideas to us. Note that the two parts are separated in the Psalter for weekday recitation. If you think the combination too artificial, then consider them as separate psalms.

[3] Matt. 12:20; Isa. 42:3.

Part One (1–7): The parable on the sun.
        (1–4): Creation praising God.
        (5–7): The sun, as a giant and the bridegroom.
Part Two (8–16): Explanation of the parable: the Law.
        (8–11): In praise of the Law (the moral code).
        (12–14): Application: I shall observe the Law.
Conclusion (15–16): Dedication of the hymn to God.

How can we sing this psalm at the crib? The antiphon provides the answer: Christ, the giant and the bridegroom. The comparison suggested is magnificent. At dawn the sun climbs the brilliant stairs of the rosy sky. Like a bride it is, adorned in shining jewels and radiant with joy, leaving the bridal chamber. But "like a giant" it pursues its course, boldly, relentlessly on, up to its zenith. Finally, blood-red, down it sinks into the west. Nothing can escape its warmth. Christ is the divine Sun. "He was the true light." [4] "I am the light of the world." [5] What the sun is for the earth, Christ is for our soul: light (truth), warmth (love), life (grace), joy and peace. Without the sun nothing but darkness, freezing cold and death, would be ours. Without Christ we have spiritual darkness, estrangement from God, and spiritual death. Christ, our Sun, our Bridegroom; indeed the long awaited Spouse of all mankind. The Old Testament favors this figure of God's marriage with His chosen people, Christ has given it an even deeper significance. He is the true Spouse of mankind, of the Church, and of the individual soul.

In this figure we find what is, perhaps, Christianity's sublimest feature: intensely intimate union with Christ: "and yet I am alive; or rather, not I; it is Christ that lives in me." Today, on this feast of Christmas, Christ celebrates what you might call His "betrothal" to mankind. Today divinity and humanity

[4] John 1:9.
[5] John 8:12.

have made an inviolable pact in Jesus the God-man. When "like a giant" the divine Sun reaches the heights of His course, the hill of Calvary, then He will celebrate the wedding with His own precious blood. Today, however, we see Him as the Bridegroom leaving the bridal chamber (antiphon). Thus the Church, in profound but tender symbolism, describes His birth from the immaculate womb of the Virgin Mary. A Christmas Preface found in the Leonine Sacramentary [6] shows that this symbolism dates even from the early years of the Church. Behold then, Christian soul, your divine Spouse, lying in the manger.

Christ is also the divine "giant-like" Sun, joyously, irresistibly pursuing His course (the path of our redemption) over the face of the earth. "Do you wish to know where this Sun comes from? He comes from heaven into His Mother's womb, from there to the manger, from the manger to the cross, from the cross to the tomb, and from the tomb He returns to heaven." [7] "He came to spread fire over the earth," and "who can escape its heat?"

Of but minor importance to our feast are the thoughts and ideas of the second part of the psalm. Still they allow of some application. In the Old Testament, the spiritual sun was the Law. In the New Testament, it is the Gospel, the teachings of Christ. Though it is a struggle for the Psalmist to find words adequate to praise the perfection, purity, and sanctity of the Old Law, his terms are even more inadequate when referred to Christ's Gospel, pure and immaculate, full of light and joy, holy, sweet as honey, more precious than gold or costly gems. And today, from the crib, we hear Christ's first sermon: "Blessed are the poor, the lowly, the suffering, the meek, and

[6] *LM.* 55, p. 148.
[7] St. Gregory, homily 29.

the humble." But let us keep in mind that all this is secondary. The birth of our divine Sun and Spouse is the important thought.

It was for the second psalm to heighten the sentiments of the first, while the third, in its turn, performs the same office for the second psalm.

Psalm 44: the nuptial song of the divine Bridegroom. Literally interpreted, this is a wedding psalm that first sings of the royal bridegroom, then of the bride. Whether it was originally a profane wedding song composed for King Solomon and an Egyptian princess does not particularly concern us. For us it is a Messianic hymn that celebrates the wedding of Christ with His Spouse, the Church and the soul. Such it was considered in the synagogue, and in the early Church; it was called the "canticle" of the psalms.[8] Its divisions are evident.

The theme. Two main divisions: the king, the queen.

Introduction (1–2)
  I The king:
    a) his beauty and grace (3);
    b) his courage and bravery (4–7). The psalmist pictures the king clad in shining armor, mounting his chariot; he shouts a wish of "good luck" to him: "Ride on triumphant, in the cause of truth and for the sake of justice";
    c) his virtue and justice (8–9);
    d) his magnificent appearance (10).

  II The queen:
    a) leaving her own home (11–13);

[8] So called perhaps because of its similarity in idea with the Canticle of Canticles. Tr.

b) her beauty and wealth (14–16);

c) her children (17–18).

What purpose does this psalm serve in the Christmas office? What is its message? The wedding. We can distinguish three stages in Christ's marriage with mankind. The first is His incarnation by means of the conception and birth. In this, so to speak, human nature was wedded with the divine nature in the person of the divine Word. The second stage followed on Calvary, where Christ redeemed and reunited mankind to God. (Redemption and reunion were realized in the individual soul by baptism and the infusion of sanctifying grace.) Through this grace that makes men children of God, He gave Himself in marriage to the souls of men. The final, perfect union of the Church and the soul with the divine Bridegroom in heaven is the third stage.

St. John described this vividly in the Apocalypse: "I, John, saw in my vision that holy city which is the new Jerusalem, being sent down by God from heaven, like a bride who has adorned herself to meet her husband." [9] Psalm 44, the nuptial hymn, sings of this triple marriage. The second stage, however, lends itself best to our feast, so that we can readily view the psalm as referring to it as we kneel before the crib. Even at that, the Church's first wish in this psalm, in my opinion, is to accentuate the thoughts that deal with the marriage of humanity to the divinity of Jesus. Then we would view the King decked out in his armor and royal insignia as the person of the divine Logos, the divinity of Jesus. The queen is His sacred humanity, raised to its lofty dignity by this union, from which there springs this progeny: redeemed mankind. It is true that such a thought offers too many difficulties to those who may be unskilled in theology. We may be inclined, then,

[9] Apoc. 21:1 ff.

to keep to the previous idea of Christ as the Bridegroom, and the Church or the soul as the bride.

Let the psalm accordingly be our bridal serenade before the crib of the Infant. We can imagine ourselves to be St. Francis of Assisi, and on his lips we can put our hymn to the divine Spouse. My soul, in this hymn renew your promise of fidelity and love to the divine Infant, your Bridegroom, as He called Himself.[10] Indeed, one must have the love of a St. Francis for the Infant to appreciate this hymn properly. Even its opening words spring from the very heart. Now the king and queen enter the scene. I paint as lovely a picture of the Savior as I can. Today it is a beautiful Babe, "the lovely little Boy with curly hair." [11] The psalm itself suggests the picture. First it describes the beauty of Jesus:

> "Fairer in beauty are You than the sons of men;
> grace is poured out upon Your lips;
> thus God has blessed You forever."

That is today's theme, as we saw in the antiphon. The Church wishes us to dwell awhile on the charm and beauty of the divine Child. Indeed, the picture has a winning charm; the eternal, changeless beauty of God wrapped in human flesh, and that, the flesh of a little Infant. But this Infant grows in stature before our very eyes. Now we see Him as a valiant warrior, fighting God's battles down through the centuries. How many fell victim to His love! And, as is to be expected, this mystery of Christmas has softened even the hardest of hearts. Reluctantly we shift our gaze from the Infant to give our attention to the bride, that is, to ourselves. We listen to the proposal. It is satisfactory; we become the new bride. Today,

[10] Matt. 9:15.
[11] From the German original of *Silent Night*.

on the feast of Christmas, God's grace stands at my door, seeking my hand. For there must be a wedding of grace with our free wills if we are to beget spiritual offspring, that is, good works.

With the repetition of the antiphon we turn our thoughts again for a moment to the wonderful Child, our Bridegroom. Even though the three psalms differ in sentiment and ideas, they are directed to a single theme, the birth of Jesus: psalm 2, where God, born of all eternity, is born now in time; psalm 18, the divine Sun, the Bridegroom leaving the bridal chamber; psalm 44, the marriage of God and man in the person of the new-born Child.

The versicle summarizes the trio of psalms. It is a repetition of the second antiphon: the Bridegroom leaving the bridal chamber.

The lessons follow now. In these God speaks to us by the mouth of Isaias, the evangelist of the Old Testament. During Advent the lessons from Isaias followed in regular order from day to day. But for this feast, the Church selects three detached, unrelated passages from the prophet. Each, then, has its own application to the feast.

The first lesson is from the famous "Emmanuel" passage.[12] The particular section chosen (9:1–6) is a separate, self-contained poem. Its general theme is the restoration of God's kingdom by Christ.

In the introduction the prophet recounts how the territory of the two tribes of Zabulon and Nepthali (afterward Galilee) had been degraded by the incursion of the Gentiles, so much so that the people even referred to it as "the land of the Gentiles." But the time would come when this region would lift its head in pride and honor. (Christ spent most of His

---

[12] Chaps. 7–12.

time teaching and healing in Galilee.) In the darkness that shrouds the pagan world a great light appears, the Messianic Sun.[13] The splendid strokes of the prophet depict the Messianic era, the time of lasting joy and peace. Joy shall reign as great as that of the harvest time, or like that of jubilant victors dividing the spoils. Here the prophet turns his thoughts back to the captivity in Babylon. He sees his people under the yoke, driven along by the captor's lash. But then the Messiah smashes the heavy yoke and the fetters that bind His people. From the story of our redemption we know that the prophet speaks here of our release from the chains and fetters of Satan. There shall be no war in the kingdom of the Messiah, no place for blood-stained garments. There shall be only peace, the eternal peace of God. We Christians understand that this peace foretold by the prophet is not external and material, but a true, spiritual, interior peace that fills the souls of the children of God. The main verse of the poem follows (the reason for its selection), the classical passage: "For a child is born to us, and a son is given to us, and the government is upon his shoulders: and his name shall be called, Wonderful, Counsellor, God the Mighty, The Father of the World to Come, the Prince of Peace."

We picture the prophet lost in reverie before the crib, gazing joyfully on the Child. But this Child grows before his very eyes, and now the sacred writer searches for names and titles to bear the burden of describing the majesty, the greatness of the Child.

The responsory is heard like an echo to the lesson. This is the place for the soul to ponder well the words of the lesson and then to give voice to the sentiments of the heart. This is the fulfillment of the prophecy: "A child is born to us." Why

[13] Ps. 18.

have we such a long responsory here? It is because in this passage the Church wishes to sing of the exact moment of Christ's birth. She tells us to picture to ourselves this great miracle; the veil of the profound mystery is removed. Today, at this very moment, the prophecy is fulfilled: the King of heaven is born of the Virgin. A few words declare the purpose of Christ's incarnation: to reinstate exiled mankind in the kingdom of heaven. Thus the explanation of the prophecy as told in the lesson. The scene opens further now. We see the joyous choirs of angels rejoicing over the redemption of mankind. We hear their song float over the plains, the Infant's lullaby: "Glory to God in the highest, and on earth, peace to men of good will." Is not this the reason for Christ's coming and the program of His life? Twice more the responsory repeats the scene, in the very same words, as though we would turn from it only with reluctance.

The second lesson is taken from the second part of the Book of Isaias. This begins with chapter 38 and contains the prophet's consolations foretold for the exiles in Babylon.

Chapter 40 treats of the fact that God definitely and surely decreed the redemption of Israel. Two distinct thoughts are in this second lesson: (a) the announcement of the Redemption (40:1–5); (b) the world is transitory, only God is eternal and immutable (40:6–8). We might consider each thought as developed by the prophet in a sort of hymn. The first hymn: literally, the prophet is promising the release from the Babylonian captivity. But looking much farther ahead, God speaks in these verses of the redemption of mankind by Jesus Christ. It is as though He would say: "Be comforted, be comforted, mankind; your misery is come to an end, your guilt is forgiven, you have received double from the hand of the Lord for all your sins." Thus the prophet declares the full significance of the redemption. The captivity under Satan, much worse than the exile in Babylon, has come to an end. Adam's guilt and our own personal guilt are both wiped away by Christ's death on the cross. In place of our sins a double measure of grace was given, so that on Holy Saturday the Church can well sing: "O happy fault, that brought us such a wonderful Redeemer!" Today this happiness has begun, with the birth of that Redeemer, as we heard in the angels' hymn.

The prophet then describes a scene for us. From the desert to the east the Redeemer-King is entering the land of the Jews. A herald (the voice of one crying) precedes and warns the people to prepare the way for the Messiah: "Every valley shall be filled and every hill brought low; the crooked way shall be made straight, and the rough ways smooth." Then the glory of the Lord; the Redeemer Himself makes His entrance, and all mankind shall see Him. We are familiar with this famous passage about preparing the way for the Messiah. We know this preparation is a spiritual one to be accomplished especially by penance. The hills are sins of commission, and must be leveled away; the valleys are sins of omission, and must be filled in. And lo! Today the prophecy is fulfilled. The glory of the Lord is revealed in the little Infant, and we men can behold Him with our own eyes. The second "hymn" in the lesson, in contrast to the God who came to serve us, describes the misery and frailty of mankind, an effect of sin. To blend this idea with the thoughts and sentiments of the feast, we need but think of the infant Jesus freely assuming this miserable nature to give it new dignity, new glory, and a share in His own immortality. Simple and straightforward, this description of man's frailty is indeed quite moving.

The responsory is, again, flowing over with joy. "*Hodie*" is the opening word for three of its phrases. "Today" the true peace came down from heaven; "today" the heavens rained down honey over the whole earth. (In a brief pause here, the Church recalls the promised land of Canaan, flowing with milk and honey, a type of the kingdom of God, flowing with the superabundant graces Christ brought from heaven.) "Today" dawned the day of the new redemption, the day of restoration to our former glory, the day of eternal happiness. We cannot help but hark back to the lesson: Your misery is come to an end; your guilt is forgiven. For your sins you have received double from the hand of the Lord.

The third lesson.[14] This too is a separate passage. Jerusalem, the humbled widow, is summoned to rise from the dust, to throw off her chains, to don her bridal robes; for the day of her release from exile is near. What a splendid picture and prophecy of mankind's longing for its redemption! As though the Church would say: "Yes, O mankind; you who lie in the dust, in the shackles of sin, disgraced and humiliated by sin, cast off those shackles and put on your festive garments. The day of your redemption by Jesus Christ is at hand. And what a price was paid for that redemption from Satan! No cost more dear. The price was the precious blood of Christ. The yoke of the evil one lay heavy on the human race. But now, from the crib the Redeemer cries aloud: 'See, here I am.' "

The responsory follows naturally on the last words of the lesson. First witnesses of the great event are the shepherds. Filled with emotion and excitement, we fling our questions at them: "Shepherds, tell us what you have seen. We have seen the little Infant and the choirs of angels singing praises to the Lord." This is a touching, pastoral "drama" enacted in the office of the sacred feast, the beginning of the Christmas plays popular especially during the Middle Ages.

[14] Isa. 52:1–6.

SECOND NOCTURN

Whereas the first nocturn meditated on the birth of our Lord, the second deals rather with the things Christ brought to earth: His kingdom, peace, salvation, and reconciliation with God.

As I pray the first antiphon I picture myself kneeling with outstretched arms here in God's house on Christmas night, waiting for God to put the divine Infant in my arms. Filled with joy, eager longing, and gratitude, "we receive, O God, here in Thy temple, Thy (incarnate) mercy."

Psalm 47. This is a hymn of thanksgiving for the deliverance of "our God's city" from the attack of the enemy. Though besieged by the foe, the city is delivered through the wonderful intervention of God. The psalm can readily be divided into four balanced strophes.

First strophe (1–4): God, the great protector of the holy city; the strongly fortified city.

Second strophe (5–8): God delivers the city. Enemy kings besiege the city; a vivid description of their sudden defeat, climaxed in the picture of a raging storm at sea, with God's sudden intervention, and the utter destruction of the enemy.

Third strophe (9–12): prayer of thanksgiving in the temple for the marvelous deliverance.

Fourth strophe (13–15): In thanksgiving, the citizens walk in procession around the city, observing that the defenses are still intact.

In the liturgy we usually apply this psalm to the invincible stability of Christ's Church. We might entitle it with the words of Christ Himself: "The gates of hell shall not prevail against it." For adaptation to our feast of Christmas, however, this psalm is more difficult than the others. In the last two lessons there was mention of the exaltation of Jerusalem. We might, then, make the following application. Along with that of her great "King" Jesus Christ, the "city of God" (the Church) is celebrating her own birthday too. The stable with the shepherds is a foretype of the Church. Note St. Ambrose' words in the eighth lesson: "Behold the beginning of the new Church!"

Great indeed is the Lord lying in the manger. Though He whimpers like a helpless babe, nonetheless He is the One who can fill kings with fear and trembling like that of one giving birth, and who can also smash their ships to pieces. Today too, a great joy floods the plains of Bethlehem, the city of the great King who is the son of David. Turning now to the enemies who lay siege to God's city, the Psalmist conjures up a few scenes from Good Friday. Herod was forerunner of all those tyrants who lay siege to Christ and His Church, and they all share the fate described in the psalm. How true it is that what Christ begins to build today (on the first Christmas), He establishes for all eternity!

Yet if we study the antiphon, we find that the Church does not wish to exaggerate this somber theme. Instead, she stretches out her arms lovingly to the Infant in the manger: "We gratefully accept this, the greatest grace God can give us, and we gladly sing Thy praises." Today indeed, there is true joy on Mount Sion. All Thy people rejoice over Thy marvelous ways, especially for Thy decree of redemption that brought us the Infant in the crib. If we were to take a stroll "around the walls of God's city" today, after 1900 years, we would find them still intact, impervious to the assaults of hell. In a spirit of joyous faith we profess: our God, the Infant of Bethlehem, lives, moves, and rules in His Church.

Psalm 71. Though the application of the first psalm was not

easy, the second (psalm 71), the psalm on the three Magi, is a genuine Christmas hymn, and directly Messianic.

Its theme:

1. Longing for the Messiah (1–3);

2. Justice and peace, characteristics of the Messiah (4–7);

3. His rule shall have no end (8–11);

4. He shall be a father to the poor (12–14);

5. The prosperity and abundance of His kingdom (15–17);

6. Conclusion: a tribute of praise (18, 19). This verse also concludes the second book of psalms.

Psalm 71 is the answer to what shall become of this Infant. Here is that answer: He is the King of Peace, the Distributor of Justice, the Father of the Poor. It is the development of this theme that makes it appropriate to pray this Messianic psalm before the crib of the child Jesus: Jesus, You are the one who shall restore justice on earth. Through the Redemption mankind can once more appear justified before God, and justice returns to the world. Man is seeking peace, and peace it is that You offer him, peace with God, with himself, and with his fellow men. For in Your kingdom two special flowers have bloomed: "The mountains shall yield peace for the people, and the hills justice." Without any display of earthly splendor, quietly and softly, like the dew settling on the grass, You came down on earth. You are that gentle, penetrating rain, too, that the prophets foretold for the dry and waterless earth: "Drop down the Just One like dew, ye heavens; ye clouds, let Him descend like the rain." Poor and small though You are here in the manger, Your kingdom shall have no limit in time or place. All peoples shall serve You, for the Magi from the East, already on their way to Bethlehem, are nothing more than the forerunners of the Gentiles who are to come to Christ. In the persons of the three Magi the whole world bends its knee in reverence before the crib. Friend and protector of the poor You are, the poor Infant of Bethlehem who have chosen poverty as Your bride. And yet You remain and You make others immeasurably rich. The abundance of Your graces surpasses that of the vast, billowy grain fields, especially the grace of the living bread: the gift of Your own body and blood. Bethlehem means "house of bread" (see the seventh lesson from St. Gregory). Let us keep in mind the theme stressed in the antiphon: Jesus, the King of Peace.

Psalm 84. Though the people have returned from exile, their hopes for a period of prosperity have not yet been fulfilled. To cheer up his people the Psalmist foretells the kingdom of peace that the Messiah will establish.

The division:

Strophe one: a) The exile comes to an end (2–4);
b) New trials and hardships (5–8).
Strophe two: a) The help that is to come (9, 10);
b) The kingdom of peace (11–14).

Psalm 84 is most appropriate for this feast. We can readily pray it kneeling before the crib: "Today, O God, through the birth of Your Son, You have removed the curse that lay on the earth and You have filled it with Your blessings. You have overthrown the dreadful tyranny of the prince of this world. You have extinguished the fire of Your wrath and have forgiven the sins of mankind." It is true that all this actually happened only on the cross, but we can still say that our redemption began in the crib on the first Christmas. The following half-strophe is a petition that the redemption may be realized and applied subjectively to each of us: Savior, turn now to help me. Merely a glance of Yours from the crib can give me new life, and my heart shall once more rejoice in You. (This verse recurs again tonight at Mass in the prayers at the foot of the altar.) And now I lean close to the Infant, and His sweet whisper falls upon my ear: Peace be to you. "He will speak of peace to His people." "Near indeed is His salvation"; rejoice you children of men, "for His glory (is) dwelling in our land." "God's fidelity to His promises (the Savior Himself) has sprouted over night like the flower from the stalk of Jesse. Appeased now for the first time since the fall of Adam, divine Justice (the Father) looks down graciously on man from His throne in heaven." This is also the antiphon. St. Bernard developed with beauty and skill in one of his sermons the striking parable that this passage (vv. 11, 12) suggests.[15] As long as Adam dwelt in the Garden of Paradise, the four "sisters" remained amicably with him: mercy, fidelity, justice, and peace. But after Adam's sin a quarrel arose, especially between mercy and justice. Mercy sought for pity and forgiveness from God. Justice demanded strict punishment of the fault. On and on the quarrel went until finally God's Son, "the wise Solomon," pronounced the decree that both justice and mercy were to be right. "I will become man and atone for man's sins on the cross." All heaven was in wonder at words of such profound wisdom, and here before the crib the quarrelling sisters were reconciled. At emnity since the day of Adam's fall, today justice and mercy embraced and exchanged a kiss of reconciliation. And at the Messiah's entrance into the world, "justice shall go before him as a herald, and peace shall follow in his footsteps."

This is certainly a masterly Christmas hymn. In the antiphon the Church makes it clear that on this feast especially she would emphasize these ideas of peace and justice.

The versicle, from psalm 44, is full of admiration for the

[15] Migne, *PL*, CXCIII, 383 ff.

beauty of the Infant: "Fairer in beauty are You than the sons of men."

The lessons follow with a sermon dating from the early years of the Church. Our preacher is the great Pope Leo I. Time and again his eloquence roused the hearts of the Roman faithful to joy and gladness during the fifth century. His sermon gives us an inkling of what sermons were like in those centuries of strong, burning faith.

The fourth responsory, following naturally on the fourth lesson, voices the Church's amazement. Lying in a manger here between brute beasts is God's own Son. What a mystery! According to God's plan man was to rule over the beasts of the earth. But by sin, Satan, disguised in the form of a beast (the serpent), dragged man down to the level of the beasts: "He resembles the beasts that perish." [16] Then to lift man up again from his sin, down from heaven came the second Adam into a stable for animals. Now the ox and the ass warm His shivering members with their breath.

The second part of the responsory is a song of praise to the Mother of God, continued in the three following responsories. The sermon proceeds in the fifth lesson, describing the battle Christ wages with Satan for our redemption. On strictly equal terms this battle is to be fought. Christ meets the prince of the world not in all His divine majesty, but as the God-man, a man without sin. For His birth as man God chose the royal Virgin of the family of David, and by the ministry of an angel He revealed to her the fact of her immaculate, virginal motherhood.

At Rome in ancient times a special ceremony accompanied the reading of this lesson. On this holy night the pope used to

[16] Ps. 48:13.

consecrate the helmet and sword of some Christian knight. Led forward to the pope, this knight unsheathes his sword, lays his helmet on the lectern, and puts on the cope over his suit of mail. He then proceeds to sing the lesson. (This fifth lesson is apt since it treats of Christ's battle with Satan.) This ancient custom took its origin in an age that still offered the sword for God's service, an age when physical force and power were tempered by the laws of morality.

The fifth responsory dovetails with the preceding lesson. The sixth lesson is a passage taken from the conclusion of the sermon. It is a joyful prayer of gratitude for our redemption: "We have been given new life in Christ, and in Him have been made new creatures." There is likewise a sober admonition to be mindful of our dignity. We are sharers in God's own nature, members of Christ's body. Lessons like this reflect the strong faith of the early Church.

The sixth responsory is a song of praise of Mary's virginity and divine maternity.

THIRD NOCTURN

This third nocturn is rather long. Though psalm 88 is for the most part appropriate, treating, as it does, of the Redeemer's human descent from David, and of the kingdom of the Messiah, yet we would prefer to have the psalm abridged, especially since the last part is a misfit in the Christmas office. The other two psalms (95 and 97) sing the praises of God's kingdom.

Psalm 88. This psalm is a lament over the downfall of the royal house of David. It is a typical Oriental prayer. When an Oriental seeks a favor, he begins by expressing his gratitude for past kindnesses. Only then does he make his request. The psalm dates from a very sad era in the history of the chosen people, perhaps the period of exile. The Psalmist's effort to instill new courage into his depressed people has him turning their thoughts to the promise God made of old to King David and his posterity: that the theocratic throne should remain in the house and family of David forever. As a result, this yet unfulfilled promise is the chief motive of the petition for the restoration of the kingdom. The division of the psalm is fairly evident:

1. The motive for the request, God's kindness to David (1–36):

   a) Praise of God's fidelity and mercy (1–5);

   b) The choir reflects on God's magnificence manifested both in the realm of nature and in the history of mankind (6–19);

   c) God's promise to David (theme of the whole psalm) (20–38).

2. Description of the present situation: the distress of the royal house (39–46).

3. Plea for the fulfillment of the promise (47–53).

Now how can we apply this psalm to our feast? The promise God made to King David is its theme, and the main reason for its choice. When the Church sings this hymn to the Infant in the crib, it is as though she would say: Today this promise has been fulfilled in Christ the Son of David, as the angel had foretold: "The Lord God will give Him the throne of His father David, and He shall reign over the house of Jacob eternally; His kingdom shall never have an end." [17] Thus we pray the psalm on Christmas night. The very first verses mention God's promise to David, and God's mercy and fidelity too. As we kneel quietly before the crib, the thought strikes us: Where can there be any greater proof of God's

[17] Luke 1:32 f.

mercy and fidelity than is seen here in the crib, the first act in the great drama of our redemption? God is certainly true to His word. In Jesus Christ, every promise from the prot-evangelium onward is fulfilled. Even though men may have proved faithless to Him, God still was merciful. Indeed, Christ is God's mercy and fidelity incarnate. These two virtues, mercy and fidelity, are mentioned seven times in this psalm. As soon as he finishes the introduction, the Psalmist sings of God's grandeur as it is reflected in nature and in mankind. It is not hard to make this passage our tribute of homage to the divine Infant. There in a straw-filled manger lies the great and infinite God. "The heavens proclaim Your wonders, O Lord, and Your faithfulness, in the assembly of the holy ones." O divine Infant, "O Lord, God of hosts, who is like You?" Your tiny hands "rule over the surging of the sea." They hold this earth as if it were a nutshell. With a single, tiny breath You snuff out the lives of the kings of the earth. Yours are the heavens, Yours the earth. North and South are the work of Your hands. Thabor and Hermon, the loftiest peaks, sing their tribute of praise and joy to You today. Mercy and fidelity are Your heralds. Happy the people who can kneel with joyous hearts before Your crib to pay their homage and to linger for a while in the radiant light of Your countenance.

Only now, however, comes the main thought. God's prom-ise to David has been kept to its fullest extent. First of all, God chose David from among his people, anointed him with oil, guided and protected him in all his pursuits, routed all his enemies. He made David the ruler of a kingdom. David was allowed to call God his Father; God spoke of David as His first-born son, raised to a dignity greater than that of all the kings of the earth. Do not these very words show that, in guid-ing the sacred author, the Holy Spirit had in mind the great

Son of David, Jesus Christ? Only in our Savior were all these verses fulfilled in their entirety. He alone could truly call God His Father in the proper sense; Him alone could the Father truly call His first-born Son. This is the thought that the Church selects for the antiphon in today's office. The same holds true of the promise God made to the royal house, to the descendants of David. His posterity was to possess the throne forever. In fact, even were David's sons to prove faithless to God, though He would punish their fault, He would not break His covenant with David. On solemn and sacred oath God assured him that his throne should remain forever.

When the Jews in exile took up the following lamentation about the downfall of the royal family of David, they were maintaining that in David's human posterity the promise certainly had not been fulfilled. David's descendants lost the actual earthly rule forever. Though from the Psalmist this "unfulfilled promise" evokes a sad lamentation and petition, for us it is a happy confirmation of the fact that the promise was made not in view of David's earthly children, but in view of the great Son of David, the Savior Jesus Christ. As the angel Gabriel expressly announced, in Him God's promise found its literal fulfillment. The last section of the psalm, then, the laments and petitions, fit but loosely into the structure of our office. (Of course, the fact that the Church incorporates an entire psalm into an office need not mean that every part of the psalm have an equally important bearing on the feast.) When we sing this psalm now before the Infant's crib, we may apply it to our redemption from the exile of sin. The psalm, then, is like our last ardent Advent cry for the Messiah. And today this cry is answered. Israel's oppressors scoffed at the "tardiness of the anointed one" (Christ, the Messiah). Today He is here. Nonetheless, in the interest of the unity of our

Christmas Matins, I would prefer to see the last two parts (vv. 39–53) omitted.

The last two psalms bring Matins to a joyous close. They are songs of joy and exultation over the new-born King. All the faithful, the Gentiles, and nature itself, are invited to greet the Infant in the manger. Both psalms are easy for us to understand.

Psalm 95 is one of the "royal" psalms, and well balanced in both strophe and contents. In the following translation the general divisions of thought are indicated at the left of the text.

Psalm 95

God's people:
1 Sing to the Lord a new song;
    sing to the Lord, all you lands.
2 Sing to the Lord; bless his name;
    announce his salvation day after day.
3 Tell his glory among the nations;
    among all peoples, his wondrous deeds.

II

Motive:
4 For great is the Lord and highly to be praised;
    awesome is he beyond all gods.
5 For all the gods of the nations are things of naught,
    but the Lord made the heavens.
6 Splendor and majesty go before him;
    praise and grandeur are in his sanctuary.

III

The Gentiles:
7 Give to the Lord, you families of nations,
    give to the Lord glory and praise;

8   give to the Lord the glory due his name.
Bring gifts, and enter his courts;
9   worship the Lord in holy attire.
Tremble before him, all the earth;

The motive: 10   Say among the nations: The Lord is
King;
He has made the world firm, not to be
moved;
he governs the peoples with equity.

IV

Nature: 11 Let the heavens be glad and the earth rejoice;
let the sea and what fills it resound;
12   let the plains be joyful and all that is in
them.
Motive: Then shall all the trees of the forest exult
13   before the Lord, for he comes;
for he comes to rule the earth.
He shall rule the world with justice
and the peoples with his constancy.

Thus the psalm. Note the three categories: God's chosen
people sing; the Gentiles bring gifts; nature rejoices. Each
time the motive is given: God is great; God is the King; God is
the Judge. Finally, note the effect of the triple repetition: sing,
bring, rejoice.

Now to apply the psalm to our feast. In a way we can call
this psalm the Christmas-tree hymn of the Psalter. The antiphon is striking. It is as though the angels were peering down
curiously from heaven, fascinated with what they saw. And on
earth at the sight of the new-born Child, both men and nature
stand enthralled, with hearts full of joy. A "new hymn" is to

be sung now, for the Old Covenant has come to an end: *recedant vetera, nova sint omnia voces, corda et opera* ("let the old withdraw; let all things be renewed, our words, our hearts and our works"). We the faithful are the first invited to greet the divine Infant, "the great God." Then the Gentiles are called. They already long for the redemption, and in the person of the Magi are even now on their way to Bethlehem. "Say among the nations: The Lord (this Child) is king." (In the early and even Middle Ages, the words *a ligno* used to be added to the verse *Dominus regnat.* . . . The verse, then, was construed to mean: "Tell the Gentiles that the Lord reigns on the wood." Of course the words applied to the wood of the cross, but we can refer them to the wood of the crib.) Inanimate creation also has its greeting for the Redeemer. It too yearns for release from the curse incurred because of man's sin.[18] The Psalmist offers a picturesque account of nature's paying homage to the Infant. Heaven and earth, the sea and the plains, all bow in reverence to their Lord. Around Bethlehem (and our own cities, too) on this holy night a whisper rustles through the leaves of the trees: "He comes to rule the earth." And that tree heard the fearful message too, which thirty-three years later was to furnish the beams of His cross.

Psalm 97. This is divided similarly into three strophes, the first referring to God's people, the second to the Gentiles, and the third to inanimate creation. Though it is the classic Christmas psalm, structurally it is not as beautiful as psalm 95. We can pray it with the same sentiments as those of the preceding psalm. The antiphon voices its joy with a double Alleluia, rejoicing that today God has announced "His salvation," our redemption, and has revealed the Savior to us. Truly He has done "wonderful things," the mercy and fidelity of God. Today

18 Rom. 8:22.

all the world can gaze on the Savior. The King, it is true, came to judge, but in a way entirely different from what we expected. He came not to punish, but to heal and to redeem.

The versicle repeats the antiphon for psalm 88: Christ is the only-begotten Son of the Father.

Once more we have a trio of lessons and, as is usual, this third nocturn offers an explanation of a passage from the Scriptures. However, since at Christmas three different Masses are said, their three Gospels are but briefly explained. We hear the comments of three eminent Fathers of the Church: Gregory the Great, Ambrose, and Augustine.

In the seventh lesson St. Gregory treats of the edict of Emperor Caesar Augustus. In the Middle Ages this lesson used to be read when the German emperors visited Rome. Accompanied by two cardinals, the emperor approached the Holy Father. Clad in a cope and girt with a sword, he listened while the lesson was read. Afterward he kissed the foot of the Holy Father. This custom was observed even as late as 1468 by Kaiser Frederick III.

From St. Gregory's homily we learn that even at his time (c. 600) three Masses were celebrated at Christmas. The lesson's three main thoughts have a strong appeal: the book of life, the house of bread, and Jesus, born "on the road," that is, away from home.

The seventh responsory repeats the praises of Mary's divine maternity and invites the Gentiles to join in the praise of the Savior. The second part came from the Greek liturgy.

The eighth lesson is a passage from St. Ambrose's homily on the "shepherd" Gospel.

The last responsory is not, as we might expect, an echo of the preceding lesson, but rather a prelude to the lesson that follows. (Something akin to the position of the Alleluja in the

Mass liturgy.) It is the climax to the prologue of St. John's Gospel which we read daily at Mass: "And the Word was made flesh and came to dwell among us." Tonight the Logos, the Second Person of the Blessed Trinity, has become "flesh" (that is, man) and (according to the Greek) pitched His tent on earth. Now we behold the majesty of God in this frail Infant, full of grace and truth. This Child is the almighty Creator of the universe: words so profound that we can never hope to plumb the depths of their meaning.

The last lesson is concerned with the prologue to St. John's Gospel. It is an explanation from the lips of the great philosopher, St. Augustine. From the very words of the prologue he proves that the Word, the Second Divine Person, is not, as the Arians maintained, a creature of the Father, but is uncreated and, in fact, is He through whom all things were created. For the rest, the lesson is rather difficult to understand, not to mention its being also rather heavy and dull for the Christmas office.

Matins closes with the solemn chant of the Te Deum, and the oration for the feast.

We might summarize our whole consideration of the Christmas Matins by saying that it is a masterpiece of prayer art, outstanding in its simple clarity and vigor of expression. The psalms are in splendid harmony with the theme and leading thoughts of the feast. Especially well chosen are the antiphons, so much so that by themselves they provide a beautiful Christmas meditation. Finally, the responsories are vivid and picturesque, and in general the lessons are of excellent caliber.

CHAPTER XVIII

The Pre-Lenten and Lenten Office

THE PRE-LENTEN OFFICE

WE speak of Septuagesima, Sexagesima, and Quinquagesima Sundays as the pre-Lenten period. They form a transition from the joy of the post-Christmas cycle to the sober penitence of the Lenten season. But in relation to Lent, or better still to Easter, these three weeks are, as a matter of fact, more a preparation. You might call this three-week period the antechamber of the Lenten season. The liturgy for these three Sundays is particularly beautiful and artistic in structure. This is true of the Mass liturgy especially. Although the Office here cannot match the lyric poetry of the Advent season, still there are features worth our noting.

Matins opens with a special Invitatory: "Let us come before His presence with thanksgiving; and make a joyful noise to Him with psalms." [1] It is thus the liturgy informs us that these three weeks are a period of preparation for the serious penance to come, so that it is important to rise a little earlier than usual. In Matins throughout this pre-Lenten period there are two focal points on which converge all the thoughts and ideas of the Office: the patriarch and the Gospel. As her principal

---

[1] In this passage, taken from the old version of psalm 94, the author is emphasizing the word *praeoccupemus*, which, however, does not appear in the new version, although it remains in the Invitatory. Tr.

287

spokesman in the Matins office on each Sunday, the Church sets before us one of the great patriarchs: Adam, Noe, and Abraham. Not merely the lessons of the first and second nocturn but the responsories also serve this purpose. These responsories, in fact, remain the same throughout the week. The Church's plan, then, is to place the figure of the patriarch vividly before our minds, and not to let it quickly vanish. The Sunday Gospels also have a special significance. In the third nocturn as is usual, there is an explanation of the Gospel by one of the Fathers. But much stronger than on other Sundays, the Gospel itself resounds throughout the day and the following week. During these three weeks the Magnificat antiphons are choice texts directly from the Sunday Gospel. Even more remarkable on these three Sundays is the liturgy's concern with the Gospel throughout the day, apportioning the main passages to the various hours so we may take our part in the Gospel drama. We could make many interesting observations on this point.

Now I call attention to the patriarch and the Gospel, the twin themes for these three Sundays.

Septuagesima Sunday: Adam; and the laborers in the vineyard. Besides being the father of mankind, Adam is also an antetype of Christ. In the Magnificat antiphon for First Vespers the liturgy gives this fact concise but profound treatment: "The Lord said to Adam, 'Do not eat of the tree that is in the middle of Paradise: in what hour thou shall eat of it, thou shalt die the death.'" Back we go now to the very beginning of our redemption, whence came all the grief and sorrow on this earth, but all the happiness too, and all salvation. Our thoughts go out to another tree in the midst of God's kingdom, the tree on which the second Adam died, the tree that bears the fruit of eternal life.

Throughout the day we take our part in the drama of the Gospel parable. At Lauds we are hired by God "early in the morning" to go to work in His vineyard. At Prime He fixes on the wage and sends us out to work. At Terce He calls us, the stragglers, into the vineyard. Later at Sext we still loll idly in the market place. Toward sundown, at None, He calls us to get our wages. At Vespers we look over our pay. Then in the Magnificat antiphons for the rest of the week we keep hearing in our souls the invitation God makes to us in this Gospel.

Sexagesima Sunday: Noe; and the sower. Noe is the sower of mankind, the man of justice in a world of sin, the builder of the ark. He too is an antetype of Christ. In the Magnificat antiphon we sing: "The Lord spoke to Noe: the end of all flesh cometh before Me; make for yourself an ark of timber planks, that every seed may be saved in it." This picture gives us the mystical foreshadowing of both the Church and the cross of Christ. In the lesson about this patriarch in the second nocturn, St. Ambrose offers a splendid commentary. Once again there is the beautiful parable drama enacted through the course of the day. At sunrise we listen to the parable's introduction and setting, as though the liturgy would say: The holy drama is about to begin now: "The sower went out to sow his seed. . . ." That is the picture of Christ today. In each of the hours that follow (Prime, Terce, and Sext) we stage a scene from the drama and sing a passage of the parable. There is absolutely no mention, however, of the "wasted" seed. It is the liturgy's wish to speak only of the good seed and of the rich fruit it yields. What a help this thought is toward a proper appreciation of the passage! Here the liturgy would concern itself not with sinners, but rather with the faithful and the just. "The seed fell on good soil, and brought forth fruit in patience" (Prime). "They that keep the word of God in a

290 THE BREVIARY EXPLAINED

good and perfect heart, bring forth fruit in patience" (Terce). Note how both antiphons emphasize "patience," as though the Church would say: the best soil for God's seed is patience in the Christian life. "The seed fell on good soil and brought forth fruit, the one a hundredfold, the other, sixty   ." (Sext). The chant stops purposely at the mention of "sixty-fold," for we are at the hour of Sext. "Brethren, if you wish to be truly rich, love true riches" (None). This passage does not come from the Gospel itself, but from the homily of St. Gregory. Thus the antiphons of the four little hours outline a rich and fruitful Christian life. In the evening the Church whispers in our ear the secret of God's kingdom: "To you it is given to know. . . ." At sundown on each of the next three days the liturgy sings its song about the sower. Strange as it may seem, this song is not from the Scriptures themselves, but again, from the homily of St. Gregory. See, for instance, how beautiful the second antiphon is: "The seed is the word of God; the Sower is Christ. All that find Him, shall live forever."

Quinquagesima Sunday: Abraham; and the blind man by the roadside. A special love characterizes the liturgy's treatment of the father of all the faithful, that magnificent foretype of Christ, Abraham. "He is a truly great man, brilliant with the badges of virtue, of a greatness worldly wisdom cannot match." Thus St. Ambrose speaks in the second nocturn. There are eight responsories in Matins that treat of Abraham. Especially beautiful is the Vespers antiphon for the Saturday preceding: "The father of our faith, great Abraham, offered a holocaust on the altar, in place of his son." With words full of sublime devotion and a melody of exquisite spiritual beauty and feeling, the Church herself composed this antiphon. Then she lets us take part again in the Gospel drama that unfolds through the course of the day. At sunrise we hear Christ Himself: "Behold, we go up to Jerusalem and all things shall be fulfilled that have been written of the Son of man. He shall be betrayed to the Gentiles, mocked, and spat upon; and after scourging Him, they will kill Him; and on the third day He shall rise again." How appropriate an antiphon for the sunrise office! In the four little hours we ourselves are the blind man begging light from the Lord. And with each hour our plea grows more earnest, more insistent. Toward evening as the sun is setting, the drama draws to a happy close. The Lord gives me, the blind man, my sight. "Immediately he was able to see, and he followed Him, praising God." In our gratitude we sing the Magnificat which today is the thanksgiving song of the blind man who now can see.

In fairly even proportion, then, these two themes dominate the liturgy for the Sundays of the pre-Lenten season. The three patriarchs, Adam, Noe, and Abraham, are the important characters, antetypes of Christ, models for us. The three Gospel dramas in which we take part suggest three distinct steps: the call, the instruction, and the enlightenment. It is evident, then, that a devout study of the Breviary and Missal liturgy for this period will yield much spiritual joy and profit.

THE LENTEN OFFICE

We found the Advent office characterized by a special richness of thought and tender emotional appeal. This showed up particularly in the happy choice of Scripture passages in Matins, Lauds, and Vespers. Advent is the preparation for a season of shorter length and less importance than Lent. Yet we find it decked out in rich and at times even extravagant finery of thought and language. Quite naturally, then, we should expect all this in an even greater degree from the period that prepares us for the year's greatest feast. Such is not the case, however. To drop a curtain, for the time being, over the liturgical masterpieces that give the Holy Week liturgy its high rank in art, and to confine our study merely to the office of the first four weeks of Lent, would, I fear, leave us more than somewhat disappointed. The last echoes of the Alleluja at First Vespers of Septuagesima and the masterly compositions of the pre-Lenten season lead us, naturally, to expect the liturgy to develop and prove itself richer with the coming of Ash Wednesday. But, as we mentioned already, this is not at all in evidence.

Before we consider the office of Lent in detail, we should outline briefly this season's idea and purpose. In the days when a youthful and vigorous Christianity was conquering the decadent metropolis of pagan antiquity and opening its arms to vast throngs of converts, Lent was a time of instruction (catechumenate) and trial for those who wished to receive baptism. At a designated church each day, and by means of reading and instructions in Holy Scripture, they were initiated into the mysteries of Christianity. There were indeed apostates even in the early Church. From this vital contact with Christ the vine, these withered branches could draw new life. Lent was a time of penance and atonement for them. Lent's idea and aim, then, was to instruct the catechumens and to exhort sinners to penance and a resolute change of heart. The supernatural stream of the sacred mysteries of the faith was to impart and restore to souls supernatural life in Christ and in His Church. But it was further meant to cleanse the whole Christian community. To their souls it would apply the instruction given the catechumens in order to stir up the grace of their own baptism; it would have them use the time of penance to cleanse their own souls from sin. Thus the grace of redemption already possessed, was brought to the fore and rendered more effective. Because nowadays there is no longer question of a special period of instruction for catechumens, or of penance for those who had been expelled from the Church, the holy season of Lent, in general, is intended as a time for renewing the grace of our baptism and for cleansing our souls of sin in a spirit of penance and contrition.

Lent is, then, the time to rouse new vigor in the soul that has been infected with sin and sensuality, the time to enliven our relation with Christ through grace. For this reason the Church dispenses her spiritual treasures far more lavishly in Lent than in other seasons. The celebration of holy Mass is, as always, her chief means of imparting supernatural life to our souls. I cannot help but think just now of the marvelous Lenten Masses that nourish our frail, diseased souls with a diet of God's word skillfully varied in the Foremass and the Sacrifice which follows. A friend of the liturgy will not hesitate a moment to prefer the Lenten Masses to those of the saint for the day. The very fact that Holy Mother Church prescribes the ferial Mass for the daily conventional Mass in cathedral and cloister churches, seems to vindicate the claim that only the ferial Masses correspond fully to the spirit of the season. And since the liturgical revival maintains that the office is meant to serve both as preparation for and echo to the Mass, it is only consistent then, to claim that the office likewise be ferial, since the sanctoral office entirely disregards the spirit of the Lenten season. Because there are no continuous Scripture lessons for the first nocturn, one must have recourse to the Common of the Saints when the office of the saint is recited during this season. Then too, the Te Deum at the end of Matins is hardly in accord with the season.

Along with the Alleluja and the Gloria, it should be reserved for Easter. I have no doubt that the points mentioned will be viewed as defects that are not to be overlooked in speaking of the Lenten office. If it is the mind of the Church that Mass and office complement each other, and if the Church herself prefers the ferial Masses to those of the saints that occur during Lent, then logically we prefer that the ferial office be recommended, even prescribed, for those obliged to choral recitation.

Done with this digression now, we can study the Lenten office itself. As we said above, it cannot compare with the Advent office for luxuriance of expression and elaborate development. A more or less bleak sobriety pervades the whole season. Shadows of guilt and penance seem to have settled over the prayers of the liturgy. Everything about Lent is overcast with sentiments of penance and contrition. Although the special Lenten Masses begin with Ash Wednesday, the proper office does not start in until First Vespers of the First Sunday of Lent. This seems to indicate that in ancient times Lent itself began on the first Sunday. It is the Sundays that form the framework for the liturgy of the whole season. Richly equipped with appropriate Scripture passages, they naturally make the weekday offices appear less prominent and less artistic. More in detail now, let us take up the individual hours.

The Vesper psalms for the Sundays have no proper antiphons. Therefore they are inferior to those of Advent, whose antiphons were carefully chosen to suit the season. Only when we reach the capitulum do we find texts proper to the day. We hear there an important part of the Sunday Epistle. The hymn too has a true Lenten character; its fourth verse treats explicitly of fasting and mortification. The principal phrase of the versicle is drawn from the Gospel for the First Sunday, and is kept as a Lenten refrain throughout the season. "For to His angels He has given command about you, that they guard you in all your ways." Each day Holy Mother Church reminds us with this versicle that God has given a special grace to encourage and spur us on in our journey through the day and through life. The Magnificat antiphons for the First Sunday were selected with a special view to the idea and purpose of the season. The one for Second Vespers embodies a practical program for Lent. The oration is borrowed from the Mass. Matins, where references to the season and characteristics of it are most conspicuous, is certainly the climax of the day's office. An expressive Invitatory stands at the beginning of this hour for the whole four weeks: "Let it not seem useless to you to rise early before dawn, because the Lord has promised a crown to those who keep watch." This overture is a clever coupling of the hour thought with the Lenten theme. Frankly the Church here suggests a wholesome sacrifice for Lent: to rise a little earlier than usual. It certainly seems in place during this season to rise half an hour earlier and to recite Matins in the morning instead of anticipating. Thus our liturgical and ascetical lives can join hands working at mutual development. In the first two strophes of the hymn we learn that there was a sort of Lent even in the Old Testament. Strophes three, four, and five give us the proper concept of a fast: something more than merely eating a little less than usual. The hymn ends with an appeal to God to have pity on our weakness. Once again the psalms have no proper antiphons. Hence they too are inferior to the Matins psalms of Advent. In the lessons for the first nocturn we continue with the Book of Genesis. Every Sunday a new figure is selected from our ancestral gallery of the Old Testament. On the First Sunday, by exception, the Church uses lessons taken from St. Paul's Second Epistle to the Corinthians to set forth the program for Lent.

The responsories for the First Sunday are exceptionally artistic, rich in thought and emotion. Their song is of contrition, penance, and the various good works that Lent should find us performing. To some extent, at least, they even match the poetry of the Advent responsories. Those of the other Sundays of Lent are, in general, echoes and reflection on the Scripture lesson just read, with special emphasis on the patriarch theme. With remarkable clarity they set forth the main events in the patriarch's life.

The Sunday lessons are well worth our attention. In the second nocturn for the First Sunday we hear a stirring Lenten sermon from the lips of Pope St. Leo I. On the Second Sunday, the Scripture lessons about the patriarch Jacob give the Church the opportunity to introduce a few passages from St. Augustine's *Contra mendacium*. On the Third Sunday it is St. Ambrose who describes the veneration which the early Church had for the patriarch Joseph, who spent so many years in Egypt. Finally, on the Fourth Sunday, in connection with the Scripture lessons about Moses, St. Basil reminds us that when Moses went up to Mount Sinai, he was fasting. He could not preach a more appropriate Lenten sermon. The Gospel homilies are likewise chosen carefully with a view to the season. We hear the words of Gregory, Leo, Bede, and Augustine, each in his turn. There is no Te Deum at the end of Matins; the Church is saving that for the vigil of Easter. For Lauds we use the second schema, that for the penitential seasons. Certain striking verses are selected from the psalms and used as antiphons. For the most part these offer a practical suggestion as to the liturgical application of the psalms. The capitulum is the same as that of Vespers.

The hymn opens with the words *"O Sol Salutis,"* that is, "O Jesus, Sun of our salvation." It is a genuine morning-hymn in which we sing of the coming day of redemption (Easter) with suppressed sentiments of Easter joy. Thoughts of the new day dawning mingle with thoughts of our spiritual renewal. The versicle for Vespers appears again at Lauds. When the liturgy wishes to accentuate an idea from the Gospels, from time to time the Benedictus antiphon is used to reassert an important passage.

Nor is it hard to discern the relation of the office to the Mass liturgy. The morning hymn for Lauds serves at the same time as the first Introit of the Mass. The principal ideas in the Scripture readings of the Mass are portioned out through the little hours. Here we can often detect a special relation between the theme of the hour and that of the day. In fact, we can assert, in conclusion, that these four Sundays of Lent, both in the Mass and in the office, form a single liturgical unit which is foundation and framework for the whole Lenten liturgy. The liturgy for the First Sunday is by far the most outstanding composition. I fear we can more admire and marvel at it than fully understand it. There are few days that can match the classic beauty and unity of this Sunday.

We have already mentioned that the weekday offices betray certain weaknesses. We would prefer to have the sanctoral offices eliminated. It often happens that the Scripture lessons proper to the day cannot be read. There is only a hint given of them in the responsories. It is because of this that we miss the most interesting parts of the stories of Isaac, Jacob, Moses, and others. The Fathers try to compensate for this, at least in one nocturn, by giving us a homily on the Gospel from the ferial Mass of the day. Every day there is a special antiphon for the Benedictus at sunrise and for the

Magnificat at sunset. These deserve our study and meditation because they single out the leading thought for the day.
Then too, they are closely related to the aims of Lent, namely,
instruction and penance. Thus they frequently give us the key
to the explanation of the day's Mass. The fact that there are
two different orations for Lauds and Vespers is another noteworthy feature. At Lauds we use the collect of the Mass, and
at Vespers the *oratio super populum*. This latter occurs after
the Postcommunion of the Mass, but only during Lent. We
note also that, according to an ancient custom, during Lent
we should recite Vespers before noon. This custom has a
historical background from the days when a strict spirit of
penance and mortification postponed the noonday meal to evening, that is, until after Vespers were sung.

CHAPTER XIX

Office for Passiontide

ON Passion Sunday the Lenten liturgy enters on a new phase. At least externally, it may be characterized by the draping of the crucifix and the statues in the church, and also by the more somber and at times soul-stirring timbre of the liturgical chants. Alongside our own penance, we might say even in its place, the Church now proposes the redemptive sufferings of Christ Himself. We commemorate His passion and death. Before our eyes stands the Savior, making the journey to Jerusalem for the Passover, re-enacting His death in the sacred mysteries of Holy Week: the King with a cross for His throne, who, if He be lifted up, will draw all men to Himself. Holy Mother Church, ever with an eye to the spiritual progress of her catechumens, her repentant children, and those who seek to renew their hearts, saves her strongest appeal to our spiritual sensibilities for the last days of Holy Week. A prayer drama reproduces the whole work of our redemption. Once more we have the Mass liturgy with its impressive ceremonies. On Palm Sunday and the last three days of Holy Week it represents and re-enacts in a mystical way the story of our salvation. And, of course, the office surrounds the whole drama, setting the stage for it and unfolding in these last three days the magnificent artistry of this prayer drama.

Thus a new period opens with Passion Sunday. Saturday's

First Vespers usher in Passiontide and are the first faint cries of anguish, that will reach their climax on the following Thursday evening. Both psalms and antiphons are taken from the regular Saturday office. The Passion drama begins in the capitulum. This is from the Epistle of the next day's (Sunday's) Mass, a most appropriate Lenten text. In this Epistle to the Hebrews, Paul describes Christ, the true high priest. Not with the blood of goats and calves (in itself of no value for expiation) but with His own blood, He sacrificed Himself to death to make satisfaction for us. In this sacrifice Christ is both Priest and Victim.

The *Vexilla Regis* that follows is a masterpiece. Its song is of the cross that serves as our divine King's throne. *Vexilla Regis,* the King's flag, a hymn of grief and sadness. Nonetheless, though the hymn voices grief and suffering, the cross predominates in our thoughts not as the pillar of shame and torture, but as the banner of victory, the Savior's royal pennant. In this hymn we glimpse the spirit of the early Church. It does not depict Christ tortured, as the friars painted Him, but royal and victorious, on a magnificently bejewelled cross that we still can see in the mosaics of the ancient basilicas.

But thoughts like these are hardly apropos in Passiontide. They smack too much of anticipated Easter joy. We had best kneel for the sixth strophe, to pay our homage to the holy cross. The versicle that follows seems to be a sigh of the Savior emitted in those last hours of agony before His betrayal: "Save me, O Lord, from the evil man"; and the response: "from the godless man, deliver me." At this reply to the versicle we might readily think of Caiphas, Pilate, and Herod. This versicle is with us each day as a sort of Passion theme up to the day of betrayal, Wednesday in Holy Week. It is a verse borrowed from psalm 139, and we can apply it profitably to ourselves. Let us picture our Savior mildly complaining of the many times when by our disloyalty and cowardice in living up to our faith, we took the role of His torturers. The Magnificat antiphon at First Vespers is a prelude to the Mass liturgy. These Magnificat antiphons during Passion Week depict vividly the mental sufferings of the Savior. But His bodily sufferings are by no means overlooked. In Vespers for the Wednesday before Spy Wednesday it is remarkable to hear our Lord sweetly complaining to Judas (and to us): "So many good works have I done for you; why do you wish to kill Me now?" And at Vespers the next day again, at the very hour of the Last Supper, we hear these plaintive words rise from the depths of His anguished heart: "With desire I have desired to eat this pasch with you." Then on the Friday before Good Friday we glimpse the crafty murderers at work, plotting the death of the Just One: "The high priests took counsel as to how they might slay Jesus." Only one week hence, at about this time when we say Vespers, the curtain will fall on Golgotha, and the work of our redemption will be accomplished. We can readily see, then, how appropriate was the choice of these Magnificat antiphons.

In the night office of Matins a special devotion and pensiveness, and a tender sympathy color the Church's meditation on Christ's passion. The overture is taken from the Invitatory psalm itself (94): "O, that today you would hear his voice: 'Harden not your hearts. . . .'" Now the liturgy appeals to our sympathy. Even if nothing else will influence us, if like the Jews in the desert in ages past, despite all His mercies and benefits, we are still faithless to God, surely the passion of our Savior will make us stop to reconsider, "today," now, while this prayer drama re-presents and relives His passion for us anew. The majestic hymn that follows sings again of the royal cross. There is a picturesque comparison made between the tree of sin and the tree of our salvation, and also between the wood of the crib at our Savior's birth, and the wood of the cross at His death. Though we might expect them, there are no proper antiphons for the psalms of the three nocturns. Only the versicle at the end of the psalms relates them to the theme of Christ's passion. They sound again like the voice of the Savior crying out from the Mount of Olives and from Mount Calvary.

Until now, that is, from Septuagesima Sunday, the Redeemer's character has been set in outline by the figures of the holy patriarchs of the Old Testament. The series closes with Moses. Now Jeremias enters on the scene. His life's tragic feature was the foreseeing and foretelling of the misfortune that was to befall the people he was sent to save, a tragedy he could not prevent because of the hardness of their hearts. In this stirring but tragic role, Jeremias is a vivid antetype of the Redeemer of the world. His prophecies, and especially his lamentations, are the very perfection of religious literature. Holy Mother Church reserves them for Passiontide to soften men's hardened hearts. In the first nocturn we listen grief-stricken to the vigorous language of this momentous message from God. Later, during the last three days of Holy Week, Jeremias will compose the swan song of the dying Redeemer. In the second and third nocturns, St. Leo and St. Gregory the Great preach homilies to us. The former suggests that we make our fasts more rigorous, out of sympathy for the sufferings of our Savior. In this matter he is merely passing on an apostolic tradition. In connection with the Gospel, St. Gregory admonishes us to examine our consciences to see if we are really opening our hearts to God's word. All three nocturns are laced with vivid responsories that depict

scenes from the Passion. We can find rich matter for reflection
here. At one time it is the spiritual sufferings, at another it is
the historical Passion which we relive by our prayerful reflections. The responsories accentuate the human side of Christ's
passion, the side that so readily evokes our sympathy, and
they give His divinity less prominence. From time to time,
nevertheless, the dogma is reasserted that we find our salvation and consequently our happiness in Christ's passion and
death. This thought is expressed forcefully in the responsory
for the first lesson where our Savior's passion is represented
to us in both its human (and therefore tragic) aspect and its
divine (and therefore redemptive) aspect.

Now in the responsories, when she speaks to us through the
Old Testament, the Church counts the days until Easter: "In
fourteen days, in the evening, there shall be the Lord's Pasch;
and on the fifteenth day, you will celebrate the solemn feast
to the Most High." After the Passion, our redemption; after
the Passion, Easter! As in the hymns of the Holy Cross, so
too here a shaft of Easter light and joy breaks through the
gloomy shadows of Lent. Yet, quite understandably, there is
no Te Deum at the end of Matins.

The bright and usually joyous hour of morning praise now
becomes a fervent Passion prayer. The psalms are from the
second schema and have their proper antiphons that let our
suffering Savior speak to us. At times they sound like the
mild reproaches He voices on Good Friday. The lesson (capitulum) is borrowed from Vespers. The hymn, *Lustra Sex*,
sings of the cross and the instruments of the crucifixion, with
emphasis, however, on the cross, the royal deathbed. As in
Vespers, so in Lauds we have a versicle that re-echoes like a
sigh from the lips of the Savior through the whole period:
"Save me from my enemies, my God, and deliver me from

my adversaries." The Benedictus antiphon strikes the tragic theme of the day's Gospel. It is particularly well chosen for the sunrise canticle, at the very time when the Light yearns to enlighten those who "sit in darkness (sin) and in the shadows of death (far from salvation)." Many, in fact most men, are not particularly interested in the Sun of salvation. They remain passive and unaffected by its light.

This same thought is voiced again on Monday in the figure of the thirsty man. Then on Wednesday, in the image of the Good Shepherd, the Sun of redemption again tries to show men the benefits of His light. The antiphons on Thursday and Friday give us a stirring preview of the events that will occur on the same days the following week: "My time is at hand, I will celebrate the pasch with My disciples at your house"; "The high priest took counsel as to how they would slay Jesus, but they feared because of the people." The first antiphon introduces the celebration of the Eucharist. The second is another picturesque parallel to the idea mentioned before about the "Light" that was snatched from men. A marvelous antiphon full of allusions to light and its spiritual significance closes the series of Benedictus antiphons on Saturday morning before Palm Sunday. Two words: *clarifica* and *claritate,* taken from the Savior's high-priestly prayer, introduce the celebration of the high-priestly act that is to begin now on Palm Sunday: "Glorify Me (the brilliant dawn is an image of this glory), Father, with that glory which I possessed with You before the world came to be." Today's sun, which will be the same tomorrow, is a figure of Christ's eternal glory.

The little hours develop and amplify the thoughts enunciated in Vespers, Matins, and Lauds. We hear the echo of the day's Epistle in the capitulum; and in the responsories once again we find scenes from our Savior's passion. The usual

Gloria Patri is omitted here. There is a special connection between the short lessons of Sext and None and their respective hour-themes and historical redemptive backgrounds. The office during the week merely develops the ideas set forth on Passion Sunday. Throughout the week in the lessons, St. Augustine explains pericopes from St. John's Gospel. We have already considered the profound and picturesque antiphons for the Benedictus and Magnificat. As in the first four weeks of Lent, so in Passiontide there is a special oration for Vespers, the *oratio super populum,* taken from the day's Mass, just after the Postcommunion. During these days the little hours too have special antiphons, intimately related to the hour-theme and to the historical redemptive background of the particular hour. At 9 o'clock (Terce), we relive the memorable scene in the courtyard of Pilate. At 12 o'clock (Sext), we hear the Savior cry out from the cross. Finally at 3 o'clock (None), we see the hole into which the cross is jammed. Together with the capitula and responsories, these antiphons lend a thoughtful unity to the weekday office. We can easily discern the special theme Holy Mother Church is developing in each hour.

CHAPTER XX

The Holy Week Office

THOUGH Passion Week's dramatic presentation of the sufferings of Christ heightens and enhances the Lenten liturgy of the first four weeks, the peak and climax of the magnificent prayer drama is Holy Week. Palm Sunday is the grand opening of this last week of Lent. That day's liturgy has two parts: the joyous blessing of the palms with the victorious procession, and the sad and somber Mass that follows. There is nothing exceptional about the office which surrounds these solemnities and which has the usual task of keeping the thoughts of the feast with us through the day. Passiontide contributes the hymn and versicle, and even the Invitatory at Matins remains the same. Only Vespers can give us a new feature: the meaningful lesson from Paul's Epistle to the Philippians. Here Paul describes the obedience of Christ "unto death, yes, to the death of the cross." In First Vespers the Magnificat antiphon, again taken from Christ's high-priestly prayer at the Last Supper, shows the Savior solemnly accepting the "death sentence" decreed from all eternity by the Most Holy Trinity. The antiphon for Second Vespers, like an echo to the morning's joyous procession, promises Christ's resurrection following His death.

There is nothing remarkable about Matins. In the first nocturn Isaias laments over Jerusalem desolate and wasted because it chose to say: "I will not serve," even though the

Lord cared for it as for "His favorite vineyard." Pope Leo holds our attention in the second nocturn with a homily on the Lord's passion. In the third nocturn St. Ambrose explains the Gospel about Christ's triumphant entry into Jerusalem. The responsories that follow these lessons are still grave and somber in character. We can see the Savior going to embrace His sufferings. Lauds too is wrapped in penitential mourning robes. Only its Benedictus antiphon rings out, like the solemn farewell which the Church bids her King as He departs for His death: "Blessed is He that cometh in the name of the Lord, Hosanna in the highest." Prime and Terce maintain the victorious tenor of the palm procession, and Sext and None are again occupied with the opening scenes of the Passion. The capitulum at Sext (it was about 12 o'clock that our Lord was nailed to the cross) recalls once again that Christ was "obedient unto the death of the cross," and at None (at 3 o'clock our Lord died) the capitulum reminds us that "every knee shall bend in heaven and on earth (before the Redeemer on the cross)." Notice here, once again, how greatly the historical redemptive background of the hours influences the ideas and thoughts of our prayers.

The office of Monday, Tuesday, and Wednesday in this great week shows a somewhat progressive development. Special antiphons add their bit to Lauds taken from the second schema. The short, crisp phrases of these antiphons are meant to rouse us to sympathetic prayer with our sorrow-laden Savior. Christ, the suffering Head, prays; and we, the suffering members of His mystical body, ought to pray along with Him. What a profound and truly liturgical thought! The rest of the office is the same as that of the preceding days. On Monday St. Augustine preaches the Gospel homily at Matins. (In preparation for His burial) Magdalen anoints the Savior. We note how beautifully Holy Mother Church teaches us the lesson of Magdalen's devoting her spare means to the service of the Lord, a not altogether inappropriate thought for our own times. The single nocturn on Tuesday and Wednesday gives Jeremias the chance to continue with his vivid scenes. The Benedictus and Magnificat antiphons are brief excerpts from the history of the Passion. We should take special note of the fact that psalm 54 in Terce on Wednesday is "dedicated" to Judas. This traitor song is well suited to the day that commemorates his sad deed. As you might expect, from Palm Sunday on, the office harmonizes with the Mass liturgy. The sanctoral offices are eliminated entirely. (As we mentioned before, we should like to see this measure prevail from Ash Wednesday through the whole of Lent.) The last stage of the preparation for the *Sacrum Triduum* closes with Vespers and Compline on Wednesday. We hear the concluding antiphon *Ave Regina Coelorum* for the last time.

In the pages that follow we shall treat in detail the Matins of Maundy Thursday, Good Friday, and Holy Saturday because they belong to the masterpieces of the Breviary. We rightly call these Matins a trilogy, since every Matins is a prayer drama, and these three all focus on the one great thought of Christ's passion. We have, then, a trilogy on the passion of the Savior.

Matins for Holy Thursday furnishes the introduction to the trilogy, the overture to the great drama. The theme is Christ's passion with the spotlight playing on its causes and its execution. The principal themes are: the events on Mount Olivet, Judas, and the institution of the Eucharist. As all this is but the opening page of the drama, the intensity of emotion and poetical ardor is purposely restrained. The second part, and

the climax of the trilogy, is Matins for Good Friday. This
gives us the great drama of the cross and sets the scene on
the hill of Calvary. Beyond a doubt, the whole week's office
has no sadder or more moving part. The third part brings
a lessening of the tension, a sort of calm after the storm. In
this Holy Saturday office there is a gradual surge of hope
for Christ's resurrection. But this vanishes as we catch a
glimpse of our dead Savior's bloody wounds.

The Tenebrae Matins have several characteristics to distinguish them from Matins for the rest of the year. At other
times Matins has its festive introduction called the Invitatory,
and also a number of short versicles and prayers to set off
the larger elements of the hour; no festive chorus of chimes
begins or ends abruptly. It starts rather with a little bell,
gradually swells into a jubilant chorus, and then tapers off in
much the same way, gradually and slowly. Just so the Church,
as a rule, introduces and closes her official prayer with short
verses that rise in our hearts like the first faint sentiments
of devotion. In the Tenebrae Matins, however, this is not the
case. They begin straightway, without any introduction; and
they close every bit as abruptly. Why is this so? What on
other days would seem a cold beginning and an inartistic ending for the office, on Good Friday provides a striking expression of grief and sorrow. We are taken aback; something is
missing. And then we remember: now Christ has left His disciples and this life. We are stricken anew with grief and sorrow. It is for this same reason that the psalms do not conclude
with the customary *Gloria Patri*.[1]

---

[1] The history of the development of the liturgy traces the absence of this
prayer to an ancient form of Matins which has endured in these three offices
of Holy Week.

Matins is, as a rule, closely followed by Lauds. At other times we might well wish to separate the two, so as to make Lauds a real morning prayer. But here we ought to recite them together. They are both parts of the prayer drama; besides, they are always recited together when the office is said publicly. On the previous night (nowadays, unfortunately, it is often the preceding afternoon) the Church gathers for its nighttime prayers, the Tenebrae Matins, or as the official terminology has it, *matutinum tenebrarum*. These Tenebrae Matins presuppose that the church is in darkness. This is the proper setting for the drama that Holy Mother Church is staging for us. The King of Light battles with the prince of darkness and his followers. Indeed, these last three days call for special ritual for the night office. The action takes place before the altar stripped of all its ornaments. The clerics lay aside customary solemn vestments and wear plain surplices. No organ accompanies the chant. Before the altar is placed a triangle that holds fourteen yellow candles and one white one. This custom had a practical origin: the candles served to illumine the darkness of the church at nightfall. Later it received a symbolic meaning. The fourteen yellow candles of the triangle and the six on the altar represent the apostles and disciples who all fled and deserted the Savior in His hour of need. That is why after each psalm one candle is extinguished until at last for the *Miserere* the church is completely dark. The one white candle that represents Christ is taken down from the stand at the end of the office (during the *Miserere*) and hidden for a moment. Then at the sound of the clapper it is brought out and put back on the candlestand. Because of the noise of the wooden clapper, in Germany the Tenebrae is sometimes called Clap-Matins. The clapper's noise should remind us of the earthquake at

Christ's resurrection. Originally the sound was made by the shutting of the choir books, to indicate to the faithful that the service was over. Then the lighted candle was restored to the triangle to light the way for the faithful as they left the church.

CHAPTER XXI

Matins for Holy Thursday

THE first part of the trilogy is an introduction to the great drama. Its theme is the Passion in its spiritual aspect, its physical causes, and its accomplishment.

1. By Holy Thursday, Christ's death was a settled matter as far as the Jews were concerned.

2. Judas betrays his Master.

3. In the Garden, Christ suffers the whole of His passion in His soul and will.

4. The institution of the Holy Eucharist and the representation of the passion of Jesus.

The action opens on the evening of the first Holy Thursday. But we must not expect the action to unfold in chronological order as in an actual drama. No; here and there the thoughts leap, only to return to the principal theme in the end. Scenes of the Passion and the days that follow occur and lack chronological order. Rather than a drama, it is a mosaic of prayer pictures unified by the general theme of Christ's passion, and especially the events of this Thursday evening.

Some general remarks on the individual parts of this Matins office are here presented.

The psalms. In festive offices, as a rule, and on these next two days, special psalms are selected which best suit the thoughts and sentiments of the feast. But on Holy Thursday this is not the case. The psalms weave an unbroken numerical pattern from 68 to 76. (In ancient times Wednesday Matins stopped at psalm 67; therefore Thursday Matins began with psalm 68). Yet not all conform to the Passion theme. This defect was probably noted but left unaltered since this office is but the beginning, the introduction to the trilogy. It does, however, make its recitation somewhat less enjoyable, and naturally causes difficulty for the beginner trying to relate the psalms to the theme of the feast. Some explanation of the text is therefore necessary. Our Savior Himself declared that many of the psalms speak prophetically of the Christ: ". . . how all that was written of me in the law of Moses, and in the psalms, must be fulfilled."

The Lamentations. It is mainly the Lamentations of the prophet Jeremias that give the Tenebrae service its profoundly moving effect. What are they? What are their position and their purpose in the Tenebrae?

In the Lamentations, Jeremias voices sentiments of the bitterest grief and mourning over the destruction of Jerusalem by the Babylonians, and over the captivity of his people. These five songs belong to the most beautiful elegies of all world literature. They are written in verses each of which begins with a different letter of the Hebrew alphabet. This is why the Hebrew letter is chanted before each verse. The introduction to the Book of Jeremias gives the historical setting for the Lamentations: "And it came to pass, after Israel was carried into captivity and Jerusalem was desolate, that Jeremias the prophet sat weeping, and mourned with this lamentation over Jerusalem. And with a sorrowful mind, sighing and moaning, he said. . . ." Understanding the literal sense of the Lamentations is not too difficult. But what about their position and purpose in the Holy Week Matins?

First of all, the Lamentations give us the proper sentiments of grief and sorrow. The Tenebrae Matins are, after all, our expression of sympathy and sorrow with our suffering Savior. Just as Jeremias mourned over his beloved city and its temple, so we are supposed to mourn the "loss" of our bridegroom.[1] But we have an even more important relationship to our Spouse, which we might better explain by this parable. Once God chose a very beautiful spouse (mankind). The wedding was soon to take place, but the bride broke faith with her Lover and eloped with the prince of this world (the fall into sin). God, of course, rejected her, and she, led along by the devil, sank deeper and deeper in misery. We see her now, shamed and disgraced in the eyes of the world, despised by the devil, chastised and afflicted by God. She sits by the roadside, an object of scorn to all passers-by. Now she grieves and laments, for she has had time to reflect on her actions. (Here the Lamentation begins.) Then something wholly unexpected happens. Her former Spouse comes and relieves her affliction. Merely to forgive her infidelity does not content Him, but He even assumes her guilt and He Himself pays the heavy price of her crime. To show His immense love for her He takes on His own shoulders the full rigor of justice demanding the penalty for her crime. See now how He grieves and laments. The full weight of the bride's sin has fallen on Him, and all the stripes fall on His back. It was with such arduous labors and sufferings (more than Jacob's in winning Rachel) that He ransomed His bride. (This ransoming was our Redemption.) Now He loves His bride with a love that is truly great. He will not treat her as a servant or a slave, though, if He wished, He certainly could rightly do so. No; she is His bride. She is the Queen, as He is the King.

So much for the parable that tells the whole story of our

[1] Matt. 9:15.

redemption. Now we can see the relation of the Lamentations to the passion of our Lord. Who, then, is the bride grieving and lamenting? (a) Taken literally, she is the faithless Jewish nation. This figure of the marriage pledge between God and the Jewish people is common among the prophets. (b) In today's office this bride is the human race which through Adam's sin forsook God and fell into the slavery of Satan. (c) The bride is also each human soul that has broken faith with God through personal sin. (d) Finally, in these Lamentations we can picture the Savior taking our place and mourning and lamenting for our sins. Then too, sinful mankind grieves over the disgrace and affliction it endures because of its sins.

Now we can understand the first nocturn of these three Matin offices. In the psalms we hear the laments of our suffering Savior; in the lessons, those of sin-ridden mankind and of every sinful soul. Then in the responsories, the Church tells us that Jesus has taken on Himself all our sorrows and afflictions. Or we might put it this way. In the psalms we see the suffering Savior; in the lessons mankind strikes its breast and says: "He is suffering all that for me." Thus, in the Lamentations the Church gives all of us a chance to hold a mirror before our souls to see and understand sin's frightful misery and wretchedness. For that reason each passage of the Lamentations closes with the stirring cry: "Jerusalem, Jerusalem, turn (return) to the Lord your God." These stirring elegies are not merely recited but are chanted in a sad and solemn melody to move us all the more to sympathy and sorrow. Unfortunately the origin of this melody is lost in the shadows of time. It may have come from Jewish antiquity.[2] Its sad, long, drawn-out tones sweep over the soul. Repetitious, yet never tiring, it is a

2 Gueranger, *The Church Year*, VI, 329.

melody that has stirred countless thousands of hearts and evoked the admiration of the greatest artists.

With all their simplicity, the responsories in the Tenebrae office are particularly attractive. They enhance the dramatic element of the Matins, besides weaving in a thread of unity through the action of the drama. In the responsories for Holy Thursday's Matins, a certain order and progressive development appears. Those of the first nocturn treat of the agony in the garden; then in the second, they tell of Judas; and in the third, of the dozing apostles and of the Jews plotting to slay the Lord. In each of the three offices the last responsory describes the actual scene of the drama.

To my mind, the weakest element in the Holy Thursday Matins seems to be the lessons of the second nocturn. St. Augustine gives an explanation of a verse of a psalm (here psalm 54) and relates it to the Passion. How much more appropriate it would be if St. Augustine were to comment on the famous "Judas verse" (15) of this psalm, especially since the three responsories deal with the traitor!

In all three offices Jeremias speaks in the first nocturn, St. Augustine in the second, and St. Paul in the third. Perhaps this is not merely coincidental. Jeremias is the foretype of the suffering Savior; Augustine and Paul both received the grace of conversion and aptly exemplify the marvelous effect of Christ's passion on their souls.

First Nocturn

First of all, let us study the three psalms.

Psalm 68 is an anxious cry for help against wicked enemies. It is a prophetical hymn which we Christians can readily regard as the Savior's Passion song. The theme is obvious: the agony of Christ in the Garden.

This psalm consists of four clearly discernible parts.

1. Background scene: Christ's agony is described in various pictures.
2. The prayer in the Garden.
3. The curse: an awful woe upon the faithless Jews.
4. Solace in the agony. Here we think of the angel sustaining the Savior in His agony. Then we cast a glance at the rich and glorious fruits of His passion.

Psalm 69 is an excerpt from Psalm 39. But even at that, it contains a complete thought pattern: prayer in time of need. The author looks to his enemies, to his friends, and to his own soul.

Psalm 70 is a prayer for deliverance. We may regard the psalm either as a harassed old man's trustful plea for help, or as the collective prayer of the Jews in exile, Israel's advent cry for redemption. A note of unswerving confidence in God pervades the psalm. It opens with an assertion of firm reliance on God's help and closes with a joyous expression of assurance of being heard. We can observe only a general progression of thought through the psalm, without any strophic divisions. The thought changes between verses 14 and 15.

1. Earnest assertion of trust in God (1–14).
2. Certainty of being heard (15–26).

The hymn begins with some verses of psalm 30. Perhaps the author recalled this ancient psalm of David's and mused: "This is how David prayed; let us do the same."

Then the liturgical application. The first three psalms are the vigorous outcries of an unhappy and sorely afflicted soul. In our office they become the prayers that fall from the lips of Jesus, revealing to redeemed mankind and to the eternal Father in heaven all the unspeakable suffering and affliction that flood the Savior's heart. So they depict the Savior praying in the Garden. It is for us to pray these psalms along with Jesus, now sympathizing with our Bridegroom, now grieving and begging forgiveness for our own sins and for those of the world; these sins but serve to crucify Him anew.

Matins begins with the masterly Messianic psalm 68. We may call it the Gethsemane psalm.

The antiphon outlines the main purpose of the Passion. (a) Jesus has come to repair God's honor. As a result, in a true sense of the word, He was "consumed," "eaten up," in His passion and death. (b) He redeemed us by vicarious satisfaction. He took upon Himself the sins of the whole world, and in this agony in the Garden of Olives they crush Him with their frightful weight.

We can hear Jesus grieving in the psalm. Strophe one: Description of the Passion, a series of pictures describing His agony. They give us some idea of the terrible extent of His sufferings.

Strophe two: Christ's prayer, the prayer in the Garden. Men's sins are like a bottomless quagmire, or a floorless sea into which He sinks and in which He can find no solid place to stand.

Strophe three: The curse. On the Savior's lips this passage is doubly forceful. Here is the fearful doom the Lord foretold for the faithless Jewish people that had chosen to slay its Messiah. It is the prophecy of Israel's punishment for all future ages, a blinded nation, fated to wander over the face of the earth, ever hated and despised, ever fearful and insecure, ever in quest of gold.

Psalm 69 is a prayer of one in great need. Here we see Jesus considering first His enemies (Judas, the Jews, and the devil) who are plotting His death; then His own innocence.

Psalm 70 also fits in with Christ's prayer in the Garden. A

hymn of trust in God, it rises to sentiments of perfect resignation and confident assurance of being heard. The antiphon is somewhat in the vein of the "Father, if it be possible, let this chalice pass from Me."

Especially from its interior spiritual aspects, the psalms have described Christ's passion in a rather uniform way. The versicle now summarizes the action so far: the enemy is at hand; inwardly Jesus struggles against His passion.

Up to this point the action was set in the Garden of Olives. Now the scene changes. We see another figure: the disowned bride sitting by the side of the road, the wasted and desolate Sion, sinful mankind. Once more we see the striking figures in triple contrast, the bride in the lesson, the Savior in the responsories.

The first Lamentation, from which our three lessons are taken, describes the ruins of the city and its temple: figures of fallen mankind and the sin-ridden soul.

First Lesson

Aleph: Mankind and the soul, once the King's child, God's child; now indentured to Satan through sin. A queen dethroned.

Beth: The figure: our first parents driven out of Paradise; mankind disinherited. Once the devil attained his goal, he abandoned them to utter misery.

Ghimel: The Jews depart as captives to Babylon. A figure of the restlessness of men estranged from God.

Daleth: Picturesque in the extreme. The past, and the present. Formerly crowds of pilgrims thronged the streets and gates of the city. The joyous welcomes of the priests filled the air. Young maidens sang in the choirs. But now, what a change! All this is an image of the history of mankind and our own souls. Nature exulted when man "walked with God" in the Garden of Eden. She mourns and grieves now, for the temple of our soul lies in ruins.

He: The prince of this world has triumphed. He rules mankind. A black and tarry flood of sin sweeps over the earth.

And I too have swollen this flood with the stream of my own personal sins. The admonition, then, is directed to me: "Jerusalem, Jerusalem, return to the Lord your God."

First responsory. Now, after letting this sad image work its full effect on our souls, we turn our attention to the reality: the Savior sweating drops of blood in the Garden of Olives. The sins of the whole world in all their wicked horror and repugnance rise up before His soul, a gigantic burden that He must shoulder though it seems to Him that He will never be able to carry it. Hence His ardent, plaintive prayer.

Second Lesson: a continuation of the first

Vau: Grace was man's ornament. Now because of sin, all such ornaments have vanished. Helplessly sunk in misery, man is driven along by Satan who is sure of his prey.

Zain: The image: our first parents reminiscing about the Paradise they lost. It is only after sin that man fully realizes the value and happiness of innocence.

Heth: Very poetical. It shows us the shame and disgrace of the disowned bride (mankind). Full of shame, she turns away.

Teth: The bride lying in the dust by the roadside. The whole lesson gives a further picture of the abasement of mankind: once so beautiful through grace; now fallen so low through sin. Once more I strike my breast, contrite; for I myself am the faithless bride: "Jerusalem, Jerusalem. . . ."

Second responsory. Another series of scenes from the Passion. First we see Christ reviewing His sufferings, afflicted with death, without solace or comfort, deserted by His disciples. Then we see Him handed over to His enemies. "Helplessly" He permits them to lead Him away. Every affliction that belongs to His spouse He takes upon Himself.

This responsory is exceptionally vivid and dramatic. Its few words convey a wealth of thought. Particularly effective is the repetition of verse two. This is the so-called *repetenda*. It usually contains the leading thought of the responsory. Note the antithesis: "you flee away; I go to be slain for you."

Third Lesson: a continuation of the second

Jod: The pagans' desecration and destruction of the temple cut the Jews to the heart. Sin desecrates the greatest of sanctuaries, the human soul. And to expiate this crime, the sacred temple of Christ's human nature is now desecrated. ("Destroy this temple . . ." Christ said. Recall, too, the stripping of the altar on Holy Thursday morning; and do not forget the next psalm, number 73.)

Caph: Famine. Gems bartered for bread. Sin deprives man of everything. (The prodigal son was barely able to scrape together a few husks, such as were eaten by the swine.)

Lamed: The bride herself speaks. A famous passage. The bride lies disgraced in the dust by the side of the road. Now we see the Savior with His sufferings there at her side.

Mem: A description of the interior anguish of the Passion.
         The frightful agony of mankind's sins. This Christ
         took upon Himself. Mankind snared in Satan's
         meshes.

Nun: (literally): The yoke of my sins never sleeps. A
         stirring image of fallen man. A heavy yoke binds
         him fast. He must carry this yoke of sin through the
         centuries, driven on by the relentless devil.

I too have added my weight to this yoke. "Jerusalem, Jerusalem . . ."

Third responsory. Another surprising series of Passion pictures. A moving passage: Jesus "the man of sorrows" stands before us. All the suffering and affliction of sinful mankind, the disinherited bride, Christ takes on Himself. The whole responsory is an adaptation of the familiar Passion prophecy in Isaias 53:2 ff. Notice the emphasis on the idea of the vicarious atonement Christ makes for us. The responsory well shows the relation between the Lamentations and the Tenebrae Matins, between sinful mankind and the suffering Redeemer. "He hath born our iniquities," He suffers for us. It is an appropriate conclusion for the first nocturn.

Second Nocturn

Let us study first the literal meaning of the three psalms.

Psalm 71: the Messias is a King of Peace. The whole psalm is Messianic.

The thought pattern:

1. A cry of longing for the Messiah (1–3).
2. Justice and peace, the trademarks of the Messiah (4–7).
3. His kingdom shall never end (8–11).
4. He shall be a Father to the poor (12–14).

5. The happiness and abundance in His kingdom (15–18).

Conclusion: a tribute of praise (19–20). This verse also concludes the whole second book of the Psalter.

Psalm 71 is evidently an Epiphany hymn. At first sight, consequently, it seems out of place used here as a Passion psalm. Probably it never would have found its way into the Tenebrae office were it not for the fact that the whole series of psalms from 68 to 75 was selected as a unit for this Matins office. However, we shall soon see that it fits quite well here. A few reflections may help to clarify this point. It is precisely in the Passion that we find a particular prominence and emphasis given to Christ's kingship. On Palm Sunday He entered the city as a king. That He claimed to be a king was the main charge against Him in Pilate's court. In His answer to Pilate's question, Christ Himself explained the point: "Yes, I am a king." And then how inspiringly beautiful, how full of awe His kingship appears in the Passion! A king of suffering and sorrow. We see Him seated there on His mock throne, the crown of thorns encircling His brow. The inscription at the top of the cross, His throne for the while, "Jesus of Nazareth, King of the Jews." Moreover, we ought not forget that Holy Thursday was the day on which Christ instituted the Eucharist. The lessons of the third nocturn commemorate this event. Especially toward the end, psalm 71 has Eucharistic overtones; mention is made of the abundance of grain in the Messianic kingdom. And it is the Holy Eucharist above all that is the continuation of Christ's kingdom of peace.

The antiphon confines itself mostly to the kingship of sorrow and suffering. It has two possible meanings. Through His death the Lord Jesus has delivered the poor (mankind) from the mighty (Satan). But it may also be regarded as: The Lord (the Father) has delivered the poor (Jesus) from His enemies by raising Him from the tomb as Victor. The psalm, then, fits in easily with the theme: Christ's solace and comfort in His agony. The angel shows Him the kingdom of everlasting peace that is to be the fruit of His passion. It could be, then, that the Church desires to give us both meanings from the antiphon.

Psalm 72: The material prosperity of the wicked. This is a didactic poem that describes the struggle that rises in the heart of the just man because of the prosperity of the wicked. There are two principal divisions:

1. The problem: a picture of the good fortune of the wicked and his haughtiness, in contrast to the wavering faith of the just man (1–16).
2. Solution to the problem:
   a) their happiness is short-lived (17–22a);
   b) true happiness consists in possessing God (22b–28).

The last part of this psalm ranks among the finest passages of the Psalter. And the psalm itself harmonizes with our theme. Christ's passion is the timeless illustration of this psalm. For Christ is defeated; the evil one triumphs. The people lose their confidence, even the apostles are scandalized. And yet, how long does the success, the triumph of the Jews, last? In very truth God has kept His word: "As though they were the dream of one who had awakened, O Lord, so will you, when you arise, set at nought these phantoms." Forty years later Jerusalem was a heap of rubble. And see how, through His union with God, even in the midst of His sufferings Jesus triumphs (verse 28). This magnificent passage might well be the victorious conclusion of His agony and the ardent prayer that accompanies it. It may be regarded also as an echo of His ever-beautiful farewell address to His apostles. It is quite true that the Old Testament cannot offer the perfect solution for the problem of suffering as Christ our suffering Savior did: "Take up the cross . . . follow Me." In the Matins for Holy Thursday this is precisely the full meaning of psalm 72.

The antiphon concerns the haughty high priests and Pharisees who are bent on slaying Christ.

Psalm 73: Desecration of the sanctuary. A poetical elegy on the destruction of the temple (by the Babylonians, perhaps).

The thought pattern is evident:

1. A description of suffering (1–10).
2. In trial and affliction, trust in God by considering the past history (11–16); and by reflecting on God's providence in the realm of nature (17–18).
3. Pleas for help and deliverance from affliction (19–24).

The application of this psalm to our Matins is easy. The ruined temple is an image of the matchless, living temple of Christ's sacred humanity. The Jews are proceeding to destroy this temple, as Christ Himself foretold: "Destroy this temple. . . ." [3] Thus, in the words of this psalm, the Church grieves for the body of Christ, this living temple of God, so frightfully broken and torn during these days of His passion. The antiphon is a cry for help placed by us on the lips of the Savior agonizing in the Garden of Olives.

St. Augustine's commentary on psalm 54 supplies the lessons for the second nocturn. Lessons four and five treat of the first verse of this psalm: "Hearken, O God, to my prayer; turn not away from my pleading; give heed to me, and answer me."

It is the outcry of a sorely afflicted soul. What is the source of this affliction? Verse three answers: "I rock with grief and am troubled"; wicked men persecute the Psalmist. St. Augustine adds the thought that the wicked are on earth for a good purpose. Either they eventually become good, or the good are

[3] John 2:19.

tried by their wickedness. The Church clearly wishes to apply this verse to our Savior in the Garden. It is His cry of anguish.

Fifth Lesson

We must not hate the wicked, for we know that a Saul may in time become a Paul. Only the devil is hopelessly lost. We have to hate him and give him ceaseless battle, for he is the king of a world estranged from God. The thoughts of the lesson are but loosely related to one another. Only the sixth lesson speaks explicitly of Christ's passion, where Augustine applies a verse of the psalm to Jesus: "For in the city I see violence and strife." Whereas the second nocturn's lessons are rather disappointing, the responsories, all treating of Judas, are most appropriate.

The fourth responsory may well be linked to the preceding lesson where we read that the wicked are here on earth that they amend. The link, Judas, unfortunately, is no longer able to amend. By way of exception, this responsory is not taken from Scripture.

Across the screen of our soul are flashed the brief, disconnected phrases of the sad fate of the unfortunate apostle. Note the antithesis: Friend—kiss; betrayal—hold him fast. The words, "It were better for him if he had never been born," occur in all three responsories. In the third they are the *repetenda* too, itself repeated three times.

The fifth responsory is borrowed from an ancient Church hymn.

The sixth depicts the solemn scenes at the Last Supper when Christ first mentioned to His disciples the fact of His betrayal. (See Leonardo da Vinci's *Last Supper*.)

All three responsories sharply depict the pain it costs Jesus to lose even a single soul.

THIRD NOCTURN

Psalm 74: God rewards us according to our deeds. A "judgment" psalm. We must note the change of persons speaking in this psalm if we are to understand its meaning.

1. Introduction: Praise to God (1–2).
2. God addresses sinners (3–5).
3. The Psalmist speaks to his enemies (6–8).
4. Conclusion: Praise to God (9–10).

The psalm tells of the punishment God deals out to the wicked. God is patient, but when the time for patience is up, His wrath breaks out suddenly and devastatingly. Hence the warning against pride and arrogance. Vividly it describes God forcing the sinner to drain the cup of His wrath to the very dregs.

Application of this psalm to Holy Thursday Matins. At first sight, evil seems to triumph in the Passion. Therefore the Jews grow even haughtier. But the day of judgment is coming for those who stubbornly remain in sin. On that day what vengeance God will wreak on those sins, when He punished His own Son so severely for them! Christ uses this psalm to admonish His haughty enemies: "Leave off sinning and be converted." It reminds us of certain parts of the Passion. The antiphon, for example: "Speak not insolently against God," makes us think of the terrible challenge hurled at Pilate: "His blood be upon us and upon our children." [4] In the psalm itself, we recall Christ's words: "Henceforth you shall see the Son of man sitting at the right hand of the Father, and coming on the clouds of heaven," as though He would say: "Now I stand before you bound like a criminal; but soon it will be you who stand before My judgment seat." The psalm develops this thought.

[4] Matt. 27:25.

When we see the cup of God's wrath that the sinner has to drain, we think almost unwittingly of the chalice of suffering Christ had to drain to the very dregs for us sinners. We can make many similar references and like relations between the psalm and the Holy Thursday office.

Psalm 75: Thanks for a recent victory of Israel (over Sennacherib, perhaps). A picturesque hymn.

The thought pattern:

Introduction: God dwells in Jerusalem (1–2).

1. The judgment to be passed on the enemy (3–6).
2. God, the Judge of the whole world (7–9).
3. Prayers of thanksgiving in the temple (10–12).

The application. We easily grasp the picture of our redemption as a tremendous battle waged between Christ and Satan. On the battlefield of Golgotha, Christ smashed the bow, shield, and sword of His diabolical enemy. But now we watch the fierce battle, the hours of Christ's agony in the Garden of Olives. Yet we manage also to glimpse already the glorious victory. The psalm describes the Last Judgment as a battlefield strewn with corpses. Even in the agony in the Garden, Christ's all-seeing eye discerned the trophies and gains of that battle for our redemption.

The antiphon is forceful. Jesus' passion was a terrible sentence passed on sin and Satan. The earth is personified, and in fear and reverent silence she watches this most unusual spectacle: the triumph of God over hell and sin.

All this points to the fact that this psalm treats not so much of the Passion itself, as of its effects. Redemption is the sentence of condemnation God passed on sin. Jesus may seem to suffer defeat, but actually He is Victor and Judge. So, for a preface to this psalm we can aptly use Christ's words: "Sentence is now being passed on the world; now is the time when the prince of this world is to be cast out." [5]

Psalm 76: The mysterious ways of God. This resembles psalm 72 somewhat, in its mirroring the soul of a God-fearing man who feels his people have been abandoned by God. It is a sad hymn, with hardly a glimmer of hope to brighten the heart of the Psalmist. Through tears he begs God for help, but in vain. Forlorn, the soul finds no comfort in its thoughts. All he can do is sigh despondently as he asks himself: "How long is this going to last? Will God reject us forever?" Finally he comes to the painful conclusion that he had so long resisted making. Now he has to admit God's dealings with His people have changed beyond a doubt.

Rather suddenly then, the Psalmist turns from the dismal present to the history of his people's past. The glorious memories swirl up before him. He sees the God of the Covenant ransoming His people and destroying the heathen. The concluding sentence brings a faint glimmer of hope in God's mercy: "You led your people like a flock."

The thought pattern:

1. Doubt and uncertainty: interior struggles (1–10).

2. Settling the doubt: reflecting on the past (11–20).

The application. The Church applies the sentiments of this psalm, its feeling of spiritual abandonment and utter lack of comfort and solace, to our Savior in His agony in the Garden. In praying the psalm we may abstract from its thought content and place ourselves beside Christ in the sad surroundings of Gethsemane. A good title for this psalm: "My soul is ready to die with sorrow." [6]

[5] John 12:31.
[6] Matt. 26:28.

In the antiphon we find the Savior on His knees with His arms outstretched, praying.

You can see how this last psalm has brought us back to the theme and sentiments of the Holy Thursday office, the agony in the Garden. It is true that the first nocturn opened with psalm 68 (the "Gethsemane psalm") and kept to this theme throughout. Still the second and third nocturns occasionally soared to other and loftier thoughts, to return finally in the ninth psalm to the sorrows and torment of the Garden.

A terse paraphrase of Christ's prayer in the Garden, the versicle summarizes the entire Matins office.

The scene of our prayer drama shifts in the lessons of the third nocturn, the institution of the Holy Eucharist. These lessons are taken from a famous passage of St. Paul's First Epistle to the Corinthians.[7] Paul is upbraiding the faithful of Corinth for a certain abuse. In the agape feast, which was closely related to the celebration of the Eucharist, some of the well-to-do faithful were bringing their own food to eat, and letting the poor go hungry. This scarcely betokened the proper sentiments and dispositions for receiving the Holy Eucharist. To remind them, then, of the priceless value of the Eucharist, Paul gives a brief account of its institution. It is because of this account, found in the second of the trio of lessons, that the whole passage was chosen for this nocturn. You would be hard put to find a more sublime section in the whole office for Holy Thursday. Note particularly the passage that links the Eucharist so intimately with the death on the cross: "So it is the Lord's death you are heralding, whenever you eat this bread and drink this cup, until He comes." [8] Abstract from the special circumstances of this letter; place yourself with rever-

[7] I Cor. 11:17–34.
[8] I Cor. 11:26.

ence in the upper room at the Last Supper, and in spirit assist at the institution of the Holy Eucharist. After this account Paul speaks of unworthy Communions and their effects. For such sacrileges God punished many at Corinth with sickness and even death.

Were it not almost certain that Judas did not receive Communion at the Last Supper, we could well think of him in reference to this passage. At any rate, we can never forget that every sacrilegious Communion renews Christ's passion in a spiritual way.

The seventh responsory, like the third, is composed of Old Testament prophecies, especially those of Jeremias.[9] The great prophet, himself a figure of the suffering Savior, describes the special hostility of his own people. His words fall naturally from our Savior's lips. The image of the Lamb of God occurs often in the Scriptures. But the next image is difficult to understand: let us put wood into his bread. That is: let us poison his bread by adding some deadly wood to it. Several kinds of wood can poison food merely by contact with it. The Fathers, and the Church herself, like to apply this figure to the Savior: "Let us put wood (the cross) in his bread (on His body, the true Bread of Life; John 6:32) and destroy Him from the earth."

The eighth responsory is perhaps the most moving of all. Jesus calls His slumbering apostles, upbraids their weakness and indifference, and compares them with the zealous Judas. A fearful contrast: "You sleep, but Judas does not sleep. He hastens to betray Me." Even today we find this contrast: the children of the world against the children of light. It could well be that Jesus upbraids our indifference too.

The ninth responsory gives a short but comprehensive pic-

[9] Jer. 11:19.

ture of the drama as far as it has progressed. Jesus is bound like a thief and led off from the Garden to the high priest.

A glance now over the whole office will reveal the drama's remarkable unity.

Holy Thursday Evening

1. The agony in the Garden predominates. Many of the psalms (68, 69, 70, 76) develop the theme.
2. The Last Supper is described in the eighth lesson, and is treated also in psalm 71.
3. Particular scenes are recalled on this evening:
   a) Judas: responsories 4, 5, 6, 8;
   b) The slumbering apostles: responsory 8;
   c) The enemies: responsory 9.
4. A general treatment of Christ's passion: psalms 72, 73, 74, 75, and the fifth lesson.

The gems of Holy Thursday Matins. First of all, the responsories every one of them; then psalm 68 and the eighth lesson; and the masterly Lamentations.

Defects or weaknesses of this office. The arbitrary use of psalms 68 to 76 in their numerical sequence; and the lessons of the second nocturn.

CHAPTER XXII

Matins for Good Friday

MATINS for Good Friday is the second part and the climax of the trilogy. This part of the drama we might entitle "The Death of Christ on the Cross." Although once again the action proceeds without strict chronological order, yet we can designate Jesus' hanging on the cross as the central and principal scene. The other scenes of the day that appear we may regard as so many pictures and memories fleeting across the mind of our crucified Savior.

The atmosphere of this office is extremely somber and sad. In fact the Psalter holds no psalms sadder than those found here. In the Lamentation even, a frequent accent on grief and affliction is noticeable. The responsories are beautiful, but also sad. And they do not follow the sequence of events in the drama very exactly. This deep sorrow that pervades the Good Friday office keeps throwing brief bits of the Passion scene before us. We do best, then, to focus our attention on the picture of the Savior nailed to the cross and to listen to the outpourings of His afflicted heart. Now it is a feeling of utter abandonment, now a heart-rending grief, as He recalls each event of the past day and of the previous evening.

First Nocturn

The first psalm (2) and its antiphon lose no time in setting us down in the thick of the battle of the Jews against Jesus.

Transported to the council chamber of the high priest, we hear the frenzied shouts of the priests and scribes. When Christ replies to Caiphas: "Yes, I am the Son of God," they throw up their arms and rage like mad men. We think too of how in their fight against Jesus the Jews join forces with the pagans. Pilate and Herod are friends now. We seem to hear the mad shouts of the populace: "Away with Him, crucify Him!" This is the picture we get from the antiphon and opening verses of the psalm.

The psalm is Messianic and describes the war the world wages against Christ and His kingdom. It describes Christ's victory too. One of the Psalter's prize pieces, this psalm is especially dramatic. (We referred to it above, in the study of the Christmas Matins.) The Holy Spirit Himself, in the Acts of the Apostles,[1] makes the application of this psalm to Matins for Good Friday: "Thou hast said through thy Holy Spirit, by the lips of thy servant David, our father: What means this ferment among the nations, why do the peoples cherish vain dreams? See how the kings of the earth stand in array, how its rulers make common cause against the Lord and his Christ." True enough, in this city of ours, Herod and Pontius Pilate, with the Gentiles and the people of Israel to aid them, made common cause against Thy holy servant Jesus, so accomplishing all that Thy power and wisdom had decreed. The first half of the psalm portrays the powerless hate of the Jews. With Jesus nailed to the cross, they have apparently won the victory. But actually, the victory is Jesus'. The second part of the psalm tells us: He who died so pitiably on the cross is the eternal Son of God; "Him we shall serve." "Yes; if only I am lifted up from the earth, I will attract all men to Myself." [2] As

[1] Acts 4:25 f.
[2] John 12:32.

the antiphon indicates, however, it is the opening verse that gives the main idea of the psalm.

Psalm 21. This, the most stirring Passion psalm of all, then follows. According to the unanimous testimony of the Fathers, and of the Church herself, this psalm is directly Messianic. In a vision David beholds the crucifixion. Our Savior Himself on His cross recited this psalm, or at least its first verse. It is the climax, the central point of the great drama of the cross. There are three parts: complaints of the suffering Savior; description of His sufferings; comfort and solace in these sufferings. In the first part we hear the prayer that issues from the lips of our crucified Savior. The Gospel gives us the original text of this prayer: *"Eli, eli, lamma sabacthani!"* It is a cry that burst from the unfathomable depths of Christ, suffering and abandoned by God. The first part wavers between utter despondency and deep trust in God. Strophes one and three are negative descriptions; strophes two and four are positive ones. Is it hard to imagine these sentiments tearing at the heart of our crucified Savior? See how He writhes, like a tortured worm. The shouts and cries of the mocking crowd are arrows to pierce His heart. We read practically the same account in the Gospel.[3] But even in the midst of this, utterly abandoned by God and man, Christ keeps returning to perfect trust in His Father.

A succession of Passion scenes pass before Christ's eyes and ours in the second part of the psalm. We are led through all the scenes of Christ's bitter sufferings, from the gruff capture in the Garden, to the last weary sigh on the cross. His enemies are depicted as ravenous beasts, and the Passion as an attack by wild boars and lions. Like wild animals, His adversaries thirst for His blood. Now it is poured out like water and all

[3] Matt. 27:43.

His strength has vanished, His blood spent to the last drop. As its own flame consumes the candle, so His fire of suffering and love consumes our Savior, the great paschal candle, burning on the candelabra of the cross. His mouth more parched than an old, dry potsherd, He suffers a burning thirst. The malicious Jews surround Him like a pack of wild dogs. Then we come upon another familiar prophecy: "They have pierced my hands and my feet." This is the psalm's climax. We can picture the Savior hurled to the ground. His hands and feet are pierced by the nails that answer to the heavy blows of the hammer. His joints are racked and stretched so that we can number every bone. All eyes are fastened on Him now as He is raised aloft. What a spectacle of misery! And yet, not a heart melts to sympathy; they delight in His anguish. Then another well-known prophecy (which is also the antiphon): At the foot of the cross His executioners cast lots for His garments.[4]

It is the third section of this psalm that tells us of the comfort and solace Christ had in His passion. The cup of suffering had been drained to the very dregs. A ray of "resurrection glory" now breaks through the gloom of Golgotha. Our Savior cries out: "It is consummated." With this He utters a last prayer of thanksgiving for the salvation of the world, and we join Him in this prayer. If we interpret and apply the next few verses properly, we hear the Savior speak of the fruits of His sacrifice on the cross: (a) mankind's salvation; (b) the Eucharist, the fruit of the tree of the cross; (c) the conversion of the Gentiles, the birth of a universal Church. Thus the whole world gathers around the cross so that Christ's very words were fulfilled: "Yes; if only I am lifted up from the earth, I will attract all men to Myself."[5] All this points to the fact

[4] John 19:23.
[5] John 12:32.

that this psalm is the climax, the high point of the Matins drama.

Psalm 26. Though it is quite appropriate, this psalm definitely eases the tension of the drama. Characterized by its unique Davidic confidence in God, it ranks with the most stirring hymns in the Psalter. There are two distinct parts; trust in God; plea for help in great need. The first strophe of the first part: trust and confidence in the midst of great affliction. Second strophe: an ardent plea; it is only the desire to remain with God that comforts the Psalmist. With God he feels strong enough to endure everything. In the second part of the psalm he sinks to the depths of suffering and distress, prays for help, and then regains his former confidence in God.

We have scarcely any trouble in placing this whole psalm on the lips of the crucified Savior. It is the very opposite of psalm 21. Whereas this latter is colored by deep suffering and abandonment that rise eventually to firm trust and confidence, psalm 26 is marked by a deep confidence in God from which, at times, it sinks to depths of suffering and affliction. But even in the greatest affliction, Christ's soul was united with the Father. Indeed this was the whole source of His strength.

The very opening verse of the psalm fits well into our scene: the darkness that shrouds the hill of Calvary, the darkness too in the soul of our Savior who cries out: "My God, why hast Thou abandoned Me?" Nevertheless, some light shines through all this darkness, the light of obedience, of love and trust in the Father. It is this light that gives the Savior strength in the midst of His furious enemies. He realizes His oneness with the Father. When He complains, then, at the height of His suffering, that God has forsaken Him, He is voluntarily taking this last, bitter draught of suffering to win for us the grace of spiritual union with God. In this mood, then, standing at the foot of the cross before the eyes of our afflicted Savior, we utter this plea for union with God.

In the second part of the psalm we hear again the laments of Jesus. At the verse: "Though my father and mother forsake me, yet will the Lord receive me," we cannot help but think of the cowardly flight and desertion of His apostles. A verse or two later we hear the false witnesses mouthing their charges in the council of the Sanhedrin and before Pilate. We recall that the Jews deceived themselves too, acting against their convictions, hurting themselves most of all (v. 12b). This verse serves also as the antiphon for the psalm. If we relate it to the crucifixion, our ears are quick to hear the Savior's laments over the ingratitude of His people, yet they do not miss His prayer: "Forgive them. . . ."

We might put the last verse on Our Lady's lips, voicing her hope in her Son's resurrection.

The versicle recalls the antiphon for psalm 21. Everything has been taken from Him, even His garments. Now He hangs on the cross in overwhelming shame and disgrace.

The lessons. It is the bride once again, sinful mankind in all her shame and disgrace, that we place alongside the pathetic figure on the cross. This is the relation that the lessons bear to the Lamentations.

Lessons one and two are taken from the second chapter of the Book of Lamentations; lesson three is from the third chapter. The first chapter of Lamentations dealt more with Jerusalem's sins, and so was appropriate for the first part of the trilogy. Chapter two, however, dwells more on the desolation and disgrace of Jerusalem and its temple; very fitting for Good Friday.

For an understanding of its symbolism: Jerusalem, devastated and disgraced, is a figure of mankind, the bride sitting in the dust by the side of the road, cast into extreme misery through sin. To redeem man and to relieve him of his misery, Jesus of His own will takes all this disgrace upon Himself. It is for this that He now hangs on the cross.

The first lesson describes Jerusalem's destruction. That is the figure; the reality we find in the responsory: the laments from the lips of the Crucified. In a trio of brief Passion scenes we listen to the cries that surge from the Savior's heart. The apostles have deserted Him, Judas is His betrayer, and His own people are His murderers. He who loved all of them unto death, in His turn must suffer from them all. And of course, the main reason for presenting these three incidents is to give us a warning: we too belong to each of these three classes.

The second lesson, again most picturesque, describes the terrible misery caused by the destruction of Sion. The "Mem" verse is particularly beautiful, and is frequently cited: "Great as the sea is thy destruction." How frightful the wound sin has inflicted on mankind! (Recall the parable of the Good Samaritan.) Terrifying the pain and anguish of Christ who hangs on the cross to heal that wound. In verse "Samech" we are quick to recall the mockeries of the Jews and the soldiers.

With a few, deft strokes the second responsory paints a masterly picture of the scene for Good Friday afternoon. The chronological order of events is purposely disregarded. From events at the foot of the cross, scenes shift rapidly to things happening before and after the crucifixion. The Church wishes these few words to strike a wholesome terror into our hearts.

In the third lesson, taken from chapter three of the Lamentations, Jeremias is spokesman for his people. Here we regard Jeremias not as the disgraced bride, but as the foretype of the suffering Savior. We hear Christ's anguished cries from the cross: Jesus, the man of sorrows, on whom the whole wrath of God weighs because He took on Himself the sins of mankind. The beauty and sentiment of this passage matches psalm 21. Both deal extensively with the abandonment and interior and exterior darkness that enveloped the Savior. All mankind's sin and all its affliction closed in upon Him like an impregnable wall.

Jesus on the cross speaks once more in the third responsory. As in the *Improperium,* where the Redeemer mournfully complains to His people, here Jesus, on the point of death, addresses a poignant question to His people, Israel. Using the familiar Old Testament figure of the vineyard, He speaks from the very depths of His heart.

Second Nocturn

Psalm 37 is one of the most pathetic psalms in the whole Psalter. The author, probably David, describes the suffering and affliction that fell on him because of sin. Since the psalm is likewise Messianic, we can readily apply it to our suffering Savior. He is afflicted and punished for the sins of the world which He wills to call His own, for He has volunteered to pay its ransom. We may picture Him either as in the *Ecce Homo,* or at the scourging pillar, or hanging on the cross, while He sorrowfully chants this song. In the antiphon we find that "the Jews used force on me, they sought to slay me." These few words give us a summary of all the violence and outrages heaped on Jesus: the arrest in the Garden, the beating and scourging in the praetorium, the crowning with thorns. And so it goes, right up to the crucifixion.

Many verses of the psalm are especially appropriate. We hear that the Father, angered by sin, cast the full weight of His wrath on His Son. A description of the "Man of sorrows" follows: not a spot on His body is left without a wound. We think immediately of the scourging and the crowning with thorns. The picture compels our attention. All His followers desert Him; His people cry out: "Crucify Him!" Yet, through it all, Jesus breathes only heavenly patience and peace. Often we think of: "Jesus, however, held His peace." His enemies gloat over their victory. For all His good works, His kindnesses, He receives only evil in return. Indeed, "What manner of man is this?" There is no need to mention that this psalm is one of the gems of the Good Friday office.

Psalm 39 consists of three parts, somewhat different in their tone. (a) A hymn of thanksgiving. The author has obtained help in a pressing need; now he sings his thanks to God. He is convinced that he can best show his gratitude by fulfilling God's will; he therefore makes this promise to God. (b) A prayer for help. New dangers and trials appear on the horizon; once more, then, he comes begging to God. (c) The third part is psalm 69 (see Matins for Holy Thursday). The Psalmist studies first his enemies, then his friends, and finally himself. How does this psalm fit into our Good Friday office? Obviously its first and second parts offer a description of the Passion from the lips of Jesus Himself. This is hinted at by the antiphon, borrowed from the first part of the psalm. This antiphon is the prayer of the Savior on the cross, asking for perseverance and ultimate victory over His haughty, taunting enemies. The second and third parts of the psalm contain several verses which can be referred to our suffering Savior with no trouble at all. They speak of the measureless depths of His affliction, of His utter abandonment, and also of His prayers addressed to the Father.

Nor does the first part of the psalm lack an application to our Matins. On the testimony of the Epistle to the Hebrews, this psalm was the morning prayer in the life of the Redeemer.[6] ". . . that sins should be taken away by the blood of bulls and goats is impossible. As Christ comes into the world He says: no sacrifice, no offering was Thy demand; Thou hast endowed Me, instead, with a body. Thou has not found any pleasure in burnt sacrifices, in sacrifices for sin. See then, I said, I am coming to fulfill what is written of Me, where the book lies unrolled; to do Thy will, O My God" (v. 10). In accordance with this divine will we have been sanctified by an offering made once and for all, the body of Jesus Christ. The entire life of Jesus, from birth to death, was one great holocaust of obedience to the Father for the redeeming of the world. The crucifixion was the final act of this sacrifice. All the animal offerings of the Old Testament were but types and shadows of this the one, true, all-atoning sacrifice. If, then, the Epistle to the Hebrews would make this psalm the morning prayer of Christ's life, the Church would make it His night prayer too. And what a profound thought that is! Now the Savior is lifted up to the rocks of Calvary ("He set my feet upon a crag"). In the midst of all His sufferings He chants a hymn of thanks for the redemption that is now accomplished. Once more, from the pulpit of the cross, He proclaims to us that His was a surrender to God's will, and that such a surrender is our life's task. From the cross He calls out, down through the centuries, that now satisfaction has been made to God's justice ("I announced your justice

[6] Heb. 10:4.

in the vast assembly"). Such a hymn of thanksgiving seems especially beautiful rising from the heart of Jesus on this saddest of all days.

Psalm 53, a prayer of petition, is easily understood. There are two distinct parts: (a) a plea for help against the enemy; (b) confidence in being heard, and a promise of thanksgiving. The antiphon suggests that we should apply the first part of the psalm to Jesus. The verse, "For haughty men have risen up against me," is strikingly appropriate. The Jews now have handed their Messiah over to the pagans and have thereby renounced the prerogative of being God's chosen people. This explains why the emphasis is on the "haughty men." In the second part, our eye fastens on the verse, "Freely will I offer you sacrifice." We cannot help but think of the sacrifice of Calvary.

The versicle is a repetition of the antiphon for psalm 26 in the first nocturn. It stresses the malice and hypocrisy of the Jews who chose to slay Jesus against their own better convictions, and indeed, to their own destruction.

The lessons once more are taken from the sermons of St. Augustine on the psalms. Unlike those for Holy Thursday, these second nocturn lessons are rich in ideas and are closely related to the theme of the day. They are an explanation of psalm 63. Because this psalm is explained in the second nocturn of Holy Saturday's Matins too, and because a knowledge of its contents is presupposed for an understanding of this lesson, and finally because the psalm itself is most appropriate for Christ's passion, we shall first give its translation, and afterward a commentary on its meaning.

Psalm 63

1   (for the leader. A psalm of David)

I

Petition:

2   Hear, O God, my voice in my lament;
from the dread enemy preserve
my life.

3   Shelter me against the council of
malefactors, against the tumult of
evildoers,

Motive, the persecution of his enemies:

4   Who sharpen their tongues like
swords, who aim like arrows their
bitter words,

5   Shooting from ambush at the innocent man, suddenly shooting at
him without fear.

6   They resolve on their wicked plan;
they conspire to set snares, saying,
"Who will see us?"

7   They devise a wicked scheme, and
conceal the scheme they have devised; deep are the thoughts of
each heart.

II

God's punishement:

8   But God shoots his arrows at them;
suddenly they are struck.

9   He brings them down by their own
tongues; all who see them nod
their heads.

The just rejoice: 10 And all men fear and proclaim the
work of God, and ponder what he
has done.
11 The just man is glad in the Lord and
takes refuge in him; in him glory
all the upright of heart.

There are two main divisions. (a) The affliction and suffering from his enemies (strophe 1–3); (b) God's reply and the
punishment of the enemy. In his treatise St. Augustine points
out how Christ's passion and resurrection give this psalm
splendid illustration. Thus Good Friday's Matins treats the
first part of the psalm where the victory of the wicked is described; the second part, God's triumph, is reserved for Holy
Saturday.

In this first part the Savior sighs and begs for help and protection against the enemy, the Jews in particular, who slay
Him not so much with the sword of their hands, as with
that of their tongues. For it was their persistent accusations
that wrung the sentence of crucifixion from Pilate. They took
counsel, they plotted their wicked schemes. Now they see their
hated adversary fastened to the cross. They exult in victory
and mock and taunt the Crucified. But how long shall this
last? The psalm gives a grand description of the overthrow.
At the height of their triumph God's wrath strikes. And what
about Jesus at this point? With Good Friday but hardly passed,
already the Jews were uneasy in enjoying their triumph, for
they feared Jesus would rise from the dead. They sealed the
tomb and set guards over it. And by so doing, of course, they
provided official witnesses for the resurrection. The guards
were seized with fear while the Savior and His followers were

smiling in the first warmth of Easter joy. Now we can readily grasp the lessons; the sixth is particularly beautiful, with its typical Augustinian vigor.

Once again it is the Jews that the Savior addresses in the fourth responsory. Not limited to any special time, the scene takes in rather the whole Passion, from the arrest in the Garden, through the scourging, to the crucifixion itself. The fifth responsory is exceptionally vivid. We are midway in the Matins office. A few, masterly strokes sketch the Lord's death. Over and over the *repetenda* emphasizes that death. Twice we hear Christ exclaim from the cross in the darkness that settles over Calvary, two verses, from psalms 21 and 30.

The sixth responsory is another lament from the Savior's lips. It is a rather difficult passage from Jeremias [7] where, taken literally, the prophet grieves over the persecution his people have inflicted on him. Since Jeremias was a figure of the Savior, the Church now applies the passage to Christ. It is a classic elegy. The tomb is the place to set the scene for our listening to the lament of the dead Savior.

Third Nocturn

This nocturn likewise opens with two rather gloomy psalms. Psalm 58 is a heart-rending cry for help against a bloodthirsty enemy. Despite his affliction, the author is animated by a firm confidence in God. It is this confidence that shoots some sunlight through the mournful atmosphere of the psalm. Two refrains occur twice in the psalm, forming its climax and summarizing its sentiments. On the one hand there is affliction and attack from the enemy: "Each evening they return, they snarl like dogs and prowl about the city." On the other hand we find deep trust in God: "For You, O God, are my strong-

[7] Jer. 12:7–12.

hold." Thus we already have the key for the interpretation
of the psalm in the Good Friday office. Infinite suffering and
sorrow; limitless trust in God: these are the two poles between which Christ's human soul wavers like a compass nee-
dle. On one side we hear the words fall from the cross: "My
God, why hast Thou forsaken Me?" On the other: "Father,
into Thy hands I commend My spirit." It is thus we put
the psalm on the lips of the Crucified and with heartfelt sympathy listen to the outcries of His sufferings, not failing to
catch His fervent prayer of confidence in God. The Jews are
rightly styled "bloodthirsty" men. Although the Psalmist
would assert his own innocence, this can hold perfectly true
only of Jesus. In the first refrain, "Each evening they return,"
we think of the devil; "at evening" when the powers of darkness unleash their might against Jesus; again, when the whole,
vast horde of hell, like bloodthirsty dogs, gather atop the hill
of Calvary. Yet in the midst of all this grievous affliction, Christ
remains closely united to the Father: "O my strength! your
praise will I sing." Indeed, it is on the harp of the cross that
He plays for the Father the greatest hymn of praise. In the
antiphon we see that the Church wishes to depict Christ's
sufferings in this hymn.

Psalm 87 can also lay claim to being one of the saddest
hymns in the Psalter. Its syllables speak not the faintest trace
of comfort. Just one wave of suffering after another, with a
triple cry for help out of an utter abandonment by God. A
feeling of complete annihilation pervades the psalm. "My
couch is among the dead, whom you remember no longer."
Even after such outpourings of grief the Psalmist fails to
overcome his suffering. He cannot raise his eyes in confidence
to God, but chooses to end with a gloomy, melancholy lament
over God's wrath. The application is evident. To put it briefly:

the psalm is a paraphrase of Christ's words: "My God, why hast Thou forsaken Me?" a cry of utter abandonment by God. Jesus sees Himself already in the grave, sealed off from the living. Death, the greatest punishment this earth inflicts, is also the penalty for sin, and thus it is the deepest humiliation for the God-man. If Christ recoiled at the grave of Lazarus, how must He, Life itself, have shaken with horror at the thought of His own death! The antiphon emphasizes the utter abandonment Christ endured. We think not so much of the apostles' desertion, as of the Father's forsaking Him also. Everything that might have offered some comfort was taken from Him.

Psalm 93 is in somewhat the same vein, a hymn of grief and earnest petition, but much more hopeful than the preceding psalms. In fact, it rises to the heights of a full realization of victory. The hymn is artistically fashioned, with three pairs of corresponding strophes. The middle strophe is an intercalary strophe.

I 1. Petition: May God punish the wicked (1–3).
   2. Picture: The activities of the wicked (4–7).

II Reflection:
   3. God sees the actions of men (8–11).
   4. God is the hope of the just (12–15).

III 5. God gives aid (16–19).
   6. God punishes the wicked (20–23).

This psalm lends a ray of light to the rather gloomy atmosphere of the hour, despite the fact that the antiphon would have us stress its dismal side. Its application to our afflicted and crucified Savior offers no special difficulty.

Nevertheless I think it worth while to suggest the following setting for the psalm. It is Good Friday evening. Christ already lies in the tomb, and the Jews exult in their triumph. Mary, the Lord's Mother and the noblest member of the grievously afflicted Church, sits near the tomb and prays this psalm. Only too well do its thoughts fit in with the sentiments of this Mother at the grave of her Son; grief, lament, and hope in His resurrection. To be sure, those thoughts of vengeance must be tempered by our Christian faith. 1. O God, how long will the wicked rejoice? 2. A picture of wickedness: the high priests and the Pharisees. 3. Finally they realize the truth. It is true that Jesus is defeated, to all appearances. His eyes are closed, His arm limp in death. Yet He is the eternal Judge. 4. God, the hope of the just. He never forsakes His own. He will rise again. 5. After Calvary, the resurrection. Indeed, were it not for God's grace, sorrow could well deprive me of my hope. Though the horror of His passion tears at my heart, my soul is at peace in its hope for His resurrection. 6. Punishment of the Jews. They have called this punishment down on their own heads. "They shed the blood of the innocent Lamb." And indeed, His blood shall come upon this people, an eternal witness of the murder of their God. This last psalm of Matins brings the action of the drama thus far.

The versicle speaks once again of the Jews slaying Christ with the sword of their tongues. It is a passage from psalm 108 which does not occur in this office.

The lessons introduce an entirely new thought for this Matins of Good Friday, a thought not altogether alien to the liturgy of Passiontide: the high-priesthood of Jesus.

Christ is our eternal High Priest who offered His one, all-atoning sacrifice on the altar of the cross. He is priest and victim in one. It is this magnificent thought that crowns our Matins office for Good Friday.

This subject is also treated in the Epistle to the Hebrews. The seventh lesson speaks first of the eternal "Sabbath rest," and of the irresistible power of God's word, topics somewhat foreign to our theme. Only then does the lesson mention Christ's high priesthood. Just as the priests of the Old Law passed through the outer courts and entered the holy of holies, so Jesus has now made His way to the very throne of God, the heavenly holy of holies. Then we must tell the world our faith in Him. Though He is the Son of God, still He does not stand at a distance from us, inaccessible and cold, with slight sympathy for our needs. He is well acquainted with our infirmity, suffering even the humiliation of temptation, "like to us in all things, sin alone excepted."

Consequently Jesus is our companion in suffering. He sympathizes with our fraility and opens the door to the throne of grace for us (eighth lesson). The High Priest stands between God and man. If He is to represent both sides worthily, He must be on close terms with both parties. That means He must be familiar with man's needs, and yet be chosen for the office by God Himself. Jesus fills this dual role. As man, He is well aware of our necessities; as God's Son, He can claim for Himself the divine appointment to the office (ninth lesson). This high-priestly office is seen at its best in Christ's sufferings. For in the Passion the Son of God practiced obedience, to His divine perfection joining His human death. It was God who humbly offered this sacrifice which, then, had to be perfect and all-atoning, guaranteeing eternal salvation to all who follow His example.

The beautiful passages about the loud cries and laments of Christ can be referred to His prayer in the Garden.

The seventh responsory, a lament of Christ on the cross, contains practically the same thoughts as the last three psalms:

handing Jesus over to the pagans; crucifying Him with two thieves; His enemies standing around the cross. The *repetenda* is an excellent choice: the battle of giants on Calvary, Christ against Satan.

The eighth responsory is a meditation or reflection for the choir. It reminisces on the events of the past night. Three scenes stand out in particular: that of Judas, of Peter, and of the council of the chief priests. Emphasis is placed on the contrast between Peter and Judas.

The last responsory once again serves to sum up the action as far as it has progressed. Exceptionally picturesque and poetical, it is easily understood. All we have to do is ask the question: Who is the subject? Who is the one who utters these poignant laments? There are three possible answers, and we have no right to foist our preference on others since each offers a very stirring picture.

1. It may be Jesus Himself who speaks. Hanging on the cross, once again He gives utterance to His great sorrow.

2. However, these words may be equally appropriate on the lips of our Mother Mary, sitting on the hill of Calvary, holding her dead Son in her arms, weeping and lamenting: "He who consoled me is now far from me." A beautiful vesper scene, the Pieta.

3. Finally, it may be the Church herself who utters these words. Good Friday, the saddest day of the year, is at hand. The Church grieves, for "her bride has been taken away." The responsory makes a grand conclusion for Matins.

And now if we look back over the whole office, we may well say that it is a genuine masterpiece of prayer art, a drama whose action centers in the agony and death of Jesus, a drama whose scenes are magnificent with grief and sublime poetry. For the most part the hill of Calvary is the stage. The psalms throughout are sad and mournful, chosen from the saddest hymns of the Psalter. We note especially psalms 21, 37, and 87, the third Lamentation, and the responsories. These are in remarkable harmony with the theme. The other parts likewise fit well into the general outline of the office.

CHAPTER XXIII

Matins for Holy Saturday

T HE third part of the great trilogy. The scene: Christ lying in the tomb, the Church near-by, weeping and lamenting. Jesus rests peacefully now after a strenuous battle. The wounds and scars of His passion show plainly. It was Christ Himself who spoke in yesterday's responsories. Today, however, it is mostly the Church we hear lamenting. Yet her lamentations already show a trace of hope. Things are more tranquil today, a bit less gloomy. But even at that, toward the end of Matins we return to yesterday's mournful sentiments. This fact should not surprise us. Holy Saturday's Matins are meant to be the Church's mourning over the loss of her divine Spouse. The wounds are still visible on His dead body, and they are continual in their cry for vengeance on the faithless Jews. The enemies of Jesus are still furious, as with lies and calumny they strive to erase every remembrance of the Messiah. Grief still weighs heavily on His Mother Mary and on His disciples. And sad to say, the Church must admit that many of her children have returned from Calvary still cold and unmoved. While she ponders all these things, it seems as though the wounds of her dead Spouse break open and bleed afresh.

Unlike the office for the two previous days, the Matins for Holy Saturday manifests a definite progress in the action of the drama. This shows up particularly in the antiphons and psalms; on the contrary, the responsories do not flow along with the course of the action. Six acts are distinguishable in this drama, or to keep to the setting suggested above, that is, the Church sitting near the tomb and weeping over her dead Spouse, we can regard these six acts as so many scenes that pass before her grief-stricken soul.

Scene one. Christ lying peacefully in the sepulcher. First nocturn, antiphons: 1. I sleep and rest in peace. 2. He shall find rest on thy holy mountain. 3. My flesh rests with hope. Versicle: In peace I sleep and take my rest.

Scene two. Jesus' descent into hell. Second nocturn, first antiphon: Lift up, eternal gates, for the King of Glory shall enter.

Scene three. Hope in the resurrection. Second antiphon: I believe that I shall see the Lord in the land of the living. O Lord, you have taken my soul from hell. Versicle: restore my life. A plea for resurrection.

Scene Four. The sealing of the tomb. Lessons of the second nocturn.

Scene five. Jesus triumphs over His enemies. Third nocturn, psalms 53 and 75.

Scene six. (Return to the basic theme of the drama.) Deep sorrow and mourning.

Psalm 87. The plea of a man handed over to the dead. The first seven responsories are similar; the eighth summarizes the action of the drama for Holy Saturday: Jesus in the tomb, with the soldiers on guard.

It is well to observe here the important role of the antiphons, and how the individual psalms are chosen not so much for their general contents as for a particular verse, which frequently serves as the antiphon. For example, psalms 4, 14, and 23.

The action moves steadily now on its rising tide of resurrection joy. At the very moment when we might almost expect to hear the "Alleluja," there is an abrupt return to lamentation, as if the office would say: Hold on now, wait a minute; your Spouse still lies in the tomb.

This Matins office has its own peculiar charm, somewhat of a mixture of sorrow, hope, and restrained joy. It is more a matter of immersing ourselves in its thoughts and sentiments than actually explaining them.

First Nocturn

Like Matins yesterday and the day before, today's office opens with the theme for the day: Jesus lying in the tomb. Thus the antiphon stresses the peaceful rest, the sacred "night-off" after a strenuous battle. The deep hues of this thought color the Church's praying of the psalm that follows. Though the proper idea of this is secondary, it is not altogether out of harmony with the theme.

Psalm 4 is a plea of David, perhaps, as he was fleeing from his son Absalom. He begs God for help (1); even in great peril he knows he is safe if he has confidence in God; he calls upon his enemies to think things over, for their scheme is useless (2). He animates his diffident followers to a firm trust in God (3). The application of the psalm to our Matins is easy. We put it on the lips of the Savior in the tomb. The first part, consequently, is a plea to the Father for the resurrection. Grant that I may escape the confines of My tomb. The second part of the psalm directs a warning admonition to the enemy. Reason this matter out for yourselves. Your battle against Me is in vain. There is still time to retreat. Finally, the third part is a word of encouragement to His rather fearful companions: Do not lose hope.

The main idea, however, is found in the antiphon, apart from the contents of the psalm: Christ rests in peace.

The next antiphon is intended to suggest a similar idea. In spirit we take our place near the "holy sepulcher." This sepulcher is now actually God's "tabernacle," housing Christ's sacred body which was always united with the Divinity. Calvary, called "the place of the skull" until today, is now "the holy mountain." Now, after a hard day's work, Christ takes His rest on this holy mountain, in order to begin His triumph in a few hours.

Psalm 14 is one of the pilgrimage hymns, composed perhaps by David on the occasion of the carrying of the Ark of the Covenant to Mount Sion, the highest point of the captured city of Jerusalem. The Psalmist urges the pilgrims to examine their consciences. When am I worthy to dwell on the holy mountain? The answer: when I am free of all sin. Then the common transgressions of the day are enumerated. From this we see that the psalm can be applied to Jesus only in a very transferred sense. We make the thought positive and say: Jesus is the purest and holiest of men. He has indeed merited rest, even the right to reign at the right hand of the Father. He is our great Model. Of course, the psalm also suggests that we examine our own consciences. Are we worthy to make the pilgrimage to the holy sepulcher?

We may answer briefly. On the sacred mountain in the holy sepulcher rests the holiest and purest of men. If I am to ascend to those heights, then I too must be holy and pure.

Psalm 15. This third psalm contains a famous Messianic prophecy about Christ's burial and resurrection. In his first sermon after Pentecost, St. Peter has the following to say about the psalm.[1]

[1] Acts 2:24–32.

But God raised Him up again, releasing Him from the pangs of death; it was impossible that death should have the mastery over Him. It is in His person that David says, Always I can keep the Lord within sight; always He is at my right hand, to make me stand firm. So there is gladness in my heart, and rejoicing on my lips; my body, too, shall rest in confidence that Thou wilt not leave my soul in the place of death, or allow Thy faithful servant to see corruption. Thou hast shown me the way of life; Thou wilt make me full of gladness in Thy presence. My brethren, I can say this to you about the patriarch David without fear of contradiction, that he did die, and was buried, and his tomb is among us to this day. But he was a prophet, and he knew God had promised him on oath that He would set the sons of his body upon his throne; it was of the Christ he said, foreseeing His resurrection, that He was not left in the place of death, and that His body did not see corruption. God, then, has raised up this man, Jesus, from the dead; we are all witnesses of it.

St. Paul, too, adduces this passage as a Messianic prophecy.[2]

These remarks of the holy apostles indicate the application of the psalm to Holy Saturday's Matins. The antiphon also refers to this Messianic text. Furthermore, the whole contents of the psalm itself can be harmonized with the theme of the day. The psalm describes the happiness of a man united with God. In spite of external sufferings, he still has the best lot: "Fair to me indeed is my inheritance." God is his portion; He walks at his side to guard him and to keep him from falling. This sublime idea of union with God (which we must try to realize in our own prayer life) finds its perfect realization only in Jesus. Not merely because of His consubstantiality with the Father, but also because of His perfect surrender to God's will, His life was immersed in God. Consequently He rejoices; He cannot remain in the tomb; His

[2] Acts 13:35 ff.

body rests joyfully, hopefully. Yes; the reward for a life of obedience and suffering will be eternal joy at the right hand of the Father. Fortunate shall I be if I, too, can make these thoughts my own.

The versicle concludes the first scene of the drama: Jesus rests peacefully in the tomb. Notice how the word *requiescam* ("rest") is purposely used in each of the three responsories, and also in the versicle, four times in all.

Then follows the reading service. The first lesson, departing from the theme of the Lamentations, breathes a trace of hope. It is human nature that speaks, waiting for the redemption and the resurrection of Jesus. How today's lessons differ from yesterday's! Yesterday, inconsolable grief; today, patient hope. The very first Lamentation reflects strikingly the sentiments proper to Holy Saturday that rise in the heart of mankind waiting and longing for its redemption. It is true that the body of our Savior is still in the tomb, but a glimmer of hope arises, like the first streaks of dawn that herald the new day. The day of our redemption is at hand: "Great is thy fidelity. God is my portion." We long for resurrection. Over and over again we give voice to our hope. To wait, quietly and somewhat mournfully: that is the theme of Holy Saturday. In the second part we find a description of the Savior. From His very youth He bore the yoke of suffering. On earth He remained ever alone and misunderstood. In all humility He kissed the dust. Willingly He gave His body to the scourgers. Like a lamb led to slaughter, He never opened His mouth.

The responsory that follows echoes these last few thoughts: the lamb at the slaughter. Note the *repetenda:* He died to give us life.

The next two Lamentations take us back to our former sorrow. Once more, in the image of the devastated city of Jeru·

salem, we see the bride in disgrace by the roadside. The loftier her former dignity, the more lamentable her present fate. The higher God lifts man by His grace, the lower man falls, and the greater the penalty for his sin. What a sentence to Jesus, the kindest, the holiest of men! In the image of the sinful city of Sodom, once again the vast guilt of our sins is set before us.

The third Lamentation is from the fifth chapter of the Book of Lamentations, and is a fervent prayer of the prophet Jeremias for his beloved people after they had been carried off into captivity. The picture he draws of the misery of his people is heart-rending. At the sight of the wounds of the dead Savior, the bride, sinful mankind, is stirred anew to a realization of the misery her sins have caused. In brief we may say: by sin man fell into disgrace and incurred God's rejection. And all this humiliation Jesus took on Himself.

Stirring and poetical, the two responsories are laments of the Church waiting near the tomb. Note how in each the *repetenda* highlights the theme: "In you (O Jerusalem) the Savior of Israel has been slain." "For the day of the Lord has come, a great and very bitter day" (the day of His death), but there comes another day, greater and sadder (the day of judgment). The Latin text allows of both these meanings.

SECOND NOCTURN

In psalm 23 the Church shows us a second scene: Jesus' descent into limbo. This psalm David composed in memory of the occasion when the Ark of the Covenant was brought to Mount Sion in Jerusalem. There are two parts, and likewise two scenes. The first is that of the procession making its way to Mount Sion. It proposes two questions: 1. Who is making this procession? And the answer: Almighty God, who made the earth. (According to the ancients' way of looking at it, God set the foundations of the earth on the waters of the sea.) 2. Who is worthy to join in this procession? The answer: He whose heart and hands are pure. The second scene opens before the gates of Jerusalem, at the moment when the procession with the ark reaches the closed gates of the city. A twofold choir gives voice to certain questions which describe the majesty of the God of the Covenant. This latter scene is of paramount importance for our Matins, as is indicated by the antiphon. However, even the first part has a relation, though secondary, to our theme.

It is a magnificent scene that the psalm unfolds. Christ the Savior is risen. Accompanied by choirs of angels bearing the instruments of His passion, He proceeds to limbo, smashes the bronze gates, and with joyous, eager expectancy, is hailed by our forefathers, from Adam onward. It is the triumphal procession of Jesus the true King of glory, the great Conqueror who survived the battle for our redemption with the archenemy of mankind. Our minds travel almost spontaneously from this scene to that of the gates of Paradise which, ever since Adam's fall, have been closed and guarded by the fiery sword of the cherubim. Today the first man will pass through those gates. Of course the guards must ask the names of all who enter. This first man is the Lord, the Mighty One, the Warrior Hero. At this response the gates to the heavenly house of the Father are opened wide. The first part of the psalm suggests a reflection similar to that proposed in psalm 14: He, the holiest and purest of all, rests in the tomb. Of Him those words hold true in their loftiest sense: "Pure hands and pure heart." And we must not lack this purity if we are to remain worthily at the tomb, or especially if we are to join the procession, following Him through the eternal gates of heaven.

The third scene of today's Matins is one of hope in the resurrection. This is shown in the two psalms 26 and 29. We prayed psalm 26 yesterday. This very fact makes it possible for us to see how the same psalm can suggest entirely different thoughts and sentiments under different circumstances. We might compare it to looking at a scene through different colored glasses. Yesterday psalm 26 was the prayer of the suffering Savior, a weary struggle to express His trust in God. Today it is a prayer of hope in Christ's resurrection, whether it comes from the lips of His Mother Mary, or of the Church herself. The antiphon tells us: I hope to see the Lord among the living. Mary is the best representative and interpreter of the Church waiting hopefully by the tomb of Christ. While all His disciples, all His apostles, failed Him, while His enemies exult in triumph and no one else hopes for His resurrection, in this the darkest of nights, the Mother of the Lord, the star of hope, "the light" was never extinguished. She maintained her hope and confidence. When the enemy and fearful thoughts oppressed her, her courage did not fail her. How beautiful the prayer for union with God that flows from her soul! The second part, of course, tells us how her heart was actually steeped in pain and sorrow. Even yet every fiber of her being trembles when she recalls those frightful scenes of the crucifixion. Nevertheless the basic and dominating sentiments of the psalm are those of firm hope in the resurrection.

Psalm 29 carries this hope somewhat further. In fact, it seems almost to anticipate Easter morning and sing a song of thanks for the resurrection. The psalm is actually a hymn of gratitude. Cardinal Faulhaber styles it "a heartfelt and lyrical *Deo gratias*." There are five equally balanced strophes:

1. Thanks for deliverance from war, sickness, death (1–3).
2. God strikes, and heals (4–6).
3. In his arrogance the Psalmist is afflicted by God (7–9).
4. Punishment and petition (10–12).
5. God's mercy; thanksgiving (13–15).

The application of the psalm to Holy Saturday Matins. We can put the psalm on the lips of the Savior. Then it becomes a song of thanks for His awaited resurrection. He sees Himself already risen from the tomb. The Church conveys this idea to us through the antiphon. However, the psalm itself suggests a number of thoughts apropos of Holy Saturday. The first strophe expresses Jesus' thanks for His victory over the enemy (we think immediately of the devil), for mankind's recovery from sin, and for His resurrection from the tomb. It is this last idea which the antiphon emphasizes. The second strophe contains two beautiful verses which aptly characterize Holy Saturday: "For his anger lasts but a moment; a lifetime, his good will." Our Lord's passion was short, like a brief moment, compared to the eternal glory it brought Him, and to the grace which was forever restored to mankind. "At nightfall, weeping enters in, but with the dawn, rejoicing." Holy Saturday is indeed the day of weeping, and Easter Sunday is the morning of rejoicing. Over strophes three and four we pass lightly since they express but general and ordinary ideas. We need not try to apply each and every verse of a psalm to our theme. The liturgy often applies only a part, or even a single verse, to a feast. The rest can be more or less disregarded. We place the fifth strophe on the lips of the Church, or of the Blessed Mother. The verse, "You changed my mourning into dancing, you took off my sack-

cloth and clothed me with gladness," suggests the transition
from Holy Saturday to Easter Sunday, the turning point of
the whole drama. Actually we seem to have run ahead of ourselves in our prayer sentiments, as if our hearts were bursting
with untimely Easter joy. The versicle concludes the nocturn,
telling us: we are on the crest of the wave of Easter joy. The
thoughts of retaliation and vengeance, based on the Old
Testament outlook, get slight stress from us, as though to
say: I will show them that I am the victor.

The lessons. We are already familiar with the lessons since
they are a continuation of those of Friday. Psalm 63, which
the lessons treat of, has two contrasting parts. The first, as we
saw, speaks of the victory of the enemy and fits in well on
Good Friday, as does the second on Holy Saturday, treating
of God's victory. Similarly the commentary on the psalm is
spread out through the lessons of the two days. Somewhat
disappointing is the fourth lesson, since the application of
the verse, "Deep are the thoughts of each heart," is rather
difficult. On the other hand, the fifth and sixth lessons fit ex-
cellently into our office. While Jesus rests in the tomb, we
watch the wicked but useless activities of the Jews. They seal
the tomb. Then when the soldiers report the resurrection,
bribery makes them spread the nonsensical lie: "The disciples
stole the corpse while we were asleep." The quick-witted
Augustine slyly remarks: "O hapless cunning, you produce
sleeping witnesses. Indeed, you yourselves must have been
asleep when you figured out such a scheme." The lessons present the fourth scene of our drama: the sealing and guarding
of the tomb.

The three responsories, one more beautiful than the other,
are lamentations. We may picture either the Church or Mary,
the best representative of mankind, as mourning and lament-

ing at the tomb. In the fourth responsory the theme of psalm 23 is further developed: Satan is captured; the bars and gates of hell are shattered. The fifth we know from yesterday. The sixth, perhaps the best of all, is sung at certain burial rites also. We hear the Church complaining and lamenting that the passion and death of the Savior make such little impression on most of us.

THIRD NOCTURN

The first two psalms flow along on the mounting tide of Easter joy and triumph; the third sinks rather suddenly again to the depths of grief that actually belong to Holy Saturday. The first two present the fifth scene: Jesus, the Victor over His enemies. In general we give more accent here to the contents of the psalm itself than to the antiphon.

Psalm 53. We prayed this psalm yesterday, but with a different outlook. Yesterday it was a matter of stressing the first half. Today we turn our eyes to the second half. Jesus is the One who speaks. In the strenuous battle, God is my helper. He will not leave my soul in hell (cf. the antiphon). My enemies lie defeated in the dust. Gladly will I offer sacrifice to You.

Psalm 75. Although this psalm occurred also on Holy Thursday, today's office is its proper place. It presents a stirring scene: Jesus in triumph over hell and Satan. The antiphon, it is true, suggests the peaceful rest of Jesus in the tomb, "the city of peace" (translation of "Jerusalem"). Still, the psalm immediately describes the battlefield. In fact, Christ's passion was a powerful struggle with the devil. On the battlefield of Golgotha the divine Hero smashed "the bow and shield and sword" of Satan, and won a glorious victory. "Resplendent You came, O powerful One, from the everlasting mountains." What is this but a reference to the glorious brilliance of the resurrection? "They sleep their sleep"; we see the soldiers falling powerless to the ground. "The earth feared and was silent." Can we not hear the earth quake "with fear" at the moment of His resurrection? The scene grows even more gripping. We have reached the day's end. "Henceforth you shall see the Son of man sitting at the right hand of God and coming on the clouds of glory," the Risen One, to pass sentence on His enemies.

At this point it might seem that we have reached the very morning of Easter itself. We practically have the Alleluja on our lips already. But no! It is still Holy Saturday, and we must "sit all alone and in silence" (first Lamentation). Up to this point we could discern a noticeable progression in the thoughts and actions of the Matins drama. But in the last psalm we retrace our steps to the tomb in grief and sorrow, for it is the saddest psalm of all, psalm 87. Again yesterday's office has acquainted us with it. In the dark depths of His abandonment on Golgotha, the Savior felt as though He had already been excluded from the land of the living. Today His body actually lies in the tomb, and His soul has descended into the kingdom of the dead. Thus the passages about the descent into the pit and the dwelling in the shadows of death find their full application in today's office. The antiphon suggests we place the whole psalm on the lips of the Savior. Death is for Jesus the greatest humiliation. And He takes it upon Himself for the sins of men. He, the Son of God, the eternal and immortal God, has become "a man without strength": "my couch is among the dead." In praying this psalm, then, we try once more to feel in our own hearts the enormous affliction Christ suffered on Good Friday. Let the waves of anguish surge up against my soul. Let the horror of

Golgotha fill my heart. The versicle leads our thoughts back to the theme of the first nocturn: Jesus resting peacefully in the sepulcher.

The lessons, somewhat more beautiful than the previous ones, continue the ideas of Good Friday about the high priesthood of Jesus. The ninth lesson, from the Epistle to the Hebrews, compares Christ's priesthood with that of the Old Testament, presenting the sacrifice of the cross in a sublime light. The seventh lesson is rather a separate passage. Christ is the high priest of the future. Mere type and shadow was the Old Testament high priest compared to Him. The former entered the holy of holies once a year and sprinkled the ark with blood of animals to atone for his own and the people's sins. For Christ, the eternal high priest, there was only one solemn, sacrificial entrance. The tabernacle He entered was not made by hand of man; it was heaven itself. The Victim He sacrificed was the most precious conceivable; not the blood of animals, but His own precious blood. And of course, the fruit of such a precious sacrifice was correspondingly valuable: man's redemption for time and eternity. The animal blood of the Old Testament imparted a certain external and ritual cleansing. The blood of Jesus, freely offered, brings an inner spiritual cleansing from sin, and sanctification as well.

The seventh responsory. These thoughts about the precious blood of Jesus remind us of scenes filled with the battle of hell against Christ, and of the hatred of the Jews.

The eighth lesson speaks of the wonderful effects of Christ's death, the death that established a new relationship for us with God, a new Covenant with these two special effects.

1. The vast accumulation of sin and guilt was now annihilated, not indeed by a mere gracious act of God's will, but by the redemptive death of His own Son.

2. Once the barrier of sin is removed, our path is clear to the glorious inheritance, the kingdom of God with all its treasures of grace and glory. This inheritance, however, is ours only on the death of the testator, Christ.

The eighth responsory explains how difficult the sacrifice of the cross was for Christ, the living Son of God, for whom there could be no greater humiliation than death.

The ninth lesson compares the blood of the Old with the blood of the New Testament. In making the old covenant with God, Moses sprinkled his people and the Book of the Covenant with blood. So too the new covenant was sealed in the blood of Jesus. Thus our Lord's blood became the great means of our forgiveness.

We note that these three lessons present not so much the action of the drama, or prayer, as they present dogma, the dogma of our redemption by the death of Jesus.

The last responsory again depicts the action of the drama as far as it has progressed.

Matins for Holy Saturday is a genuine masterpiece of progressive development in thought, sentiment, prayer, and doctrine. The action proceeds from the burial to the threshold of the resurrection. Its underlying sentiment is grief, illuminated by peace and firm hope.

A few words remain to be said of the other hours of Holy Week. Lauds are taken from the second schema (penitential Lauds). Consequently they are not the usual joyous morning prayer, but they continue the somber atmosphere of Matins. Throughout Lauds the antiphons, whether taken from the psalms themselves or borrowed from other prophetic passages of Sacred Scripture, speak of the passion of our Savior. The Benedictus, of course, is the climax of the hour, with appropriate antiphons to describe an event that occurred on each of the three days. On Holy Thursday it is the traitor's kiss; on Good Friday, the inscription on the cross; on Holy Saturday, the mourning of the pious women. The conclusion of Lauds is striking. The whole choir kneels to sing a short chant which is further developed on each of the three days; its few words summarize the entire contents of the day's Matins. "Christ, for us, became obedient unto death." On Friday we add: "yea, unto the death of the cross"; and on Saturday: "wherefore God exalted Him and gave Him a name which is above all names." These additions harmonize well with the character of each day.

Holy Thursday: Christ's passion in general.

Good Friday: His death on the cross.

Holy Saturday: hope in the resurrection.

In this background the choir sings the *Miserere*, the Church's hymn of contrition. It is as though the liturgy would say that the fruit of all this reflection on Christ's passion should be contrition and amendment. As a final conclusion we find a simple but stirring oration which occurs throughout the office of these three days. The little hours for the sacred Triduum have no ornament whatever. By this total lack of ornament the Church wishes to arouse in us the proper sentiments and atmosphere for the day's office. Vespers for both Thursday and Friday are a sad, mournful evening song. Specially chosen psalms with appropriate antiphons become the laments and mild reproaches the Savior addresses to His people. This hour is likewise bereft of all ornament. The antiphon for the Magnificat on Holy Thursday consists of the sacred words: "When they were eating, Christ took bread, blessed it, broke it, and gave it to His disciples." Here the Church sings her thanks for this "souvenir" that Christ left to remind us of Himself. We might entitle Vespers for Good

Friday, "The Evening on Golgotha." The Magnificat antiphon would suggest this: "He said: 'It is consummated,' bowed His head and died." We give thanks for the accomplishment of our redemption. The office maintains its somber character and its rather ascetic form until None on Holy Saturday, to burst forth then in the Mass for Easter night, with the jubilant Alleluja for Christ's resurrection and our redemption. Our hearts should live the prayer of the Church during these days. We should immerse ourselves in the hymns and poetry of the liturgy, that we may be able to celebrate with deep, spiritual convictions the great feast of our redemption.

CHAPTER XXIV

The Easter Office

WE can scarcely imagine a more dramatic or more vigorous change of sentiment and atmosphere than that between Holy Saturday and Easter Sunday. From the depths of grief and sorrow Holy Mother Church leaps to the heights of joy and exultation. Christ casts off the gloom of His passion, death, and burial in the tomb to put on the brilliant garments of His resurrection that brought with it for Him eternal joy and eternal life. It is true that the short Vespers of Holy Saturday presented a definite strain of Easter joy, but only in the Matins office of the great feast itself is the full grandeur of this joy revealed. Let us study it in detail.

EASTER MATINS

"Lord, open my lips." After three sad days we hear again the Invitatory, the solemn, festive introduction to Matins. I thank You, my God, for opening my lips again that I may sing a joyous song of praise to You. What boundless joy shall be mine when, after the "Holy Week" of this life, I celebrate my first Easter in heaven and pray there for the first time: "Lord, open my lips"! "And my mouth shall proclaim Your praise." Now we can sing God's praises again, for especially Eastertide is the time to praise God. "Alleluja" is the Easter greeting: "Praise the Lord!" "Glory be to the Father . . ." The last three days we could not say this. But we pray it now with new fervor and devotion. Alas, how easily such little prayers escape our attention! "Alleluja!" Again our lips open to utter this favorite greeting. It is our companion through the whole year, except for these last two months, from Septuagesima to Easter, or rather to Holy Saturday, when in the Mass we take it up again with joyous hearts. From now on it is our constant companion, reminding us of Christ's resurrection and the joy it brought to God's children, until the day when we shall sing it forever in the heavenly Jerusalem. What a contrast between yesterday and today! Yesterday Matins began quietly, sadly, and without any introduction. Today it opens with a jubilant Invitatory, like a magnificent pealing of chimes.

Surrexit Dominus vere, alleluja ("The Lord is truly risen, alleluja"). Let us keep in mind that the Easter Matins were sung at night. Holy Mother Church goes about by candlelight to spread the word among her children: "The Lord is risen. Be not unbelieving, as the apostles. The Lord is truly risen, and so too shall be your own resurrection." We have already considered the Invitatory psalm. The strains of the Invitatory fade away, and, though usually the Church gives vent to her emotions in a hymn, we find no official hymn in the whole octave (except the Sequence, and that is an inconsistency). This is the earlier form of Matins in the Roman rite where there were no hymns at all. And today we have only one nocturn. This may be explained by its historical development. In the early Church there was no liturgy celebrated on Holy Saturday. The ceremonies did not begin until nightfall. We may well study the marvelous symbolism of the blessing of the new fire and of the paschal candle, all at night. The greater part of the night was then devoted to the baptism of the catechumens, so that there was time left for only one nocturn, and that the last, just before the time of Christ's resurrection.

When we first study the psalms of the Easter Matins we are somewhat disappointed to find no more appropriate selection than the first three psalms. The following are apparently the reasons for their choice. 1. By this selection the Church wishes to say: At Easter we start from the very beginning, since we have become "new men," living new lives again in Christ. Logically then, we should say the first three psalms. 2. The second reason is that on this day of great joy and gladness the Church declines to use any external aids to produce the effect she desires. So she used the first three psalms in their numerical order. 3. Finally, these first three psalms are to represent the entire Psalter. As though the Church would say: All the psalms sing the praises of our risen Savior.

The antiphons try, and quite successfully, to apply the psalms to our risen Lord.

The first psalm is the preface or subtitle of the whole Psalter. It contains the general theme of the entire collection of psalms: Happy the way of the good; woe to the wicked! Today, in the person of the just man, the Church sees the risen Savior, the model of all just men. Christ, far from ever committing sin, is the archenemy and conqueror of sin and Satan. He is the One whose life's principle, indeed whose very meat, was to do the will of Him who sent Him. Christ has become our tree of life from the fruit of which we receive the graces of eternal life, "planted near running water," that is, the sacraments, the grace-laden streams of His precious blood. Before His death the fountain of grace was dried up. Now, through His death and resurrection, we have been redeemed. We may also regard this tree as the mystical Christ and His Church. ("I am the vine, you are its branches." John

15:5.) Christ is the main trunk; we are the living branches, provided we are united with Him through grace. It is true of this vine, too: "yields its fruit in due season." Every good deed, every good thought and desire, although unseen and unappreciated and unrewarded here on earth, will have its "success" with God. No leaf will wither on this tree, a thought all the more encouraging in the light of the past week. Did not our ministry over so many months seem fruitless, our efforts thankless? Today we glimpse the brighter side of the Passion: resurrection, eternal bliss for the chosen children of God. Indeed, no leaf has withered away, "Whatever he does, prospers." There is also a practical lesson for us: Look for the fruit at the proper time. It has to ripen first. We men have so little patience. On the other side, we can also study the "godless" man. How all his efforts eventually come to nothing! At Christ's death, in the very moment hell believed itself victorious, it suffered its greatest defeat. The Jews sealed the tomb and set guards to watch it, and thus provided witnesses for Christ's resurrection. Here on earth the evil man will not succeed. But if perchance he should, he will certainly not succeed in heaven. The last few verses cast a ray of light on the day of judgment. Men shall rise from the dead; the just to eternal bliss, the wicked to judgment. The moral of the psalm is: "Risen, then, with Christ, you must lift your thoughts above." [1]

We can also understand the antiphon better now. The risen Savior uses a part of the psalm to speak to us. Christ calls Himself: "I am, who am." This is the translation of the divine name "Jahwe" which God revealed to Moses in the burning bush. "He who exists eternally." The Savior consequently calls Himself God. Through His victory over sin and Satan

[1] Col. 3:1.

He proved that He does not "follow the counsel of the wicked," and also that all during His mortal life God's will was His "delight."

Psalm 2. This is a hymn we sang two days ago, on Good Friday. We heard the cries, "Crucify Him!" ring out from the assembly of the Jews. We take up the hymn again today, but with entirely different sentiments. The battle that the Jews (hell) waged against Christ was in vain. We can readily make the psalm a resurrection song. Hell raged in all its fury against Jesus, and God "laughed" all Saturday. Then on Sunday morning, "He struck the guards to the ground." Now the risen Savior Himself lifts up His voice: "The Father has made Me the ruler of the kingdom of God." His first request of the Father: Give Me the nations, the Gentiles, for My inheritance. As the Jewish nation proved itself unworthy of Him, now He turns His eyes to the Gentiles, and to us, the children of the Gentiles. In spirit He saw the great, universal Church, the *ecclesia catholica,* for this is the prize of His victory. The antiphon lays special emphasis on this thought, while Holy Mother Church repeats the joyous Alleluja three times. My Savior, lead and guide me by Your staff (*virga ferrea*) and be the King of my heart. Then the Psalmist lifts a warning finger: "And now, O kings, give heed." Who are these kings? Ourselves. We are, and always must be, true kings, rulers of ourselves and our passions. Let us note especially the beautiful verse, "Serve the Lord with fear, and rejoice before Him." Joyous but reverent fear of God; that is the proper relation for us with the risen Savior.

Psalm 3. This is one of David's songs, full of confidence in God, even in the midst of great affliction. Though surrounded by his enemies, David sleeps soundly in God's arms. From the antiphon we learn to put the psalm on the lips of our risen

Savior; and indeed it makes an excellent resurrection hymn. Jesus could well sing the first strophe on Holy Thursday or Good Friday, when everyone and everything seemed to conspire against Him. In the midst of His passion He prays the second strophe. What a frightful struggle the Passion meant for Him, especially in the Garden of Olives! But He places His trust in God. Then on Holy Saturday He prays the third strophe: "When I lie down in sleep. . . ." Early Sunday morning He could say: "I awake again, for the Lord sustains Me." Christ is the Victor, and in Him we shall also conquer hell and sin if we have a similar trust in God. His resurrection is the pledge of our own final victory.

The versicle relates Holy Saturday with Easter Sunday, Holy Week with Easter Week: He who hung on the cross for us, Alleluja, has risen from the tomb, Alleluja!

The lessons. In these three lessons the Church explains parts of the Gospel for the Mass of the feast. "Good tidings" is the Gospel today indeed. "You have come to look for Jesus of Nazareth, who was crucified; He has risen again, He is not here." [2] The great Pope St. Gregory I gives us the explanation of the Gospel.

In the first lesson he applies the Gospel to our own lives. As the pious women came to the tomb with spices, so we must come to Jesus with the fragrant odors of virtues and good works. Then we too shall be able to see the angels, the citizens of heaven.

The more than customary length of the first responsory makes it somewhat resemble the responsory for Christmas. Here too, the Church wishes to single out the theme of the feast and to celebrate the very moment of Christ's resurrection from the tomb.

[2] Luke 16:6.

Both responsories in today's Matins fulfill the role of the ideal responsory, that is, they echo the thoughts of the lesson and the Gospel, and both consist of passages from Sacred Scripture. They tell of what occurred immediately after Christ's resurrection: the holy women visiting the tomb and the appearance of the angels. In the Middle Ages the faithful used to dramatize these responsories, and they are, in fact, the origin of the cherished Easter plays presented in the church.

The second lesson offers an allegorical interpretation for the Gospel. The angels sit on the right, and this right side signifies the eternal life the risen Savior began after His mortal life. The dazzling white garments the angels wore symbolize our joy at being redeemed, and also the angels' joy at seeing that once more the empty mansions in heaven are filled.

In the third lesson we hear the angels addressing the holy women.

After a week's omission, once again we conclude Matins with the jubilant chant of the Te Deum. And there is no day in the year when it is more appropriate. Today we lift our voices in joyous, exultant thanksgiving for Christ's resurrection. First we give praise to the Most Holy Trinity, and today we have a special motive for this praise: the Resurrection. Thus Matins draws to a close. It is magnificent in its simplicity, because it is composed of the most sublime prayers and readings in all Christian literature. If we recite Matins separately from Lauds, we conclude the hour with the oration, and finally, the Easter antiphon to Our Lady, *Regina Coeli* ("Rejoice, O Queen of heaven").

EASTER LAUDS

Lauds is the Church's "resurrection song" par excellence. This hour has her daily recalling thoughts and sentiments of Easter and the resurrection. With its striking symbolism it is, perhaps, the most beautiful hour of the office. Dawn is breaking, and as the sun sends its first red shafts of light up on the horizon, night crawls away in defeat. Nature celebrates its resurrection. The flowers open their petals, the birds begin to chirp and sing. It is the very hour of our Savior's victory over death and resurrection from the tomb. Even man leaves his bed now. The risen Savior and reawakened nature appeal strongly to him for his own spiritual resurrection. "Risen, then, with Christ, you must lift your thoughts above." [3] We might thus summarize the symbolism of Lauds. Christ is risen from the tomb; nature has its reawakening; man, too, should experience a spiritual resurrection. Now we can understand why this hour is so full of songs and references to nature, and why the Alleluja is so often repeated. It is so that we may celebrate the triple resurrection each day. Another feature of the resurrection theme is the fact that every Sunday is a little Easter. Hence the many Allelujas. Finally, in this hour of Lauds on Easter Sunday itself, the idea of resurrection is trebly emphasized. It is the resurrection hour on the very day of the Resurrection. Now we can the better appreciate this beautiful hour.

Whereas on great feasts special psalms are selected for Matins, on all feasts and Sundays the psalms for Lauds are always the same. The reason is that Matins is somewhat of a meditation or a prayer drama on the feast, but Lauds is essentially a morning prayer. The psalms of Lauds therefore

[3] Col. 3:1.

generally sing God's praise, without special reference to the theme of the feast. They are meant to serve only the thought of the hour and not that of the feast. The antiphons take care of the latter, for they are intended to direct our thoughts to the feast. However, in Lauds the antiphons generally have a function other than in Matins. In the latter the antiphons furnish the key to the interpretation and application of the psalms. They indicate the particular message that the psalm conveys for the feast at hand. In Lauds, however, the antiphons serve but to frame the psalms, as a rule, without any special reference to them. They encircle the psalm like pretty garlands, and have the sole purpose of linking the idea of the hour with the main theme of the feast. Actually they form a rich mosaic in the Easter Lauds. I rejoice over my own spiritual resurrection along with reawakened nature; and after each psalm, by means of the antiphons, I share likewise in the joy of the great feast. It is precisely because of this coincidence of resurrection themes that the relation of the idea of the hour with the theme of the feast is so easily made.

The antiphons for today's Lauds are short but vivid accounts of the events that surrounded the resurrection and that occurred at this hour of Lauds. These narrate the action of the drama, but the psalms supply the accompanying chorus of praise on the part of the Church and inanimate creation. In fact the psalms are reflections or meditations, something like the responsories between the lessons. Thus on Easter, Lauds is not merely the morning prayer, but also the tribute of praise that all creation offers to God for the resurrection of the Savior.

When we set out to pray this hour, we should try to picture for ourselves Mary's prayerful longing to see the Lord on the first Easter morning. Let us try to capture her sentiments as we recite the hour, if possible, early in the morning. We can picture Mary walking out toward the Garden of Olives in the early hours of the morning. Over yonder, the hill of Calvary is still shrouded in darkness. Even while she moves her lips in prayer, the great event recounted in the antiphon occurs: Christ rises from the dead, His resurrection unseen by human eye. Only the angel, dazzling white, attested the fact of the great miracle by rolling back the stone and appearing to the guards in front of the tomb. Meanwhile we unite with Mary to sing the resurrection song of all creation, psalm 92. Nature, too, offers a figure of Christ's resurrection. Daylight wrestles with night, and finally masters the darkness. In the psalm God battles against the raging flood that threatens to engulf the earth once more. But God is victorious, and the flood-waters cannot reach the throne of the heavenly King. How well this figure describes the resurrection of Jesus! The Savior is victor over the raging flood of sin and hell and death. Indeed "the floods lift up their tumult," but "powerful on high is the Lord." And now He is enthroned, the risen King; all creation is His raiment, the powers and forces of nature are His sword. Thus the first psalm presents a graphic picture of the resurrection.

The action then proceeds. We hear about the earthquake that accompanied the resurrection, and about the appearance of the angel (antiphon two). In psalm 99 we rejoice with Mary and hasten to greet the risen Savior. This is a beautiful and artistically balanced prayer that was said in the joyful processions to the sanctuary. I begin now to realize who the Risen One is: the infinite God, Creator of the universe. And today He is likewise the Good Shepherd gathering His flock that had been scattered by the enemy. Before I meet Him I ask myself again: What does this person mean to me today?

He is good and kind and true to His word. How appropriate for this great feast of the resurrection! The second psalm, like a crescendo, deepens and develops the sentiments of the first. As the events unfold, I see the angel standing before the empty tomb (antiphon three).

The climax, however, comes in the third psalm (62), a splendid hymn, full of affectionate longing. We can sing it with Mary as she yearns for her Jesus: "And my soul thirsts like the earth, parched, lifeless and without water." Nor is her longing, any more than our own, left unfulfilled. Jesus appears to her. Oh, the ineffable bliss of a soul united with God! The second strophe gives us the cue to interpret the psalm for the feast. The climax: Mary in the loving embrace of Jesus. Verse 9 beautifully describes our Easter Communion: "My soul clings fast to You, Your right hand upholds me."

Once more we turn our thoughts to the empty tomb. We see the guards paralyzed with astonishment, a sign of their defeat (antiphon four).

Our hearts are so full that they leap for joy. We now invite all creation to join in our song of praise to the risen Savior. Both of the next two psalms are like choral chants in which the different elements of creation celebrate their own future resurrection along with that of the Savior. These psalms are magnificent in their simplicity and uniformity, especially if we have the opportunity to recite them outdoors in the early hours of the morning. Everything teems with life, and all lift their arms in prayer. All the thousands of animals and plants, all the hidden forces of nature, the murmuring brook, the drone and hum of the bees, the chirping of the sparrows, and the leaves rustling with the wind, the hills wreathed in mist, all join in the prayer; and I am the leader, their representative before God. What a magnificent feast!

As a rule, the so-called capitulum (a brief passage from Sacred Scripture) follows the psalmody at Lauds as a sort of summary of the leading ideas of the feast. However, this is not the case in the Easter Lauds. We have instead a short psalm verse that recurs at each hour during the following week and that reveals the full significance of the feast: "This is the day the Lord has made." This verse was sung at Eastertime from the early years of the Church.

The Benedictus follows. With this canticle, every day at Lauds the Church welcomes the Savior as "the Orient on high" and greets this new day given to work out our salvation. We promise to "serve Him without fear, in holiness and justice before Him all our days." As we sing the Benedictus today, we greet the risen Savior who shines on those who sit in darkness and in the shadow of death, to guide their feet into the way of peace. What beautiful symbolism lies here! We sing this canticle as the sun mounts in the heavens. The antiphon depicts the holy women setting out for the sepulcher "as the sun was rising." In this image of the rising sun, the *"oriens ex alto,"* we see our risen Savior Himself.

With the oration the hour draws to a close. This prayer summarizes the whole hour in a few words. It states the theme both negatively and positively: Jesus has triumphed over death, and He has reopened the gates of eternity. All we have to do is supply these two figures: the victor of Calvary, and paradise reopened. Though unexpressed, the petition is obvious: Give the victory over death and sin to me also, and open the gates of paradise for me also. Then the oration mentions that we can ask God for nothing, but that first by His grace He must inspire us with the desire for it.

Finally, throughout the week we add two "Allelujas" to the concluding verse, *Benedicamus Domino* ("Let us bless the Lord").

EASTER VESPERS

The celebration of the feast concludes now with Second Vespers. As usual the psalms are taken from Sunday, and the antiphons are repeated from Lauds. These also have the same purpose as in Lauds, that is, to enclose the psalms without any special reference to them. Again they narrate the events that occurred at the resurrection. We can consider the psalms again as meditations or reflections woven into the series of antiphons and try, as best we can, to apply them to the feast. Nor is this too difficult.

First, let us glance at the literal meaning of the five psalms.

Psalm 109. This is a directly Messianic psalm which Christ applied to Himself.[4] Its brilliant pictures describe the victory of the Savior. We may divide the psalm according to the following thoughts of the contents.

1. Christ as King (1–3).
2. Christ as High Priest (4).
3. Christ as Judge of the world (5–7), all during the history of mankind, as well as on the Last Day.

Remarks on the individual verses. 1. According to Oriental custom, the vicar takes his place at the right hand of the ruler.[5] 3. Out of my womb, even before the stars began to shine, before all creation, I begot thee of My very essence and being. 4. God does not regret it. Though some of mankind scorned and scoffed at the priestly office of the Messiah,

[4] Matt. 22:43.
[5] Matt. 26:64.

He did not retract His oath. 5. This day of wrath, *Dies irae* (whence the well-known sequence *Dies irae, dies illa*), is actually the whole long history of the human race, one great "day" of wrath and judgment. The final chapter of this history will be written on the Day of Judgment. 7. "From the brook." A rather obscure verse for which various interpretations are given. Perhaps it is a realistic scene of the great victory. "He will heap up corpses and smash their skulls; these roll along in the torrent where they stop to drink." This verse certainly has no bearing on Christ's passion.

In spite of its obscurities, this psalm will readily blend with our thoughts and sentiments for the feast if we keep our attention focused on the three offices of the Savior.

Psalm 110. A hymn of thanksgiving to God for His marvelous favors to the chosen people, especially on the occasion of their deliverance from Egypt. It is an alphabetical psalm; that is, each verse (in the Hebrew) begins with a different letter of the alphabet. This feature explains its rather sententious form and its lack of a definite thought pattern.

The division of the psalm.

Thanks to God

Why? a) For His great favors (deliverance from Egypt) (2–4).
      b) For the miraculous manna (leading the Jews through the desert) (5).
      c) For the conquest of the Promised Land (6).

Conclusions

God. His attributes: fidelity, justice, and holiness (7–9). We should both love and fear him (10).

Psalm 111. A counterpart to the preceding psalm: the good

God (Ps. 110), the good man (Ps. 111). It also is alphabetical, and consequently rather loose in its structure and thought pattern.

The song of the upright man. Its division is quite loose.

1. Love of God (1–4).

2. Love of one's neighbor (5–10).

Psalm 112 is a simple but expressive hymn that bears some resemblance to the Magnificat. The most high God exalts the lowly and enriches him with favors.

The song on humility and lowliness. Division:

1. Praise to the great God (1–6).

2. The greatness and excellence of God is manifested also in His exalting the lowly (7–9). Two examples from sacred history are cited: David and Anna, the mother of Samuel the prophet.

Psalm 113 is a combination of two hymns which, however, actually do belong together. We can thus picture the situation for ourselves. The people are in exile, and the Psalmist chants one of the folk songs of Sion (Ps. 136) about God's mercy and kindness in the past (part one). Then, inspired by this remembrance in the midst of his sorrow, he bursts forth with a song of confidence in the merciful God, of utter contempt for the deceitful idols (part two). The first hymn is profoundly poetic in its frank simplicity. Nature exults at the sight of God accompanying His people in the Ark of the Covenant. The second hymn shows definite traces of development from an antiphonal chant between priest and people.

Children of the True God; Children of Idols

I. Nature pays its homage to God on the occasion of the Exodus from Egypt (1–8).

II. Prayer for deliverance from exile, Ps. 113B; verses
(1–18).
   1. Motive for the prayer: not because of our own
      merits, but for the glory of Your name among the
      Gentiles (1–3). Otherwise they would believe
      that You were powerless.
   2. Helplessness of the idols (4–8).
   3. Our trust in God (9–11).
   4. The priests' blessing: God bless you (12–15).
   5. Let us see the holy land in this life (16–18).

How can we apply these psalms to our feast?

Psalm 109. This psalm should be particularly sacred to us
since Christ Himself declared it to be Messianic. It offers
a splendid portrait of the Messiah; not the mild, meek Savior we read of in the Gospels, but the eternal King of the
heavenly kingdom, making conquest after conquest through
the course of the centuries; the High Priest who continues
His redeeming sacrifice in heaven before the throne of the
Father in an unbloody manner, and on earth through the
Sacrifice of the Mass; the eternal Judge who has stood in
judgment over mankind throughout its history and who will
judge it for the last time on the Day of Judgment. How aptly
this portrait fits the risen and glorified Savior! In the very
midst of His passion did He not prove Himself a Conqueror,
a King, and a Priest? The helpless amazement of the guards
at the tomb was a symbol of His utter victory over all His
adversaries. We should ponder this psalm frequently and
recite it with reverence and devotion. Thus the very first
psalm brings before our eyes the picture of the risen Savior.

Psalm 110 is a hymn of thanks to God for His favors. There
were certain themes which dominated Old Testament poetry:

the deliverance from Egypt, for example, or the journey through the desert and the conquest of the Promised Land. In fact, the Jewish feast of the Passover is a commemoration of their release from bondage in Egypt. For us Christians, of course, all these favors God granted His people were but figures, according to God's plan, of the kingdom of God. The first Pasch was to prefigure our feast of Easter. In those days the feast was to celebrate their liberation from slavery in Egypt. Here we celebrate mankind's release from the slavery of Satan. Nor was it without God's design that Christ was crucified at the time of the Passover. The long journey through the desert was a figure of the pilgrimage of the Church through time, and of the children of God through this life. Jesus Himself adduced the miraculous manna as a figure of the Holy Eucharist. And finally, the entrance into the Promised Land prefigured our entrance into heaven. We can easily see how this psalm becomes our own prayer of thanks for the redemption which Christ won for us by His death and which He confirmed by His resurrection. In the second part of the psalm we extol the various perfections of God displayed in the work of our redemption, in particular fidelity, justice, and sanctity.

Psalm 111. I have entitled this psalm "The Song of the Upright Man." It depicts the good, just man who fears God and is kind and fair to his fellow men. In accord with Old Testament views on the matter, he is rewarded by God with temporal prosperity. We naturally think of supernatural merit and the eternal reward. Who is this "just man" of the psalm as we apply it to our feast? First of all, it is the risen Savior Himself. He is the "just man" in the highest sense, He who offered Himself as a victim for mankind, whose only "delight," in fact whose very "meat," was to do the will of the Father, He who so freely and bountifully gave to the "poor," that is, to us, who took pity on us and not merely "lends" but gives us unstintingly of His treasures. And in the fullest sense, has not our Savior become a light, indeed the light that illuminates us all in the darkness, "gracious, merciful, and just"? However, each one of us must also be a "just man" so that the psalm actually becomes a paraphrase of St. Paul's words: "Risen, then, with Christ, you must lift your thoughts above." [6]

Psalm 112. This is the hymn on humility and lowliness. God is indeed great; but He shows His greatness especially in this, that He singles out and exalts the lowly. How fit the psalm into our Easter office? What is its special message? The same message as in a famous passage of St. Paul's Epistle to the Philippians: "Yours is to be the same mind which Christ Jesus showed. His nature is, from the first, divine . . . (yet) He dispossessed Himself, and took the nature of a slave . . . and then He lowered His own dignity, accepted an obedience which brought Him to death, death on a cross. That is why God raised Him to such a height." [7] We must learn humility from the Savior. Thus our psalm enunciates the one great feature and principle of the kingdom of God: it is the humble and lowly whom God exalts. We see before us the Church, "the sterile mother," and yet exalted as the mother of thousands of God's children. We see also the "Man of sorrows," exalted today to the kingship of God's kingdom. This psalm finds no better illustration than Easter. It gives us some practical advice. Will you follow a path different from that of your Savior? Then try always to be humble.

[6] Col. 3:1.
[7] Phil. 2:5 ff.

Psalm 113. The first four psalms fit well enough into the Easter office. But the fifth is rather difficult to apply to the feast since it is for the most part foreign to the Christian mentality. However, we may explain it in this way. The first part described the journey of the Jews with the Ark of the Covenant. This is Holy Mother Church journeying through the long desert of time. The risen Savior has His place in the procession. Today He commences His victory march. Thus we see all nature join in the triumph: mountains, hills, and seas cower and tremble before this "Corpus Christi procession" (the earthquake that occurred at the resurrection). And we (application of the psalm to ourselves) are overjoyed to march along in this procession. The second part: the procession of God's Church makes its way over the earth. On the way we see the pagan idols of the world. Everything the world glories in, concupiscence of the eyes and the flesh, culture, wealth, honor, power, and pomp, all stand by the side of the road, intent on diverting us from our path. We shout our answer to them: "Vain and helpless are these idols, and equally powerless their worshipers." We place our trust in the risen King, Jesus Christ. Jesus, bless your flock; on this long journey, do not let us lose the divine life we possess ("It is not the dead who praise the Lord"; in the mind of the ancient Jews, once one went to limbo he could no longer praise God), but keep us in your grace. If, however, you prefer to make the application to Easter more personal and proximate, the following thoughts may appeal to you. Easter was in olden days the special time for baptism. We should therefore renew our baptismal promises at Easter. The second part of the psalm thus becomes a renunciation of the devil ("I renounce . . .") and a pledge made to Jesus: "Do you believe in Jesus Christ?" "I believe and trust in Him."

Instead of the usual capitulum and hymn, we find the Easter theme song: "This is the day . . ." The Magnificat antiphon continues the narrative begun in the psalm antiphons. The hour reaches its peak at the Magnificat in which, full of ardor, we thank God for the bountiful graces of the feast. These graces bear some resemblance to those granted to our Mother Mary. Together with the grateful prayer of His own Mother, the prayer of God's children mingles with the sweet clouds of incense and rises up before His throne. We thank God especially for making us His children, the greatest fruit of Christ's death and resurrection. Again, in this canticle as in psalm 112, we hear the admonition: Be humble, and then you will be exalted.

CHAPTER XXV

Office for Paschaltide

Paschaltide extends in the liturgical year from Low Sunday to None of the Saturday before Trinity Sunday. Although the office for the Easter octave is the same as that of the feast itself, still we find certain peculiarities that characterize the paschal season, beginning with First Vespers of Low Sunday. I will enumerate these peculiarities and make a few pertinent remarks.

1. The Alleluja is the leading feature. Nearly all the antiphons consist of one or three Allelujas, or at least conclude with this Easter cry. We can say the same thing of the versicles and responsories (the long responsories at Matins as well as the short ones for the little hours), for each ends with one or even two Allelujas. We understand its significance, that it is the theme song of Easter and the resurrection, an Easter greeting. Consequently it is repeated over and over again in the liturgy of the season.

2. Another peculiarity of the period is that all the psalms of Matins, Lauds, and Vespers are enclosed in a single antiphon, after the manner of the little hours. Thus, for example, at a ferial Matins office, all nine psalms are framed in a single antiphon. I find no satisfactory reason for this peculiarity. It does not occur during Easter Week itself, but only from First Vespers of Low Sunday on. During this period the

only exceptions to this peculiarity occur on feasts of Christ or of the saints.

3. The Ordinary for Paschaltide contains a number of beautiful passages. Matins for Sundays and ferial days opens with the joyous song: *Surrexit Dominus vere, alleluja* ("The Lord has truly risen, Alleluja"), just as we heard it on the feast of Easter itself. The Matins hymn (*Rex sempiterne*), is also full of Easter vitality and enthusiasm. After a tribute of praise to the risen Savior, it goes on to sing of our own spiritual resurrection through baptism. The thoughts are sublime: "You, once born of a virgin, rise now from the tomb, and bid us also who were buried with You, to rise from the dead." "You, the eternal Shepherd, who wash Your flock in the waters of baptism, this is the cleansing of our souls, the sepulcher of all our sins." In all three of the ordinary hymns for Paschaltide, a special verse (*Ut sis perenne*) is inserted just before the doxology. It expresses a request for true Easter joy. Another notable feature of the ferial Matins for this season is the Te Deum. Throughout the rest of the year at the end of Matins in a ferial office there is no Te Deum. Paschaltide, however, is marked out definitely as a season of joy by the presence of this solemn hymn at the end of Matins. The three ordinary capitula for the season repeat three important Scripture texts about the risen Savior. Both of the other hymns are of remarkable beauty, too. The Vesper hymn represents the newly baptized, all clad in white, making their way from the baptistery to the church where they assist at their first Mass and for the first time share in the eating of the Lamb. It is well here to observe that this hymn (as most of them) has much more appeal and originality in its primitive form.

At Vespers all during this season we hear the beautiful

and appropriate versicle: "Remain with us, O Lord, alleluja: for evening is at hand, alleluja." It is as though the drama of Emmaus were re-enacted each evening for us, while we join the disciples in the prayer that the Savior may not leave us in the evening of trial and temptation, and in the evening of our life.

4. The liturgy for the Sundays of the paschal season is much simpler than that of the Sundays of Lent and Passiontide. In the latter, even the little hours had special antiphons. This is not the case here; only the capitula are proper to the season. These are taken from the Sunday Epistle so that the practical lessons and important thoughts re-echo through the whole day. The Magnificat and Benedictus antiphons are always taken from the Sunday Gospel. (This holds true even for First Vespers.) Thus the Gospel narrative rings in our ears from morning to evening. In other words, Christ, as portrayed in today's Gospel, stands before our eyes from sunrise to sunset. Another remarkable feature of the season is that special Magnificat and Benedictus antiphons are provided even for weekdays. They are taken either from the Gospel itself or (more often the case) from accounts of the various apparitions that occurred after the resurrection. These antiphons make exceptionally beautiful liturgical aspirations. But unfortunately they are generally unnoticed, chiefly because the ferial office occurs so seldom.

5. We should also make mention of the current Scripture readings for the paschal season. These are taken exclusively from the New Testament. This principle holds true for the Easter season: *Omnia nova*. These lessons are beautiful indeed, and during these weeks we can profitably use the current books for our daily Bible reading. Two weeks are devoted to reading the Acts of the Apostles, one to the Apocalypse,

and one to the Epistle of St. James. We have little trouble understanding how appropriate the first two books are for this season: the history of the infant Church and the account of St. John's revelations, the hope and solace of the early Christians. The classic responsories of this season are also worth our attention. In the responsories for the Third Sunday after Easter, for example, the Church is represented under various figures: that of the fruitful vine, that of the bride decked out in all her finery, and that of the holy city of Jerusalem.

Like a vine, I gave forth a pleasant odor, alleluja:
Come to me all of you who desire me, and fill yourselves with my
    fruit, alleluja, alleluja.

In me is every grace of the way and of truth:
In me is every hope of life and virtue.

Your streets, Jerusalem, will be paved with pure gold, alleluja:
And a song of joy shall be sung in you, alleluja.
And all shall call out in all your streets, alleluja, alleluja.
You shall shine with a brilliant splendor and all the ends of the
    earth shall venerate you.[1]

One of the seven angels spoke to me, saying:
Come and I will show you the new bride, the spouse of the Lamb.
And I saw Jerusalem coming down from the heavens, decked out
    in her jewels, alleluja, alleluja, alleluja.

The responsories for the fourth week after Easter are a continuous canticle on the Alleluja.

O God, I will sing a new song to you: Alleluja.
I will play for you on the psalter of seven strings, alleluja, alleluja.
You are my God, I shall praise you;
You are my God, I shall exalt you.
I will play for you on the psalter of seven strings; alleluja.

---

[1] These four lines are taken from the first responsory of feria quarta in the third week after the octave of Easter. [Ed.]

If I ever forget you, alleluja,
Then let my right hand wither.
Let my tongue cleave to my jaws,
If I do not remember you, alleluja.
Sing us a hymn: alleluja.
How can we sing the hymn of the Lord in a foreign land?
    Alleluja, alleluja.
For there those who led us away captive, asked for the words of
    our songs:
How can we sing the song of our Lord in a foreign land, alleluja?

6. Another peculiarity of the paschal season is the special
Common of Martyrs for both Missal and Breviary. At any
rate, this seems to suggest that "the white-robed band" of
martyrs forms the retinue of the Conqueror of death and hell.

In commemorating the martyrs during Paschaltide, the
Church is exemplifying the words of St. Paul: "Being partners of His sufferings, you shall be partners also in His encouragement." For this reason the Common of Martyrs for
this season is full of joy and triumph. Its texts breathe an
ancient Christian spirit and enthusiasm. The following lesson from a sermon of St. Ambrose offers a key for the interpretation of this Common: "It is quite appropriate, brethren,
now that we have celebrated the joyous feast of Easter in
the Church, to share our joy with the holy martyrs and proclaim the glory of the resurrection of the Lord to those who
shared in His passion" (Common).

The office for this Common of Martyrs contains many gems
of prayer and poetry.

His consecrated (*Nazarei*) are dazzling white, alleluja:
They give glory to God, alleluja;
They are white as milk, alleluja, alleluja, alleluja.
They are brighter than snow, whiter than milk, more brilliant than
    old ivory, more beautiful than the sapphire.

The Church invites us: "O daughter of Jerusalem, come and see the martyrs with the crowns, with which the Lord crowned them on the great day of solemnity and joy, alleluja, alleluja" (Benedictus antiphon).

The letter of St. Cyprian the martyr, addressed to the martyrs and confessors (in the ancient sense of the term) makes an excellent lesson for the season.

We summarize what we have considered by saying that, as reflected in the Breviary, the paschal season is indeed of early Christian simplicity, but also of a genuine if distinctive appeal and beauty.

A word now about the two feasts of the Ascension and Pentecost. The feast of the Ascension concentrates fully on Christ's kingship. The whole feast is concerned with His enthronement at the right hand of the Father. Again, the office is a pleasant blending of beauty and simplicity. As at Christmas and Easter, the feast's antiphons at both Vespers and Lauds recount the historical event. Note the emotion and vigor of the hymn *Salutis humanae,* especially the beautiful stanza,

Tu dux ad astra, et semita,
Sis meta nostris cordibus,
Sis lacrymarum gaudium,
Sis dulce vitae præmium.

In the Magnificat antiphon for First Vespers we see Christ standing at the threshold of the heavenly mansion, talking to the Father: "Father, I have manifested Your name to the men You have given me out of the world: and now I pray for them, not for the world, because I am coming to You, alleluja." For the most part, Matins is a collection of "royal" psalms, while the antiphons highlight the words: *ascendit, elevare, exaltare.* The fitting Ascension psalm (46) is used as a complete unit and also in separate verses. The Magnificat antiphon for Second Vespers provides a splendid conclusion for the feast: *O Rex gloriae.* Together with its octave, this feast has much in common with the feast of our Lord's Epiphany, inasmuch as both focus our attention on Christ's kingship.

Pentecost is the second highlight of the Easter season. This feast's office has several special features. Matins, as at Easter, consists of but one nocturn, and for the same reason. Pentecost used to be the end of the catechumenate and also the time for baptism. That left time then, during the night, for but one nocturn. We sing the hymn *Veni, Creator Spiritus* at Terce, the time of the descent of the Holy Spirit. Then at Vespers we find all the Pentecost themes: the historical events of the first Pentecost, the effects of the Holy Spirit, and also baptism (fourth antiphon).

Matins is not so easy to understand. Its three psalms may be compared to a triptych with the three following scenes. Scene one: the historical event, and the significance of the miracle of Pentecost. We see the powerful effect of the "wind" in the imagery of psalm 47. Scene two: the operation and influence of the Holy Spirit in His Church. Though psalm 67 is difficult (the most difficult of the whole Psalter, in my opinion), this much is clear: it describes God's victory march in the Ark of the Covenant from the desert into the Promised Land as far as Sion, whence the God of the Covenant extended His rule over the whole world through His Son and His Church, under the guiding influence of the Holy Spirit. Scene three: creation renewed by the Holy Spirit. In psalm 103 we find an exceptionally vivid account of the six days of creation. The magnificence and grandeur of the visible creation is a token and figure of the invisible, spiritual "creation" that takes place in the Church and in our souls through the Holy Spirit. The feast concludes with the Magnificat antiphon which, as it frequently happens, is a *hodie-*chant.

CHAPTER XXVI

Office for the Feast of Corpus Christi

AMONG the other festive offices I shall treat only that for
the feast of Corpus Christi, mainly because it is one of the
most beautiful offices of the whole Breviary. It was composed
in 1274 at the request of Pope Urban IV by the great doctor
of the Church, St. Thomas Aquinas. Unquestionably a classic masterpiece of liturgical prayer art, this office takes its
place among the finest treasures of the Roman Breviary. The
vast difference between this office, however, and that of the
ancient feasts is immediately discernible. The latter resemble a magnificent vale of beautiful but wild flowers and ferns,
whereas the Corpus Christi office is more like a trim, exquisitely cultivated garden. Older feasts and offices that date
from the early ages of Christianity are easy to distinguish
from more recent ones that originated in the Middle Ages
or in modern times. The old feasts breathe the spirit of the
vigorous age of the martyrs. They are not so artistic and
exquisite in their composition. On the contrary, careful and
methodical composition and different structural and artistic
patterns characterize the later feasts. Corpus Christi fits in
among these later feasts, and its office is undoubtedly a finished masterpiece. Every new effort discloses a new beauty
and a new depth of thought.

398

The antiphons are, as they should be, the key for interpreting the psalms. The most beautiful and appropriate were selected and, through the antiphons, given an intimate, vital relationship to the feast. The responsories are particularly artistic and well balanced structurally. The first three treat of the figures of the Holy Eucharist; the next three of its institution; and the last two treat of the fruits and effects of the Eucharist. Each is so arranged that one part is from the Old Testament, and the other from the New, like a prophecy and its fulfillment. The hymns, too, came from the pen of St. Thomas, and there is no question but that they belong among the masterpieces of world literature. Here we have an example of perfect art: unity in variety, and variety in unity.

It is only after singling out the theme that we can truly understand and appreciate the office of a particular feast, since this theme is the focal point of all the prayer texts. Corpus Christi is the feast of the institution of the Blessed Sacrament of the Altar. It is our tribute of thanks and homage to Christ who revealed His limitless kindness and love in the institution of the Holy Eucharist. As a matter of fact, Holy Thursday is really the day the Sacrament was instituted. But the sad memories of Christ's passion that enshroud this feast are scarcely compatible with the great joy and celebration such an event deserves. For this reason the Church gives us the feast of Corpus Christi, to commemorate the brighter side of Holy Thursday. This feast occurs on the first Thursday after the end of the Easter cycle. Its office emphasizes the early Christian ideas of the Eucharist as food and as sacrifice.

Vespers

First and Second Vespers, the same except for the Magnificat antiphons, open and close the celebration of the feast.

Both are joyous canticles of praise and thanksgiving to God.

Christ Himself cited the first psalm (109) as being Messianic. It portrays the Redeemer in His three offices: as King enthroned at the right hand of the Father, as Priest offering an unbloody sacrifice, and as Judge of the world. The psalm is very poetic and full of vivid imagery.

What message does the psalm convey for our feast? To the question: "Who is present in the Holy Eucharist?" it answers: "Jesus Christ, the Son of God." And though He makes Himself a helpless prisoner under the species of bread, yet He is the mighty Conqueror, the King, and the Judge. Full of reverence and gratitude, Holy Mother Church turns her eyes to her Spouse. We pray: 1. Jesus, You are the King of our hearts; subject them entirely to Your sway. There is still much pride and arrogance in us. Give us some day a place in Your retinue "in holy splendor." 2. Jesus, You are our High Priest. This is the main theme of our office today; hence the antiphon. Just as You offered the sacrifice of redemption on the altar of the cross, so now You renew and represent this sacrifice of love every day on our altars. Today with grateful hearts, we commemorate the institution of the Holy Eucharist. You are the true Priest at every Mass; the human representative merely lends You his hands and his tongue. 3. In conclusion, You are also our Judge. Now the mild and meek Lamb hidden under the appearance of bread, one day You will come as the roaring lion of Juda. But even now You act as Judge. You fill the hungry and turn the rich away empty. Jesus, be a lenient Judge. "He who eats . . . unworthily, eats . . . judgment to himself."

We ought to pray this psalm with great reverence. (Melchisedech, the mysterious priest-king of Salem, offered a sacrifice of bread and wine in the days of Abraham. This was a figure of the unbloody sacrifice of Jesus.)

The theme: Christ, the Priest of the unbloody sacrifice.

Psalm 110 is a thanksgiving hymn, hence an ideal Vesper psalm. It is the Church's way of thanking God for the graces of the day, but in particular for the great grace of the Eucharist. Only after grasping its literal sense shall we be able to apply this psalm properly to the feast. In their songs and hymns the Jews loved to sing about the deliverance from Egypt, about God's marvelous guidance in their journey through the desert, their rescue from the clutches of Pharaoh, the passage through the Red Sea, the miraculous manna, and the conquest of the Promised Land. All these were favorite themes, the everlasting miracles and monuments of God's loving solicitude for His chosen people. These were the motives for their faith and trust in God. So also in this psalm. But for us the only difference we make is that God's marvelous works and favors are antetypes of the future redemption and of the wonderful kingdom of God. Line for line we can apply this psalm to ourselves and translate it into our own Christian language. The deliverance out of Egypt for us is the redemption from the slavery of Satan. The journey through the desert is our journey through life on this earth. Oftentimes the figure becomes a reality, for frequently enough the earth offers God's children "little bread but many stones." And God is our leader too, not in the form of a pillar of fire or a cloud hovering over the ark, but in the person of the Savior Himself accompanying us through life. Moreover, we too have a lasting reminder of His love and solicitude. In order that we may not faint on the way, He feeds us each day with the miraculous manna of life, the true bread of heaven. That is the highlight of the psalm, and likewise the theme of the feast that is stressed in the antiphon. For us the entrance into the Promised Land becomes our entrance into heaven. Then, if the Jews could praise God as being faithful, kind, and holy, what must we Christians say of Him when He has given us in Christ the whole wealth of His grace and favors?

The theme: The Holy Eucharist is our manna for the journey through life.

Psalm 115 is another hymn of thanksgiving, one that the Jews sang after their release from captivity in Babylon. The Psalmist vows to offer a solemn sacrifice of thanksgiving in the temple, and the sacrifice is represented here as a libation. For us the psalm becomes a Eucharistic hymn for two reasons. 1. At the Last Supper it was sung as a hymn of thanksgiving for the first Holy Communion. It belongs to the so-called Hallel psalms sung, according to Jewish custom, during the paschal ceremonies. Thus this psalm is sacred to us because Christ and His apostles used it on such a momentous occasion. 2. It is used also in the Mass liturgy. After consuming the body of our Lord, the priest says: "How shall I make a return to the Lord for all the good He has done for me? The cup of salvation (that is, the precious blood) I will take up, and I will call upon the name of the Lord." For these two reasons, therefore, the psalm becomes a true Eucharistic hymn of thanksgiving for us. As a result, it is appropriate for the Vespers of Corpus Christi. It tells us that the best way to thank God for all the graces conferred on us during the past day is by the Holy Sacrifice of the Mass (eucharistia, "thanksgiving." It is Christ Himself who thanks the Father for us).

The theme: The Mass is Christianity's great sacrifice of thanksgiving.

Psalm 127 in its literal sense gives a lovely picture of a household pleasing to God and a blessed family life. It concludes with a prayerful wish for the favors and graces of the Messianic era. The Fathers liked to apply this psalm in a mystical way to Christ and His Church. In a similar fashion we can apply it in our office. Christ is the father of the family that is, mankind; the family He won by submitting His will to the Father. He built the house of His Church by the bloody labor on the cross, and we reap the fruit of His sweat and blood. The Church is His beloved spouse. She came forth from the wound in the side (*in lateribus domus tuae*) [1] of the second Adam's body. Countless thousands of children she has given to her divine Spouse, "the true vine." And her children, too, are gathered around His table. Then the antiphon presents a beautiful scene: the vast family of God gathered around the table of the Lord. Jesus the father, Holy Church the mother, and we the children, all ranged about the holy table, fed with the bread of the Holy Eucharist. We give thanks for all the graces received in Communion, and we ask for a further grace: that the Church may see many children gathered around her table.

The theme: The Lord's table.

Psalm 147 is another hymn of thanksgiving for the return from the Babylonian exile. God has restored the city and repaired its gates. Blessings, peace, and prosperity once more flood the land. God fills His people with bread again. Now the Psalmist turns his thoughts back to the period of the exile. God deserted His people because of their sins. It was

[1] Old version.

like winter then, as far as their souls were concerned: everything stiff, with cold, ice, and snow everywhere. But now God has forgiven them. Spring comes to the soul, and its warm winds melt the snow and ice so that now the brooks and streams are swollen. Thus God sends His people back to their homeland in little groups. In a spirit of heartfelt gratitude, the Psalmist acknowledges that God has not shown such love and solicitude for any other people.

How does this psalm fit into our office? It is a figure of the kingdom of God. At one time on earth it was "deep winter," in the souls of men, too. Everything was frozen, far removed from God by sin. Then spring came to earth with Christ, and the once frozen streams of grace began to flow again and to fructify the soil of men's souls. Jerusalem, God's favorite; this is the Church and the soul. Both can sing: "Glorify the Lord, O Jerusalem, . . . for He has strengthened the bars of your gates," that is, He protects you from the devil. He gives you the long awaited peace and fills you with the best of the heavenly wheat, the Holy Eucharist. This, then, you must gratefully acknowledge: to no other people has God shown such love and care as to us Christians.

The theme: the prosperity of the kingdom of God; the Holy Eucharist, the food of the children of God.

Let us now summarize the beautiful description of the Holy Eucharist given in the Vesper psalms. First we see the Priest of the unbloody sacrifice; then the Church making its pilgrimage through the desert of time, with the precious manna as her sustenance; then Christianity's thanksgiving sacrifice; likewise the Savior at the Last Supper, and the charming scene of God's children grouped around the holy table; and finally Jerusalem, rebuilt and flooded with God's blessings, her people filled with the marrow of the heavenly wheat.

We can distinguish three stages in the structure of our Vesper office. First the psalmody; secondly the capitulum; and thirdly the climax, the Magnificat. The theme of the feast, so well developed and amplified in the psalms, is neatly crystallized in the capitulum. It is the famous passage from St. Paul's First Epistle to the Corinthians about the institution of the Eucharist. In these few words we find the whole sum and substance of our feast. The subject matter, the institution; the special theme, food and sacrifice. The hymn follows as a reflection or lyric overflow of the capitulum. It is related to the capitulum somewhat as the responsory is to the lesson. This particular hymn, the *Pange lingua*, perhaps the most famous of St. Thomas' compositions, is characterized like the others by its classic form and profound thought. Its main idea is found in the third stanza: the description of the institution of the Eucharist.

The climax of the hour, of course, is the Magnificat, Mary's own hymn of thanksgiving. We observe that our motive for thanksgiving is very like hers. With her Son Jesus under her heart, Mary gives thanks for being chosen to be the Mother of God. Today the Church carries her Eucharistic Savior in her hands, and we carry Him in our hearts. Together we give thanks for this divine "visitation." Mary, better than anyone else, can teach us how to honor the Holy Eucharist properly and to receive it worthily. That is the purpose of the Magnificat: to remind us that this canticle would make a beautiful thanksgiving prayer after Communion. The Magnificat antiphon of First Vespers draws attention to another important point: the exaltation of the lowly and the humiliation of the proud. In fact, this thought is expressed in the

Magnificat itself, one of the features or principles of God's kingdom. This principle is marvelously exemplified in the Holy Eucharist, the sacrament of humility, where the humble find all strength and sweetness, while the proud look on with scorn and contempt. Thus the Eucharist is itself a condemnation of all pride and arrogance.

The Magnificat antiphon for Second Vespers is a masterpiece, crystallizing in four brief phrases the whole dogma of the feast: 1. the Eucharist as our food; 2. our sacrifice; 3. imparting grace; 4. pledge of eternal glory. This antiphon is the grand finale of the whole feast.

First Vespers concludes with the oration, divided like the ancient orations, into two parts: 1. the motive, and 2. the petition.

1. The motive. We should note that it is God the Son whom we address in this oration (*passionis tuae*). In the older orations we always address the Father. "You have left us a memorial of Your passion in this wonderful sacrament." "Wonderful," being full of wonder and mystery. This is meant especially of the Eucharist as a sacrifice. Do we actually recall the Passion at the time of Mass? Jesus emphasizes this here in order that we ever may be mindful of His blessed passion.

2. The petition. What do these words mean: ". . . so venerate that we may always experience the fruits of Thy redemption"? The Holy Eucharist will always produce its effect in us. What is expected of us is the "veneration"; not mere external piety, but true, interior devotion. That is the only way we can assimilate this spiritual food so that it will give life and growth and protection against spiritual maladies. Now, how do the motive and the petition fit together? In the Mass, and therefore in the Eucharist, we find a memorial of Christ's passion; not merely a lifeless commemoration of a

long-past event, but an actual re-presentation and renewal of our Savior's death. When we celebrate Mass we actually have before us the tree of the cross bending its grace-laden branches down to us that we may enjoy the fruits of redemption. Consequently the main petition of the oration is that we may be of the proper dispositions to receive this fruit. There are three distinct thoughts:

1. The tree of the cross, standing before us in the Eucharist (Mass).
2. May we be able to reap the fruit of redemption.
3. Give us the dispositions necessary to do so.

The *jugiter* ("always," "every day") tells us that the Eucharist is to be our daily food for the journey through life.

Matins

This is the real meditation on the feast. As usual, the drama opens with the Invitatory, in this case a magnificent example of prayer art. Then the theme of the feast is woven into the majestic psalm 94. The Invitatory is perhaps the tersest expression of the theme: Christ present in the Eucharist as the food of our souls. This brief chant voices our homage to Christ, the King of God's kingdom. The emphasis, however, is on the contrast. He, the Lord of the world, gives Himself to be our food, food which imparts to us divine life, full and abundant life. In psalm 94 we are especially concerned with Jesus as the Good Shepherd who feeds "the sheep of His flock." Finally, we recall the manna in the desert.

Through this majestic archway with its splendid tableaux of the Eucharistic King, the Good Shepherd, and the manna, we pass on to the hymn with its scenes from the Last Supper. After its joyous introduction (note, too, the frequently quoted verse: *recedant vetera, nova sint omnia, corda, voces, et opera*), the hymn takes up the theme of the Last Supper. First the passover meal (stanza two), then the institution of the Holy Eucharist (stanzas three and four), the commission to the priests to perpetuate the Eucharist (stanza five), the bread of angels, of heaven, the slave eating his Master (stanza six).

The three nocturns of the office for the feast are arranged in a progressive pattern of ideas. The first treats of the symbolism of the Old Testament prefiguring the Eucharist. The second is concerned with the theme of the feast. And finally, the third nocturn gives us the climax: the Gospel. The lessons for the first nocturn, surprisingly enough, are taken from the New Testament. Their responsories outline three of the most outstanding figures of the Holy Eucharist: the paschal lamb (1), the manna (2), and Elias' hearthcake (3). In all these responsories the first part is taken from the Old Testament, and the second from the New. In the responsories of the second and third nocturns the opposite holds true.

There is no special thought pattern or sequence in the psalms. They follow in numerical order, highlighting now one aspect of the Eucharist, now another.

First Nocturn

Psalm 1 is an even-tempered, quietly moving, instructive hymn. It treats of the two ways: the way of life, and of death; of the just man and the sinner, of their reward and punishment. We are already familiar with this psalm from the Easter office where we saw the Savior Himself as the "just man." We can make the same application here, giving special attention to the figure of the fruitful tree. Before us stands the tree of life in the paradise of God's kingdom, the tree planted near

the stream of Christ's own blood. It spreads its boughs wide
to us children of God that we may pick the wholesome fruit
of the Holy Eucharist. We know, of course, that there were
two special trees in Paradise: the tree of knowledge of good
and evil, and the tree of life. The latter was meant to nourish
and sustain the physical life of our first parents. It was a figure
of the Holy Eucharist,[2] given to nourish and sustain the
divine life of the children of God. Truly may we say of this
tree of life: it "yields its fruit in due season," that is, according to the antiphon, the "season" that came at Christ's death.
We may consider it either as the time of His death on the
cross, or of the Last Supper. This "tree" of the Eucharist is
also "always green," bearing blossom and fruit alike.

The theme: The Eucharist, our tree of life.

Psalm 4 is somewhat more emotional. Again, we are already
familiar with this psalm from our study of the Holy Saturday
office. Its application, however, is quite different. The psalm
describes the happiness of the godfearing man. While the
joy of the wicked vanishes as swiftly as a soap-bubble, the
upright man is loaded with favors. "The Lord does wonders
for his faithful one, . . . the Lord will hear me when I call
upon Him." God's countenance smiles down upon him like
the warm, energizing rays of the sun. His spiritual joys far
surpass the material happiness of the worldlings. Profound,
sweet peace of soul and a lively hope of heaven are his great
comfort and solace. If those of the Old Law can use such
language, how much more reason have we Christians to exult
over the graces and joys of the kingdom of God! Of course
the greatest of all these joys is the Holy Eucharist. With it
and through it we receive all the other favors and graces

[2] Apoc. 2:7; 22:2.

enumerated in the psalm. The antiphon suggests the proper
application. Let the children of the world rejoice over their
material wealth as they would over an abundance of wine
and grain. We children of God exult in the Eucharistic wine
and in the bread of life. These nourish our souls and give us
rest in the peace of our Savior, in the arms of our Jesus.

The theme: The Holy Eucharist, the true riches of the kingdom of God.

Psalm 15. This psalm we know already from Holy Saturday.
If possible, it has even more warmth and feeling than the
preceding psalm. One of the priests or Levites sings a song
of gratitude for his happy "portion." The first few verses are
rather obscure, but St. Thomas helps us to understand them
by means of the antiphon. Under the Old Law it was the
blood of animals that united men in sacrifice, and consequently with one another and with God, but in the New Law
God unites His people through the blood of His own Son. The
Old Covenant was ratified and sealed by the blood of animals; the New, by the blood of Jesus Christ. And whereas
the Old Covenant effected but an external union with God,
in the New Covenant the blood of Christ makes of us all one
mystical body. The very blood of Jesus flows in our veins too,
making us "sharers in His divinity." Thus from the antiphon
we learn that the blood of Jesus is in the fullest sense the
blood that ratifies our Covenant. Of course, the rest of the
psalm admits of many references and allusions to the Holy
Eucharist. We also find our greatest delight in the Eucharist.
This and the divine life it imparts are our "portion" and our
"cup." For us too, "the measuring lines have fallen on pleasant sites." (When the territory of the Promised Land was
apportioned, each family received a tract of land by lot; one
a good section, another not so good.) We children of God

have reason to rejoice, for "fair indeed is our inheritance," our Savior, Jesus Himself.

This joy and gratitude over the "portion" that has fallen to us is so great that we ourselves are constrained to ponder over it even during the night. The Eucharistic God, the true Emmanuel ("God with us"), is ever at my side, my food and sustenance for the journey and battles of this life on earth. But not only on earth, even in heaven He will not suffer His faithful one "to undergo corruption." The Eucharist is the pledge of our resurrection. "The man who eats My flesh . . . I will raise him up at the last day." [3] Happiness on this earth, eternal bliss in heaven: such are the fruits of the Holy Eucharist.

The theme: The Eucharist is the sacrifice of the New Covenant and our marvelous "portion."

In the versicle the Eucharist is referred to as the bread of angels, the bread of heaven; the Alleluja that accompanies the versicle voices our spiritual joy and happiness. This verse comes from psalm 77 (24 and 25), and speaks of the manna, a figure of the Holy Eucharist.

The lessons of the first nocturn contain the well-known passage about the Lord's Supper from the Epistle to the Corinthians. We met it before in the Holy Thursday office. In these lessons we have the kernel of our doctrine on the Holy Eucharist. The first lesson is merely the introduction, giving the historical background: the abuses of the faithful at Corinth. The second lesson, giving the account of the Last Supper, is actually the highlight of Matins. Note especially the last sentence. It shows the connection between the Eucharist and Christ's death, and thus affirms that it is essentially sacrificial in character. Finally, the third lesson offers some admonitions

[3] John 6:55.

about unworthy Communion, which we ourselves may well take to heart. This is, consequently, the somber side of an otherwise joyous office.

There is no special connection between the responsories and the lessons they follow. Each responsory explains a figure of the Eucharist: the paschal lamb, the manna, and the miraculous bread of Elias. The first part of each responsory is taken from the Old Testament and contains the figure. The second part is from the New Testament and indicates the fulfillment.

First responsory. On the eve of the Passover the Jews have to slaughter the paschal lamb and eat the meat with unleavened bread.[4] Then St. Paul, in the beautiful passage from the Epistle to the Corinthians, shows that this paschal meal was a double figure: the lamb prefigured Christ, and the unleavened bread prefigured the purity of us Christians.

Second responsory. The manna is a figure of the Eucharist. In His sermon at Capharnaum the Savior Himself explained the manna in this way. The theme of our prayer is the Eucharist now, instead of the manna. Besides the special properties of the manna, He also indicated the effects of the Eucharist, the bread of heaven and the bread of life.[5]

Third responsory. The hearthcake of Elias. This figure is less familiar to the laity. The prophet flees from the wicked queen Jezabel into the wilderness. He is ready to die from grief over the godlessness of his people. Tired and hungry, he lies down to sleep under a juniper tree. Suddenly an angel of God comes and touches him, saying: "Rise now and eat." There at his head he finds a hearthcake. He eats it, and from the energy and strength it gives him, through the next forty days he walks all the way to Mount Sinai, as the angel had

[4] Exod. 12:3, 5, 8.
[5] Exod. 16:12, 15; John 6:32.

commanded.[6] This miraculous bread is a figure and also a symbol of the Holy Eucharist. With the strength of this heavenly bread, we can accomplish our journey through life to the heavenly mountains. The Eucharist preserves our eternal life, that is, the life of grace.[7] Throughout the responsories, antiphons, and lessons, therefore, the emphasis is on the Eucharist as our food, although other ideas accompany the main theme.

Second Nocturn

Psalm 19 is a patriotic prayer before battle. Before riding off to battle, the king offers a sacrifice to God. The priests bless his weapons and then offer prayers for victory. Firm in their trust in God, the soldiers are sure of victory. We have little difficulty in applying this hymn to our feast. Christ is our King. At the head of mankind He wages a continual battle against Satan until the end of time. It is not we who conquer, but Christ, conquering in us. And every day before we ride off to battle, we utter our battle prayer: Father, "we call upon You"; and as does our King, we too bring a sacrifice. We are sure of victory then, for we are battling not "with chariots . . . and horses," but "in the name of (Jesus) the Lord our God." The antiphon explains our sacrifice, the Holy Sacrifice of the Mass. We are all priests offering as our victim the Lamb of God, and so we pray that our sacrifice may be fruitful for us. Notice here how the emphasis has shifted to the Eucharist as a sacrifice.

Theme: The Mass, our sacrifice before the day's battle with Satan and the world.

Psalm 22 is a surpassingly tender and emotional psalm that

[6] III Kings 19:6 ff.
[7] John 6:52.

the Church has made a Eucharistic hymn: "The Lord is my Shepherd." The Lord is my host in the Holy Eucharist. Here two lovely pictures portray our Eucharistic Savior. 1. The Good Shepherd. We have already seen this picture as we passed through the "archway" of the Invitatory. His own flesh and blood are the pasture, the green meadow, where He refreshes our souls. In the Holy Eucharist our Good Shepherd leads us safely through this life. Even when we "walk in the dark valley," we "fear no evil," sheltered beneath His watchful eye. The Holy Eucharist is our "rod and staff" in life and in death. 2. The good host: another picture of our Eucharistic Savior. This is the reality, the fulfillment of the parable in the Gospel, where the master himself waits on his servant.[8] Each day a table is prepared for us where Christ is both host and food. In fact, this table is spread "in the sight of (our) foes." The Eucharist, the bread of the strong, our medicine and antidote against sin. Our cup overflows with the wine that inebriates us for heaven, the wine that produces virgins. We gather around this table in a spirit of genuine friendship and loving union with Jesus. We live in God's house, for we ourselves are the temple of the Most High. Nearly every word of this beautiful psalm bears some reference to the Holy Eucharist.

Psalms 41 and 42. These belong together. Originally they formed one psalm. True gems of liturgical prayer, they combine to form an elegy that can well take its place among the pearls of world literature. In my explanation I shall follow Zenner-Wiesmann (*Die Psalmen,* Munster, 1906). The author of this psalm must have been highly gifted, enjoying in addition a rich interior life. In this masterpiece he reveals the inner movements of his soul. We find eager longing mingled

[8] Luke 12:37.

with sad remembrance, joyous hope and anxious hesitation, earnest plea and soul-wringing lament. The psalm strikes us almost like a passage from a modern emotional ballad. So natural are its sentiments, so true to life, that we ourselves are constrained to experience the Psalmist's inner conflict and struggle. The refrain is exceptionally effective. Repeating it three times is the author's clever means of keeping before us the psalm's main sentiment and dominant atmosphere, while the psalm proper unfolds the thoughts and emotions of the Psalmist.

We need to study the historical setting and literal meaning of this psalm if we are to appreciate it properly. The occasion is the Babylonian captivity. Far from their sanctuary where God Himself dwelt among them, the Jews are driven into exile by the Gentiles, who lord it over them. Now the Psalmist rises from the depths of his anguish to a firm hope and long-ing for God and his homeland. He runs the whole gamut of emotions and affections. Here we see one of the exiles lost in melancholy reverie, standing on one of the insignificant hills that flank the Euphrates. His eye scans the horizon. Far off to the west the lofty Mount Hermon lifts its snow-capped peaks to the sky. These same peaks had once followed the poor exiles day by day as they made their weary journey eastward, until finally, like a last farewell from their beloved homeland, they disappeared from view. Now the exile dwells here amid the endless plains, far from the source of his life. As he ponders these thoughts, he feels like a hind, hunted and chased out into the desert, straying through the wilder-ness. He pants and thirsts for water, but in vain. Thus the poor exile panted and longed for Sion, the temple of his God. All the more painful, the more consuming is his "thirst," be-cause he must listen to his captors' taunts: "Where is your

God?" As though God had forsaken him. How well he knew where God was!

But then happy scenes from the past flash across his mind, memories of magnificent feasts in God's honor. Men came to Jerusalem from far and near. As the people filed in procession into the forecourt, the lofty halls of the temple resounded with the joyous chant of psalms. Truly festive times they were, like the joy and exultation of a grand wedding. Such feasts were the highlights of his life. God seemed so close at such times, so near at hand. In fact, he used to "behold the face of God." Of a sudden he wakes from his reverie. Once more he realizes his bitter plight, all the sadder in the light of such glorious memories. And so he utters the stirring query: "Why are you so downcast, O my soul? Why do you sigh within me?" But his grief does not get the best of him. With manly vigor he rises to new trust and confidence in God. "Hope in God. For I shall again be thanking Him, in the presence of my Savior and my God" (I still have hope of returning to my homeland).

A heavy burden bows down his soul. In spite of everything, he cannot get rid of it. He cannot deny it, for it is certainly there. But now he takes up the matter with God. The river of Babylon flows along down below, uninterruptedly, wave after wave. It is a symbol of the suffering and oppression that have surged over the exiled people. Once more his thoughts turn homeward. He is living in Jerusalem again. By day the sun of God's grace shines down on them, and at night the lovely melodies of the psalms rise up to heaven. And now? "Why do You forget me? Why must I go about in mourning, with the enemy oppressing me?" Why? "My foes mock me, as they say to me day after day: 'Where is your God?'" His soul is brimful of love for his God and it feels the keen knife of their scorn. But he will not go astray. Come what may, he knows how to control himself. Now he comforts himself: "Why are you so downcast, O my soul? Why do you sigh within me?" Then encouraged, he adds: "Hope in God" for you will return again to your homeland (this strophe is the peak and climax of his grief). Now trust and confidence win out. Now he relies firmly on God. Since his cause is God's cause, so God has to take up the fight in his behalf to avenge the mockery of his enemies: "Do me justice, O God, and fight my fight against a faithless people." "For You, O God, are my strength." But now? Does not this seem to be a contradiction? "Why do You keep me so far away? Why must I go about in mourning, with the enemy oppressing me?" Is my enemy to triumph over me? No! "Send forth Your light and Your fidelity; they shall lead me on, and bring me to Your holy mountain (Sion), to Your dwelling place." See how beautifully he portrays his thoughts. Delivered from the privations of exile, his longing satisfied, with his heart fairly bursting for joy, he hastens to the altar to praise God and to sing a jubilant hymn of thanks amid the music of the zithers, just as he used to do in the happy days of his youth.

Only in the future, however, is this glorious picture to be an actuality. Now, then, there is still room for fear and doubt in the anxious soul: "Why are you so downcast, O my soul?" Nonetheless, in view of the glorious future, his soul pulses with new life and animation, and so concludes on this impressive note of encouragement: "Hope in God."

Now that we find such a beautiful elegy in our office for Corpus Christi, let us see how we may apply it to the feast. We can consider the psalm as a parable and single out, accordingly, the points of comparison, disregarding the others. The exile is a figure of our own life on earth, this "valley of tears" and misery where the child of God has one great solace, one great hope and longing, the Holy Eucharist. In this respect we are much more fortunate than the Jewish exiles. We have a "sanctuary," and in this sacrament our God is always near us. For this reason we pass lightly over the parts of the psalm that deal with the sorrow and dejection of the exiles, and concentrate our attention and devotion on the parts that speak of hope and longing. Thus our longing for the Holy Eucharist is presented in these two psalms as our solace in the exile of our earthly life. This desire and longing are the best preparation we can make for the reception of the Eucharist, and the best way we can repay Christ's longing to dwell in our midst, in our very souls: "I have longed and longed to share this paschal meal with you before My passion." [9]

The longing of the exiled Jews for their "sanctuary" should be the norm of our desire for the Eucharist. How fervently might we pray that first verse: "As the hind longs for the running waters. . . ." I need no sad reflection on past happiness and joy to kindle this desire in my soul. I have my "sanctuary" always before me, the great comfort of my life. Each morning every day I can say: "I will go in to the altar of God, . . . to your dwelling place . . . amid loud cries of joy and thanksgiving, with the multitude keeping festival." The antiphon presents the following thought: let us rejoice at the holy table where we eat of the bread of life. Between the sufferings of this life and the spiritual joy and happiness we receive from the Eucharist, there is no comparison. For this reason we need not "go about in mourning," because through the storm and clouds there shine down on us the warm, bright rays of the Eucharistic Sun. And though there

[9] Luke 22:15.

well may be hours of trial and affliction, the "Gethsemanes" in our lives, when "the breakers and billows" of suffering surge over us, we have a place to pour out our troubles, where we can always find comfort and peace.

Psalm 42 belongs to the third nocturn, but we will treat of it here instead. It was selected for our office because of the important role it plays in the Mass, in the prayers at the foot of the altar. The antiphon is the same there as for our feast, though in the latter it has more direct application to the Eucharist. In both settings (in Mass and feast) the psalm is one of those sung by the pilgrims on their way to "the holy mountain" of the Eucharist. From the soul's depths we hear the cry: "Fight my fight against a faithless people" (my unruly passions), and: "from the deceitful and impious man (within me) rescue me." Am I strong enough to climb the steep path? "For You, O my God, are my strength." The enemy shall not block my path. "Send forth Your light and Your fidelity, they shall lead me on and bring me to Your holy mountain, to Your dwelling place." And thus I shall approach the altar of God, to receive Christ Himself, who will renew my gladness and joy (antiphon) that I may give thanks to Him upon the harp of my soul. How then can the trials of this life depress my soul?

These two psalms (41 and 42) are the highlights of the office.

The lessons for the second nocturn were written by St. Thomas himself. They are taken from the works on which Christ Himself passed judgment: "Thomas, you have written well of Me." The first two responsories speak of the institution of the Eucharist. The first part of each, we find, is taken from the New Testament; the second, from the Old. The fourth responsory is from Job 31:31. The friends of Job protest their great love, that is, their desire for lasting friendship and companionship with Job. This "love" is a figure of the love and eager longing the faithful soul has for Jesus in the Eucharist. What is expressed in the figure as mere "desire" ("Who will give us of his flesh that we may be filled?") finds its fulfillment in the person of Jesus in Holy Communion. Fifth responsory. In the first part Christ commissions His followers to celebrate this memorial of Him. The Church replies in the second part with the words of the Lamentation: "I will be mindful and remember, and my soul shall languish within me." [10] What better answer could she make? In every Mass we commemorate Christ's death on the cross, and shall not our hearts also languish with sympathy for our beloved Savior? This particular responsory is the midway point of Matins. Is it merely coincidental that the *repetenda* should contain Christ's command to commemorate His death? The sixth responsory is the only one taken entirely from the New Testament, though the first part does speak of "manna." Its main thoughts are about the *panis vivus et vitalis* ("the living and life-giving bread"). (See the Sequence of the Mass.)

Third Nocturn

Psalm 42. We have given this psalm consideration already in connection with psalm 41.

Psalm 80 is a festive song used on the occasion of the solemn pilgrimages to Jerusalem. It has two parts: the invitation to the feast; God's address to the assembled people. This literary device is especially effective. As the King who made a covenant with them, God calls His people into the temple in order to address them. It is a serious, threatening sermon. (a) The text of the sermon: I rescued you from your slavery in Egypt,

[10] Lam. 3:20.

and led you through the desert into the Promised Land. (b) The application: "Hear, My people. . . . I, the Lord, am your God. . . . Open wide your mouth, and I will fill it." (c) The punishment if His command is neglected. (d) The reward for its fulfillment: "If only My people would hear Me, . . . quickly would I humble their enemies. . . . I would feed them with the best of wheat, and with honey from the rock I will fill them." Then the psalm concludes rather abruptly, though the final verse keeps echoing in our ears.

Now let us apply the psalm to our feast. We, too, are celebrating a great feast (*die sollemni nostro*). So the first part can be the joyous invitation to celebrate the feast (see the Introit of the Mass). Then our Savior preaches the sermon for the feast. He recalls to us the graces of our redemption. On the cross He rescued us from the slavery of Satan. He spoke to us so often from within "the cloud." Now He offers us either life or death. It is for us to choose. If we choose life, we shall be rich, powerful, invincible. How appropriate the words of the antiphon: Christ feeds us and fills our soul with the bread of life and the honey of the Holy Eucharist! We ought not stress this one verse in our application, but concentrate on the whole idea of the bountiful prosperity and joy of the kingdom of God.

The last psalm (83) caps the psalmody for the Matins office. It is a warm, tender hymn of longing for the Holy Eucharist. In its literal sense it was one of the pilgrimage songs sung on the way up to Jerusalem. We can easily adapt the Old Testament allusions and make it a genuinely Christian, Eucharistic hymn. Its antiphon suggests that in the psalm we open the floodgates of our joy over the great mystery of our faith. Several of the verses would make excellent ejaculations. "How lovely is Your dwelling place, O Lord of hosts; my soul yearns and pines for the courts of the Lord; . . . even the sparrow finds a home, and the swallow a nest; . . . Your altars, O Lord of hosts, my king and my God."

The lessons for the third nocturn are St. Augustine's explanation of the Gospel for the feast. The profound doctor has given us a priceless commentary which the Church makes free use of in expounding the Gospel of St. John. Again, the two last responsories have several special features. 1. Like the earlier ones, their first part is from the New Testament, and the second from the Old. 2. They have the ideal relation to the lessons they follow, that is, besides being taken from the day's Gospel text, they fit logically into the words of the lessons. Thus responsory seven flows naturally into lesson eight, and responsory eight, into lesson nine.

It is once again the grandiose hymn Te Deum that concludes our Matins. This is the common prayer of the entire redeemed Church. It brings our grand celebration of the Eucharist (that is, the Matins office) to its climax and its close.

Lauds

In Matins and Vespers the theme of the feast (the Eucharist) predominates, with the hour thought (night; evening) somewhat subordinated. Just the opposite occurs in Lauds. The hour thought (creation's morning prayer) takes the lead, while the theme puts in but an occasional appearance. It is as though I were praying my usual morning prayer, but with this difference: from time to time I recall that today is Corpus Christi. The antiphons take care of this for me, and as a result they do not have the function, as in Matins and Vespers, of supplying a clue for the interpretation of the psalms. As they are merely a Eucharistic frame for the psalms, they have varying degrees of relation to them.

Psalm 92: Christ as King and Victor. The earth is His throne, creation His raiment, the powers of nature His sword, the whole universe His domain. The antiphon conjures up another picture before our eyes. Christ, Wisdom personified, the Logos, the wise architect and builder of the universe, has built another house, the Church, the kingdom of God on earth. Here He sits not enthroned as a King, but the Good Shepherd who feeds us, His guests, with His own body and blood.[11]

Psalm 99 is a song of praise to God our Savior who is likewise our Creator, Redeemer, and Good Shepherd, good, kind, and faithful to His word. In spirit I enter the house of the Lord to celebrate the feast of the Eucharist. Today, on Corpus Christi, I must give a special greeting to the Good Shepherd, who feeds "His people, the flock He tends" with the sweet "food of the angels," the "bread of heaven."

Psalm 62 is our morning hymn, full of longing for God. We can apply it easily to the Holy Eucharist, using its poetic phrases to express our own longing and desire for union with Jesus in this sacrament. In the dry, waterless valley of this earthly life our souls thirst for Him. Eagerly we think of Him as we lie on our couches. In the shadow of His wings we shout for joy. For indeed, only in the Holy Eucharist are the words truly realized: "My soul clings fast to You; Your right hand upholds me."

We might say, in fact, that only in the light of this sacrament can this psalm be fully and properly appreciated. The verse, "And with the riches of a banquet shall my soul be satisfied," suggested the third antiphon: "Rich is the bread of Christ, it shall yield dainties to kings." The passage is borrowed from the patriarch Jacob's last blessing to his sons. For

[11] Prov. 9:1 ff.

his son Aser, Jacob prophesies that his family will eventually obtain a rich and fruitful land whose fruits will yield dainties to kings.[12] The liturgy adapts this passage to the Eucharistic bread which offers such rich food to our souls and which makes spiritual kings of men who were slaves to sin. This psalm is the highlight of Lauds and, of course, fits perfectly into the office for the feast.

The Canticle of the Three Youths is creation's grand symphony of praise to God. All creatures are invited to sing God's praises. There is a special reason for doing so today: the Holy Eucharist. Today, indeed, nature has much more reason for praising its Maker. The King of all creation laid aside the mantle of His divinity to don the simple clothes of an inanimate creature, in the forms of bread and wine. This is a special distinction conferred on creation, and a token of its eventual resurrection. Thus today, the Canticle of the Three Youths encircles the Holy Eucharist like a beautiful garland woven by all the creatures of heaven and earth alike.

The antiphon follows naturally on the words of the psalm: "O ye priests of the Lord, bless the Lord God." It goes on to say that the priest who is holy, that is, consecrated to God, can best praise Him by offering the incense of liturgical prayer and the bread of the Holy Eucharist.[13] But this truth holds true of all Christians, since they are "a royal priesthood, a consecrated nation." [14]

Psalm 148 continues creation's song of praise: heaven and earth praise the Lord. Here, too, we can easily relate the hour thought with the theme for the feast. The antiphon is but loosely related to the psalm, yet directs our thoughts heavenward. (We can notice this frequently in Lauds, that toward

[12] Gen. 49:20.
[13] Lev. 21:6.
[14] I Pet. 2:9.

the end of the hour our thoughts and sentiments are concerned with the next life.) This particular antiphon is somewhat obscure: "To the victor, I will give hidden manna, and a
new name." [15] This hidden manna is a foretype of eternal
bliss, a sort of Eucharistic Communion in heaven. The victors
are all the saints in heaven (the Church triumphant, as distinguished from the Church militant on earth). The new
name likewise signifies the happiness of the future life, according to the words of Isaias: "You shall no longer be called
'forsaken,' but you shall be called 'my beloved.'" [16] Thus
from the antiphon we learn that the Eucharist is also a foretype of the eternal union with God in heaven.

Now we can see that the five antiphons of Lauds have
heightened the various aspects of the Eucharist: food, effects,
sacrifice, and pledge of eternal happiness. If we join these five
to the Magnificat antiphon for Second Vespers, there appears
an excellent mosaic portraying the Eucharist: O sacred banquet (first antiphon), in which Christ is eaten (second antiphon), the memorial of His passion is celebrated (fourth
antiphon), the soul is filled with grace (third antiphon), and
a pledge of future glory is given us (fifth antiphon).

The capitulum brings our prayer to the second stage. We
leave the hour thought for a while, to find ourselves now at
the scene of the Last Supper. The hymn is a vivid, lyrical reflection on the capitulum. The few phrases of the first stanza
describe Christ's appearance on earth and His work here. In
the second, third, and fourth stanzas the hymn describes the
Last Supper. The fifth designates our weapons for defense
against the wicked enemy. The last two stanzas are particularly beautiful. The poet Santolius said he would gladly have

[15] Apoc. 2:17.
[16] Isa. 62:4.

sacrificed all his works could he have been the author of these four lines:

> Se nascens dedit socium,
> Convescens in edulium,
> Se moriens in pretium,
> Se regnans dat in praemium.

What a treasure of thought in these few words! The fifth stanza is unusually forceful, a prayer "before battle."

The third stage and also the climax of the hour is the Benedictus. With the rising sun we greet our Savior, the Light of the world who illumines our hearts and grants us true peace. Today we greet the Eucharistic Sun which rises in the Holy Sacrifice of the Mass and which, according to the antiphon, imparts to us the eternal life of grace. Then we are no longer "in darkness and in the shadow of death." Then He guides "our feet into the way of peace." Then He gives us the strength to "serve Him . . . in holiness and justice . . . all our days." Our joyous morning prayer concludes with the oration for the feast.

CHAPTER XXVII

The "Tempus per Annum"

NOW for a few remarks about those two periods in the liturgical year which we call the *tempus per annum,* that is, the period after Epiphany, and the twenty-four Sundays after Pentecost. The expression itself, *tempus per annum,* suggests that the office for the period has no special characteristics. As a matter of fact, during this time the office is quite simple, with few variable parts.

For the Sundays after Epiphany, Matins opens with the following Invitatory: *Adoremus Dominum, quoniam ipse fecit nos,* and the hymn is the well-known hymn of St. Ambrose which we have already studied, *Aeterne rerum Conditor.* The psalms remain the same, but the lessons, of course, change from day to day. Those of the first nocturn are selected from the Epistles of St. Paul, and usually the second nocturn lessons have some bearing on those of the first, by way of explanation, homily, and the like. Lastly, the third nocturn contains a homily on the current Gospel. Even the responsories for this period show little change, repeating themselves throughout the whole six weeks. They are borrowed from the psalms, in a kind of numerical order: psalms 6, 9, 15, 17, 23, 24 (Sunday); psalms 30, 26, 33 (Monday); psalms 38, 39, 40 (Tuesday); Oratio Manasse, psalms 56, 58 (Wednesday); psalms 70, 70, 70 (Thursday); psalms 85, 85, 17 (Friday); psalms 100, 101, 101 (Saturday). As far as senti-

ment and contents are concerned, these responsories are
notably varied. Sometimes they are full of contrition and petitions for aid, sometimes radiant with joy and gratitude. They
make a splendid example of the typical Christian soul hiding
within its depths the whole range of sentiment and emotion.

Lauds and the other hours follow a similar pattern, with
few variable parts. For Lauds and Second Vespers it is only
the Benedictus and Magnificat antiphons, and the oration,
that change. In First Vespers, even the Magnificat antiphon
remains the same: *Suscepit Deus Israel, puerum suum, sicut
locutus est ad Abraham et semini ejus in saecula.* Here we
show our gratitude for being made "children of God." The
likewise invariable capitulum is well worth our attention and
consideration, as also are the responsories and verses in the
little hours for both Sundays and weekdays. The latter are
brief "axioms" from the Scriptures. For example, at Terce:
"God is love, he who dwells in love dwells in God, and God
in him." [1]

The Sundays after Pentecost have a structure similar to
that of those just treated. Few of their parts are variable, although more than of the Sundays after Epiphany. A caesura
occurs in the period after Pentecost inasmuch as from the
twenty-eighth of September on, the Invitatory verse and the
hymn at Lauds change. Until September twenty-seventh
the Invitatory is, *Dominum qui fecit nos, venite adoremus*
("Come, let us adore the Lord who made us"). Thereafter it
is, *Adoremus Dominum, quoniam ipse fecit nos* ("Let us
adore the Lord, because He made us"). Of course, we find
little difference in their contents. In the hymns, however,
there is a difference. The summer hymns are much shorter
than those sung in the autumn. We can readily surmise the

[1] I John 4:16.

reason for this difference. The prayers were shortened in the summer because of the need of greater manual labor and exertion. September twenty-eighth was traditionally the day when the transition to winter began.

In Matins only the lessons and responsories vary from day to day. We remember the order of the books read during the time after Pentecost. Until July 31, the Books of Kings; during August, the sapiential books; in September, the four books: Job, Tobias, Judith, and Esther; in October, the two Books of Machabees; in November, the prophets Ezechiel and Daniel, and the minor prophets. This arrangement of the lessons according to the months is a peculiarity of this season. It does not appear elsewhere in the liturgy. The month is not a liturgical unit. The responsories follow a schedule somewhat like the lessons, with this difference, that the same responsories recur the whole time a certain group of Books is being read. The longest period with the same set of responsories is that which accompanies the reading of the Books of Kings. Under certain circumstances (if Easter occurs at an early date) this period may extend as long as eleven weeks (since the reading of the Books of Kings stops with the first Sunday of August). Eleven responsories are sung during that time and they continue through Matins for both Sundays and weekdays. A study of their contents shows us that they treat of the important incidents narrated in the Books of Kings, especially such as concern David, Solomon, and Elias. During August we have another set of eleven responsories that treat throughout of wisdom. On the other hand, there are special responsories for each of the four books: Job, Tobias, Judith, and Esther. For the Book of Machabees read during October we find another group of thirteen responsories. And finally, in November there are fourteen responsories for all the prophets together. We see, then, that so engrossed does the liturgy become in the readings from the Old Testament that it reflects on them and sings of them through the whole week, without there being so much as a single responsory for the Sunday Gospel. In fact, the lessons even of the second nocturn almost always have some bearing on the reading from the Old Testament.

We find, with regard to the other hours, that both First and Second Vespers and Lauds of the Sunday offices have special antiphons for the Magnificat and Benedictus. Invariably the one for First Vespers is selected from the current Scripture lessons. It is usually a short sentence giving the kernel of the message conveyed in the lesson. (In this respect the time after Pentecost is superior to that after Epiphany.) The other two antiphons (for Second Vespers Magnificat and for the Benedictus) are culled from the day's Gospel. Their purpose is to extend the sacred Gospel drama into the whole day. Thus it often happens that the Benedictus antiphon proclaims the beginning of "the action," and the Magnificat antiphon its close. This is the Church's way of teaching us that in spirit we should join in the Gospel drama throughout the day. For example: On the tenth Sunday after Pentecost we take the part of the publican who "stood far off; he would not even lift up his eyes toward heaven; he only beat his breast and said, God be merciful to me; I am a sinner." [2] That was the beginning of the drama. In Vespers we hear the conclusion: "This man went back home higher in God's favor than the other." [3] The oration is the only variable part for the other hours. It is precisely during this "season" (the *tempus per annum*) that our prayer can follow the whim and mood of our heart almost unrestrictedly.

[2] Luke 18:13. Benedictus antiphon.
[3] Luke 18:14.

CHAPTER XXVIII

The Common

BESIDES the Proper of the Time in the Breviary, there is
a Proper of the Saints. This section includes all the proper or
special texts for the feasts of the individual saints. Almost
anyone who prays the Breviary is familiar with its contents.
As a rule we find only a brief account of the saint's life, and
a special oration. Some, however, have more proper texts,
and a few have even a whole special office. The antiphons
and responsories in such a case are taken from the "life" of
the saint. These texts we call *historiae*. They are unquestionably gems of liturgical prayer. By way of example we might
mention such proper offices as those for the feasts of the
apostle St. Andrew (November 30), St. Lucy (December
13), St. Agnes (January 21), St. Agatha (February 5), The
Finding of the True Cross (May 3), and The Exaltation of
the True Cross (September 14), The Birth of John the Baptist (June 24), SS. Peter and Paul (June 29), St. Lawrence
(August 10), Our Lady's Assumption (August 15), the Holy
Archangel Michael (September 29), All Saints (November
1), St. Martin (November 11), and St. Cecilia (November
22). A lover of the Breviary will study these offices carefully
and prayerfully, and assuredly will find much that is admirable and inspiring.

As we mentioned, however, such proper offices are rare. By
far the majority of the saints' feasts draw their prayer texts

431

from the Common. After the reform of Pius X, the ferial arrangement of the Psalter determined the use of the psalms in the Common of Saints. Since this Common plays such a notable part in our Breviary prayers, we shall make a few remarks about its contents and significance.

Generally the term *Commune Sanctorum* is used to designate that part of the Breviary which contains the texts regularly employed for feasts of saints. The saints are divided according to rank and sex into various classes: apostles, martyrs (three Commons for this group: one martyr, several martyrs, martyrs in Paschaltide), confessors who were bishops (and abbots), confessors who were not bishops, doctors, virgins, and non-virgins. The Common for the Dedication of a Church and that for feasts of the Blessed Virgin Mary follow after the Common of the Saints.

The practice of classifying the saints according to rank is quite ancient in the liturgy. We find the beginning of this division as early as the time the Te Deum was composed: "The glorious choir of apostles praises Thee . . . the renowned line of prophets . . . the white-robed band of martyrs . . ." At the time the Te Deum was composed, no special veneration was shown to confessors. The Litany of the Saints also follows the arrangement of the *Commune Sanctorum*. How beautifully these various classes would combine with their foretypes to furnish responsories at Matins for the feast of All Saints!

Now let us try to grasp the full significance and the special characteristics of the various classes. History sheds some light on the matter. Christians in the beginning did not celebrate the feasts of the saints. In fact, liturgical veneration of the saints began only with the memorial services in honor of the martyrs. Mass was celebrated every year, on the anniversary of his death, at the tomb of the martyr to commemorate his triumph.

The celebration of the apostles' feasts was introduced afterward, and, as the Te Deum indicates, for a long time apostles and martyrs were the only ones to receive veneration in the early Church. "Martyr" in those days was a synonym or equivalent for "holy" or "just." Thus he alone was to receive a saint's cult. It was some time before the Church decided to venerate publicly those who were not martyrs. St. Sylvester and St. Martin of Tours were the first "confessor saints."

The Church's concept of "sanctity" contributed substantially to the formation of certain classes of saints. What was this concept in the early Church? The ancient Christian ideals of sanctity were the martyr and the virgin: a life of virginity crowned with the martyr's crown to proclaim his faith in Christ.

This ideal or concept of sanctity sprang from two basic notions: every Christian, of course, is a "copy" of Christ, an *alter Christus,* and he is also Christ's Church in miniature. The Church and the individual soul should resemble each other as mother and daughter. Christ is the King of martyrs "from whom every martyrdom takes its beginning." The martyr "helps to pay off the debt which the afflictions of Christ leave still to be paid, for the sake of His (mystical) body, the Church." [1] The martyr is consequently the most perfect "copy" or "replica" of Christ.

Again, the Church was regarded as the spotless bride of Christ, represented therefore in the virgin or in the widow who preferred to forego a second marriage for love of Christ. The most perfect model of the spotless bride, Holy Mother Church, was the Blessed Virgin Mary.

[1] Col. 1:24.

When about the fourth century martyrdom disappeared, the Church's ideal of sanctity suffered some modification. It was then that the "confessors" made their appearance. This word "confessor" has a history of its own. In the early Church it was something like the martyr who indeed "openly proclaimed the great name of the only-begotten Son before kings and potentates" (Preface for the blessing of the palms). In those days confessors were such Christians who indeed had suffered for Christ in persecution, but had not died. It was but a short step from this concept to that of a spiritual or bloodless martyrdom, that endured by the Christian who renounces the pleasures of the world and gives himself entirely to the Lord. The "vigilant servant who stands, loins girt and lamp in hand, awaiting the return of his master" is a striking example of this. Here we can see that the liturgy was reverting to the ideal of sanctity set forth in the Gospel, as accepted in the first years of the Church, before the advent of the persecutions. In fact, Christ Himself proposed this ideal in His great discourse on the Parousia.[2]

Out of the Common of Confessors developed several other groups of saints: pontiffs, doctors, and abbots. Bishops perpetuate Christ's high priesthood; the holy doctors continue His sacred office of teaching. Thus evolved the formation of the various groups. Rooted in the ideas of ancient Christianity, they appeared one by one in the course of the Church's history.

From the moral or ethical viewpoint, the reason for the excellence of the *Commune Sanctorum* is precisely the fact that, in proposing its ideals of sanctity in the various classes, the liturgy concentrates on the general ideal of the prototypes

[2] Matt. 24:25.

rather than on the peculiar qualities and traits of the individual saints. Every Christian can imitate this ideal in his own way, while the Church focuses our attention on the ideal as a whole, on the essentials rather than on the accidental details. From this we can judge the profound wisdom the Church displays in the instruction imparted through the Common of Saints. The second nocturn "lives" of the saints are meant to counterbalance a possible tendency to put all the saints into set molds. Thus against the general background of the *Commune Sanctorum* the detailed pattern of the saint's life stands out in relief. In this way we can see how the general ideal of sanctity is realized in the individual.

Now for a word about the origin of the texts of the Common. We ought not imagine that at the beginning the Church merely compiled a group of texts or prayer formulas for the *Commune Sanctorum*. The fact is that these texts we have now for the Common originated in a special office for a certain saint's feast. Gradually the texts were used for other saints of the same class, until finally they crystallized into the Common of the Breviary and of the Missal. We shall single out now the characteristic features of the various Commons.

The Common of Apostles is distinctive. Two main ideas or themes predominate in all the texts: the apostles are the close friends of Christ; they are the rulers, the princes of the Church. One of the characteristic verses often repeated is: *Nimis honorati sunt amici tui, Deus: nimis confortatus est principatus eorum.* This text is from psalm 138, according to the old version of the Psalter. It is the reason for the psalm's being used in the Introit and at Second Vespers. The psalm itself has little connection with the apostles. In fact, the above-mentioned text is based on a faulty rendering of the original.[3] The First Vesper antiphons speak warmly of the friendship of Christ. They are taken from the Gospel for the Mass of the vigil: "You, if you do all that I command you, are My friends." [4] In addition to the dignity of the apostles, the Common also sets forth their commission, and the sufferings they endured for Christ. Their task is to establish and extend the kingdom of the Savior on earth. They are, then, the first missioners. We note how this idea is expressed in the typical verse from psalm 18: "Through all the earth their voice resounds, and to the ends of the world their message." Psalm 18 in olden times was entitled "the Apostle," it was so appropriate for the feasts of the apostles. St. Augustine also mentions in one of his sermons that "the apostles, like 'other heavens,' have declared the glory of God" ("The heavens declare the glory of God": thus the opening words of psalm 18). The so-called capitulum for Vespers and Lauds is also appropriate: "You are no longer exiles, then, or aliens; the saints are your fellow citizens, you belong to God's household. Apostles and prophets are the foundation on which you were built, and the chief cornerstone of it is Jesus Christ Himself." [5] In the sublime spiritual edifice of the Church, Christ is the cornerstone, the apostles are the foundation, and we are the stones out of which the rest of the building is fashioned. The feasts of the apostles, consequently, are feasts of the whole Church, of man's redemption in general, rather than feasts of particular saints.

Sharing in Christ's friendship means sharing in His passion and sufferings too. Thus the apostles have "drunk deep of the

[3] According to the new version of the Psalter, this verse (17) reads: "How weighty are your designs, O my God, how vast the sum of them!" Tr.
[4] John 15:14.
[5] Eph. 2:19 f.

cup of the Lord." They have voluntarily suffered martyrdom. Their feasts should always be a time of great celebration for us. Let us note the beauty of the famous hymn, *Exultet orbis gaudiis,* and also the admirable lessons of the first nocturn on the sufferings endured by the apostles.[6]

From the Common we may also learn the dignity and honor shown the martyrs in the ancient Church. There were three groups: one martyr, several martyrs, and a special Common for martyrs in Paschaltide. The last two are exceptionally beautiful and picturesque. Over and over we hear the theme: the triumph in suffering, and the crown they have won in heaven.

A confessor, according to the Gospels, is the ideal Christian who in the night of this life, with loins girt and lamp lit, awaits the return of his Lord. This picture recurs over and over in the Common of Confessors. The liturgy gives us four main groups: confessor pontiffs, doctors, abbots, and confessors who are not pontiffs. The pontiff, or bishop, is the faithful administrator of the fountains of divine life in the Church, that is, of the word of God and the sacraments. In him Christ's high priesthood finds its fullest expression. Using as a comparison "God's anointed," King David (Ps. 131 in Second Vespers), the Common thus frequently refers to Christ's priesthood. The vigilant servant is the favorite model in the Common of confessors who are not pontiffs.

Lastly, we have the distinctive Common of Virgins, with its principal theme: the five prudent virgins. The Lord's spotless bride is the virgin, setting out in the night of this life with the bright lamp of her love for Christ, to meet her Bridegroom coming to wed her. One of the characteristic

[6] I Cor. 4:1–15.

psalms of this Common is psalm 44, the bridal song of the Church.

We make the following observations on the office for feasts of Our Lady. Mary is the queen, the paragon of saints, so that we can scarcely speak of a "Common" in the sense of a number of special texts for a group of saints. Mary's position is unique. She cannot be ranked with any group of saints. Rather, she is queen of all the groups: Queen of Apostles, of Martyrs, of Confessors, and of Virgins, as the Litany of Loreto indicates. Here when we speak of "Common," we mean the texts usually applied to Mary on all her feasts, though, in addition to this, each feast emphasizes some particular aspect. Thus we can readily see how important an understanding of this Common is for an appreciation of the individual feasts. Only in the light of the more general ideas of the Common does the special theme stand out best.

What are the fundamental ideas of the Common for feasts of Our Lady? Perhaps the briefest expression of these basic notions is found in the Invitatory for Matins: "Holy Mary, Virgin Mother of God, intercede for us." This is an excellent summary of Mary's sublime dignity. 1. Holy Mary: her personal sanctity; 2. Mother of God: the greatest honor Mary enjoys, the basis of all her prerogatives; 3. Virgin: this is the liturgy's favorite title of Our Lady, for with her it is unique since, being a virgin, she is also a mother; 4. Intercessor: this is the reason for our unbounded trust in the "Help of Christians." These four ideas are the basic themes of the Common of the Blessed Virgin. Nearly all the individual texts can be related to these themes.

Both the Common and the various feasts of Our Lady are picturesque. The liturgy is a master at representing our beloved Mother to us by means of certain figures. Three of these

recur most frequently and so deserve special consideration.
Mary is represented under the figure of the Spouse, of
Wisdom, and of the city of Jerusalem.

1. The Spouse. The Common of the Blessed Virgin contains many passages from the Canticle of Canticles. This is
one of the Books of Scripture that comes under the name of
Solomon. According to its literal sense, this canticle sings of
the love of King Solomon for a shepherdess. The "drama's"
main points are: the ardent longing of both for union in marriage, and their various efforts to achieve this; the songs and
responsories that voice their mutual affection; the great ob-
stacles that hinder their union.

This literal sense, however, is only the outer shell. Within
we find the kernel of a profound religious truth. By this figure
the Canticle describes God's love for His chosen people, and in
a fuller, Christian sense, the love of Christ for His Church
and for the soul united with God through grace. This image
of bride and bridegroom is a favorite in the Bible, in both
the Old and the New Testament. It speaks of God as "es-
poused" to the Jewish people; He is referred to as "a jealous
God"; idolatry was called "adultery."

Christ, and St. Paul after Him, lent even greater significance to this image of "wedlock." John the Baptist introduces
Christ as the bridegroom of Israel, and Christ spoke of Himself as the bridegroom of the Church.[7] In this figure we have
one of the loftiest features of Christianity: men made children of God, and the union of Christ with man's soul, a union
that reaches its perfection in the saints. Now we can more
easily see why the idea of the bride and bridegroom, especially as found in the Canticle, is so appropriately applied
to the Common for the Blessed Virgin. This intimate union

7 John 3:29; Matt. 9:15.

with God and with Christ found its fullest realization in Mary. Not only is she the holiest and most perfect of God's creatures, but she had that unique relationship with God whereby she bore the Son of God Himself in her womb for nine months.

2. Wisdom. Mary is compared to divine wisdom. In the sapiential books of Scripture the wisdom of God is personified, now in the guise of a child frolicking in the presence of the Father in the very beginning of time, aiding Him in the work of creation, again as God's angel or messenger teaching mankind wisdom and virtue, and, in fact, the true religion. By this "wisdom" the sacred authors mean, first of all, the divine attribute, the wisdom itself of almighty God, whereby He created and ordered all things in the universe. Then, in addition they mean the divine, eternal ideas which in varying degrees of perfection God realized in creatures. The Fathers of the Church saw in this personified wisdom, the Son of God Himself "through whom God created the world." Lastly, Sacred Scripture has in mind also a created "wisdom," the virtue of wisdom which God imparted to the Jewish people through the revealed religion. As used in the Scriptures, then, the term "wisdom" has a much greater significance than we usually attribute to it in every-day speech. In Scripture it designates a sort of spiritual common sense, holiness and virtue in general, as contrasted with folly and wickedness.

The liturgy, therefore, likes to relate to Our Lady these passages about wisdom. And how is that? Creatures are copies or reflections of divine wisdom. The more perfect they are, the better they mirror God's beauty, wisdom, and holiness. Thus, as the most perfect image of God in creatures, Mary is, so to speak, divine wisdom itself. Then we have God's decree from all eternity, to accomplish in Mary the incarnation of His Son. Arrayed thus in all her perfections, Mary took her place before God's face from all eternity. Finally, she possesses created wisdom, that is, holiness and virtue, to such a degree that even in this sense she well deserves to be called "wisdom."

3. Jerusalem. Thirdly, Mary appears under the figure of the city of Jerusalem or Sion (the chief defense of the city). What is the reason for this comparison? Jerusalem was unique among all cities. God chose to establish His throne in it. The chosen city it was, the favorite city of God. What a supremely appropriate figure for Mary! In Jerusalem we find the temple, the dwelling of the Most High. Mary is the living temple of God. Jerusalem, the favorite city of the great King. Mary, "blessed among women." Jerusalem, the "mother of many peoples"; all nations, even the Gentiles, journey to her. Mary, the mother of Christendom. Jerusalem, harassed and beleaguered by the enemy. Mary, the Mother of Sorrows. Jerusalem, so dear and so beloved for the Jews. Mary, most beloved (after God) for us Christians.

CHAPTER XXIX

The Breviary and the Laity[1]

W E may surely number this matter among the problems and aims of the popular liturgical revival: the Breviary and the laity. First of all, let us clarify the question. Our Catholic people are well aware of the existence of an official prayer of the Church. In fact, on the greater feasts (for example, on the last three days of Holy Week and on Christmas, and in many places even on the ordinary Sundays of the year) they themselves attend Matins or Vespers, as the case may be. Thus they become familiar with the Office, of course without understanding much if anything of what they hear. They believe that this prayer is the concern of priests and religious.

Few pastors have introduced this official prayer to their flocks. It was only gradually, at the beginning of the liturgical movement, that the layfolk were acquainted with the Office in some of the larger Benedictine abbeys. The monks actually put the texts into the people's hands so that they could assist at the Office intelligently. Even here, however, it was not a matter of proving the reasonableness or possibility of the laity's participating in the official prayer of the Church.

This question was first raised by the "popular" liturgical movement. At a "Liturgical Day" conference for priests in

[1] The following remarks, considered in the light of *Mediator Dei*, should not be construed as proposing a lay participation in the Office which is the same as that of priests, who are specially deputed for this task by the Church. Tr.

Vienna in 1926, I read a paper on "The Breviary and the Laity." This same question was discussed at a convention for both clergy and laity at Klosterneuberg in 1927. With a view to a practical solution, the problem was studied since that time by the "Popular Liturgical Apostolate" in Klosterneuberg, so that Breviaries for the laity and special texts of the Office for all the liturgical seasons were published in rapid succession. There is no further question now of a "problem." The participation of the laity in the Office of the Church is an accomplished fact.

For the fact that the laity is justified in joining in the Office there is no further need of proof. A cursory glance at the early Church makes this clear. From its Lord and Master the whole Church received the obligation to pray, indeed "to pray always and not to lose heart." In the early Church, as a matter of fact, the "parish" as a whole took on this duty of prayer. Each parish was, so to speak, a "prayer and sacrifice community." Every day the faithful gathered in the churches, morning and evening—at night especially, in the time of the persecutions—to pray and offer sacrifice together with their pastors. In those days the obligation to pray in common was not the task of the priests alone, but of the parish or congregation as a whole. However, in addition to the community prayer, the faithful also recited certain hour prayers privately at home, as, for example, we learn from the *Apostolic Tradition* of Hippolytus (*c.* 220). Thus, in the early Church, the laity as well as the clergy felt themselves obliged, and hence entitled, to recite the official prayers of the Church.

It was only at the dawn of the Middle Ages that the situation began to change. Gradually the layfolk took part in the community prayer less and less frequently, especially since now the language was unintelligible to them. At this point the cleric and religious took over the obligation of common prayer, a development that gradually proceeded so far that eventually the laity felt excluded from the community prayer, and the Breviary became a monopoly in the hands of the priests and religious. In fact, it fell to the liturgical revival to remind priests that they were praying their Breviary in the name of the whole Church and for their whole parish. In the fulfillment of its obligation to common prayer, therefore, the laity is represented by its priests. If this is true, then it is evident that the laity has at least the right to join in the recitation of the Breviary. I feel, indeed, that there is no longer need of posing the question whether they are entitled to participate or not. That they have the right is clear.

A different question is of much more importance to us now: What kind of Breviary is best for the laity? Several possibilities present themselves. We could give the layfolk a simple translation of the entire Roman or monastic Breviary, and let them select for themselves what parts to pray. This would certainly be a simple solution of the problem. I do not believe, however, that this would be practical. The layman would see this vast array of prayer texts before him, without knowing where to start or stop. Rather than be left to his own choice, he would prefer to have some prayers designated by the Church. He wants something that will in effect be an official hour-prayer of the Church.

A second possibility is a private selection and compilation of different parts of the Office, accommodated to the laity as to length and intelligibility. Several such Breviaries have appeared in recent years with more or less success. I cannot, for my part, favor such a Breviary. It is too far removed from the official hour-prayer. Besides, it is a private composition, lacking the full approbation of the Church. Our wish is to have the laity form a single choir with the clergy so that they can actually participate in the official prayer of the Church. Naturally, with such a Breviary, this is impossible.

A third possibility is this: that the Church herself choose certain parts from the Office for the lay Breviary. To me, this plan seems quite worth-while.

It is by no means a new idea. In fact, it has long since been provided for by Holy Mother Church. As we know, there is the "long" and the "short" or little office of the Blessed Virgin. The long office is found in the regular Breviary and contains all the hours, as recited by the priest. In contrast with the three nocturns of the long office, the little office has but one nocturn for Matins. This is the usual office for most sisterhoods. The votive office of the dead is somewhat the same. It consists of one nocturn, Lauds, and Vespers. Thus we see that the Church has already set the pattern for a lay Breviary. While priests and religious are to pray the entire Office with all its hours, the laity can make its little office out of a single nocturn for Matins, then Lauds, then Vespers.

Such a plan can be defended historically and theoretically, too. The vigilia (Matins), Lauds, and Vespers are the oldest of all the hours. Originally they were recited even by the laity, whereas the other hours (Prime, Terce, Sext, None, and Compline) were recited only in the cloisters. Furthermore, the former (Matins, Lauds, and Vespers) are the more festive and solemn hours, which were therefore sung or recited publicly in the churces. Finally, these three hours embody the finest elements of the whole day's office, as far as content is concerned. Matins is the day's or the feast's prayer drama. Lauds and Vespers are the solemn morning and evening prayers, closely related to the theme of the feast.

We may still ask: What benefit can the laity hope to derive from praying the Office? Every layman ought to say at least some morning and evening prayers. And surely he ought to set for himself a sort of supernatural tone for the day by some spiritual reading. All this he can accomplish by praying these three hours. Matins supplies, for the most part, an excellent spiritual reading. Lauds and Vespers are the proper morning and night prayers. The layman can hardly be concerned with the other hours during the day; that is, Terce, Sext, and None. And after all, they fulfill their purpose only if prayed at the proper time. Then too, the length of these three hours (Matins, Lauds, and Vespers) is just right for the laity. No hour would take more than ten minutes or so.

Perhaps someone, however, may still feel that we have slighted two important hours: Prime and Compline. It is true that they are ideal morning and night prayers. Prime is also a consecration of the day's labor to God, and Compline is full of references to night and darkness. Vespers, on the contrary, has very few such references. From history however, we know that both of these hours (Prime and Compline) were born in the cloister. Prime is really the second morning prayer and the chapter session. Similarly, Compline is a second night prayer, recited in the dormitory of the monastery just before bedtime. A double morning and night prayer would be unnatural and superfluous, indeed unbearable, for the laity. I readily admit that these two hours are more personal, hence easier to grasp, than the older, more objective hours of Lauds and Vespers. I maintain, however, what I stated above: Matins (one nocturn), Lauds, and Vespers are the proper hours for the lay Breviary. Of course I would by no means object if, for example, Sunday Compline and perhaps the festive office for Prime were also included in the lay Breviary; to be recited, however, *ad libitum*.

Now, what sort of Breviary shall we have for our laity? Matins is to have but one nocturn with three psalms and three lessons. We must still decide which of the three nocturns it shall be. We might always take the first nocturn. Or, as in the office of Our Lady and of the dead, on Monday and Thursday we might take the first nocturn, on Tuesday and Friday the second, etc. It would also be possible to select our three psalms from the whole three nocturns. Here, however, the subjective element would be invading our plan again. Certainly the simplest way would be to take both psalms and lessons from the first nocturn of the day. Thus we could follow the current Scripture readings. Perhaps the third lesson could be the account of the life of the day's saint (the *lectio contracta*). Concerning the lessons from Scripture, I must admit that I would prefer a better selection of material than that found in the Roman Breviary at present. We know this is owing to the mechanical hacking of the lessons at the time the Curiale Breviary was compiled. So much for Matins, opening with Invitatory and hymn, and concluding with the Te Deum or a responsory. Lauds and Vespers ought to be the same as those of the regular office, so that at these hours the laity can join in the public prayer of the Church.

With regard to the language of this lay Breviary, I think it best to make only the vernacular and not the Latin language a part of the plan. If eventually there should be a printed lay Breviary, then of course this could have both Latin and English, side by side. However, the layfolk for the most part will use the vernacular in reciting the hours, whether in choir or in private. Nor, we must admit, is the matter of a good, readable, and prayerful translation to be overlooked.

There is something, however, of even more importance. When we discuss the matter of a lay Breviary, we must not think in terms of private prayer for the laity. At least, this should not be our primary consideration, simply because first and foremost the Office is a community prayer. Since even the priests pray their Breviary almost exclusively for themselves, we have the idea that this is the prayer task of the individual. Of course this idea is wrong. The Office is the prayer of the community. It is the community that prays for those individuals who are not on hand to join in the common prayer. This general idea must be revived in us, just as primarily the lay Breviary must be a book of common prayer. In every church and parish the faithful should assemble, morning and evening, to pray the Office in the name of the whole community. And naturally, as head of the community, the pastor will, and should, participate in this prayer in the vernacular tongue.

You may think these ideas utopian, but I can assure you that all this is quite possible. In fact, such practices have flourished in our parish of St. Gertrude in Klosterneuberg for some years now. Every morning before the community Mass we pray Lauds, and on Sundays, Matins besides. This custom has become so entrenched in the parish that it is an essential part of our worship.

Now you will ask: How can I realize this plan of the lay Breviary? I believe that the religious sisterhoods must take the initial step. They already use this sort of Breviary except, of course, that it is exclusively Marian. But everyone knows how monotonous this invariable office can be. So, instead of the Little Office of the Blessed Virgin, the congregations of religious women could well take over the "little" Roman

Office: Matins (one nocturn), Lauds and Vespers of the day. The necessary permission should be fairly easy to obtain, especially since it lies within the competency of the Ordinary. The layfolk would soon follow their example.

What a magnificent accomplishment this would be: the faithful having their own official prayer that agrees substantially with that of the priests and religious! Then we would be able to say once again: We Christians are "a praying people," a vast choir embracing the whole Church through our prayers.

References

Geschichte des Breviers, P. Suitbert Bäumer, Herder, Freiburg, 1895.

Das Brevier im Dienste der Seelsorge, Linus Bopp, Kösel-Pustet, Munich, 1939.

De Breviarii Romani Liturgia, C. Callewaert, C. Beyart, Brussels, 1939.

Handbuch der katholischen Liturgik (2 vols.), Ludwig Eisenhofer, Herder, Freiburg, 1933.

Das Kirchenjahr (15 vols.), Prosper Gueranger, Kirchheim, Mainz, 1904, tr. by Dom Lawrence Shepherd. O.S.B., *The Liturgical Year,* Benziger Bros., New York, 1910.

Die liturgische Feier, Joseph A. Jungmann, S.J. Pustet, Regensburg, 1939, tr. by a monk of St. John's Abbey, Collegeville, Minn. Fred. Pustet Co., New York, 1941. *Liturgical Worship.*

Praktischer Brevier-Kommentar (2 vols.), Dr. Karl Kastner, Goerlich, Breslau, 1922–24.

Carmina Scripturarum scilicet Antiphonas et Responsoria, Carol. Marbach. Le Roux, Strassbourg, 1907.

Liturgische Studien, Beiträge zur Erklärung des Breviers und Missale (4 vols.), Bernhard Schäfer. Pustet, Regensburg, 1912–15.

Liber Sacramentorum, Ildef. Schuster, tr. by A. Levelis Marke, and Mrs. W. Fairfax-Cholmeley, *The Sacramentary.* Burns, Oates, and Washbourne, London, 1930.

Psallite sapienter, Psallieret weise (5 vols.), Maurus Wolter. Herder, Freiburg, 1904–7.

Dictionnaire d'Archeologie Chretienne et de Liturgie, F. Cabrol and H. Leclerq. Letouzey et Ane, Paris, 1924.

Bibliography

ENGLISH WORKS ON THE BREVIARY

The Church's Daily Prayer, Dom Ernest Graf, O.S.B. Burns, Oates & Washbourne, London, 1938.

The Divine Office, Rev. E. J. Quigley. B. Herder Book Co., St. Louis, 1920.

The Divine Office, Bacquez, ed. by Rev. E. L. Taunton. Burns Oates & Washbourne, London, 1885.

Autobiography of an Old Breviary, Heuser. Benziger Bros., New York, 1925.

History of the Roman Breviary, Batiffol, tr. by Atwell Baylay. Longmans, Green and Co., New York, 1898.

Liturgical Prayer, Its History and Spirit, Abbot Cabrol, P. J. Kenedy & Sons, New York, 1922.

Hymns and Canticles of the Roman Breviary, Britt, O.S.B. Benziger Bros., New York, 1948.

ON THE PSALMS

The Book of Psalms and the Canticles of the Roman Breviary (New Version of 1945) tr. by members of the Catholic Biblical Association of America. St. Anthony Guild Press, Paterson, New Jersey, 1950.

The Psalms (New Version of 1945), Ronald Knox. Sheed & Ward, New York, 1947.

The Psalms, a Prayer-book (English and Latin of the New Version of 1945). Benziger Bros., New York, 1945.

452

Towards Loving the Psalms, C. C. Martindale, S.J. Sheed & Ward, New York, 1940. Old Version of the Psalms, but still very helpful.

On the Martyrology

The Roman Martyrology (a translation). John Murphy & Co., Baltimore & New York, 1897.

The Roman Martyrology, tr. by Rev. Raphael Collins. The Newman Bookshop, Westminster, Md., 1946.

Index

455

Paul IV and the reform of the Breviary, 26
Paul the Deacon, hymn by, 139
Pentecost, feast of, 395
Pius V and Breviary reform, 26
Pius X, reform of Breviary by, 27, 204
Pray the Breviary, why, 3-9
Prayer: of Christ, 4; community, 6; family, 5; parish, 5
Praying the psalms, 62-70
Preces, the, 108
Pre-Lenten Office, 287-98
Prime, 34: history of psalms for, 206 note; in monastic chapter hall, 35; monastic origin of, 202; origin of, 20, 30
Psalms, the, 48-84
    difficulties in the, 52
    explanation of the, 214-21
    for Lauds, 207
    the maledictory, 54
    praying the, 62-70
    for Prime, 206 note
    responsory method of reciting the, 119 ff.
    St. Augustine on the, 120
    theology in the, 49
    understanding the, 58-62
    value of the, 48
Psalms explained
    1, 70-74, 259, 333, 372, 374, 408
    4, 222, 355, 409; St. Augustine on, 66
    14, 356
    15, 356, 410
    21, 335
    23, 359
    26, 337
    29, 361
    37, 340
    39, 341
    41, 414
    42, 414, 419
    44, 264
    47, 272
    53, 343, 364
    58, 346
    62, 423

Psalms explained (*continued*)
    63, 344
    68, 316
    69, 317, 318
    70, 317, 318
    71, 273, 322, 323
    72, 324
    73, 325
    74, 327
    75, 328, 364
    76, 329
    80, 420
    83, 421
    84, 275
    87, 347, 354
    88, 278
    90, 225
    92, 214, 217, 423
    93, 348
    94, 155-59, 256
    95, 282
    97, 284
    99, 83, 218, 423
    109, 382, 385
    110, 383, 385, 401
    111, 386
    112, 387
    113, 384, 388
    115, 402
    127, 403
    129, 79-83
    136, 74-79
    147, 403
    148, 424
Psalter: a book of prayer, 51; structure of the, 204-11
Psalter, the new, 211 note

Quignonez (cardinal)
Quinquagesima Sunday, 290

Rabanus Maurus, *Veni Creator Spiritus* by, 139
Rector potens, verax Deus, 152-54
Reformers of Breviary, 24
Regi saeculorum, 34
Regina Coeli Laetare, 179
Responsories: on Corpus Christi, 133; on feast of St. Agnes, 132;

Printed in Great Britain
by Amazon